IN OUR TIMES

5th edition _____

IN OUR TIMES
America Since World War II

Norman L. Rosenberg
Emily S. Rosenberg
Macalester College

Prentice Hall, Englewood Cliffs, New Jersey 07632

Library of Congress Cataloging-in-Publication Data

Rosenberg, Norman L.
   In our times : America since World War II / Norman L. Rosenberg.
Emily S. Rosenberg—5th ed.
     p.   cm.
   Includes bibliographical references and index.
   ISBN 0-13-106447-0
   1. United States—History—1945-   I. Rosenberg, Emily S., 1944-   II. Title.
   E741.R667   1994
   973.92—dc20   94-35248
                                                                            CIP

Editorial/production supervision and interior design: Shelly Kupperman
Cover design: DeLuca Design
Buyer: Nick Sklitsis
Acquisitions editor: Steve Dalphin
Editorial Assistant: Tamara Mann
Cover photo: Flip Schulke/Martin Luther King Picture Collection

© 1995, 1991, 1987, 1982, 1976 by Prentice-Hall, Inc.
A Simon & Schuster Company
Englewood Cliffs, New Jersey 07632

Printed in the United States of America
10   9   8   7   6   5   4   3   2   1

ISBN 0-13-106447-0

PRENTICE-HALL INTERNATIONAL (UK) LIMITED, *London*
PRENTICE-HALL OF AUSTRALIA PTY. LIMITED, *Sydney*
PRENTICE-HALL CANADA INC., *Toronto*
PRENTICE-HALL HISPANOAMERICANA, S.A., *Mexico*
PRENTICE-HALL OF INDIA PRIVATE LIMITED, *New Delhi*
PRENTICE-HALL OF JAPAN, INC., *Tokyo*
SIMON & SCHUSTER ASIA PTE. LTD., *Singapore*
EDITORA PRENTICE-HALL DO BRASIL, LTDA., *Rio de Janeiro*

To the memories of Joseph and Dorothea Rosenberg and of Albert A. and Helen Griggs Schlaht. Also to our children, Sarah, Molly, Ruth, Joseph.

Contents

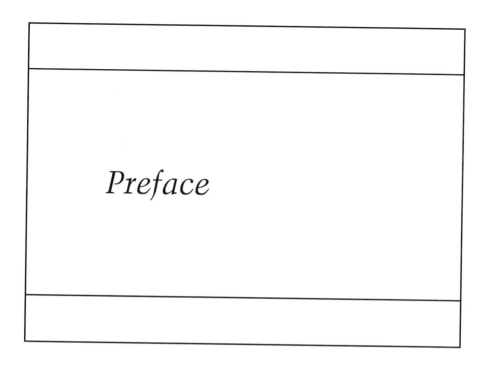

Preface

In preparing this fifth edition of *In Our Times*, we have tried to follow our initial design: to offer students and instructors an interesting framework on which they can construct their own views of the history of the postwar United States. As always, we remain heartened by the many positive responses and humbled by the legitimate dissents. In this edition, we have responded to suggestions for change and to recent scholarship by revising sentences and paragraphs, by rewriting complete sections, and by reconstructing several portions of the book's basic framework. The final chapter has been completely rewritten.

We wish, once more, to thank our colleagues and students at Macalester College for their advice and support.

Shelly Kupperman has served as a kind and expert production editor. And special thanks go to Prentice Hall's history editor, Steve Dalphin. We have worked with Steve almost as long as we have worked with *In Our Times*, and his encouragement, support, and patience always help to smooth the process of revision. We want to thank the Prentice Hall reviewers for their helpful suggestions: Arnold Rice, Kean College, New Jersey; Lee Dew, Kentucky Wesleyan College; and Melvin Small, Wayne State University.

In Our Times is still a joint production. Although we take individual initiative for re-reviewing and rewriting specific sections, we continue to work together on the final results. One of us will often complete the sentence or paragraph that the other began. And, as always, we offer our traditional response for the errors and omissions that remain in this edition: "You must be looking for the other Professor Rosenberg."

Norman Rosenberg
Emily Rosenberg

IN OUR TIMES

1

The World's Superpower

COLLAPSE OF THE OLD ORDER, RISE OF THE NEW

The war was over! Japan had surrendered! At seven in the evening on August 14, 1945, President Harry S Truman made the official announcement. Across the country people began to celebrate the end of World War II. Outside the White House, a crowd that had been waiting all day struck up the chant, "We want Harry, we want Harry!" The president appeared, said a few words, and left, only to be called back twice more by repeated shouts. Finally, he sank into a chair and expressed the universal sentiment: "I'm glad that it's over."

However, pressing problems and hard decisions did not end with the war. Postwar reconstruction and the development of a cold war between the United States and the former Soviet Union kept international affairs in perpetual crisis.

Before World War II Europeans believed they occupied the center of progress, civilization, and world power. London and Paris set the trends in world culture, held the reins of government for colonial peoples throughout the globe, and provided financial institutions for the business of far-flung empires. But World War II, coming only two decades after the tremendous strain of World War I, dramatically altered Europe's position. The costs of the long struggle left the nations of Europe—both the victors and the vanquished—exhausted and bankrupt. As Europeans spent their military and economic strength in what some historians have called a European civil war, their grasp over colonial areas weakened. Worldwide fighting strengthened local nationalist movements and whetted tastes for independence and self-determination. Anticolonial revolutionary movements were poised to dismember the European empires and to create a host of new nations in Asia and Africa.

As the old order of European dominance and colonialism disintegrated after the war, few dared to predict what would happen. Cordell Hull, Franklin D. Roosevelt's secretary of state, warned that "the people of many countries will be starving . . . homeless . . . their factories and mines destroyed; their roads and transport wrecked. . . . Disease will lurk everywhere. In some countries confusion and chaos will follow the cessation of hostilities." Hull advised that "victory must be followed by swift and effective action to meet these pressing human needs."

It fell to America, Hull and other internationalists believed, to supply the blueprint for a postwar order. Untouched by battle, enriched by wartime profits, and free from scarcity and instability, the United States emerged as victor of the victors. With much of the world in its debt, America became the undisputed superpower. American leaders tried to devise ways of using this power in postwar diplomacy. The supposed folly of isolationism and the "lessons" of appeasement during the 1920s and 1930s had turned many American policymakers into internationalists. Throughout the war they planned for postwar reconstruction.

One of the architects of American policy, Undersecretary of State Dean Acheson (later Truman's secretary of state), entitled his memoirs of this period *Present at the Creation*. The title was revealing. It reflected the belief that Americans would have to construct a new world order. It also displayed confidence—even arrogance—in America's ability to shape events. To policymakers like Acheson, forming a postwar settlement would involve little give-and-take diplomacy; it would be primarily an act of creation, a monumental American-directed effort affecting the well-being of future generations.

The American Vision

How did American policymakers envision the postwar world? Two articles of internationalist faith—maintenance of open access for trade and investment and creation of an international organization—provided the cornerstones of America's plan for lasting peace.

A trading nation with a dynamic, expanding economy, America had always opposed restrictions to the free flow of its overseas trade and investment. During the depression decade of the 1930s, Americans watched uneasily as economic restrictions threatened to close large parts of the world to their businesses. Great Britain moved toward an "imperial preference" system that placed nations outside the British Empire at a commercial disadvantage; Japan's expansionist leaders threatened to create a closed economic sphere in Asia; fascist Germany reached out to encompass new sources of raw materials. American leaders hoped to eliminate restrictionist trends in the postwar world. They believed that unhampered commerce brought peace, whereas economic restrictions—such as unequal tariffs, preferential commercial arrangements, and currency inconvertibility—bred jealousy and war. "If we could get a freer flow of trade," Cordell Hull wrote, "the living standards of all countries might rise, thereby eliminating the economic dissatisfaction that breeds war." While ushering in prosperity and peace, freer trade would, not incidentally, also enhance United States influence worldwide because of America's dominant financial position. In planning a postwar world, as in most other endeavors, ideology and self-interest dovetailed.

During World War II, Roosevelt also revived the Wilsonian dream of an international peacekeeping organization. The notion that a free exchange of ideas promoted understanding, compromise, and consensus had been a persistent American belief, and many influential Americans became convinced that an international body would serve, not undermine, national interests in the postwar world. The U.S. refusal to join the League of Nations after World War I, policymakers believed, had contributed to the breakdown of peace in 1939. Behind their convictions lay certain assumptions: that international conflicts often stemmed from breakdowns in communication, that free debate would produce a consensus in support of the most convincing argument, and that the American point of view would invariably triumph in an open forum. A representative world assembly, policymakers believed, would provide a means of moderating tensions and building a world community under the aegis of the United States, Britain, France, and the Soviet Union. These powers would become the collective guarantors of postwar peace.

American postwar plans sounded selfless and impartial. Nonrestrictive trade and investment policies and an open international forum for debate

V-J Day in Omaha. All across the country, people were celebrating victory over Japan. *Source:* Nebraska State Historical society.

appeared to give everyone an equal chance and to set aside narrow nationalism. But critics of American policy claimed that those policies would inevitably advance the interests of the nation that was economically and politically the strongest—the United States. Americans used internationalist rhetoric, critics charged, only to camouflage self-interest and their own globalist designs.

Did American policy serve the world or itself? Could it do both? These questions have formed the basis for many of the debates on postwar American foreign policy. They have also been central to interpreting the cold war that developed between America and the Soviet Union. In the period immediately following the war few American observers doubted that their country's policy was righteous and benign. But a newer generation of analysts, writing mostly after the debacle of Vietnam, severely criticized an America that tended to identify its own self-interest with the world's well-being. The nature of America's role in the postwar world remains a contentious issue.

Reconstructing an International Economic System

Secretary of State Hull made America's position on economic issues clear: It expected equal access to trade and raw materials in the postwar world. As a condition for receiving lend-lease assistance from the United States during the war, Allied nations had to promise to work toward the "elimination of all forms of discriminatory treatment in international commerce." And in July 1944 representatives from forty-four countries gathered at Bretton Woods, New Hampshire, to work out a postwar economic structure. The Soviet Union did not attend. Although the Bretton Woods delegates did not adopt every American proposal, they did formulate a system that generally reflected American goals.

Stable monetary exchange rates and full convertibility among the world's currencies seemed essential to free-flowing trade and investment. The delegates consequently created the International Monetary Fund (IMF) and charged it with maintaining a stable international system of exchange in which each national currency was convertible into any other at a fixed rate. A country could alter its exchange rate (that is, adjust the value of its money in relation to other currencies) only by agreement with the IMF. The architects of the IMF hoped that the system would combat the economic nationalism of the 1930s and believed that it would forge an interdependent world economy that would contribute to peace. The system of exchange rates did provide the foundation for unparalleled growth and prosperity in the developed nations of the Western world.

The delegates to Bretton Woods also created the International Bank for Reconstruction and Development, now called the World Bank. This institution was to encourage loans for postwar economic recovery. Loans would help restore war-ruined economies and bring resumption of normal trading patterns; financial stabilization, it was believed, would also help curb radical political movements that fed on economic discontent. Since its creation, the World Bank has been dominated by American capital and headed by an

American director. Perhaps its most prestigious head was Robert McNamara, former secretary of defense under presidents Kennedy and Johnson, who directed the bank between 1968 and 1981.

United States support for the World Bank stemmed not only from a desire to stabilize and assist needy nations but also from the pragmatic realization that its own trade would suffer unless other countries had the money to buy its products. In addition, the World Bank advanced American interests by promising to foster private investment. The bank would participate in or guarantee private American loans made in foreign nations. America was by far the richest nation in the postwar world, and the bank helped many Americans invest their excess capital around the globe, particularly in the development of raw materials needed by American industry. The outflow of American investment reduced the pressures toward inflation at home and greatly increased America's financial holdings abroad. Americans believed that the World Bank served world reconstruction and America's domestic prosperity equally well.

The Bretton Woods agreements stabilized the international economy and helped revive trade and investment. They helped sustain America's postwar economic predominance, and the American dollar became the kingpin of international finance. Until 1971, when a system of floating exchange rates replaced the fixed system set forth at Bretton Woods, the economic agreements of 1944 remained the foundation for the world economy outside the Soviet bloc. For the developed nations, Bretton Woods provided a structure for nearly three decades of dynamic growth and global economic integration.

The Creation of the United Nations

During World War II, American officials revived Woodrow Wilson's idea of a League of Nations. They proposed an international body that would mediate disputes and create a multinational force to deter potential aggressors. They hoped to substitute collective security for old-style balance-of-power diplomacy.

At Dumbarton Oaks in Washington, D.C., in August 1944 and at San Francisco in April 1945, the wartime Allies hammered out the structural details of the United Nations. They established a General Assembly, in which all member nations had one vote; a Security Council comprising five permanent members (the United States, Great Britain, France, the Soviet Union, and Nationalist China) and six rotating, temporary members; a Secretariat to handle day-to-day business; and an Economic and Social Council comprising committees for worldwide social rehabilitation and economic development.

The Security Council, which according to the UN charter had the "primary responsibility for the maintenance of international peace and security," consisted of the major victors in World War II. The inclusion of China, at American insistence, always seemed incongruous. At the time of the UN charter, China had an unpopular and corrupt government led by Jiang Jie-shi (formerly spelled Chiang Kai-shek). Many observers doubted that Jiang could maintain control at home, much less play an active role in international affairs. But the inclusion of Jiang's China represented the Roosevelt administration's desire to turn China into a friendly Pacific power that would fill the vacuum left by Japan's defeat. In 1949, however, Jiang's Nationalist government fled to the small island of Formosa and a communist regime headed by Mao Zedong (formerly spelled Mao Tse-tung) came to power. Under Mao, China did become a major power, but the Nationalist regime continued to sit on the Security Council until 1971. This discrepancy between the realities of world power and Security Council membership proved to be a weakness of the United Nations.

The provision for veto power within the Security Council also undermined the UN's effectiveness. The charter provided that each permanent member of the Security Council could exercise an absolute veto over UN decisions. None of the great powers would have joined the UN without this means of safeguarding their national interests. But the veto provision meant that the UN could act only when all five permanent members agreed, and unanimity was rare in the postwar world. The UN's strongest action, sponsoring a military force to assist South Korea in 1950, was approved during the absence of the Soviet Union's delegate.

If the Security Council did not always fulfill the peacekeeping role that its founders envisioned, other UN bodies did serve useful functions. The humanitarian programs of the UN's various social and economic agencies boosted UN prestige. In addition, the General Assembly provided a forum in which nations could articulate their positions; it was a barometer of international tensions and a gauge of shifting views on various issues. It also provided a platform for smaller nations whose viewpoints might not otherwise be heard.

THE ONSET OF THE COLD WAR

The political and economic order that American leaders had planned depended on cooperation among the great powers. But divisions within the wartime Grand Alliance eventually undermined the kind of world that American policymakers hoped to create.

Mounting Distrust

Throughout the war, tensions had existed between the Soviet Union and the other Allies. The greatest disputes centered on the issue of wartime strategy. British planners, eventually supported by the United States, favored peripheral campaigns against Germany, first into French North Africa and then up through Sicily and Italy. Soviet Premier Joseph Stalin denounced these Anglo-American offensives because they delayed the opening of a second front to the west of Germany and forced the Soviet Union to bear the main thrust of German power. Stalin suspected that his allies were carving out spheres of influence in North Africa, Italy, and the Middle East while allowing Germany and the Soviet Union to exhaust each other. The long delay in opening a second front, Stalin reasoned, indicated that the wartime alliance against nazism had not softened capitalist hostility toward Soviet communism. The fierce fighting on the eastern front and the Soviet army's tremendous casualties helped shape Stalin's postwar policies. The Soviet leader wanted to eliminate the German menace that had repeatedly threatened his country. He viewed the creation of a pro-Soviet zone in neighboring Eastern Europe as vital to his country's national security.

During 1944 and 1945 Stalin believed he had some Allied support for his goal of creating a Soviet sphere of influence. At a meeting in 1944, Winston Churchill and Stalin secretly reached an informal agreement: Churchill would grant Soviet predominance in Romania and Bulgaria in return for British preeminence in Greece. Roosevelt did not protest the arrangement. Publicly, Americans talked of eliminating spheres of influence; privately, American policymakers seemed to understand their inevitability. At the Yalta Conference in February 1945, Allied harmony reached its high tide with the implicit recognition of spheres of influence: Germany was divided into four zones of occupation; the Soviet Union agreed to sign a treaty of friendship with America's ally in China, Jiang Jie-shi; the Allies agreed to a vague promise to hold "free elections" in liberated Europe, but Anglo-American negotiators implied their understanding of Stalin's need to have Poland as a friendly neighbor.

In the end, the course of battle largely determined the postwar power situation. Soviet troops marched into Berlin from the east as American and British forces advanced through Germany from the west, and the separate zones of occupation eventually hardened into a divided Germany. The nationality of occupation forces likewise helped determine the destiny of the countries surrounding Germany. Anglo-American influence was strong in France, Italy, Greece, and the Middle East; Soviet power predominated in Eastern Europe. The United States assumed exclusive control of the Japanese-dominated Pacific islands and of defeated Japan itself.

Stalin largely ignored the Yalta declaration supporting free elections in Eastern Europe. Pro-Soviet governments came to power in Romania, Hungary, Bulgaria, Albania, and Poland; Latvia, Lithuania, and Estonia were absorbed completely by the Soviet Union. Stalin refused to include an Anglo-American–sponsored group in the new government of Poland, and some Americans cried that Poland had been betrayed.

To Stalin, a Soviet-dominated zone in Eastern Europe represented a minimal guarantee of future security. It seemed a just reward for having borne the brunt of Germany's force and for having suffered staggering casualties. (The Soviet Union lost more than ten times as many soldiers as the United States.) Stalin also recalled that Anglo-American commanders had not allowed Soviet participation in governments under their military influence. In Italy after Benito Mussolini's overthrow, for example, Britain and the United States had installed a rightist regime committed to purging any leftist or pro-Soviet sentiment.

Stalin may have regarded his Eastern European policy as defensive, but to many people in the United States it appeared aggressive. Republicans blamed President Roosevelt, especially, for failing to obtain stronger guarantees for Eastern Europe at the Yalta Conference. They felt he had betrayed the cause of democracy. Americans of Eastern European descent and others who had expected the war to open all Europe to American trade and ideas began to view the Soviet Union as a new threat to peace similar to Nazi Germany. Both Roosevelt and Truman had acknowledged the importance of the 6 million Polish-Americans to the Democratic party's strength. And Stalin's brutal, iron-handed suppression of domestic dissent made him a convincing villain. Accustomed to thinking in terms of an evil and aggressive enemy, a growing number of Americans substituted the Soviets for the Germans as the new archenemies. A former State Department official, William C. Bullitt, expressed this attitude: "The Soviet Union's assault upon the West is at about the stage of Hitler's maneuvering into Czechoslovakia." This analysis could have only one conclusion—that there could be no appeasement, no compromise with Soviet power.

American-Soviet relations thus degenerated from an atmosphere of cooperation at Yalta in early 1945 to one of deep distrust by the end of the same year. Stalin's Eastern European policies provided the backdrop to this cooling of relations, but events in the United States also contributed.

Harry S Truman, who had become president in April 1945 following the death of Roosevelt, lacked FDR's cool self-confidence, easy affability, and cosmopolitan worldview. He had not been close to Roosevelt and knew little of his policies or intentions. In attempting to form guidelines for his new administration, Truman quickly sided with those advisers who advocated a harder line against the Soviet Union, and he rejected the notion of a Soviet sphere of influence in Eastern Europe. Setting a style for his successors, he began to talk tough to the Russians, especially at the Potsdam Conference of July 1945.

Truman and his advisers had two potent weapons in bargaining with Stalin. The first was atomic power. Even before Roosevelt's death, some advisers had suggested that the bomb might be an effective diplomatic lever. After demonstrating the horrible power of this weapon at Hiroshima and Nagasaki to bring about Japan's rapid surrender, some officials believed that Stalin could no longer ignore American demands to open Eastern Europe. Truman also hoped that the Soviet's need for postwar economic assistance would bring Stalin into line. After the termination of lend-lease, Stalin requested additional aid to help rebuild Russia's war-damaged economy. But Truman's tough tone indicated that assistance would be contingent on a change in the Soviet Union's Eastern European policy. Possessing overwhelming nuclear and economic power, American leaders were in no mood to compromise.

Rather than forcing Stalin into accommodation, Truman's hard-line policy reinforced Stalin's apprehensions about Soviet security and Western hostility. Fearful of the strings America might attach to any economic aid package, he eased his country's difficulties in other ways: a new Five-Year Plan to rebuild Soviet industry and an expropriation of materials from occupied territories, particularly East Germany. Just as the United States had removed thousands of tons of military materials and scientific documents from West

The A-Bomb, 1946. The tremendous power of the atom bomb created a terrible new military weapon; it also stimulated false hopes of a bountiful and cheap energy source in peacetime. *Source:* National Archives.

Germany, so the Soviet Union carried away whatever it could use—in some cases whole factories. More and more, Stalin closed the Soviet zone to Anglo-American influence.

Some Americans believed that Truman's hard line was at least partially responsible for Stalin's growing hostility. Secretary of Commerce Henry A. Wallace, for example, advocated a more cooperative attitude toward the Soviet Union, warning that the United States had everything to lose by "beating the tom-toms against Russia." In a speech in 1946 he pleaded "[We] should recognize that we have no more business in the political affairs of Eastern Europe than Russia has in the political affairs of Latin America." Wallace argued that a secure and prosperous Russia would be more accommodating than a frightened and hungry one. But this view ran counter to Truman's foreign policy. Angered by the public display of disunity within his administration, the president asked for Wallace's resignation.

From allies in a hot war the United States and the Soviet Union became enemies in a "cold war." In 1946 Stalin publicly expressed distrust of his old capitalist allies. Their objections to Soviet policy in Eastern Europe, he believed, indicated their intention to crush socialism and isolate the Soviet regime. On the other side, Winston Churchill denounced Soviet actions, charging that Stalin had dropped an "iron curtain" across Europe. With the collapse of the wartime alliance, the world plunged into a period of bipolar politics in which America and the Soviet Union vied for worldwide influence.

Cold War Aid Programs

By 1947 the American government faced a dilemma. It had almost completed a period of rapid military demobilization, and the public longed for the "normalcy" of peace. At the same time, government policymakers perceived the Soviet Union as a new aggressor and decided to adopt a hard line. In 1946 Secretary of State James Byrnes wrote, "We must help our friends in every way and refrain from assisting those who either through helplessness or for other reasons are opposing the principles for which we stand." But would the American Congress and public approve the appropriations that such help required?

By early 1947 the issue could no longer be postponed. A leftist revolution threatened the conservative regime in Greece, and Great Britain, which had previously considered Greece within its sphere of responsibility, announced that it could no longer provide economic and military assistance. The State Department wanted to grant extensive military aid to Greece and Turkey, a move that would have established a precedent for America's entry into other areas as a replacement for European power. But the chances that Congress would support such a commitment seemed slim. Senator Arthur Vandenberg correctly assessed the situation: "If Truman wants it, he will have to go and scare hell out of the country."

Truman was equal to the task, and he set out to sell Congress and the public on both the aid program and his cold war viewpoint. A leftist victory in Greece, he explained, would lead to communist takeovers in other parts of Europe. Before a joint session of Congress in March 1947, the president advanced the Truman Doctrine. He portrayed the struggle in Greece as a conflict between two ways of life, one "distinguished by free institutions, representative government, free elections, guarantees of individual liberty, freedom of speech and religion, and freedom from political oppression." The other system relied on "terror and oppression, a controlled press and radio, fixed elections, and the suppression of personal freedoms." By failing to act, Truman concluded, "we may endanger the peace of the world—and we shall surely endanger the welfare of our own nation." These arguments cast anticommunism in global terms and brought a $400 million authorization to extend assistance, primarily military aid, to Greece and neighboring Turkey, strategically located on the Dardanelles.

The rationale for the Truman Doctrine set the terms of Americans' analysis of foreign affairs for years to come and formed the core of a policy called *containment*. The classic and most sophisticated statement of containment came in a 1947 article in *Foreign Affairs* written by George Kennan, a respected foreign service officer. Writing under the pseudonym "Mr. X," Kennan analyzed the Soviet Union's "expansive tendencies" and advocated a "firm and vigilant" application of counterforce to meet Soviet maneuvers until internal change in Russia moderated the threat to the West. Kennan stressed the importance of ordering strategic priorities; concentrating strength only in the locations deemed truly critical to national interest; and of seeing the Soviet Union, not some vague ideology called international communism, as the threat to be "contained." But these crucial subtleties became lost as containment evolved into a global, ideological crusade.

In December 1947 the president again requested a strong commitment of economic aid—this time to European nations, including Germany. Initially Congress balked, but a procommunist coup in neutralist Czechoslovakia convinced many people that Soviet aggression threatened Europe and that containment had to be implemented. The new aid program—the Marshall Plan—passed by an overwhelming margin.

The Marshall Plan sprang not only from a genuine desire to alleviate human suffering but also from a very practical assessment of America's national interests. The entire economic and political system that American policymakers had arduously constructed in postwar conferences depended on the economic revival of European nations. But European economies were faltering, and Germany remained a weak and defeated nation. American leaders recognized that their own country's prosperity ultimately required a prosperous and stable Europe. In addition, as hostility toward the Soviet Union mounted, it seemed increasingly necessary to counter Soviet power with a strong, industrialized West Germany. Germany, the Nazi enemy that had once united capitalists and communists, now became the focal point of the cold war, ominously divided between the two competing camps. As the Soviet Union changed from ally to enemy, West Germany changed from enemy to ally.

Following the enunciation of the Truman Doctrine and Marshall Plan, the U.S. government would continue to employ economic and military aid as instruments to advance its global power. Money often brought needed assistance to poverty-ridden areas and helped boost America's trade and investment abroad. American aid helped revitalize Europe. But the policy also frequently led to expensive or impossible commitments. Whereas the Soviet Union sometimes took advantage of global postwar disruption by backing revolutionary and anticolonial movements, the United States tried to "contain" instability. Threats to the status quo became suspect, and nationalist movements in the Third World, even when they had little connection with Moscow, were too often viewed solely as part of a cohesive international communist conspiracy. At a time when Europe's empires were breaking down, the United States moved into these power vacuums and often continued to back unpopular regimes. The United States increasingly pitted its might against any change that it did not control.

COLD WAR CRISES

The cold war grew more menacing during Truman's second term, and Dean Acheson, who became secretary of state in 1949, confronted a series of foreign-policy crises. In each of these, Truman and Acheson nurtured a virulent anticommunist sentiment that then came to justify suppression of dissent at home and new techniques for extending American control abroad. Acheson hoped that later generations would recognize the "truly heroic mold" of the Truman administration's cold war policies, and many later historians have indeed applauded the "wise men" of this era who charted the anticommunist course. But many other historians have viewed these years as ones of lost opportunities, when complex global realities were forced into the simplistic mold of an ideological battle between Soviet "slavery" and U.S. "freedom."

The Berlin Crisis

By 1947, American policymakers had accepted the need to contain Soviet aggression by stabilizing Europe through economic assistance. The reestablishment of Germany as an industrial power and its reintegration into Europe's economy seemed essential for the continent's full recovery. Consequently, the United States, Great Britain, and France decided to merge their zones of occupation into one federal republic and to institute a program of economic rehabilitation. On June 18, 1948, the three powers announced a currency reform for what would become, in 1949, the Federal Republic of Germany.

The Soviet Union saw the strengthening of West Germany as a provocation. Stalin wanted Germany to remain weak and divided; he desired German reparations for war damage; and he sought to dismantle the country's industrial capacity, not to rebuild it. In retaliation for the West's actions, he formed the German Democratic Republic in East Germany and closed off West Berlin, an Anglo-American–controlled sector of the capital city that was wholly within the Soviet zone.

Only one way remained into the blockaded city—by airplane. Planes began flying around the clock to deliver food, fuel, and medicine to the 2.5 million people in West Berlin. In Montana pilots practiced landings at a flight-training center with an air corridor, runways, and navigational aids exactly duplicating those in Berlin. Assisted by the latest radar techniques, Operation Vittles, as the pilots dubbed the airlift, landed almost 13,000 tons of provisions during its peak day. By the spring of 1949 the airlift was bringing as much into Berlin as water and rail had provided before the blockade. To underscore how seriously he viewed the crisis, Truman also reinstated the draft and sent two squadrons of B-29s to Great Britain. In the face of this commitment, the Soviet Union backed off. In May 1949 Stalin reopened certain corridors of surface travel into West Berlin, and the city returned to its uneasy equilibrium. But the divided city would remain a symbol and point of tension throughout the cold war.

During the year-long Berlin crisis, which had closely followed the communist coup in Czechoslovakia, the nations of Western Europe grew increasingly anxious about cold war tensions. With United States encouragement, Britain, France, Belgium, the Netherlands, and Luxembourg signed the Brussels Pact, pledging cooperation in economic and military matters. They also appealed for a stronger U.S. commitment to their security. Finally, in the spring of 1949 twelve nations, including the United States and the Brussels

Pact countries, established the North Atlantic Treaty Organization (NATO). This collective-security pact provided that an attack against one of the signatories would be considered an attack against all. Furthermore, the contracting nations promised to encourage economic ties with one another. NATO laid the groundwork for America's long-lasting military presence in Western Europe and formed a pattern for later collective-security pacts, CENTO and SEATO, in other parts of the world. NATO, together with the Marshall Plan, brought Western Europe under America's economic and military umbrella.

The Chinese Revolution

Throughout World War II, China not only fought against invading Japanese troops but was also embroiled in a civil war between the Nationalist government of Jiang Jie-shi and communist forces under Mao Zedong. The United States supported Jiang's government, providing it with arms, money, and advisers. After the war, it secured the Nationalist government a prestigious position on the new UN Security Council. Throughout the war and into the postwar period, however, many American diplomats in China predicted that Jiang's government was too corrupt and incompetent to prevail. Mao's forces were both more popular with the peasants and had been more effective in fighting against the Japanese.

Statistical comparisons made Jiang's victory over the communists seem a sure thing: By 1947 he had twice the number of men under arms and three or four times the number of rifles. From 1945 through 1948 the United States extended him a billion dollars in military aid and another billion in economic assistance. Yet these figures only measured his incompetence and lack of support. Despite American help, Jiang's armies rapidly lost ground; Chinese peasants flocked to the communist side, which promised land reform and popular government. At the end of 1948 the director of the American military advisory group in China, Major-General David Barr, reported that "the military situation [had] deteriorated to the point where only the active participation of United States troops could effect a remedy." And this adviser "certainly [did] not recommend" allying with what he termed "the world's worst leadership" to attempt the impossible: regaining the enormous expanse of Chinese territory that Jiang had lost to the communists. Still, although many officials in China believed Jiang's downfall inevitable, both the Roosevelt and Truman administrations continued supporting Jiang and his corrupt clique.

Early in 1949 the Nationalist government was forced to withdraw to the island of Formosa (Taiwan), leaving Mao Zedong in complete control of the mainland. To Secretary Acheson the turn of events was disturbing, but in a white paper presented to the president he wrote that the situation in China was "beyond the control of the government of the United States." Still, the U.S. government was trapped by its previous attempt to strengthen Jiang. Not wishing to harm the Nationalist cause, American officials had failed publicly to acknowledge the full extent of Jiang's unpopularity and ineptness. What seemed inevitable to officials knowledgeable about China looked to Americans who had come to view Jiang as the strong and respected leader of "free" China like a sellout to communism. By the time Jiang retreated, it was too late to revise the public's view of him.

The news of China's "fall" hit the United States like a bombshell. The Truman administration's Republican opponents, especially members of a powerful China lobby financed by conservative Republican business leaders, began charging that Truman and his State Department were responsible for "losing" China. Both policymakers and their opponents pictured the uneasy and short-lived alliance between China and the Soviet Union of 1949 as an ideological bond that cemented an international communist conspiracy to conquer the world. For twenty years the United States refused to recognize or deal with the communist Chinese government, even after the Sino-Soviet split totally shattered myths about a monolithic threat called international communism.

The Anticommunist Crusade

Following swiftly on the news from China came word that the Soviet Union had exploded a nuclear device. America no longer had sole possession of the ultimate weapon. Publicly, the Truman administration issued reassuring comments that the announcement had been expected and necessitated no change in America's own policies. Privately, however, Truman tilted toward his hard-line advisers and made the fateful decision to escalate atomic competition by developing a hydrogen bomb, a device based on the still-hypothetical concept of nuclear fusion.

The constant crises of 1949—Berlin, China, and Russia's new bomb—unsettled many Americans. The communist threat appeared to be everywhere; American power seemed in retreat. Many Republicans and some Democrats sought the source of America's problems not in the world at large but in traitors in their midst. The charge seemed to gain credibility when a former State Department officer, Alger Hiss, was accused of passing government papers to the Soviet Union. The search for Soviet spy rings became the order of the day; Republican Senator William E. Jenner of Indiana charged that the Truman administration consisted of a "crazy assortment of collectivist cutthroat crackpots and Communist fellow-traveling appeasers." Acheson's assessment regarding China—that America could not control all world events—sounded to some like a new doctrine of appeasement, and many Republicans demanded Acheson's resignation. The cry for an all-out crusade against communism, including suppression of dissent at home and of revolution abroad, would affect American life and policy for years to come.

The international shocks of 1949 and the fire from Republican leaders prompted senior officials in the State and Defense departments to draw up a paper outlining foreign-policy assumptions and future strategy. The report, called NSC 68, was approved by the National Security Council and the president. In 1950 Acheson traveled throughout the country trying to regain his credibility as a tough anticommunist by preaching the assumptions on which

NSC 68 was based. The report's logic eventually became the conventional wisdom of the cold war. According to NSC 68, the Soviet Union was determined to stamp out freedom and dominate the world. Negotiation with the communists was futile, for they did not bargain in good faith. And there could be no valid distinction between national and world security. The United States could not, as Acheson put it, "pull down the blinds and sit in the parlor with a loaded shotgun, waiting." The country had to embark on a massive military buildup at home and create "situations of strength" abroad, regardless of cost. NSC 68 provided the blueprint for a "national security state": a leviathan with overwhelming military power, a wide variety of economic weapons, and an extensive capacity for covert operations.

In his cold war speeches Acheson argued that freedom meant simply anticommunism. Those people who wanted to go from ally to ally "with political litmus paper testing them for true-blue democracy" were "escapists." Furthermore, domestic consensus served freedom whereas differences of opinion aided the enemy. The "fomenters of disunity" who advocated negotiation with the Soviets, Acheson explained, contributed to American weakness. Other observers, noting how often "freedom" was invoked to support dictators abroad and to suppress dissent at home, suggested that language, and therefore communication, became a serious casualty of the cold war.

Korea

Koreans, long dominated by Japanese power, had looked forward to liberation and independence after Japan's defeat in World War II. By 1946, however, zones of occupation, as in Germany, had hardened into political jurisdictions. The communist North under Kim Il Sung allied with the Soviet Union and carried out land and labor reforms on a communist model. The South, under the elite-based rule of Syngman Rhee, allied with the United States and resisted reformist challenges.

In June 1950, communist North Korea attacked South Korea across the thirty-eighth parallel dividing line in an attempt to unify the country. Committed to a policy of containment, possibly even a rollback of communism in Asia, the Truman administration invoked the assumptions and fears articulated in NSC 68. Americans viewed the Korean conflict as a showdown with international communism. Using the logic outlined in his Truman Doctrine for Greece and Turkey, the president announced that "if aggression is successful in Korea, we can expect it to spread through Asia and Europe to this hemisphere." One weak spot in the "free world" defense would start the dominoes falling.

In line with this worldwide containment policy, Truman responded globally. He gained UN support for an American-controlled defense of Syngman Rhee's South Korean regime (the Soviet delegation was boycotting the United Nations and could not exercise its veto); he also announced protection for Jiang Jie-shi's exiled regime in Formosa and ordered support for the French in their efforts to hold off communist-led nationalists in Vietnam. Assistance was extended to the Philippine government's attempts to suppress leftist Huk rebels, and the administration accelerated its efforts to encourage Japan's emergence as a strong economic and anticommunist bastion in the Far East. In Europe, more troops were added to the NATO military force, and a program for rearming West Germany was announced. The front line against communism lay everywhere, and America committed its power, prestige, and treasure as though there were no limits.

American policymakers were torn between two goals during the Korean War: simple containment (which would leave Korea divided) and rollback (which would unite it under American influence). As long as South Korean and American troops were retreating southward early in the war, restoration of a boundary at the thirty-eighth parallel seemed victory enough. But when a regrouped force under General Douglas MacArthur landed at Inchon behind enemy lines and drove the North Koreans back from the thirty-eighth parallel, decisions became more complicated. Could MacArthur "liberate" North Korea, and would the Soviet Union and China intervene if he did? The president gave MacArthur authority to pursue the war in the north as long as it did not bring a wider war with China, but the general underestimated Chinese reaction. After crossing the thirty-eighth parallel, American soldiers began to encounter Chinese "volunteers." Then, as American forces penetrated farther into North Korea and approached the border of China, the provocation became too great for China to ignore. Chinese troops streamed into Korea and sent MacArthur's armies reeling backward across the thirty-eighth parallel once again. When MacArthur regrouped and once more pushed northward, Truman ordered him to seek a negotiated settlement.

Truman's order provoked a dramatic clash between civilian and military authority. The general publicly opposed Truman's "limited war" and balked at his instructions. He pressed for a full-scale commitment to victory over North Korea, even over China, and claimed that this was America's chance to roll back communism in Asia. Truman, however, held to his position that a lengthy conflict in Korea would weaken America's defense posture in other, more vital areas. He viewed the Soviet Union as the real enemy and believed a costly Asian land war would only play into Stalin's hands. Responding to MacArthur's challenge to presidential authority, Truman had only one choice: He removed the general from command.

Those "Asia-firsters" who had denounced Truman following Jiang Jie-shi's fall in China now had new ammunition and a popular martyr. They condemned the "no-win policy" against communism, and MacArthur returned home a hero. Telegrams demanding Truman's impeachment flooded the Capitol. Huge crowds greeted the general in San Francisco, Washington, and New York. A parade in New York on his behalf attracted 7.5 million people (compared with 4 million for Eisenhower at the end of World War II) and produced over 3,000 tons of litter. George Gallup reported that only 29 percent of those polled supported President Truman's action against MacArthur.

The outpouring of support, including a MacArthur-for-president booklet, subsided quickly. Senate hearings on the general's dismissal convinced the public that most military strategists opposed a wider conflict in Asia, and few Americans wanted full-scale war. Admiration for MacArthur's military achievements remained, but most Americans welcomed negotiation. When the 1952 Republican nominee for president, General Dwight D. Eisenhower, promised to go to Korea and end the struggle, he received applause and votes. By the end of Truman's presidency the war in Korea had grown less intense and both sides had gathered around a conference table. Hammering out the details of a negotiated settlement (which eventually reestablished the thirty-eighth parallel as a dividing line) would fall to the new Republican administration.

New Policies in New Areas of Concern

The rise of America's global power and the decline of European power in the Middle East, India, Africa, and Southeast Asia necessitated developing policies toward new areas hardly considered by American policymakers of the past. Significantly, decisions were forged less out of experience, which was scant, than out of the bipolar, cold war thinking of NSC 68. Whereas during World War II American policymakers had frequently formed ties to anticolonial movements and encouraged allies to plan for decolonization, the growing conservatism and preoccupation with anticommunism that characterized the late 1940s and early 1950s tilted American policies into misunderstanding, even hostility, toward popular nationalist movements.

In Southeast Asia, Americans severed their wartime contacts with the popular Vietnamese communist-nationalist Ho Chi Minh and supported French efforts to maintain the old colonialist order.

In India, U.S. policymakers persistently confused Jawaharlal Nehru's nationalist policy of nonalignment with Soviet sympathizing. American policymakers and media pictured Nehru, a widely respected leader of Third World nationalist aspirations, as a slightly befuddled mystic who lacked the clarity of vision to recognize the Soviet threat and ally with the United States. Dean Acheson, after meeting Nehru during his goodwill trip to the United States in 1949, wrote, "I was convinced that Nehru and I were not destined to have a pleasant personal relationship. . . . He was one of the most difficult men with whom I have ever had to deal." Such condescending attitudes and the policies that emerged from them hardly provided a promising basis for future U.S. relations with the Third World.

Issues of race and international politics emerged with special clarity in the late 1940s in South Africa. The white, Afrikaner-based Nationalist party came to power in 1948 and began erecting apartheid—an elaborate system of racial separation and systematic, legally sanctioned discrimination against the nonwhites, who made up more than 80 percent of the South African population. Although some American policymakers, fresh from fighting Nazi ideas of a "master race," questioned the wisdom and morality of such a racially based government system, the desire to open South Africa to growing American trade and investment and to maintain friendly access to South Africa's copious store of strategic raw materials took precedence. The South African government also garnered U.S. support by portraying black aspirations as communist-inspired and casting its own minority rulers as stalwart defenders of capitalism in Africa. In addition, strong criticism of South Africa seemed difficult in light of America's own racially segregated society.

America's burgeoning economic presence in South Africa after 1948 attracted by the cheap labor supply that apartheid ensured, provided the basis for a growing alliance between the United States and the white South African government. Within the next two decades nearly fifty African nations became independent, and American policy toward these states—nearly all black-ruled and determinedly hostile to South Africa's racially repressive regime—took shape within the context of the close South African–U.S. alliance.

The Middle East also presented new issues. Only in Saudi Arabia, particularly through oil investments, had the United States maintained a substantial presence before the war. After 1940, strategic and economic bonds with that desert kingdom increased dramatically, and U.S. interests expanded into other areas as well. When, in 1946, the Soviet Union attempted to extend its own economic and political influence into northern Iran, for example, the United States made it clear that Britain's postwar weakness in this traditional zone of British influence should not mean gains for the Soviets. The Soviets retreated, leaving Iran and its rich oil fields within the perimeter of Anglo-American power and interest. Policies in this area would continue to be shaped through the prisms of anticommunism and the maintenance of access to oil.

Elsewhere in the Middle East, the Truman administration's support for the creation of Israel proved to have far-reaching implications. In Western Europe the problem of homeless Jewish refugees, displaced by Nazi atrocities, pressed urgently on policymakers, and Truman supported large-scale resettlement of Jews as part of his concern over the social stability of Europe. At the same time, powerful Jewish groups in the United States and abroad stressed the world's moral obligation and recalled certain assurances given to Jews during World War I to provide a Jewish homeland in Palestine. Over the objections of Middle Eastern experts in the State Department, who urged that the interests of Palestinian Arabs and others in the Middle East needed to be given more consideration, the Truman administration recognized the state of Israel in May 1948, just minutes after it was officially proclaimed by the Israeli forces, who had wrested the land in a bloody fight with Arab inhabitants. The tangle of hatreds, of demographic and boundary problems, and of new refugee issues remained to fester and provide the seeds of future conflicts and foreign-policy dilemmas.

LONG-TERM TRENDS IN FOREIGN POLICY

World War II vastly changed the U.S. government bureaucracy. Before the war the federal government employed about 800,000 civilians, 10 percent of whom were involved with national security; by the end of the war the figure had risen to nearly 4 million, with 75 percent working for national security agencies. Although the new government bureaus were designed to increase the efficiency of wartime operations, their sheer size and complexity often complicated decision making. New photocopying techniques brought additional problems associated with a "paper revolution."

The State Department, the agency traditionally responsible for creating and executing foreign policy, was transformed during the war. The department and its related agencies outgrew old quarters and, during the 1950s, expanded into twenty-nine buildings throughout Washington, D.C. When all of these offices were finally brought together in 1961, it took eight stories covering a four-block area to house them. Before the war a few people would meet in the secretary of state's office, discuss world problems, and set policy. By the end of the war, cozy familiarity and easy communication had given way to faceless bureaucratic routine. Truman's secretary of state, Dean Acheson, once asked Cordell Hull, Franklin Roosevelt's secretary of state, to come by the department and meet the assistant secretaries. Hull declined, wryly commenting that he had never done well in crowds.

The cold war also helped swell the State Department's support staff. In its new role as global superpower, the United States seemed to need a resident expert on every conceivable topic so that it could react quickly to a wide variety of situations. In this era of confrontation, the most casual decision could suddenly mushroom into a matter of major importance.

After 1949 the crisis atmosphere of the cold war delivered strong blows to the State Department's effectiveness. Mao's victory in China in 1949 outraged those Americans who believed that communism could never triumph on its own merits. The China lobby, with its close ties to the popular media, drummed the refrain that the State Department officials "sold out" China, and pressure mounted to purge the "old China hands" who had advised against an open-ended commitment to Jiang Jie-shi. Throughout the 1950s many seasoned diplomats lost influence to newer people who took a harder anticommunist line. The immediate suspicion of anyone who questioned cold war verities quashed healthy differences of opinion. The State Department became less involved in forming policies according to world realities and more caught up in interpreting the world according to a preestablished cold war viewpoint. The cold war consensus of the early and mid-1950s, combined with the attacks on experienced diplomats, damaged the effectiveness, and ultimately the prestige and power, of the State Department.

Other agencies challenged the State Department's primacy in foreign policymaking. Before the war, nearly all foreign-policy functions were centralized at State; after the war, other departments and agencies assumed major responsibilities. Policymaking became a complex process involving many different bureaucracies, each with its experts and points of view.

The military establishment became the most powerful rival in handling foreign affairs. During the war Roosevelt had increasingly turned to the military for advice, and the Joint Chiefs of Staff, created in 1941, eroded the State Department's position as the preeminent body in foreign policy. In 1947 the National Security Act reorganized the military establishment and also created a new National Security Council to advise the president. These reorganizations, housed in the huge new Pentagon building, further boosted the military's input into policymaking.

The Central Intelligence Agency (CIA) also rivaled the State Department. The CIA grew out of the Office of Strategic Services (OSS), a wartime intelligence-gathering agency. After the war the State Department, the armed services, and the FBI all sought to assume the functions of the OSS. As a compromise in 1947, the CIA was created as an independent agency under the new National Security Act. Under the influence of its activist director, Walter Bedell Smith, the CIA began to narrow into a preoccupation with anticommunism. (Smith reportedly once confided that he believed even Eisenhower was a communist.) Although the CIA's finances and operations were kept secret, scholars have estimated that the agency rapidly surpassed the State Department both in number of employees and in budget. Most CIA work involved intelligence collection and analysis, but it also delved into covert operations. American ambassadors in foreign lands complained that their ignorance of the CIA's clandestine activities sometimes undermined their prestige.

Some elements of foreign policy were altogether external to the government. Although private businesspeople in foreign lands had always influenced international affairs, the giant U.S.-based multinational corporations that mushroomed in the postwar era exerted an unparalleled impact on foreign relations. For example, the great oil giants—the so-called seven sisters—profoundly affected the world's economy through their agreements that set the world price of oil and divided up spheres of production and distribution. Many companies with far-flung investments began to view themselves as wholly new forces in international relations, developing company interests that could surpass national loyalties.

SUGGESTIONS FOR FURTHER READING

There are numerous studies of the U.S. role in the cold war world. Thomas J. McCormick, *America's Half-Century: United States Foreign Policy in the Cold War* (1989), places the cold war in a twentieth-century context; Melvyn Leffler, *A Preponderance of Power: National Security, the Truman Administration, and the Cold War* (1992), is a comprehensive study; and Thomas Paterson, *On Every Front* (rev. ed., 1992), offers a brief overview. Other broad treatments include Walter LaFeber, *America, Russia, and the Cold War, 1945–84* (rev. ed., 1985); Stephen Ambrose, *Rise to Globalism: American Foreign Policy Since 1938* (rev. ed., 1988); John Gaddis, *The Long Peace* (1987); Gabriel Kolko, *Confronting the Third World: United States Foreign Policy 1945–1980* (1988); and H. W. Brands, *The Devil We Knew: Americans and the Cold War* (1993).

On national security policy during the late 1940s and early 1950s, consult Leffler, *A Preponderance of Power*; Daniel Yergin, *Shattered Peace: The Origins of the Cold War and the National Security State* (1977); Gar Alperowitz, *Atomic Diplomacy* (rev. ed., 1985); Martin Sherwin, *A World Destroyed* (1985); Gregg Herkin, *The Winning Weapon: The Atomic Bomb in the Cold War* (1981); and John

Gaddis, *Strategies of Containment* (1982). For broad cultural views of national security, see the relevant essays in Michael Rogin, *Ronald Reagan, the Movie* (1987); the relevant chapters of Richard Slotkin, *Gunfighter Nation* (1992); and Robert J. Corber, *In the Name of National Security: Hitchcock, Homophobia, and the Political Construction of Gender in Postwar America* (1993).

On specific areas, see Terry H. Anderson, *The United States, Great Britain and the Cold War, 1944–1947* (1981); Bruce Kuklick, *American Policy and the Division of Germany* (1972); Akira Iriye, *The Cold War in Asia* (1974); Robert J. McMahon, *Colonialism and Cold War: The United States and the Struggle for Indonesian Independence* (1981); Nancy B. Tucker, *Patterns in the Dust: Chinese-American Relations and the Recognition Controversy, 1949–1950* (1983); Thomas M. Leonard, *The United States and Central America, 1944–1949* (1984); Thomas Noer, *Cold War and Black Liberation: The United States and White Rule in Africa, 1948–1968* (1985); Michael Schaller, *The American Occupation of Japan* (1985); Gary Hess, *The U.S. Emergence as a Southeast Asia Power* (1986); David Painter, *Oil and the American Century* (1986), on the Middle East and Latin America; William Roger Louis and Hedley Bull, eds., *The Special Relationship: Anglo-American Relations since 1945* (1986); June M. Grasso, *Harry Truman's Two-China Policy* (1987); Nathan Godfried, *Bridging the Gap between Rich and Poor (1987)*, on the Middle East; Howard Schonberger, *Aftermath of War: America and the Remaking of Japan, 1945–1952* (1989); Gordon Chang, *Friends and Enemies: The United States, China, and the Soviet Union, 1948–1972* (1989); E. Timothy Smith, *The United States, Italy, and NATO, 1947–52* (1991); Frank Costigliola, *France and the United States: The Cold War Alliance since 1945* (1992); Thomas Borstelmann, *Apartheid's Reluctant Uncle: The United States and Southern Africa in the Early Cold War* (1993); W. Michael Weis, *Cold Warriors & Coup d'Etat: Brazilian-American Relations, 1945–1964* (1993); and Ronald McGlothlen, *Controlling the Waves: Dean Acheson and U.S. Foreign Policy in Asia* (1993).

On particular aspects of U.S. policy, see Richard Freeland, *The Truman Doctrine and the Origins of McCarthyism* (1971); Michael Sherry, *Preparing for the Next War* (1977); Fred J. Block, *The Origins of International Economic Disorder* (1977); Lawrence Kaplan, *The United States and NATO* (1984); Robert A. Divine, *Since 1945: Politics and Diplomacy in Recent American History* (3rd ed., 1985); Robert A. Pollard, *Economic Security and the Origins of the Cold War* (1986); Michael Hogan, *The Marshall Plan* (1987); James Edward Miller, *The United States and Italy, 1940–50* (1987); Louis Liebovich, *The Press and the Origins of the Cold War, 1944–1947* (1988); Howard Jones, *A New Kind of War: America's Global Strategy and the Truman Doctrine in Greece* (1989); Erik Beukel, *American Perceptions of the Soviet Union as a Nuclear Adversary* (1989); Ronald L. Filippelli, *American Labor and Postwar Italy, 1943–1953: A Study of Cold War Politics* (1989); and Sallie Pisani, *The CIA and the Marshall Plan* (1991).

There are excellent studies of the Korean War. Burton I. Kaufman, *The Korean War* (1986), is a brief synthesis. A more detailed analysis may be found in several volumes by Bruce Cuming: *The Origins of the Korean War* (1981); *Child of Conflict* (1983), a series of essays that he edited; and, coauthored with Jon Halliday, *Korea: The Unknown War* (1988). See also William S. Stueck, Jr.,

The Road to Confrontation (1981), and Joseph Goulden, *Korea: The Untold Story* (1982).

   Biographical studies include Ronald Steel, *Walter Lippman and the American Century* (1980); Robert Ferrell, *Harry Truman and the Modern American Presidency* (1983); Walter Issacson and Evan Thomas, *The Wise Men* (1986), which looks at six leading architects of cold war policy; Mark A. Stoler, *George C. Marshall* (1989); Walter Hixson, *George F. Kennan* (1989); Anders Stephanson, *Kennan and the Art of Foreign Relations* (1989); Townshend Hoopes and Douglas Brinkley, *Driven Patriot: The Life and Times of James Forrestal* (1992); and Howard B. Schaffer, *Chester Bowles: New Dealer in the Cold War* (1993).

2

Postwar Readjustments, 1946–1953

The years from 1945 to 1952 seemed peculiarly marked by a popular mood that oscillated between visions of unprecedented peril and almost unlimited promise. The American film industry, facing the challenge of television, brilliantly captured the deep ambivalence in postwar society. On the one hand, Hollywood turned out films celebrating happiness, innovation, and prosperity. *Singing in the Rain* (1952) epitomized this mood. The brightly colored musical traced Hollywood's own transition from the silent era to sound, driving home the theme that upbeat, flexible people could adapt to changing times. The film became a great popular and critical success. Yet Hollywood also found millions of filmgoers drawn to motion pictures that emphasized the dark corners of postwar life. A whole cycle called *film noir* tore away at the easy optimism of pictures like *Singing in the Rain* and portrayed deeply troubled people fighting among themselves, confronting sinister forces, almost never succeeding, and oftentimes even failing to survive. In many of these films, the pursuit of the American Dream seemed a blind, foolish, fatally flawed obsession. Only a fool would want to sing about the joys of rain-soaked city streets, suggested *noir* films like *The Asphalt Jungle* (1950).

The tension between promise and peril appeared in almost every area of postwar life. From the programs of the Truman administration that simultaneously trumpeted both the nightmare of a vast communist menace and the dream of a domestic welfare state, to the problems of American workers, who faced both the perils of technological innovations and the promise of higher living standards, the postwar era seemed shot through with contradictory hopes and fears.

RECONVERSION, 1946–1948

Postwar Tensions

Throughout World War II, most Americans sacrificed to preserve the "American way of life." But as the global conflict dragged into 1945, it became evident that the United States had changed in fundamental ways. The war's end would terminate one struggle but would also usher in new problems, both at home and overseas.

President Harry S Truman and his close advisers had awaited the end of the war with both hope and fear. The return of peace, they hoped, would allow the Democratic party to retrieve the fallen standard of domestic reform, to revive the New Deal spirit. But the end of war also brought fears of economic stagnation. Economists recognized that it was not New Deal programs but World War II, with its huge government expenditures, that had finally ended the Great Depression of the 1930s. Remembering the sharp economic downturn that had followed the first Great War—and the bitter social conflicts that the depression of 1919 had brought—many national leaders dreaded the transition from war to peace. What would happen when wartime production slowed? Only a few weeks after the final victory, almost 100,000 defense workers in Detroit alone lost their jobs. Could production for civilian consumption take up the slack and put people back to work?

Wartime mobilization had touched most areas of American life. During World War II more and more women had entered the wartime labor force, where they sometimes took traditionally male jobs and received equal pay with men. "Latchkey children," kids who returned from school while parents were still at work, became a familiar sight during the war, and the national government, under the Lantham Act, even provided federal financing for a limited number of child-care centers. Although wartime publicists tried to portray such changes as temporary, many women held a different view. The Women's Bureau of the United Auto Workers Union reported in April 1945, "In one shipyard, 98 percent of the women want to continue working in shipyards." Other surveys confirmed that women overwhelmingly hoped to retain their wartime positions and wages.

More independence for women and children, however, provoked great controversies. Some social observers blamed working women for new strains on the family, including discontented husbands and an allegedly rising tide of juvenile delinquency. Traditionalists argued that in the postwar period, women must abandon the workplace to restabilize family relations and to alleviate the prospect of male unemployment and potential labor strife over job seniority. Returning male war veterans, they argued, "needed" jobs to bring home a "family wage." Despite attempts by the Women's Bureau in the Department of Labor and a variety of women's groups within labor unions to support women's employment concerns, men who were hostile or indifferent to the needs and desires of female workers dominated the numerous committees charged with planning postwar reconversion. Very quickly after the war, psychologists, economists, politicians, and the media all endorsed closing the doors of economic opportunity for women in the workplace. For many women, the decision to center their work around home involved no meaningful choice at all; for many who continued to work outside the home, opportunities were again narrowed to low-paying jobs in domestic service or clerical positions.

Issues of war and reconversion also intertwined with racial conflicts. Japanese-Americans, who had been stripped of their property and forcibly relocated from their West Coast homes to internment camps during World War II, faced the prospect of rebuilding their once prosperous communities. While Japanese-Americans were being restrained behind barbed wire, large numbers of African-Americans, American Indians, and Mexican-Americans were eagerly pursuing wartime job opportunities, which often necessitated moving from rural farm areas to urban industrial centers. These rapid demographic and occupational shifts stirred racial hostility between newcomers and established residents and jobholders, and most parts of the country saw significant racial conflict during World War II. African-American service personnel who insisted on wearing their uniforms in public, for instance, risked becoming the targets of racist violence; and full-scale racial conflict, which claimed lives, rocked Detroit in 1943.

Racist violence did not stop antidiscrimination efforts. Following their pledge to President Franklin Roosevelt, prominent civil rights leaders, such as A. Philip Randolph, did postpone plans to march on Washington in search of greater job opportunities for people of color; instead, they trusted that Roosevelt's Fair Employment Practices Committee would fight discriminatory hiring practices in the burgeoning war-production sector. But smaller-scale, grass-roots protests against discrimination continued during the 1940s. The so-called "zoot-suit" incidents, for example, provoked large-scale violence in Los Angeles in 1943 and smaller conflagrations elsewhere. The zoot-suiters, young Mexican-American and African-American men, adopted a clothing style that featured yards of elaborately draped pants and jackets; their zoot suits served as a symbolic, sartorial protest against racial discrimination by flaunting the wartime rationing of fabrics. At the same time, working-class black women stepped up their protests against the discrimination that marked the daily operation of many public transportation systems, especially in the Deep South, where even during a war for democracy, racial segregation remained the law of the land.

Although socioeconomic issues such as work opportunities for women and new demographic and racial trends failed to capture the kind of consistent media coverage reserved for foreign-policy questions, they deeply affected the lives of millions of Americans in the postwar era. Questions of gender and race thus symbolized a broader point: Social changes of the war years affected postwar society in all kinds of ways that had never been expected during the early 1940s.

In addition, the disorders and tensions of the immediate postwar period forcefully raised the question of the government's future role in postwar social policy. Liberal economists and many Democratic politicians argued that the national government should continue the social and economic programs—and also solidify the political gains—of the Roosevelt era. Government welfare measures could not be limited to times of acute economic depression, liberal economists contended, but must become a permanent part of the postwar economic system. Increased spending for social welfare programs would pump money into the economy, easing the problem of reconversion and providing a cushion against social conflict. Unless the national administration took decisive action, some forecasters claimed, postwar unemployment might reach 11 million workers.

Only three weeks after Japan's surrender, President Truman proposed twenty-one domestic spending programs. These included an increased minimum wage, money for hospital construction, funds for small businesses, permanent government price supports for farmers, and legislation to ensure full employment. The Truman administration faced congressional opposition from a coalition of anti–New Deal Republicans and southern Democrats, but the Seventy-ninth Congress did pass a number of Truman's proposals, including the Hospital Construction Act, the Veterans Emergency Housing Act, funds for power and soil conservation projects, and a modified version of the highly controversial Full Employment Bill of 1945.

The Full Employment Bill produced bitter political and economic debates. The bill's drafters hoped to "establish a national policy and program for assuring continuing full employment," largely through continual planning, direction, and spending by the national government. Washington would take responsibility for ensuring that the "free enterprise" system would produce full employment. But the specter of government planning and massive spending in peacetime alarmed many conservatives; to them the Full Employment Bill seemed another giant leap toward a centrally planned economy, even toward socialism.

The employment bill and similar economic proposals drew their inspiration not from socialism but from disciples of British economist John Maynard Keynes. A complex capitalist economy, Keynesians argued, required active government intervention. Whenever consumer spending declined, for example, increased spending by the government could take up the slack, maintain full employment, and prevent recession. Funds for public housing, hospitals, schools, and social welfare would provide assistance for low-income people while maintaining a high level of economic growth. In addition, government officials could use controls over taxation as an economic tool: In times of slow growth they could lower personal and business taxes to stimulate buying power and output; when inflationary pressures developed, they could raise taxes as one way to reduce the amount of spending. Keynes's American disciples did not follow all of his ideas—political pressures, for example, made it difficult to raise taxes or reduce government expenditures—but the Keynesians' "new economics" became orthodoxy to most Democratic liberals after World War II.

By the late 1940s most Americans also accepted some type of continuing economic role for the federal government, and a modified, renamed version of the Full Employment Bill did become law in 1946. Economic oversight and heavy government spending became prominent features of the postwar welfare state. The modern free enterprise system seemed too fragile to be left entirely to marketplace mechanisms.

Although it did not satisfy advocates of centralized planning or promise full employment, the Employment Act of 1946 established an important precedent and provided the institutional framework for more extensive government action. Congress created a new executive body, the Council of Economic Advisers, and charged it with advising the president and establishing policies to "promote free competitive enterprise, to avoid economic fluctuations . . . and to maintain employment, production, and purchasing power." Citizens soon came to expect that the national government, especially the presidency, would confront economic problems. Any administration that failed to develop effective programs, to maintain high levels of employment, or to curb inflation invited political disaster. In retrospect, the Employment Act of 1946, with its authorization of positive action by the national government, assumed almost the status of an informal constitutional amendment, signaling a new political-constitutional order that one legal analyst has called "the positive state."

Inflation, Black Markets, and Strikes

Despite greater government involvement, a variety of problems still beset the nation's economy following the war. Most liberal economists had feared that peacetime consumer spending would not maintain wartime levels of production and employment, but the gloomy forecasters were proved wrong. Consumers took the money in their savings accounts—funds that they had been unable to spend because of wartime rationing and production controls—and went on a buying spree. They wanted all the items that had been scarce or out of production during the war: refrigerators, new-model cars, nylon stockings, cameras and film, rubber-centered golf balls, wire coat hangers, and toy electric trains. Taking advantage of greater supplies of gasoline, Americans began to travel again, and hotel and motel owners complained that they could not handle the crowds of tourists.

In most areas of the economy, though, supply could not equal demand, and a steep inflationary spiral began. As prices soared, supplies dwindled. Producers could not provide enough meat, cars, or housing. In June 1946 a deliveryman in Denver lost an entire truckload of bread to a crowd that overpowered him outside a grocery store; rumors of a shipment of meat produced an angry, shoving crowd of over two thousand in front of a Brooklyn store; and a Detroit supermarket served coffee and doughnuts to placate angry shoppers who were waiting in line. A thriving black market soon developed. If people wanted a new car or a juicy steak, they often had to tip the automobile salesperson or the butcher. Some people tried a barter system: A meat cutter in Atlanta offered steaks and roasts in exchange for nails, flooring, and plumbing fixtures for his new home. Everywhere, people found it difficult to find homes or apartments.

Harry Truman received much of the blame for postwar economic problems. While Republicans berated him for rising prices and black-market conditions, he also faced opposition from labor unions, which had been firm supporters of the Democratic party and Roosevelt's New Deal.

In 1946 bitter labor disputes occurred in most major industries. During the year following V-J day, more than 5 million workers were involved in nearly 5,000 work stoppages. One of these, the United Auto Workers (UAW) strike against General Motors (GM), lasted almost four months. Here, the UAW's leader, Walter Reuther, advanced an idea abhorrent to management: He tried to include a provision in the new GM-UAW contract pledging GM not to raise the price of cars. Reuther argued that such a clause would prevent GM from using wage gains by the UAW as an excuse for price hikes that would affect the entire economy. GM stoutly resisted, claiming that this provision impinged on one of the company's "managerial prerogatives." GM expressed special displeasure at the UAW's insistence that the company open its books so that the union could verify its contention that the auto giant could easily absorb any of the union's gains out of corporate profits.

The UAW's stand enraged the business community and drew little support from the Democrat in the White House. The editors of *Business Week*, the widely read bible of American industry, expressed a common theme. The "time had come," argued *Business Week*, to beat back decisively "further encroachment into the province of management." A GM attorney used even stronger terms: To accept the UAW's position "would mean the end of free enterprise and efficient management." And Reuther's claim that his position actually bolstered Truman's own drive for price stability and social justice failed to move the president against GM. In the end, the UAW won a wage increase, but Reuther's dream of gaining for organized labor a broader role in determining basic political-economic decisions collapsed.

As November 1946 neared, Truman seemed to be losing support within his own party. A number of labor leaders questioned Truman's capabilities; many liberal Democrats also became disenchanted, dismissing Truman as an inept politician who lacked a social conscience.

Throughout his first year in office Truman did appear confused and inept. Seeking political popularity by promising rapid discharges for service personnel, his administration mishandled demobilization of the armed forces. At one point the navy found it lacked the ships to transport the large number of soldiers scheduled to return to the United States. By Truman's own admission the process soon "was no longer demobilization . . . it was disintegration." Although he did face extremely difficult economic decisions, Truman made things even worse by failing to develop clear and consistent policies. He hesitated, for example, to support the Office of Price Administration (OPA), an executive agency that regulated wages and prices, and listened instead to people who favored a quick end to economic controls after the war. In June 1945 Truman vetoed a bill that would have renewed the OPA's authority while limiting its powers. But after a short period with no controls at all, he signed a second bill that differed very little from the first. Finally, in

November 1946, Truman proclaimed an end to virtually all controls. Thus, Truman seemed indecisive, a person who leaned too heavily on old political cronies and representatives of special-interest groups. Even Truman's supporters could find few examples of effective leadership during his first year in the White House.

Truman Takes Command

Republicans hardly lacked campaign issues in 1946: soaring prices, black-market conditions, labor strikes, an unpopular president. By October the Gallup polling organization reported that only 32 percent of their sample approved of Truman's performance, compared with a figure of 87 percent a little over a year earlier. After years as the minority party, Republicans found themselves almost back in control. Summing up all the Democratic sins, Republican posters asked, "Had Enough? Vote Republican!" In the November 1946 elections Republicans gained control of the new Eightieth Congress and captured twenty-five governorships. Jersey City's political boss, Frank Hague, was expecting the defeats. "The Republicans would have won even had they put up a German," an aide quoted Hague. And 1948 promised to be an even better election year for Republicans.

Truman, however, rebounded from his problems. In foreign affairs, of course, his administration embarked on a vigorous anticommunist crusade, one that eventually carried over to the domestic front as well. And Truman warmed up for the domestic battles of 1947–1948 by thrashing John L. Lewis, the colorful leader of the United Mineworkers Union and by attacking the Republican-dominated Congress.

Lewis's union was trying to go beyond traditional wage issues and raise basic questions about safety and health conditions in the mines. The supposedly prolabor Democrats, Lewis argued, should be prepared to join the battle on the side of the miners. With his unruly lion's mane of white hair in constant disarray, Lewis denounced both the mine owners and the Truman administration. In response to Lewis's decision to call the miners out on strike, Truman obtained a federal court injunction in late November 1946 against both the union and its officers. Lewis initially defied the injunction as illegal but ultimately backed down from a test in the Supreme Court.

The Truman-Lewis confrontation carried considerable significance. First, Truman's action provided yet another sign that labor unions lacked political support, even among Democrats, for pushing labor-management negotiations into new areas. In the final analysis, political leaders would line up to protect management's traditional bargaining prerogatives. To the president's close advisers, the defeat of John L. Lewis also signaled Truman's arrival as a political force. "There was a big difference in the old man from then on," one aide remembered. "He was his own man at last."

The president proved particularly feisty with the new Republican-controlled Eightieth Congress (1947–1949) on domestic issues. He challenged Republicans to pass legislation he knew they opposed and refused to seek common ground on such measures as a higher minimum wage and labor legislation. At the same time, the president consulted congressional Democrats infrequently, failing to give them any clear indication of the White House's domestic priorities. At one point Democratic Senator Alben Barkley grumbled that working with Truman was like playing a night baseball game without lights: "I'm supposed to be the catcher and I should get the signals. I not only am not getting the signals, but someone actually turns out the light when the ball is thrown." Thus, while Truman proposed expensive social-welfare programs, he also urged reductions in federal expenditures. Such double-talk passed little social legislation, but it helped Truman build the image of a reactionary Republican Congress against which he could run in 1948.

In reality, Truman could cite few instances in which Republicans tried to tear down the popular programs of Roosevelt's New Deal. By the late 1940s many Republican leaders agreed that outright opposition to liberal Democratic measures such as Social Security offered little hope for increasing the GOP's vote totals. This pragmatic attitude gained most of its support from younger Republicans, particularly those who came from large northern cities or held state offices. Increasingly, they battled older, more tradition-bound Republicans in Congress for influence within the party.

Ridiculed by Truman as a do-nothing body, the Eightieth Congress actually passed several significant pieces of legislation. The National Security Act of 1947 reorganized the armed forces and the entire military establishment. In recognition of its new importance, the air force became a separate branch of the military; a new military establishment, which was retitled the Department of Defense in 1949, replaced the old departments of War and Navy; and the new National Security Council and Central Intelligence Agency assumed important tasks in planning and executing foreign policy. In a highly popular move, the Eightieth Congress also approved and sent to the states the Twenty-second Amendment, which prohibited presidents from serving more than two terms. In addition, Congress accepted Truman's suggestion to create a special commission to study reorganization of the federal bureaucracy. Under the leadership of former President Herbert Hoover, the commission submitted a plan that became the basis of the Reorganization Act of 1949. By clarifying lines of authority and reducing the number of executive agencies, the Hoover Commission hoped to make government administration more efficient.

Robert Taft, Republican majority leader in the Senate, emerged as the dominant figure in the Eightieth Congress. Son of President William Howard Taft, the middle-aged Ohioan was a shy, thoughtful man who seemed uncomfortable in the glare of national politics. Certainly he lacked the charm of Roosevelt or the fire of Truman. But Taft's close attention to detail won respect from Senate colleagues, and a reputation for honesty and integrity gained the admiration of older, more conservative Republicans. "Mr. Republican" argued that liberal Democrats were abandoning the New Deal measures of Roosevelt and moving toward socialism. Their programs, he charged, threatened to bankrupt the country and to place individual liberties at the mercy of an overbearing federal bureaucracy. But by 1946 Taft was moderating some of his more extreme anti–New Deal views: To the consternation of reactionary Republicans, he even supported some federal aid to education, a limited program of public housing, and some social-welfare measures. In view of Truman's increasing problems, Taft expected his vision of "modern Republicanism" to make him the GOP's nominee in 1948.

Passage of the Taft-Hartley Labor Act of 1947 demonstrated the Ohio senator's economic ideas and legislative skills. The law, clearly aimed at reducing the political and economic power of organized labor, outlawed the closed shop (the practice of hiring only union workers), prohibited the use of union dues for political activities, and authorized presidential back-to-work orders whenever labor strikes threatened national security. The law, Taft claimed, would not destroy labor unions; it would actually help workers by curbing the abuses of corrupt labor bosses. Taft skillfully managed the bill through the Senate and worked out a compromise with House Republicans who wanted a stronger antiunion statute. Truman vetoed the measure, but Taft collected the votes to override. Labor leaders denounced the bill as "a slave-labor act" and the "Tuff-Heartless Act"; pickets even appeared at the wedding of Taft's son.

Enactment of Taft-Hartley epitomized the ambiguous place of organized labor in the postwar political economy. On the one hand, the act struck at certain gains that labor had made during the 1930s and early 1940s; on the other, Taft-Hartley acknowledged that labor unions would retain more power than conservatives considered acceptable. In time, with the law courts and political leaders supporting the overall structure, an informal labor-management settlement emerged. Management expected labor unions to press aggressively on wage issues, including cost-of-living increases, and other compensation questions such as pension plans and fringe benefits. In exchange, labor would become more productive, turning out more products in the same units of time, and concede management's prerogatives over a wide range of basic issues including the organization of the work process and investment decisions about where to locate and move plant facilities. This arrangement offered union members the promise of higher wages, more benefits, and greater job security; at the same time, however, it removed a whole range of crucial issues from the process of collective labor-management bargaining and assigned them solely to the prerogatives of industry. Negotiations between the UAW and the Detroit automakers in 1948 followed this general outline and set the pattern for labor-management relations during the first three decades of the postwar era.

The Election of 1948

The congressional and presidential elections of 1948 produced even more conflict than the UAW–auto industry negotiations of that same year. Despite his impressive leadership in Congress, Robert Taft lost the 1948 presidential nomination to Governor Thomas E. Dewey of New York, the GOP's standard-bearer in 1944. Taft's reputation as a poor vote-getter and a midwestern conservative worked against him. Republicans, who had not nominated

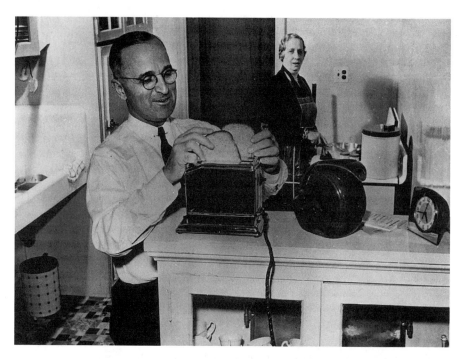

The man from Independence. Harry Truman projected an image as an ordinary citizen, one who never lost the common touch after he gained office. *Source:* National Archives.

a winning candidate in twenty years, desperately wanted a winner, and Dewey and his running mate, Governor Earl Warren of California, appeared to be shoo-ins. Dewey had done reasonably well against FDR in 1944, had won a smashing victory in the 1946 New York gubernatorial race, and belonged to the more progressive, eastern wing of the GOP.

But the victor in 1948 was not Tom Dewey: Harry Truman surprised almost all the political "experts," his Democratic critics, and the entire Republican party. "You've got to give the little man credit," admitted Republican Senator Arthur Vandenburg. "Everyone had counted him out, but he came up fighting and won the battle. That's the kind of courage the American people admire." To the extent that the presidential sweepstakes was a "beauty contest" between competing images, Truman emerged the clear winner. Dewey displayed little of Truman's warmth and personality. "I don't know which is the chillier experience—to have Tom ignore you or shake your hand," claimed one of his detractors. "You have to get to know Dewey to dislike him," another complained. Overconfident and overly cautious, "Thomas Elusive Dewey" made far fewer personal appearances than Truman. When Dewey did speak, he relied on familiar platitudes and bland appeals to national unity.

In contrast, Harry Truman slashed away at the Eightieth Congress. With his arms in perpetual motion, Truman denounced Republican representatives as "errand boys of big business" and bragged that he had vetoed more legislation than any other president of the twentieth century. During the brief interval between the Democratic convention and the November election, Truman even called Congress into special session and presented it with a list of "must" legislation. When the Republican-controlled body predictably adjourned after passing only a few minor bills, Truman escalated his attacks on Dewey and the Eightieth Congress. The president's seventeen-car, armorplated campaign train whistlestopped across the country to shouts of "Give 'em hell, Harry."

When he was not roasting the "no-account, do-nothing" Republican Congress, Truman emphasized his own version of the positive state. His chief strategists, especially Washington lawyer Clark Clifford, urged an aggressively liberal stance. Truman called for a higher minimum wage, repeal of Taft-Hartley, more public housing, and higher farm prices. During the final week of the campaign he became the first president to appear in Harlem, where he told a crowd of 35,000 African-Americans that he supported the "goal of equal rights and equal opportunities" for all Americans.

The civil rights question, which would become a more pressing political issue after 1948, did cost Truman some southern votes. His advisers wanted the party convention to adopt a mild statement in support of civil rights, but urban liberals, who were courting black voters, pushed through a stronger proposal. Following the heated floor fight, delegates from Alabama and Mississippi stalked out of the convention, and segregationists eventually formed the States Rights, or "Dixiecrat," party. The Dixiecrat platform denounced "totalitarian government" and advocated "segregation of the races." With Strom Thurmond of South Carolina as their presidential nominee, the Dixiecrats hoped to gain one hundred electoral votes in the South—enough ballots, they thought, to throw the presidential election into the House of Representatives. Thurmond, however, lacked enough financial support for an effective campaign, and the strategy failed. Most southern Democrats stayed with Truman, and Thurmond gained only thirty-nine electoral votes.

Truman survived another revolt within his party: the Progressive party candidacy of Henry Wallace. Truman had fired Wallace as secretary of commerce because Wallace had publicly criticized the administration's hard-line anti-Soviet foreign policy. With support from a wide range of left-wing groups, including the Communist party, Wallace launched a new party that advocated greater cooperation with the Soviet Union, an end to the military draft, more federal money for social and economic programs at home, and American support for a UN Reconstruction Fund to promote worldwide economic recovery. If the United States could avoid conflict with the USSR, Wallace believed, American liberals could not only revive the New Deal at home but also extend its spirit of social reform overseas. Progressive party rallies resembled old-time revival meetings, as folk singers such as Pete Seeger and Woody Guthrie campaigned for Wallace and his running mate (another guitar player), Senator Glen Taylor of Idaho. One of Guthrie's songs, sung to the tune of "The Wabash Cannonball," expressed the class-based appeal of Wallace's left-wing supporters.

There's lumberjacks and teamsters and sailors from the sea,
And there's farming boys from Texas and the hills of Tennessee,
There's miners from Kentucky and there's fishermen from Maine,
Every worker in the country rides that Wallace-Taylor train.*

But the Wallace-Taylor special never reached the White House. Following Clark Clifford's advice, Truman highlighted his own role as the nation's commander-in-chief while allowing subordinates to tie Wallace to the enemy in Moscow. "A vote for Wallace," the Democratic National Committee claimed, "is a vote for the things for which Stalin, Molotov, and Vishinsky stand." The acceptance of support from the Communist party of the United States, bitter opposition from large labor unions, the defection of anticommunist liberals, his forthright stand on civil rights, and the insurmountable problems of any newly formed party all caught up with Wallace. In December 1947 a poll showed that 13 percent of the electorate favored Wallace's candidacy; by election day his campaign had collapsed, and he received less than 3 percent of the popular ballots and not a single electoral vote.

Most fundamentally, Truman's victory demonstrated the staying power of the old Roosevelt coalition. Midwestern farmers, urban ethnic voters, organized labor, African-Americans, and even most southerners continued to support the Democratic party. Many voted Democratic because of family tradition and out of loyalty to social and economic programs begun during the New Deal. Truman's energetic campaign did not suddenly convince great numbers of voters to support the Democratic party; rather, it revived many Democrats' party loyalty and raised fears that GOP reactionaries would mount a general assault on New Deal measures. The four-way contest also apparently confused some voters. The 1948 election was what political scientists would call a "decline election," with only 54 percent of the electorate turning out. The election maintained the basic political configuration of the late 1930s and provided a mandate for the New Deal's positive welfare state. But left unsettled in 1948 was the more difficult issue of the precise scope of this welfare state.

THE FAIR DEAL

Truman's Domestic Program

After their victory, Truman and his advisers planned a new set of domestic proposals that they hoped would move beyond the New Deal. Franklin Roosevelt's programs had been designed to stop the Great Depression and to restore the prosperity of the 1920s; Truman's Fair Deal offered measures aimed at sustaining an ever-expanding economy in the new postwar era.

Truman's liberal economists believed that they had solved the mysteries of economic management. One aide, Charles F. Brannan, championed an am-

* *The Farmer-Labor Train* by Woody Guthrie © Copyright 1947 by Woody Guthrie Publications, Inc. All rights reserved. Used by permission.

bitious proposal that he claimed would give farmers higher prices while providing consumers with cheaper food. Under Brannan's program the government would lift New Deal restrictions on the number of acres planted and would maintain farm income through direct price supports.

Another of Truman's economic advisers, Leon Keyserling, predicted that the national government could guarantee full employment, higher wages, and greater profits through well-planned and well-executed spending programs. Americans had no need to take from the rich to care for the poor. Properly managed, America's capitalist economy could outproduce any socialist system in the world. In 1948 nearly two-thirds of all American families lived on incomes of less than $4,000 a year; by 1958 it would be possible, Keyserling predicted, to generate enough economic growth to make $4,000 the minimum income for *every* family. "The people of America need to be electrified by our limitless possibilities," he proclaimed.

In addition to government measures designed to stimulate economic growth, Truman's Fair Deal promised programs to promote social and economic justice. Truman proposed the expansion of Social Security, generous federal funding for public housing projects, a national plan for medical insurance, federal aid to education, and civil rights legislation. Truman and his liberal advisers touted the Fair Deal as the middle way between socialism and fascism. "Between the reactionaries of the extreme left with their talk about revolution and class warfare, and the reactionaries of the extreme right with their hysterical cries of bankruptcy and despair, lies the way of progress," Truman declared. The Democratic historian Arthur Schlesinger, Jr., provided an appropriate label for this postwar liberalism—"the vital center."

The Truman administration achieved some of its social programs, and economic conditions improved. Congress passed measures that extended Social Security benefits; raised the minimum wage (to seventy-five cents an hour); and appropriated federal funds for soil conservation, flood control, and public power. Despite some fluctuations, the economy performed fairly well during the late 1940s and early 1950s. The United States came nowhere near Keyserling's optimistic predictions, but most peoples' real incomes rose steadily. People who had survived the Great Depression of the 1930s, with help from the New Deal, continued to do well in the era of the Fair Deal.

The Fair Deal: An Assessment

Sandwiched between FDR's New Deal of the 1930s and LBJ's Great Society of the 1960s, the Fair Deal of Harry Truman is often ignored. Many historians have viewed it as an addendum to the New Deal, as a grab bag of social-economic programs left over from the 1930s; others have seen it primarily as a tepid prelude to the burst of legislation enacted during Lyndon Johnson's Great Society. But the Fair Deal deserves its own assessment. The Fair Dealers' optimistic assumptions about economic and social policies helped to shape the dominant postwar assumptions about the nation's future and about the role of government.

The Fair Deal rested on an abiding faith that the U.S. economic system, so severely criticized during the 1930s, was far superior to any type of planned economic order. Capitalism, not democratic socialism or Soviet communism, represented the wave of the future. Classical defenders of the free enterprise system, of course, had always argued that a marketplace economy maximized individual freedoms and efficiently allocated resources and finished products. But during the cold war era, capitalism's liberal defenders also claimed that it could advance the cause of social justice, the banner under which the political left marched. One of the main virtues of America's economic system, postwar liberals argued, was its apparently unlimited ability to generate economic growth, a side of American life that economists proudly measured by a relatively new statistical gauge, the gross national product (GNP). A steadily rising GNP—the total dollar value of all goods produced and services rendered—attested to the fact that the economic collapse of the 1930s would not recur. Indeed, given the new economic wisdom now available, it could not!

Visions of economic growth bedazzled postwar social planners. An ever-expanding economy, Truman's advisers promised, ensured security for those people and for those organized interests that had already benefited from legislation of the New Deal era. More important, the promise of an ever-expanding economic pie offered hope to those Americans, estimated in 1937 by Franklin Roosevelt himself to be one-third of the population, who had been largely untouched by New Deal programs. In seeking to advance social justice, the United States could deftly sidestep difficult issues involving redistribution of wealth, income, and political power. As long as there was a growing GNP, new economic growth could provide the material basis for aiding those who had somehow fallen behind in the race for success. As later explained by Walter Heller, an economist who began his distinguished career during the Truman era, economic growth was both "the pot of gold and the rainbow."

But as the dwindling band who still embraced classical laissez-faire economics complained, proponents of this new economic wisdom did not place their faith in capitalism alone. As passage of the Employment Act of 1946 suggested, even a majority of Congress, hardly a body known for its radical economic ideas, agreed that government officials had some responsibility to intervene in the free enterprise economy. Liberal economists welcomed this responsibility. Brandishing their new tools for monitoring the economy and for diagnosing its health, postwar economic doctors were generally confident that they could administer the kind of remedies—including measures to adjust interest rates, levels of taxation, and amounts of government spending—that could cure an ailing economy or merely pep up a sluggish one.

Confidence in the essential soundness of American capitalism and in their own expertise allowed the Fair Dealers to think beyond the old goals of the New Deal—economic recovery and reform. Instead, they could frame programs and establish bureaucratic institutions that could ensure steady economic growth; they could then use the results of this growth to attack ancient social problems, such as the grossly unequal access to medical care. Truman's proposals for domestic reform, more than anything envisioned by FDR, remained the basic aims of the Democratic party for almost two decades. A whole generation of Democratic liberals—politicians like Hubert Humphrey and John Kennedy—began their careers during the Fair Deal. Most never moved beyond it or questioned its basic assumptions.

However, the Fair Deal, and the larger postwar liberal vision, contained significant limitations. Despite the general affluence, especially in contrast with the economic situation in other parts of the postwar world, the American welfare state expanded its boundaries relatively little in the two decades after 1945. In 1962, Michael Harrington's *The Other America* reminded affluent liberals that nearly one-fourth of the population of their country still lived in deep poverty, largely unaided by federal programs.

Defenders of the Fair Deal's approach could, of course, argue that the more ambitious portions of Truman's program never got through Congress. Determined lobbying by the American Medical Association, which raised the cry of "socialized medicine," and apathy among middle-class voters, who were benefiting from the expansion of private medical plans like Blue Cross, helped kill the plan for national health insurance. Opposition from other powerful pressure groups encouraged a coalition of Republicans and conservative southern Democrats to block general federal aid to state school systems and the Brannan plan for agricultural subsidies. In short, many of the Fair Deal's programs lacked effective political support. Most middle-class Americans, the people who made up the bulk of the active electorate, wanted to enjoy the benefits of expanding economic production themselves—in the form of new homes, second cars, new consumer goods, and greater recreational opportunities.

But the limits of the Fair Deal cannot be blamed solely on the conservative coalition in Congress, on special-interest groups, or on voter apathy. The Truman administration itself placed greater weight on foreign than on domestic issues. America's national security and its economic well-being, Truman and his internationalist advisers believed, depended on the successful conduct of a global foreign policy. Preoccupied with foreign affairs and often clumsy in his dealings with Congress, Truman failed to provide vigorous leadership on domestic social issues. America's liberal crusaders focused most of their attention, and most of their energies, on problems overseas.

Civil Rights

The limited enthusiasm among liberal elites for new domestic crusades was most evident in the fate of civil rights legislation. Revulsion against Nazi racism helped encourage greater rhetorical denunciations of discrimination at home; wartime economic gains produced a desire among African-Americans for broader attacks on discrimination; and the outbreak of racial violence immediately after the war intensified liberal efforts to calm racial tensions. Even the climate of the cold war seemed to call for measures to improve race relations at home. As the United States proclaimed that it, not the Soviet Union, offered the proper model for other nations to follow, continued legal discrimination against nonwhites in the United States itself proved difficult to explain. Despite these forces for change, however, the Fair Deal meant only small gains for the antidiscrimination effort.

As part of his broader domestic program President Truman pushed for a variety of civil rights measures, including a ban on poll taxes, an antilynching law, and legislation to guarantee equal employment opportunities. During the 1948 presidential campaign he issued executive orders that ended (at least on paper) discrimination in federal employment. Truman took great pride in his civil rights record, claiming that desegregation of the armed forces, which began during his second term, was "the greatest thing that ever happened to America."

The Truman administration also became involved in several important Supreme Court decisions that expanded the legal remedies for discrimination. In *Shelly* v. *Kraemer* (1946) the justices unanimously held that no court could enforce restrictive covenants, legal agreements that prevented real estate from being sold to members of minority groups. In two other cases—*Sweatt* v. *Painter* (1950) and *McLaurin* v. *Oklahoma Board of Regents* (1950)—the Court ruled that a separate law school established for blacks violated the Fourteenth Amendment's requirement for equality in education and that graduate schools could not segregate students according to race. Although these cases did not declare all segregated educational facilities inherently unequal, they did point the way toward the broader school-desegregation decision in *Brown* v. *Board of Education* (1954). In all these cases Truman's Justice Department supported the claims of African-American plaintiffs.

Despite these positive marks on Truman's record, civil rights provided another example of the gap between promise and performance in the Fair Deal. Some civil rights activists blamed Truman himself for the lack of new legislative initiatives: They claimed that the president gave their cause a low priority and too often deferred to the feelings of southern Democrats. Truman did try to avoid a direct stand on civil rights; only the threat of African-American voters defecting to Henry Wallace in 1948, for example, prompted his executive orders on the military and on federal hiring. But Truman was not entirely to blame for his administration's failure to achieve more. The conservative coalition in Congress effectively bottled up legislation that would have aided African-Americans, and some military officials did their best to delay desegregation of the armed forces. Similarly, the president's initiatives in ending job discrimination ultimately depended on the attitude of other officials in the federal bureaucracy. No executive order could be self-enforcing.

There was also popular opposition to even these limited moves toward racial equality. In the southern states the Confederate flag became the symbol of resistance: One flag company boasted that Virginians owned more Confederate banners in 1951 than during the Civil War, and a New York City firm reported that the demand for rebel flags exceeded orders for the Stars and Stripes. Throughout the nation, racists violently opposed the drive for integration. When an African-American couple attempted to move into an apartment in Cicero, Illinois, a mob of about five thousand angry whites broke through National Guard lines and set the building ablaze. In the same year,

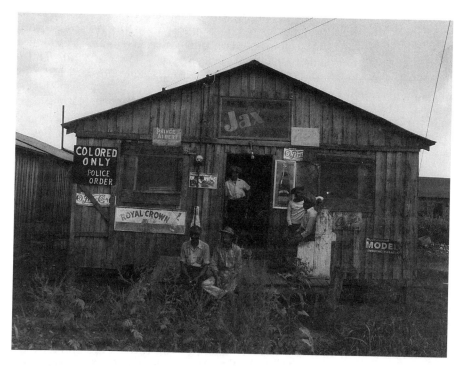

A store for "colored only." The rural South in 1945. *Source:* National Archives.

1951, a black school principal and civil rights leader died when explosives destroyed his Miami home on Christmas Day. Decrying the increased use of explosives in racial attacks, Walter White of the National Association for the Advancement of Colored People (NAACP) observed that "the bomb has replaced the lynchers' rope" as the main weapon of racist resistance.

The upsurge in white violence was one more impediment to the pace of national action against racial discrimination. Advances in the commitment to legal equality came slowly during the Truman years. Still, Truman's record looked better than that of any previous twentieth-century president. He was the first chief executive to make civil rights a national political issue, and his administration at least proposed a comprehensive legislative program. After 1948, the issue of race would inexorably move to the center of the national political stage and dramatically alter politics in the United States.

ANTICOMMUNISM AT HOME

The Communist Issue

Although the Truman administration moved cautiously on civil rights and social welfare issues, it acted decisively against communist "subversion." In 1947 Truman established a comprehensive "internal security" program designed to uncover "subversives" in the federal bureaucracy. Employing broad definitions of disloyalty, agencies purged supposed security risks. The president did oppose suggestions for more Draconian measures—such as abolition of the Fifth Amendment in national security cases—but the White House often failed to restrain the Department of Justice. J. Edgar Hoover's FBI, with the administration's consent, pried into the private lives and political beliefs of alleged subversives. Extending a practice begun during the Roosevelt years, the FBI also used wiretaps in violation of the Federal Communications Act of 1934. In 1949 Truman rejected suggestions that a special commission investigate the FBI. "Hoover has done a good job," the president told a press conference. The Attorney General's List of Subversive Organizations, first issued in 1947, demonstrated the Justice Department's propensity for establishing guilt by association. Noncommunists who happened to belong to one of these groups sometimes found themselves branded as "reds," "pinkos," or "fellow travelers." Civil libertarians charged that the government too often equated legitimate political dissent with communist subversion.

Fears of subversive elements in the United States helped to justify the creation of a massive surveillance–national security state. Citing the dangers the nation faced in the postwar era, members of the new CIA, FBI, military intelligence, and other surveillance agencies began to broaden their oversight of domestic dissenters. Those on the political left, who could be most easily linked to a vague "communist conspiracy," came under intense scrutiny. Phones were tapped, dossiers collected, innuendos spread. Summing up the activities begun after World War II, the civil liberties lawyer Frank J. Donner called the postwar period "the age of surveillance."

How real was the domestic threat of communism? Did the White House and the Justice Department exaggerate the dangers? Although no researcher has uncovered any evidence that procommunists shaped U.S. policies, the government did possess intelligence about the activities of communist agents and the passing of military information to the Soviet Union. The FBI captured several authentic spies, and J. Edgar Hoover firmly believed that "the ignorant and the apologists and the appeasers of Communism in our country" consistently minimized the "danger of these subversives in our midst."

Still, the amount of spy activity and its actual danger to national security remain open questions. Historians, for example, continue to debate whether the Justice Department possessed sufficient evidence against Ethel and Julius Rosenberg, two members of the Communist party who were executed in 1953 for giving atomic secrets to the Soviets, or the couple fell victim to anticommunist hysteria. Similarly, controversy continued into the mid-1990s over the guilt or innocence of Alger Hiss, a prominent Democratic leader accused, nearly fifty years earlier of passing secret documents to the USSR. Defenders of the Rosenbergs and Hiss claimed that government officials and witchhunters largely manufactured the cases against these alleged spies, assertions that increasingly seem impossible to prove or to disprove. Greater access by scholars to previously classified materials, released through new government regulations or through suits under the Freedom of Information Act of 1974, have only provided new ammunition with which to refight the old cold war battles. New books and articles have helped to intensify, not to settle, disputes over the nature of the communist threat during the 1940s and the 1950s. Although classified material about nuclear weaponry was passed to the Soviet Union, historical studies suggest that the information received by the Soviets in the late 1940s contained badly flawed data. Ironically, argues one study, these atomic "secrets" may have hindered, rather than assisted, Soviet efforts to acquire an atomic arsenal.

Whatever the extent of Soviet spying, the Truman administration had other reasons to mount a vigorous anti–red crusade. Since the late 1930s, anti–New Deal Democrats and conservative Republicans—particularly members of the House Committee on Un-American Activities (HUAC)—had claimed that communists and fellow travelers infested the Roosevelt administration. Charges of communist influence in the federal government often accompanied general attacks on the "socialistic" New Deal welfare programs. Responding to Republican taunts of being "soft on communism," the Truman administration hoped that its own hard-line stance would prevent Republicans from seizing the anticommunist issue for themselves.

Fears of an active communist conspiracy within the United States also dovetailed with the administration's strong anti-Soviet foreign policy. During the period immediately following World War II, public opinion polls revealed that few Americans considered communism a major problem. Truman's advisers feared that such attitudes—along with the strong popular sentiment against expensive overseas commitments—might hamstring an activist foreign policy. A tough stand against communism at home and a constant barrage of anticommunist rhetoric, administration strategists hoped, would counteract domestic resistance to Truman's sweeping foreign-policy proposals.

Consequently, the Truman administration dramatically publicized its plan for dealing with internal subversion, officials continually stressed the need for greater vigilance, and the government orchestrated a vigorous pro-American campaign. In 1947, for example, Attorney General Tom Clark developed the Freedom Train program. This historical society on rails carried important documents, including a copy of the Truman Doctrine, to more than two hundred major cities. When the train returned to Washington in the fall of 1947, the government staged a "week of rededication." At a series of patriotic demonstrations, government employees took a "freedom pledge" and everyone sang "God Bless America." In a similar vein, the Office of Education promoted its Zeal for Democracy program: Washington encouraged local schools "to vitalize and improve education in the ideals and benefits of democracy and to reveal the character and tactics of totalitarianism."

Government leaders could not manufacture this crusade by themselves; but the anticommunist effort in Washington did help to shift attention from a specific problem, the extent of Soviet espionage, to the less tangible fear of an "alien" communist "invasion" of the nation's institutional and cultural life. Partly encouraged by government leaders, many Americans became less concerned about foreign agents than about communist sympathizers spreading dangerous ideas through an unsuspecting, overly tolerant society.

During the 1940s, a variety of official anticommunist activities began. The Post Office Department banned communist materials from the mails; many states adopted laws banning subversives from state government jobs; bar associations and school boards required prospective attorneys and teachers to sign loyalty oaths. Congressional committees looked into "red webs" that supposedly stretched from Hollywood to Washington, D.C. Members of HUAC, including young Richard Nixon, claimed that their committee had discovered extensive procommunist networks in the United States; even if it stopped short of espionage, this procommunist activity allegedly hindered execution of the nation's anticommunist containment policy. Critics of HUAC and of Truman's Justice Department countered with claims that not only had very few dangerous people been fingered but also far too many innocent reputations had been smeared. Moreover, overzealous witch-hunters seemed less focused on rooting out subversives than on stigmatizing political dissidents, especially those who considered containment of the Soviet Union unnecessary and unwise or those who favored more rapid social change at home.

Hollywood and the entire entertainment industry became an important focus of debates over the legitimacy and efficacy of postwar anticommunism. In 1947, HUAC began its effort to find communist infiltration of the movie colony. The committee's widely publicized hearings, which featured both "friendly" witnesses (who testified about an allegedly extensive communist involvement in filmmaking) and "unfriendly" ones (who refused to say anything about political affiliations), badly divided the motion picture community. The Hollywood Ten, a group of witnesses that included past and present members of the Communist party, went to prison, after being found guilty of contempt of Congress, for defying HUAC by refusing to "name names" of suspected communists.

After some early resistance, studio heads cooperated with the red-hunters. Ultimately, several hundred people suspected of dangerous ideas or affiliations found themselves on an entertainment blacklist; blacklisted writers and performers found it difficult, if not impossible, to find work. (Typing away in anonymity, writers could be luckier than well-known performers; under an assumed name, one of the Hollywood Ten even won an Oscar for screenwriting while still on the blacklist.) The easiest way to escape the blacklist was to appear before an investigative committee, admit political errors, ritually condemn communism, and name at least one alleged subversive. In time, many prominent people in Hollywood and throughout the entertainment industry cooperated with anticommunist groups.

This search for subversives became—and remains to this day—a highly controversial subject. Despite overwhelming evidence to the contrary, some participants have tried to deny even the existence of blacklisting. Ronald Reagan and John Wayne, for example, denied knowing anything about a blacklist; yet both actors proudly talked about helping to rid Hollywood of people they considered subversives. Reagan served not only as the anticommunist head of the Screen Actors Guild during the cold war years but also as a secret informant for the FBI, known to the Bureau as Agent T-10. Such activities, observers and historians sympathetic to the anticommunist effort insist, represented a legitimate effort to root out pro-Soviet Stalinists and others who dishonestly tried to conceal their true political loyalties. The vast majority of "victims," they insist, actually had been associated with the Communist party or with other procommunist organizations; they were political hacks who betrayed their own artistic independence for a dubious political cause.

But the anticommunist probe of the entertainment industry also has its critics. Not surprisingly, writers and artists on the left, such as the writer Lillian Hellman (whose companion, the writer Dashiell Hammett, went to jail for refusing to cooperate with HUAC), condemned the "immoral" behavior of the "scoundrels" who testified about the affiliations and ideas of one-time friends and political allies. The anticommunist crusade in Hollywood, critical historians have further noted, coincided with a conservative assault on labor unions and the progressive political coalitions that had developed in the movie capital during the 1930s and early 1940s. In this view, industry leaders not only wanted to eliminate political opponents but also to recast Hollywood as a symbol of the postwar possibilities of anticommunism, corporate production, and mass consumption—the same set of values that Ronald Reagan subsequently carried from Hollywood into national politics.

The search for subversives, then, fed upon itself. Fueled by powerful social and political pressures, investigations of the entertainment industry became "degradation ceremonies," ritualistic exorcisms in which dissident ideas and the people who held them could be formally labeled as deviant. The whole process of overseeing people's political ideas thus created powerful pressures for conformity: Rather than risk the ordeal of being accused, many individuals simply decided to censor themselves.

A series of disturbing events appeared to give credence to wild tales of communist machinations. Mao Zedong's success in China in 1949 and Russia's first atomic test frightened those who wrongly believed that the United States had "lost" China to the communists and that the "backward" Russians had stolen vital atomic secrets from the United States. Stories about communists in the State Department and atomic spies offered attractive explanations. The year 1950 brought new shocks: The government uncovered a Soviet spy ring in the United States, and American troops entered the Korean conflict. If these developments were not troubling enough, there were a series of scandals within the Truman administration, corruption in the Internal Revenue Service, a televised investigation of organized crime, and even an assassination plot against the president by Puerto Rican nationalists.

McCarthyism

Militant anticommunism reached its apogee in—and eventually took its name from—Senator Joseph McCarthy of Wisconsin. Red-baiting existed before McCarthy ever discovered the anticommunist issue, and other witchhunters made even wilder charges. But McCarthy dominated the headlines. His tactics were disarmingly simple: He flung accusations as fast as the media could broadcast them but avoided specific proposals for fighting the communist "menace." When an acquaintance asked McCarthy how he would change the Voice of America's allegedly ineffective programs, "the Senator looked blank; obviously he had never thought about it." Nor did McCarthy spend much time documenting his sensational charges. His famous Wheeling, West Virginia, speech of 1950—in which he charged that the State Department employed more than two hundred communist sympathizers—rested on a hodgepodge of questionable evidence from old congressional files. Even though the Senate later gave him broad investigatory powers, McCarthy never bothered to pursue his allegations against the State Department. Instead, he went after new demons, who he claimed were hiding in other government bureaus.

Because of widespread publicity, McCarthy soon gained an undeserved reputation as a powerful political force. Looking more like a heavy in a B movie than a tribune of the people, McCarthy pressed his image as a tough guy and a rebel. He railed against "establishment Democrats" such as Alger Hiss and Dean Acheson. All these "bright young men who were born with silver spoons in their mouths" and all those "striped-pants diplomats," McCarthy charged, were "selling the nation out." As he escalated his attacks, anticommunist liberals and moderates worried about a new threat from the "radical right." The Wisconsin senator, his opponents feared, led a massive right-wing movement that seemed to appeal to great numbers of lower-middle-class people with little formal education.

McCarthy's power, however, did not come from a mass movement of fanatics. Instead, McCarthy gained attention because important people, such as members of the U.S. Senate, either supported his attacks or failed to oppose him. Influential midwestern Republicans, who formed the traditional base for anti–New Deal conservatism, gave McCarthy vital political assistance. Republicans who would not personally stoop to McCarthy's smear tactics—Robert Taft of Ohio, for example—tacitly encouraged the Wisconsin senator. Anything that hurt the Democrats, Taft reasoned, would help the Republican party regain power. In addition to aid from conservative Republicans, McCarthy received help from other important sources. Most newspapers, regardless of political allegiances, splashed McCarthy's charges over their pages. Sensational scoops about communist influence provided good copy—and greater sales. And many prominent liberal politicians avoided direct confrontation with McCarthy and his supporters for fear of being labeled soft on communism.

The passage of the McCarran Internal Security Act of 1950 demonstrated the fear of opposing anticommunist measures. Rather than denouncing Senator Pat McCarran's harsh proposals, the White House and congressional Democrats offered their own internal-security bills. In so doing, they accepted the McCarthyites' basic position: Communists should not expect the same civil liberties as other Americans. In its final form, the McCarran Act required communist and "communist-front" organizations to register with the attorney general, barred foreign communists from entering the United

States, and authorized secret prison camps for detention of domestic subversives during wartime. Only seven senators and a handful of representatives voted against the McCarran Act. Truman vetoed the bill, but Congress quickly overrode the president's action. McCarthyism and McCarthy continued to influence national policy.

Eventually, however, McCarthy ran out of obvious targets and overstepped even his fertile imagination. By 1953 he was charging the Voice of America, the new Republican administration of Dwight Eisenhower, and the U.S. army with playing into the hands of the communists. In one celebrated incident, two of McCarthy's aides traveled around Europe to search for procommunist literature in libraries run by the United States Information Service. His agents and other witnesses charged that these libraries contained shelves of communist books and only a handful of pro-U.S. works; one investigator even suggested that libraries manipulated card catalogs so that readers would not find books critical of communism.

McCarthy's charges of communist influence in the army resulted in a special Senate investigation. The Army-McCarthy hearings, an ongoing television spectacular, speeded McCarthy's demise. With McCarthy exposed to the harsh glare of television, many viewers tired of his brash manner and bullying tactics. Many others simply became bored with the whole communist issue. Emboldened by McCarthy's problems, critics escalated their attacks. Republican allies began to temper their support, and some anticommunists even claimed that McCarthy's extremist position discredited the fight against Moscow and unwittingly aided the Kremlin. Finally, the U.S. Senate, the source of his prestige, turned against him. In 1954 a majority of senators voted to "condemn" McCarthy for conduct unbecoming a member of the Senate. Stripped of his prestige and influence, McCarthy disappeared from the headlines, continued to drink heavily, and died in 1957 at the age of forty-eight.

McCarthyism represented one of the more extreme examples of the anticommunist culture of the 1940s and early 1950s. Fears about subversion and invasion by "alien" elements flourished, to one degree or another, in many parts of postwar life. Put simply, a wide spectrum of opinion considered communism—which different groups defined in very different ways—a domestic as well as a foreign danger and supported various efforts to contain it.

McCarthyism, in this view, even produced its own literary genre, the detective novels of Mickey Spillane. By 1950, consumers had bought more than 6 million copies of Spillane's books. With a single-minded devotion to conventional values, his fictional hero, Mike Hammer, mowed down communists, crooks, and corrupted women. Though a lady-killer, in the mold of Dashiell Hammet's Sam Spade and Raymond Chandler's Philip Marlowe, Hammer lacked the chivalric code attributed to these hard-boiled detective heroes from the prewar era. Hammer slashed away at sexual "perverts," civil libertarians, and "bleeding heart" liberals with almost the same gusto with which he smashed communists. To liberal literary and political critics, Spillane's broadly popular series of Mike Hammer novels—which began with *I the Jury* in 1947— expressed the same the-ends-justify-any-means approach as McCarthyism itself.

In time, even committed anticommunists saw their faith veering out of control. A growing conviction that McCarthy, after his foray against the army, had stepped over the line speeded his downfall. Similarly, even many anti-communists dismissed groups on the "radical right," such as the John Birch Society, as purveyors of hysteria. With their wild claims about communist subversion—even Dwight Eisenhower became a target of the Birch Society in the mid-1950s—the extreme anticommunists had the power to injure the reputations of individual liberals and moderates but not the political support to influence the day-to-day shape of anticommunist policies. At best, they gave anticommunist politicians a reserve army of committed loyalists; at worst, they projected a fanaticism that embarrassed the larger anticommunist effort.

The New Conservatism

McCarthy did receive cautious praise from a new source of conservative, anticommunist activism: William F. Buckley, Jr., who established the magazine *National Review* in 1955. The precocious product of a wealthy family, Buckley saw promotion of anticommunism, at home and abroad, as his religious and patriotic duty. Moreover, Buckley detested the liberal–Democratic welfare state; its programs, he insisted, threatened the liberty of individuals at home while underestimating the communist threat both at home and overseas. In this sense, Buckley considered Joe McCarthy—and even many of his tactics—as a justifiable response to a dangerous political world, one that liberals, and even most Republicans, failed to acknowledge. Buckley provided a powerful conservative magnet and eventually attracted a number of talented right-wing writers to his magazine.

Before Buckley entered the scene, however, a number of other writers had set the stage for a "new conservatism." Frederick von Hayek's *The Road to Serfdom* (1944) condemned the New Deal welfare state—with its programs for using government power to supplement the "natural" workings of the economic marketplace—as a major step toward totalitarianism. Offering academic support for an argument that conservative Republicans had been making since the 1930s, Hayek's scholarly publication gained a broad audience when *Reader's Digest* issued a condensed version. Much to his surprise, the Austrian-born scholar became a popular source of postwar conservative ideas, especially on economic issues. Other conservative writers championed strict construction of the Constitution, respect for the concept of states' rights, and concern about a possible "tyranny of the majority." Conservatives thus insisted that the activist New Deal dishonored the nation's intellectual heritage and endangered traditional liberties.

During the 1950s conservatives tried to enter public-policy debates. The Foreign Policy Research Institute, headed by Robert Strausz-Hupe, wanted a stronger anticommunist foreign policy, one that would go beyond simply containing to rolling back communism. Strausz-Hupe urged the United States aggressively to "carry the battle to the vital centers of communist defense." William F. Buckley took up another important conservative theme in his 1951 jeremiad, *God and Man at Yale.* His alma mater, Buckley charged, typified institutions of higher education in the ways that its faculty championed liberal, collectivist ideas and derided conservative, Christian ones. Thus, Buckley and other postwar conservatives launched an effort that would continue into the 1990s: a concerted campaign to interject conservativism into public discourse, especially on college campuses.

This new conservatism, from the very outset, covered a wide range of ideas and personalities. Russell Kirk, one of the most cerebral and pessimistic of the postwar conservatives, criticized democratic government and wanted a greater sense of deference, among the unruly masses, to the nation's "natural leaders." In contrast, other prominent conservatives such as Peter Viereck and Clinton Rossiter praised democratization and even much of the New Deal. Viereck, for example, saw welfare-state programs, such as Social Security, providing the stabilizing influences that conservatives should favor. And whereas Russell Kirk advised censorship of "dangerous" ideas, libertarian conservatives often joined liberals in urging broad interpretations of constitutionally protected civil liberties.

During the 1950s, conservatism also began its troubled alliance with charismatic religious leaders. Billy Graham, a spell-binding young evangelist, had become a religious celebrity in the late 1940s when the conservative publisher William Randolph Hearst ordered his newspapers to "puff Graham." In 1950 Graham launched a weekly radio program, called the "Hour of Decision," and the following year he embarked upon a television ministry that carried him into the 1990s. Very quickly, other religious figures followed Graham into the mass media and, also cautiously, into conservative politics.

The new conservatives would differ in their evaluations of the Dwight Eisenhower administration, which held the white House from 1953–1960. Some prominent conservatives, including Billy Graham, strongly identified with Eisenhower, but others were more critical. Barry Goldwater, who replaced Robert Taft (who died in 1953) as the voice of conservatism in the United States Senate, supported some of Eisenhower's policies but staked out positions that were substantially to the right of those espoused by the Eisenhower administration.

The National Review increasingly championed Goldwater and criticized Eisenhower. Eisenhower's presidency, Buckley charged, represented "an attitude, which goes by the name of a program, undirected by principle, unchained to any coherent responses to domestic and foreign dangers." Following a policy that came to be called "fusionism," *The National Review* opened its columns to a broad range of conservative attacks upon both Fair Deal liberalism and Eisenhower's moderate Republicanism. Even the CIA seemed too liberal for some of the magazine's contributors. Although *The National Review* often published criticism of the civil rights movement, and even defenses of segregationist policies, Buckley ultimately succeeded in distancing the new conservatism from the shrill racist and anti-Semitic diatribes that had tainted right-wing politics since the 1930s. He also helped to form a new organization, Young Americans for Freedom, that supported conservative principles on college campuses. By the end of the 1950s, the new conservatives stood poised to offer, through the Republican party, what Goldwater would come to call a real "choice" rather than simply an "echo" of Democratic liberalism.

Anticommunism and Intellectual Life

The dominant ideology of the late 1940s and 1950s posited communism as the major threat to the "American way of life" and dismissed Marxism as a pernicious doctrine without any intellectual respectability. As the liberal journalist Tom Braden put it, the cold war was being "fought with ideas instead of bombs." A number of prominent postwar intellectuals consequently joined the Congress for Cultural Freedom (CCF), an international organization pledged to promote ideas of liberty and oppose "state-sponsored ideologies" such as Soviet communism. Behind the scenes, however, the CCF received secret CIA funding. Although the CIA never told members of the CCF what to believe or what to print in their influential publication, *Encounter*, the organization rarely, if ever, endorsed intellectuals who opposed the anticommunist foreign policies of the United States. Overall, the dominant anticommunism helped to narrow social debate in the United States.

Consider, for example, the postwar media. Certainly the press remained free from direct government censorship, and many journalists, especially those on the political right, vigorously criticized official execution of specific cold war programs. Yet, after the collapse of Henry Wallace's Progressive party movement in late 1948, it became difficult to find people within the mainstream media who criticized the claim that the greatest threat to the nation came from international communism. Attending Washington cocktail parties, listening to officials' "off-the-record" justifications, and accepting government handouts at face value, influential journalists might be seen, in effect, as part of the ideological apparatus by which the state encouraged a culture focused on anticommunism. Truly independent writers like I. F. Stone, who subjected government explanations to critical scrutiny, seem to have been the exception. In contrast to his one-person operation, *I. F. Stone's Weekly* (which assumed every official statement to be suspect until independently confirmed), the mainstream media rarely scrutinized cold war orthodoxies.

A similar pattern emerged in academic life. During the 1930s, for example, scholarship stressing social conflict, the limits of capitalist institutions, and skepticism of received wisdom had figured prominently in academic debates. By the late 1940s, in contrast, the horrors of Stalinism, fears about radicals from both the right and left, and the hopeful performance of postwar capitalism all helped to produce an academic culture that ignored perspectives that might be labeled "radical."

Like prominent journalists, academic leaders proudly proclaimed their cold war, anticommunist credentials. University-based research labs, after some early postwar debates about the role of scientists in nuclear weapon making, enthusiastically enlisted in the anticommunist fight. Similarly, academics in the humanities and social sciences often lent their talents to the containment crusade. Historians of U.S. foreign relations, for example, embraced containment as a continuation of the internationalist, antitotalitarian thrust of enlightened, post-1937 foreign-policymaking. And in the social sciences, the dominant trend called for objective, disinterested, and value-free analysis; any passionate work of social criticism, such as C. Wright Mills's *Power Elite* (1956), risked being labeled as old-fashioned and out of step with currently scholarly standards.

Leading intellectuals still proclaimed themselves skeptics, but in retrospect this postwar skepticism had clear limits. Most prominent academics, in the words of one later scholar, were "believing skeptics," people whose distrust of left-wing pieties did not produce an equally rigorous scrutiny of the pragmatic political ideas they believed guided the United States. Once deeply committed to Marxism and left-wing politics, the sociologist Daniel Bell spoke for most postwar intellectuals when he proclaimed an "end of ideology." Welfare-state programs of both the New Deal and the Fair Deal offered everything needed to fix the nation's problems. Through economic and social fine-tuning, done in accordance with the best scientific and social science expertise, political managers could advance social and economic justice without any fundamental restructuring of capitalist institutions. Within higher education, a celebratory mood dominated: The United States should be praised for its many virtues rather than criticized for its few vices.

This general mood of celebration, according to mainstream intellectuals, did not mean that academic freedom had been compromised. While admitting a few cases in which left-wing academics lost their jobs, the postwar liberal academy emphasized that prominent dissenters, such as Mills, were not totally silenced as they would have been in a communist state.

In recent years, however, histories of academic culture have suggested that the cold war brought considerable surveillance of campus life by the FBI and CIA. In one case, for example, J. Edgar Hoover's agents pilfered a draft copy of a law-review article that criticized the FBI as a threat to civil liberties, a move that enabled the bureau's director to begin planning a campaign to discredit the article's author. In other cases, prominent academics covertly worked with anticommunist agencies much more closely than they admitted at the time, or subsequently. As in the entertainment industry, the history of higher education seems to have involved more dismissals, a longer blacklist of suspected radicals, and a wider history of cooperating with surveillance institutions than once thought.

THE PERILS OF PROGRESS

Publicists for the giant electronics firm of General Electric coined a phrase that captured the essence of postwar optimism: "Progress is our most important product." (In 1954 Ronald Reagan became GE's primary spokesperson.) According to the widely shared vision, the future, largely defined in terms of the increased consumption of goods and services, seemed preordained: It would be a bigger, better, streamlined version of the present. Public-spirited business corporations, employing the latest scientific and technological advances, would produce an ever-expanding array of improved products for wealthy, middle-class and even low-income families.

In time, thanks to the miracles of mass production and the mechanics of mass consumption (including expanded installment buying), the lifestyles of the nation's diverse population would ultimately converge. New "communities" would emerge, based on the mutual consumption of similar products. The richest Americans, to be sure, would always have the most, but even those at the bottom of the socioeconomic scale could live increasingly comfortable lives. Skilled technocrats, the kind of people who had proved so adept at harnessing science and technology for wartime production would ensure that this vision became reality. And if technocrats and the private sector failed to accomplish all this by themselves, postwar futurists observed, the national government stood ready to act as the cheerleader and banker for the new future.

Science and Technology

Postwar discussions of science and technology raised both fears and hopes about new developments. The atomic explosions that ravaged Japan, for example, initially produced terrifying images of worldwide destruction alongside optimistic pictures of how America's growing nuclear prowess might open an entirely new age in human history. After several years of fierce debate, in which vastly different images of a nuclear future competed against one another, opposition to full-scale nuclear development by the United States faded away. Critical scientists gradually found themselves marginalized and, in the more extreme cases, ostracized by colleagues and the increasingly powerful nuclear research lobby. For years, the government conducted experimental tests of nuclear weapons on islands in the South Pacific and in the western United States. But it kept secret until 1993 the devastating effects of radioactive fallout on humans—islanders, service personnel, nuclear industry workers, and westerners—who were downwind of the explosions or who came in contact with radioactive materials. At that time, under Secretary of Energy Hazel O'Leary, the government began to declassify revelations of government-sponsored research programs that tested the effects of radioactivity on people, often without their consent or knowledge.

By 1950, the case for bigger bombs and a domestic nuclear power industry effectively dominated public discussion. Correctly developed and properly harnessed, atomic energy, it was claimed, could power the nation's growing cities, propel its naval vessels, and carry explorers into outer space. In a similar way, radioactive technology in medicine promised exciting new advances, including victory in the fight against cancer.

By the early 1950s, a comprehensive legal network helped to legitimize the nuclear industry. The Atomic Energy Act of 1946 gave the president sole authority to order the use of nuclear weapons but vested day-to-day control over nuclear materials to a new executive agency, the Atomic Energy Commission (AEC). Run by civilians, the AEC initially conducted research and made basic policy decisions about the use of nuclear technology. Under the Atomic Energy Act of 1954, however, this system of tight federal control was modified in favor of an arrangement by which the AEC would grant licenses to private users of nonmilitary atomic energy. The goal of this new system, according to its supporters, was rapid growth of privately owned but government-regulated nuclear generating plants. Few people questioned the wisdom of this important step toward the creation of a private nuclear power industry in the United States.

The national government became more involved in a wide range of other, nonnuclear scientific activities after World War II. The wartime experience suggested the need for peacetime support of military research, and advocates of federal aid also urged the government to appropriate more money for nonmilitary experimentation. In a report to the president entitled *Science—The Endless Frontier* (1945), Vannevar Bush, who had managed scientific projects for the government during World War II, called for a single national agency to administer grants for scientific research. Scientists, he argued, would go on to make important new discoveries that could protect the nation from foreign enemies and dramatically improve the quality of citizens' daily lives. In 1950 Congress established the National Science Foundation, and NSF grants soon allowed scientists to explore subjects unknown a generation earlier. By the 1960s, federal funds underwrote most scientific research in the United States.

Encouraged by government funds (and by grants from tax-exempt private foundations), scientific activity accelerated in the postwar era. Ever since the late nineteenth century the number of scientists and technicians had been growing faster than the general population, and this trend continued after 1945. The United States had once been a nation of basement tinkerers. But the corps of highly trained specialists who dominated science and technology after World War II could not build their own laboratories, as Thomas Edison had once done. The new discoveries—in fields such as chemistry, biology, electronics, and nuclear energy—rested on highly sophisticated equipment and complex scientific theories about the physical universe.

Popular enthusiasm for scientific and technological innovation overwhelmed doubts about the social impact of new developments. The postwar era seemed to promise almost unbelievable, and overwhelmingly positive, changes. Instead of merely adapting human institutions to the natural environment, scientists celebrated their ability to go beyond the natural to create an artificial world. Knowledge of scientific theories permitted them to rearrange molecular structures and to produce synthetic fibers, high-strength adhesives, synthetic construction materials, and many other new products. In 1944 scientists at Rockefeller Institute isolated a compound called DNA, which opened the secrets of genetic reproduction. Throughout the 1940s biochemists tried to unravel the molecular structure of DNA, and finally in 1953 scientists constructed a model of a DNA molecule. Abstract theoretical knowledge and sophisticated technology were becoming important national resources, like iron and coal; indeed, scientific knowhow and up-to-date technology now seemed the most vital resources of all.

Developments in the computer-electronics industry, however, suggested ambiguities in the dominant, postwar vision of "progress." From management's perspective, for example, the ideal factory seemed one almost totally devoid of workers. In 1946, *Fortune* magazine featured a section on the Automatic Factory, including an article entitled "Machines Without Men." By the use of new, computer-assisted technology, this article predicted, the factory could be emptied of dirty, troublesome laborers and run by a handful of skilled technocrats who looked after the "accurate," "untiring," and highly efficient "electronic gadgets." The following year an executive at Ford Motor Co. offered a term that has remained, depending on one's point of view, either a threat or a promise—"automation."

What, for example, would be the fate of workers who faced computer-assisted technologies? Viewed from the vantage point of corporate managers and other apostles of progress, the answer seemed obvious. A more efficient production process was eminently democratic: More consumers would obtain more goods and services at lower prices. But if one reversed the perspective and looked at this kind of "progress" from the position of workers, substantial difficulties appeared. New technologies, developed by management (often with hefty government subsidies), controlled by management, and explained to the public by management, promised to strip workers of a good deal of power and control over both the work process and ultimately their job security.

In 1952, a youthful GE publicist-turned-author, Kurt Vonnegut, Jr., criticized the "progress as our product" vision in his novel *Player Piano*. Based on many of Vonnegut's own experiences at GE's complex in Schenectady, New York, *Player Piano* fantasized a future in which automation obliterated the skills, self-confidence, and human spirit of workers; Vonnegut imagined a world in which one-dimensional technocrats presided over a moral and spiritual wasteland. The future, he warned, might not be characterized by evolutionary progress, as corporate publicists confidently predicted; instead, postwar America could be headed down a dark, dangerous, and disorderly path of "devolution." Although *Player Piano* became a cult classic, Vonnegut himself later recalled that the GE technocrats he so bitterly lampooned remained wedded to the mainstream, postwar vision: New technologies were automatically good, and automation would bring the benefits of consumerism to a wider audience, while relieving workers of the burdens of repetitive labor.

The story of postwar medicine also showed the ambiguous nature of scientific "progress." Undeniably, there were positive breakthroughs. After World War II, for example, the United States experienced severe, unprecedented epidemics of poliomyelitis. Between 1947 and 1951 this disease, which generally crippled those it did not kill, struck an annual average of 39,000 Americans, mostly children. (Between 1938 and 1942 the annual average had been only 6,400, a figure that rose to 16,800 between 1942 and 1947.) In 1952 doctors reported some success using gamma globulin as a preventative, and three years later Jonas Salk pioneered the first truly successful vaccine. A nationwide program to inoculate people with this and the later Sabin vaccine resulted in the virtual elimination of polio by the 1960s.

After World War II, doctors also introduced a series of "wonder drugs." Penicillin, an antibiotic discovered in the 1920s and refined during the war, came into general use between 1945 and 1952; a powerful set of antibiotics—streptomycin, aureomycin, terramycin, and magnamycin—appeared after World War II; and antihistamines, which proved important in the treatment of allergies, became available in the late 1940s. These drugs and new surgical techniques allowed many Americans to lead longer and sometimes more comfortable lives. They also encouraged more determined research into cancer and heart disease, two afflictions that became increasingly common as the United States became more urbanized and industrialized. Nearly a half century later, cancer and heart disease, though treatable, remain serious public health problems, while the overuse of antibiotics has created new strains of super bacteria that are largely immune to traditional super drugs.

The postwar period also brought innovations in mental-health care. During World War II, psychiatrists won acclaim for successfully dealing with mental stress among military personnel, and in 1946 hospitals run by the Veterans Administration were still treating more than 100,000 people for neuropsychiatric disorder. Against this backdrop, a new generation of practitioners sought to expand their profession's mission beyond that of caring (in the words of one mental-health activist) for "a hopeless and hapless few." Instead of caring only for people in mental institutions, a group of young activists hoped to treat everyone who suffered, needlessly they argued, from the stresses of an increasingly complex society.

These activist psychiatrists gradually prevailed within their own profession and in congressional politics. Overcoming opposition from more conservative colleagues, who wanted to retain the emphasis on treatments within mental hospitals, the young Turks foresaw new social and communal roles for psychiatry. Confident of their ability to diagnose mental problems with scientific accuracy and anxious to dispense cures from a variety of different places, including community clinics and educational institutions, they helped push the National Mental Health Act of 1946 through Congress. Enjoying broad support, even from political conservatives such as Robert Taft, this law committed Washington to "the improvement of the mental health of the people of the United States" by supporting research into "psychiatric disorders," by training new personnel, and by awarding states money to help establish treatment centers. In 1949, activists secured the establishment of the National Institute of Mental Health (NIMH), which played a vital role in encouraging both Congress and state governments to fund community mental-health clinics. Within ten years, NIMH's annual budget topped $50 million, and by the early 1960s it neared $200 million.

Changes in medicine, however, did not automatically mean better health care for everyone. Exotic new drugs, complicated treatment procedures, and lavish hospital facilities increased the costs of medical care. Those with low incomes and many elderly people simply could not afford the new "wonder" cures; many rural areas and small towns, unable to compete with metropolitan areas for younger physicians, lacked competent doctors and adequate hospital facilities. Largely as a result of this maldistribution of medical services, the United States was actually losing ground, compared with other industrial nations, in reducing its infant mortality rate.

In addition to the unequal distribution of medical treatment, postwar technology created other problems. New developments accelerated the disappearance of the family doctor—the general practitioner celebrated in Norman Rockwell's paintings—and the proliferation of specialists—doctors trained to diagnose and treat only a limited number of conditions. Indeed, after World War II new medical technologies meant that large hospital complexes, with their costly equipment and their large staffs of specialists, replaced the home and the doctor's office as primary treatment centers. Fewer and fewer doctors made house calls; more and more people went to hospital emergency rooms or outpatient centers. At the same time, those who needed extensive medical care found that the new medicine often meant a costly stay in the hospital. In 1946 only 1 of every 10 Americans was admitted to a hospital for inpatient care; twenty years later the figure had risen to 1 of every 6.5 persons.

Unfortunately, a hospital visit did not always result in either an instant cure or, in some cases, even the proper treatment. According to numerous studies, perhaps half of many common surgical operations, particularly those performed on women and children, were unnecessary. Other critics of the postwar medical establishment cited the proliferation of iatrogenic illnesses, ailments brought on by the "treatment" for some other malady. Many iatrogenic illnesses, these critics argued, resulted from a naive faith in new medicines, from improper testing and regulation of new drugs, and from the popular belief that doctors possessed a miracle cure for every ache and pain. Assessing the impact of exotic medical technologies would, by the 1990s, require a complex dialogue in which philosophers who specialized in medical ethics, as well as the medical community and the general public, would take part.

Agriculture

Postwar science and technology affected all segments of American society, and even farmers, supposedly the slowest to alter settled ways, saw significant changes. Farming became more mechanized and scientific than ever before. Sophisticated biological research produced new types of seeds, such as hybrid corn. Introduced in some areas during the 1930s, hybrid corn spread to all parts of the country by the 1950s. Equally important to grain producers, the chemical industry produced cheaper fertilizers and pesticides. Farmers quickly turned to these chemicals to boost output: They used three times as much fertilizer in 1950 as they had ten years earlier. Farmers also began to adopt labor-saving machines on a massive scale. Between 1940 and 1960, for example, the number of tractors increased by more than 200 percent, and the number of grain combines rose nearly as much. Meanwhile, engineers were increasing the size of these machines, boosting their horsepower with higher-compression engines, and offering a variety of attachments. The new machinery and chemicals drastically reduced the number of farm laborers needed to bring in key crops (see Table 2–1).

As a result, farm output exploded after World War II. For many years agricultural production had been increasing, but now—with hybrid seeds, better equipment, cheaper fertilizers, and new irrigation facilities—output rose at a much faster rate than before. Farmers could cultivate hitherto unproductive land and areas once set aside as pastures for horses and mules. (In 1920 farmers had used more than 90 million acres of potential croplands to graze draft animals; by 1960 they needed less than 10 million acres for pasturage.) In addition, the new agricultural methods permitted farmers to utilize their old land more effectively, and the yield per acre rose substantially after World War II. But irrigation required massive amounts of water, and fertilizers and pesticides raised serious health hazards for both farm workers and consumers.

Meanwhile, steadily increasing production yields kept farm prices low, thereby decimating the rural economy. Whereas most of the world's people spent almost half their incomes for food, Americans needed only about 20 percent of their paychecks to feed their families. Most farmers did not enjoy the rising incomes of most other Americans, and only the largest and most efficient operations could show substantial profits. Although Washington tried to support farm incomes by updating the programs devised during Roosevelt's New Deal—direct subsidies and various plans for restricting acreage—nothing really succeeded. Low prices and steadily rising costs continually plagued small operators. Taking advantage of their private economic power and their ability to secure federal assistance, larger corporate farmers

TABLE 2-1   Declining Demand for Farm Labor Accelerated the Rush to Urban Areas and Left Pockets of Rural Poverty

MECHANIZATION OF AGRICULTURE: WORKER-HOURS PER 100 BUSHELS OF SELECTED CROPS

Crop	1945–49	1955–59	1962–66
Corn for grain	53.0	20.0	9.0
Sorghum grain	49.0	20.0	9.0
Wheat	34.0	17.0	11.0
Hay	6.2	3.7	3.0
Potatoes	12.0	6.0	5.0
Sugar beets	6.3	2.9	2.1
Cotton	146.0	74.0	39.0
Tobacco	39.0	31.0	25.0
Soybeans	41.0	23.0	20.0

Source: Agricultural statistics.

gained larger shares of the agricultural market while the number of smaller family farms declined steadily (see Figure 2–1).

All parts of the country felt the social impact of the revolutionary changes in agricultural production, but no region was affected more than the South. During the 1940s and 1950s, because of the new emphasis on corporate farming and mechanization, millions of African-Americans who had worked as agricultural laborers, especially in the cotton-growing industry, left the South for the Middle West, the Northeast, and (increasingly) the West Coast. Similarly, those families in the rural South, both African-American and white, who had tilled their own small holdings, found that they could no longer sustain themselves by farming. At the same time, up-country from the Deep South, white farm families were being forced, because of the economic changes in farming, to leave Appalachia for midwestern cities like Dayton, Cincinnati, Cleveland, Detroit, and Chicago. The people who stayed behind, whether in the rural South or in Appalachia, struggled to keep families together and to meet their financial obligations. For millions of people who had once sustained themselves on the land, the postwar era's much-touted "progress" seemed merely a distant dream.

FIGURE 2-1   In the postwar period the trends toward fewer but larger farms and toward a much smaller rural population accelerated. By 1980 three out of every four Americans lived in a metropolitan area.

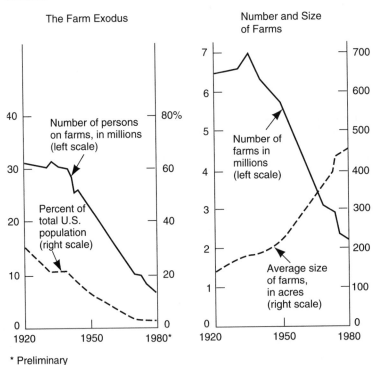

The Farm Exodus

Number and Size of Farms

* Preliminary

The United States at Mid-century: The Taint of Scandal and the End of Truman's Presidency

The ambiguous results of developments in science and technology, along with domestic and international tensions, produced considerable unease about everyday life in mid-twentieth century America. The promise of the postwar era also seemed marred by signs of widespread corruption. In 1950 and 1951 an ambitious Democratic senator from Tennessee, Estes Kefauver, dramatically unveiled the shadowy world of organized crime. Skillfully using television, Kefauver brought underworld figures—from top mobster Frank Costello to petty gamblers and prostitutes—into millions of living rooms. The Kefauver hearings held all the drama of a Hollywood production. "It was difficult at times to believe that it was real," marveled *The New York Times*.

Other stories of corruption appeared during the postwar period. In 1950 the U.S. Military Academy, the citadel of gentlemanly honor and patriotic values, expelled ninety West Pointers, including nine starting members of the football team, for cheating on examinations. That same year, prosecutors in New York uncovered a point-shaving scandal in college basketball. Star players on several top teams—including national champion City College of New York and the University of Kentucky—were found to have taken bribes in exchange for rigging game scores in favor of professional gamblers. Bernard Malamud's novel *The Natural* (1952) captured at least some of this mid-century disillusionment: A talented but gullible baseball star, Roy Hobbs, falls prey to corrupt owners and mysterious gamblers, eventually disgracing the national pastime. (In contrast to the film version of the 1980s, Malamud's novel of the 1950s ends on a note of despair: Hobbs fails to redeem himself and comes to symbolize an unreflective, naive national spirit.)

By the 1950s, big-time sports had become an important part of cultural life, and revelations about scandal at the highest levels produced widely different reactions. Some blamed the corruption on a decline in moral principles and demanded a vigorous response. The National Collegiate Athletic Association (NCAA) banned from further competition the basketball players who had taken bribes, and the National Basketball Association blacklisted them forever. But others were not so quick to accept or to assign moral blame. The West Point cadets refused contrition, claiming they were being punished for a practice followed by most of their classmates. Army's football coach, Colonel Earl Blaik, whose son had been one of those dropped from the academy, refused to condemn his players and publicly reaffirmed his faith in football as a character-building sport.

In time, the search for corruption reached into the White House. Along with McCarthyite charges of being soft on communism, accusations about "the mess in Washington" eroded Truman's popularity. During his last years in office, scandals seemed to pop up everywhere. An old crony, Harry Vaughan, was accused of accepting illegal gifts; the Senate uncovered examples of apparent political favoritism in the Reconstruction Finance Corporation, including one celebrated case in which the wife of a former RFC official received a mink coat as part of a questionable transaction; the *New Republic* leveled charges of bribery or political favoritism at six different federal agencies; the head of the Democratic National Committee appeared guilty of influencing a government decision in exchange for legal fees; and Republicans charged that the Truman administration was full of "five-percenters," who traded their political influence for kickbacks on public contracts.

Cantankerous and stubborn as ever, Truman lashed out at his critics. Despite clear evidence to the contrary, he proclaimed that "my house is always clean." Although no one ever linked the scandals to Truman himself, he left Washington with his reputation as a presidential leader badly tarnished. Only after the passage of time and the uncovering of far greater scandals in subsequent presidential administrations would Harry Truman become a national folk hero, a president lionized by both Republicans and Democrats, liberals and conservatives, for his feisty independence.

Meanwhile, as the nation passed the midpoint of the twentieth century, the perils of the postwar years appeared to have passed; the great promise of "the American century" seemed in view. To be sure, even the most optimistic observer conceded lingering problems: the Soviet threat overseas, McCarthyism at home, economic problems at the fringe of a growing affluence, and the explosive issue of race relations. But even social critics generally accentuated the positive: Though hardly tranquil, labor-management conflict now centered on clearly defined issues; the welfare state, assisted by newly developed social science expertise, seemed firmly in place; the capitalist economy appeared to have outgrown traditional cycles of boom and bust; a new scientific-technological elite promised to produce progress for all; the national security establishment seemed entirely capable of safeguarding the nation's global interests. And perhaps most important, the apparent "end of ideology" suggested a future in which rational planners and practical compromisers could solve remaining difficulties. During the mid-1950s, public-policy debates would generally focus on questions of how best to adjust to the self-evident promise of the United States, but beneath the surface the unresolved postwar tensions remained.

SUGGESTIONS FOR FURTHER READING

Lary May, ed., *Recasting America: Culture and Politics in the Age of the Cold War* (1989), offers essays on different aspects of postwar life; and Stephen J. Whitfield, *The Culture of the Cold War* (1991), and William Graebner, *The Age of Doubt* (1991), provide brief overviews. Two still useful accounts, especially for labor and mass culture, are Marty Jezer, *The Dark Ages* (1982), and George Lipsitz, *Class and Culture in Cold War America* (1982). Alan Wolfe, *America's Impasse* (1981); Margaret Weir, Ann S. Orloff, and Theda Skocpol, eds., *The Politics of Social Policy in the United States* (1988); and Steve Fraser and Gary Gerstle, *The Rise and Fall of the New Deal Order, 1930–1980* (1989), all take longer views of postwar themes.

Robert Ferrell, *Harry Truman and the Modern American Presidency* (1983); William Pemberton, *Harry S Truman: Fair Dealer and Cold Warrior* (1989); and David G. McCullough, *Truman* (1992), offer good introductions. Truman's own account can be found in *Memoirs* (2 vols., 1955–1956); Robert H. Ferrell, ed., *Off the Record: The Private Papers of Harry S Truman* (1980); and Merle Miller, *Plain Speaking* (1974), a series of interviews that helped spark the rehabilitation of Truman's reputation. Michael J. Lacey, ed., *The Truman Presidency* (1989), offers interpretive essays; and Alonso Hamby, *Beyond the New Deal* (1973), remains a useful look at Truman's Fair Deal, but it should be supplemented by the relevant chapters of the same author's *Liberalism and Its Challengers* (2nd ed., 1992). Specialized studies include R. Alton Lee, *Truman and Taft-Hartley* (1966); Allen J. Matusow, *Farm Policies and Politics in the Truman Administration* (1966); William C. Berman, *The Politics of Civil Rights in the Truman Administration* (1970); Maeva Marcus, *Truman and the Steel Seizure Case* (1977); Monte Poen, *Harry S Truman versus the Medical Lobby* (1977); Andrew J. Dunar, *The Truman Scandals and the Politics of Morality* (1984); and Steven M. Gillon, *Politics and Vision: The ADA and American Liberalism, 1947–1985* (1986).

Economic and labor issues may be traced in Robert Leckachman, *The Age of Keynes* (1966); John Bernard, *Walter Reuther and the Rise of the Auto Workers* (1983); Gerald D. Nash, *The American West Transformed* (1985); Robert H. Zeiger, *American Workers, American Unions, 1920–1985* (1986); Milton Derber et al., *Labor in Illinois: The Affluent Years, 1945–1980* (1989); Mark Friedberger, *Farm Families and Change in Twentieth-Century America* (1989); Kim McQuaid, *Uneasy Partners: Big Business and American Politics, 1945–1990* (1993).

There are many excellent studies of the postwar red scare. Joel Kovel, *Red Hunting in the Promised Land* (1993), and M. J. Heale, *American Anticommunism* (1990), take the long view, whereas Fred Inglis, *The Cruel Peace* (1991), offers an international perspective. Richard M. Fried, *Nightmare in Red: The McCarthy Era in Perspective* (1990), and Ellen Schreker, *The Age of McCarthyism* (1994), are recent syntheses; but David Caute's *The Great Fear* (1978), still offers a good, more detailed account. Specialized studies include Michael Belknap, *Cold War Political Justice* (1971); Frank J. Donner, *The Age of Surveillance* (1980); Peter Steinberg, *The Great "Red Menace"* (1982); Stanley I. Kutler, *American Inquisition* (1982); Larry Ceplair and Steven Englund, *The Inquisition in Hollywood* (1983); Ronald Radosh and Joyce Milton, *The Rosenberg File* (1983); David Oshinsky, *A Conspiracy So Immense: The World of Joe McCarthy* (1983); Gerald Horne, *Black and Red: W. E. B. DuBois and the Afro-American Response to the Cold War* (1986); Ellen Schrecker, *No Ivory Tower: McCarthyism & the Universities* (1986); Herbert Mitgang, *Dangerous Dossiers: Exposing the Secret War Against America's Greatest Authors* (1988); Bernard Dick, *Radical Innocence: A Critical Study of the Hollywood Ten* (1989); Robert P. Newman, *Owen Lattimore and the "Loss" of China* (1992); and Sigmund Diamond, *The Compromised Campus* (1992).

Athan Theoharis has a number of outstanding studies on the culture of surveillance and anticommunism; see, for example, *The Truman Presidency:*

The Origins of the Imperial Presidency and the National Security State (1979), *Beyond the Hiss Case* (1982), and *From the Secret Files of J. Edgar Hoover* (1991), three volumes that he edited. See also the relevant chapters of Theoharis and John Stuart Cox, *The Boss: J. Edgar Hoover and the Great American Inquisition* (1988), and Curt Gentry, *J. Edgar Hoover and the Secrets* (1991).

On cold war cultural and intellectual trends, see Whitfield, *Cold War Culture*; Robert Booth Fowler, *Believing Skeptics* (1978); Mary Sperling McAuliffe, *Crisis on the Left: Cold War Politics and American Liberals* (1978); Serge Guilbaut, *How New York Stole the Idea of Modern Art: Abstract Expressionism, Freedom, and the Cold War* (1983); Richard Pells, *The Liberal Mind in a Conservative Age* (1984); Paul Boyer, *By the Bomb's Early Light: American Thought and Culture at the Dawn of the Atomic Age* (1985); Alexander Bloom, *Prodigal Sons: The New York Intellectuals & Their World* (1986); Alan Wald, *The New York Intellectuals* (1987); Lawrence H. Schwartz, *Creating Faulkner's Reputation: The Politics of Modern Literary Criticism* (1988); Robbie Lieberman, *"My Song Is My Weapon": People Songs, American Communism, and the Politics of Culture, 1930–1950* (1989); Thomas Hill Schaub, *American Fiction in the Cold War* (1991); Daniel Horowitz, *Vance Packard and American Social Criticism* (1994); Allan M. Winkler, *Life Under a Cloud: American Anxiety About the Atom* (1993); and Michael Wreszin, *Rebel in the Defense of Tradition: The Life and Politics of Dwight McDonald* (1994).

Science, medicine, and technological issues are discussed in Daniel Ford, *The Cult of the Atom* (1982); George T. Mazuzan and J. Samuel Walker, *Controlling the Atom: The Beginnings of Nuclear Regulation* (1984); David Noble, *Forces of Production* (1984); Bryan Jennett, *High Technology Medicine: Benefits and Burdens* (1986); Howard Ball, *Justice Downwind: America's Atomic Testing Program* (1986); James Patterson, *The Dread Disease: Cancer and Modern American Culture* (1987); Jonathan Liebenau, *Medical Science and Medical Industry: The Formation of the American Pharmaceutical Industry* (1987); Rosemary Stevens, *In Sickness and in Wealth: American Hospitals in the Twentieth Century* (1989); David A. Hounshell and John K. Smith, Jr., *Science and Corporate Strategy: DuPont R&D, 1902–1980* (1989); Brian Balogh, *Chain Reaction: Expert Debate and Public Participation in American Commercial Nuclear Power* (1991); Andrew Polsky, *The Rise of the Therapeutic State* (1991); Gerald N. Grob, *From Asylum to Community: Mental Health Policy in Modern America* (1991); Stephen P. Waring, *Taylorism Transformed: Scientific Management Theory Since 1945* (1991); Daniel M. Fox, *Power and Illness: The Failure and Future of American Health Policy* (1993); and Stuart W. Leslie, *The Cold War and American Science* (1993).

3

Politics and Culture in the 1950s

MODERATE REPUBLICANISM

The broad smile of Dwight Eisenhower dominated electoral politics during the mid-1950s. A successful general in World War II, Eisenhower was shrewder than his simple popular image suggested. Army promotions and success as a commander required ambition and a politician's keen sense of timing, and Eisenhower put the political skills he had learned in the army to good use during his presidency. But to his admirers of the 1950s, he simply radiated good, down-home common sense rather than political guile. Even his nickname, "Ike," had a folksy ring, lacking the efficient staccato of JFK and LBJ or the distant formality of Richard M. Nixon. Though old doubts persisted and new problems emerged during the Eisenhower years, from 1953 to 1960, Ike himself emphasized a faith that traditional values remained the key to tapping the full possibilities of postwar life.

The Elections of 1952 and 1956

In 1952, encouraged by the Truman administration's many problems, Republicans anticipated the electoral victory that had slipped away four years earlier. Still, GOP leaders wanted to take no chances, and the desire to pick a winner worked in favor of Dwight Eisenhower.

Some people doubted that Eisenhower would ever run. In 1948 the popular general had firmly rejected a presidential race because of the "necessary policy" of subordinating the military to civilian rule. And despite a Republican background, his postwar political affiliation remained a mystery. As late as

1951 Truman suggested that Eisenhower become the Democrats' standard-bearer.

But while president of Columbia University from 1948 to 1951, Eisenhower formed close ties with influential members of the Republican party's eastern establishment. He came to share their belief that another GOP defeat would embolden the more conservative and the McCarthyite wings of the party. A moderate on almost every issue, Eisenhower did not want the GOP to swing so far to the right. He also believed that the United States must play an active role in Europe, and he feared that Senator Robert A. Taft, the leading contender for the Republican nomination, was not firmly committed to NATO. When eastern supporters convinced Eisenhower that Taft's reputation as a midwestern reactionary would prove a serious political liability, the old soldier decided that both the GOP and the nation needed him. After twenty years of Democrats in the White House, the GOP could not pass up a seemingly sure winner: Eisenhower won a first-ballot victory at the 1952 Republican convention. To soothe ruffled feelings, he selected Richard Nixon, a Republican regular and anticommunist crusader, as his vice-presidential candidate. The thirty-four-year-old Nixon was also expected to attract younger voters.

During the 1952 presidential campaign, Eisenhower encountered some difficulty transforming himself from general of the army to good old Ike. Gradually, though, he mastered the rituals of American politics. To the displeasure of some, he made symbolic concessions to right-wing Republicans, holding a reconciliation meeting with Senator Taft and campaigning alongside several outspoken McCarthyites. In a Wisconsin speech Eisenhower deleted a favorable reference to General George Marshall, a close friend but one of Joe McCarthy's favorite targets. And though Ike piously announced, "I shall not and will not engage in character assassination, vilification and personalities," Nixon and other surrogates sought votes by extravagant attacks on communist influence in Washington, corruption in government, and the "no-win" war in Korea. Nixon returned to the communist conspiracy theme when stories about his political slush fund threatened his place on the GOP ticket. His televised reply to the charges featured insinuations that the "reds" wanted to deny him the vice-presidency and contained self-pitying comments about his wife's "Republican cloth coat," his worn-out Oldsmobile, and his one political payoff—his daughters' little dog, Checkers. The "Checkers speech" saved Nixon's career and boosted his appeal among GOP leaders. It even gave him a reputation as a skilled television performer.

By contrast, Democrats found few bright spots in 1952. Their presidential nominee, Governor Adlai Stevenson of Illinois, won the plaudits of liberal columnists for his cleverly phrased speeches, but critics complained that the erudite Stevenson aimed his addresses well over the average voter's head. His image as an intellectual and a recent divorce became frequently noted handicaps. In addition, Stevenson had to outrun the unpopular shadow of Harry Truman, who insisted on taking part in the campaign. Political pollsters, who had substantially revised their techniques after the miscalculations of 1948, discovered that many voters simply felt that the Democrats had been in power too long. Election results corroborated their predictions. Eisenhower carried all but nine states, and the Republicans also gained control, though by very narrow margins, of both houses of Congress.

Eisenhower appeared to be a person who could restore old-time virtues to government, and most voters seemed satisfied with his leadership. In 1956, when the Eisenhower–Stevenson presidential contest was replayed, Eisenhower's popularity remained undiminished. Retaining Richard Nixon as a running mate (after several unheeded hints that Nixon might prefer a cabinet post), Eisenhower received almost 10 million more popular votes than Stevenson. Ike's popularity, however, did not carry over to his own party. The Democrats had regained control of both houses of Congress in 1954, and they solidified their position in 1956.

The Eisenhower Presidency

Eisenhower promised a "constitutional presidency." Extolling a preference for local government and state autonomy, he felt that Democratic administrations had extended national power too far and had spent the public's tax dollars too freely. Eisenhower also believed that Harry Truman, whom he held in very low esteem, had provoked Congress, needlessly embittering relations between the White House and Capitol Hill. Ike came to Washington determined to get along with Congress; such cooperation became a necessity after the Democrats gained control of both houses in 1954. Eisenhower instructed cabinet members to avoid antagonizing members of Congress. The art of leadership, he told one associate, did not require "hitting people over the head. Any damn fool can do that. . . . It's persuasion—and conciliation—and education—and patience. That's the only kind of leadership I know—or believe in—or will practice." During his two terms he received considerable help from congressional Democrats led by two cagey Texans, Sam Rayburn and Lyndon Johnson. Political centrists themselves, Rayburn and Johnson approved of many of Eisenhower's policies; one historian described their version of "loyal opposition" as three parts loyal and one part opposition. Although the executive branch and Congress often clashed, there was little of the bitterness that characterized relations between them during the Truman era.

Eisenhower also sought harmony within his administration. Believing that Democratic administrations had ignored sound managerial practices, he filled his first cabinet with Republican business leaders. "Engine Charley" Wilson, secretary of defense, came from General Motors; Treasury Secretary George Humphrey had headed the giant Mark Hanna Company; Postmaster General Arthur Summerfield owned a huge car agency in Michigan. A liberal magazine dismissed Eisenhower's appointees as "eight millionaires and a plumber." The plumber was Democrat Martin Durkin, president of the United Association of Plumbers and Steamfitters. Eisenhower hoped that a union leader might smooth relations between his administration and organized labor, but appointment of a Democrat as secretary of labor only angered conservative Republicans. Within eight months Durkin was gone.

Eisenhower also drew heavily from business and the military to fill White House staff positions.

The president shrewdly managed his corporate team. He picked Sherman Adams as his chief aide (some people called Adams the assistant president) and gave him broad authority. Adams acted as gatekeeper, allowing Ike to see people who had important business but blocking those who might waste his time. He also handled many sensitive duties that Eisenhower wished to avoid. Adams soon became notorious for his brusque phone calls—he made more than two hundred every day—in which he barked orders and then hung up without waiting for a reply. This style gained Adams many enemies in Washington, but it also allowed Eisenhower himself to avoid some ticklish situations. In foreign affairs and in economic policy, Eisenhower adopted a similar strategy, letting Secretary of State John Foster Dulles and Treasury Secretary George Humphrey take the heat while he remained above the battle.

Eisenhower's skillful use of subordinates as political lightning rods reflected his deep conviction that, after all of Harry Truman's troubles, he must restore the image of the presidency and support for traditional values. Although he had formed no church ties during his army career, Eisenhower quickly joined Washington's National Presbyterian Church (seven previous presidents had been members) and became a Sunday regular. He opened cabinet meetings with a silent prayer and began the tradition of "prayer breakfasts" at the White House. His inaugural parade contained a hastily constructed entry called "God's Float." Flanked by slogans proclaiming "In God We Trust" and "Freedom of Worship" and topped by a curious structure that was supposed to resemble a nondenominational church, the creation struck one minister as "an oversized model of a deformed molar left over from some dental exhibit." But Eisenhower rarely stumbled in his public relations efforts. Unlike Richard Nixon, who would unsuccessfully invoke many of the same symbols during his stormy presidency, Eisenhower convinced most people of his sincerity. Although liberal critics questioned the wisdom of his policies, few doubted his integrity or decency. And through his much-publicized addiction to golf and bridge, pastimes that millions of ordinary citizens also enjoyed, he projected the image of the common man.

In recent years, many presidential scholars have revised earlier estimates of Eisenhower's abilities. For a long time historians believed that strong figures such as Dulles, Humphrey, and Adams dominated Eisenhower and really ran the government. Early in Eisenhower's first term a familiar joke asked, "What if Ike died and we got Nixon as president?" "Yes," went the punch line, "but what if Adams died, and we got stuck with Ike?" But Eisenhower now gains higher marks. He skillfully presided over cabinet sessions and meetings of the National Security Council, and he apparently retained a firm, though often unseen, rein over those areas he considered critical. During his second term all three of his key advisers resigned (scandal forced Adams's resignation, Humphrey returned to business, and Dulles fell victim to cancer), yet Eisenhower carried on without any noticeable disruption in the presidential routine.

President Dwight David Eisenhower's emphasis upon his leisure-time activities was part of the "hidden-hand presidency." Often pictured on "the golf course, he also fished and dabbled in painting. *Source:* National Archives.

Still, many questions about Eisenhower's presidency remain unanswered. Did Eisenhower, who left office with an extremely high rating in the opinion polls, simply ignore controversial domestic problems like environmental pollution and urban decay? Did his obvious lack of sympathy toward the civil rights movement help inflame racial tensions? (See Chapter 5.) And was he as shrewd a president as his close associates would later recall, or did he simply have extraordinarily good luck in handling the affairs of state? All these questions and many others await further research and contemplation. But one point seems clear: At a time when many people wanted a respite from the perils of the immediate postwar period, the former general from the Great Plains provided a symbol of old values, traditional virtues, and hopes for a bright future.

Eisenhower and the Corporate Commonwealth

Evaluating the political and economic policies of the 1950s, one historian characterized Eisenhower's two-term presidency as devoted to the creation of a "corporate commonwealth." During his career in the military bureaucracy, Ike came to share the managerial perspective of sophisticated corporate leaders. He saw increased efficiency, streamlined organization, self-discipline, and cooperation as the keys to both good business and good government. Eisenhower also came to accept, as did most business executives, a role for organized labor in the postwar economy and the popularity of Democratic social-welfare programs. Consequently, Eisenhower's brand of moderate Republicanism aimed at creating an economic prosperity that rested on harmonious relations among business, government, and labor.

Accepting the basic premises of the New and Fair Deals, Eisenhower worked with Congress to raise Social Security payments, minimum wage rates, and unemployment benefits. Congress created, with Eisenhower's support, a new cabinet Department of Health, Education, and Welfare (HEW). Moreover, he tried to achieve good relations with union leaders and, he hoped, to win some of the rank and file over to the Republican party.

Eisenhower did, however, oppose expensive, new government programs. Two weeks after taking office, he announced that the "first order of business" should be "the elimination of the annual deficit" in the federal budget. Guided by George Humphrey, who headed the Treasury Department during Ike's first term, the Eisenhower administration tried to limit federal expenditures, even if this meant turning its back on the kind of economic management that disciples of the new economics were urging on the White House. Eisenhower's economic team preferred to finesse the political problems that accompanied a sometimes sluggish economy and even rising unemployment rather than to face the difficulties it associated with increased government spending and a growing federal bureaucracy.

However, especially during his first term, Eisenhower accepted some new domestic spending programs. In response to an economic downturn in 1953–1954, he permitted the acceleration of spending for public-works projects as a way of stimulating the economy. He also endorsed new government projects that did not require inordinate outlays of federal monies. His administration, for instance, fully supported the Interstate Highway Act. The timing of new highway construction, Eisenhower even suggested, might be used so it could "have some effect in leveling out peaks and valleys in our economic life." Financed by taxes on gasoline purchases, which were earmarked for a federal highway trust fund that supplemented state expenditures, this vast public-works project aimed at crisscrossing the nation with a planned system of controlled-access expressways. A major national commitment to Detroit's gas guzzlers, the interstate program, in effect, subsidized the trucking industry and those individuals who could afford long-distance travel in their private vehicles.

The Interstate Highway Act of 1956, arguably the largest public-works program in human history, produced a host of spinoffs. Construction companies prospered; new gas stations, restaurants, and motel chains sprang up near the exit ramps; and the mobile home industry, symbolized by the sleek Airstream trailers, entered the era of mass production. Metropolitan areas soon experienced dizzying mazes of on- and off-ramps, monuments to the increasingly sophisticated techniques of highway planners.

But the positive effects of the interstate highway program often obscured its drawbacks. Railroads, a less expensive and less polluting means of transportation, could not compete with truckers who used free interstate highways, and rail lines fell into deep financial trouble. In New York City mass-transit facilities decayed; in Los Angeles and many other cities, light-rail transit was ended; and miles of concrete and asphalt crisscrossed the landscape. Americans became more car-crazy than ever, and the more they drove, the more there seemed to be no alternative to driving. Those without cars—especially the elderly and people with low incomes—were the losers. The highway lobby, an informal alliance of auto manufacturers, oil producers, and construction companies, were the winners. The graft sometimes associated with the purchase of right-of-ways and the award of contracts tainted local politics and recalled the railroad corruption of the late nineteenth century.

Despite the Eisenhower administration's desire to restrain federal spending, the economy still grew at a generally steady pace. The GNP (measured in constant dollars) expanded nearly 25 percent during Eisenhower's eight years in office, while consumer prices rose by an annual rate of less than 1.5 percent between 1953 and 1960. Unemployment figures, unfortunately, also rose, from a rate of about 3 percent in 1953 to one of more than 6 percent in 1959–1960. Although Eisenhower had accepted some responsibility to respond to the recession of 1953–1954, he showed no such inclination in 1957–1958, when a much more severe downturn occurred.

As the Eisenhower presidency wound down and new economic problems emerged, the president himself became more fiscally conservative. By the spring of 1958, signs of recession were everywhere, and the official unemployment rate reached 7.5 percent. Even leading business people, who had been among Ike's strongest supporters during his first term, became restive and urged a more energetic response, such as a tax cut, from Washington. Although Eisenhower endorsed the National Defense Education Act (NDEA) of 1958, which created a loan program for college students as a means of ultimately strengthening instruction in science and mathematics, he blocked efforts by Secretary of HEW Arthur Fleming to support federal funding of classroom construction at the elementary and secondary levels. Spurning the advice of Arthur Burns, who had helped to guide Eisenhower's more vigorous response to the 1953–1954 recession, the president insisted that the recession would eventually cure itself, without either tax cuts or increased social-welfare expenditures. Fearful that increased spending would spark an inflationary spiral, Eisenhower remained committed to balancing the federal budget. Despite the complaint of liberal Democrats that he should do more to stimulate additional economic growth, he congratulated his administration for overseeing eight years of general prosperity.

Certainly, the president and his defenders could credit his cautious approach to the economy with helping to sustain broad-based economic gains during the 1950s. During that decade, according to most estimates, large segments of the blue-collar, working-class population saw their incomes and lifestyles raised to levels that could be called middle class. If the Pentagon became the center of a military-industrial complex, the suburbs became the focus of what might be called the auto-house-electrical-appliance complex. Both home ownership, especially in the new postwar suburbs, and a host of new consumer products, made available by credit buying, became real possibilities for millions of people.

Liberal devotees of the new economics still considered the rate of economic expansion too slow to keep up with population growth. America's economic growth rate, they pointed out, lagged behind that of the Soviet Union, and the large baby-boom generation would soon demand a greatly enlarged job market. Moreover, Germany and Japan were beginning to rebuild the infrastructures of their war-shattered economies while economic planners in the United States were resting on their laurels, apparently blind to their increasingly outdated industrial plants and deteriorating infrastructure. Finally, social liberals charged that the lack of new federal spending programs stemmed not from the lack of pressing problems—such as urban and rural poverty, air pollution, central-city blight, and an inequitable system of health care—but from a determination to ignore them.

By the mid-1950s, liberal social observers became more critical of the direction of postwar society. Breaking with the celebratory tone of the immediate postwar period, they increasingly pointed to tears within the social fabric. Much of this attention first focused on the alleged discontents of the middle class: their lack of purpose, sense of aimlessness, and desire for greater peace of mind. The sociologist Daniel Bell, who had earlier proclaimed the "end of ideology," gradually became less sanguine about technological expertise as the solution to all social problems, especially those related to work. In 1956, he cataloged the discontents of the work process, criticizing preoccupation with issues of efficiency and managerial control. Beneath the semiofficial public tranquility, social critics observed a seething strata of private tensions.

A few liberal social critics shifted the focus from private discontents to public social problems. In *The Affluent Society* (1958) John Kenneth Galbraith denounced the parsimony of public-welfare programs. He contrasted the personal affluence of most Americans with the lack of decent public services, writing of the travelers who steer their "mauve and cerise air-conditioned, power-steered and power-braked car" through badly paved and littered streets; who "picnic on exquisitely packaged food from a portable icebox by a polluted stream and go on to spend the night at a park which is a menace to public health and morals." Galbraith scathingly attacked the American tax system, which permitted such a disparity between public services and private comfort. He called for higher levels of taxation and greater government spending.

Ignoring such criticism, Eisenhower and his economic advisers, especially William McChesney Martin of the Federal Reserve Board (FRB), held fast to their conservative economic policies. The first FRB head to exploit the intricacies of monetary policy, especially the board's control over the amount of money in circulation, Martin shared Ike's fears about inflation and his fondness for balanced budgets. Eisenhower could remind himself that he had entered politics to soothe and assure, not to reform and crusade. Many years later, he still proudly remembered his principal presidential accomplishment as having created "an atmosphere of greater serenity and mutual confidence."

Yet, as critics within and outside his administration noted, all was hardly serene and calm during the 1950s. On one level, Ike's own successes as "the

Coney Island, 1950. Though the old-style amusement park would not last, prosperity and the baby boom ensured that other youth-oriented forms of leisure, such as massive theme parks like Disneyland, would flourish. *Source:* National Archives.

manager of prosperity" ironically rebounded against him and the Republican party when many people, who were coming to enjoy the prosperity of the 1950s, accepted the Democratic argument that more aggressive government intervention could have produced even greater economic growth during the Eisenhower years. Because of his moralistic commitment to balanced budgets, many people came to see Eisenhower as an impediment to a vibrant, rapidly expanding economy.

Eisenhower's opposition to new domestic initiatives also undercut his initial hopes of constructing a presidency that was conservative on economic matters but liberal to moderate on social questions. The 1950s, far from being a period of serenity and mutual confidence, was a decade in which rapid social and cultural changes placed considerable strain on the nation's political and social institutions. Eisenhower appeared to be a person whose understanding of social issues, especially ones involving race, lagged behind new ideas.

GENDER, FAMILY, AND YOUTH

The Baby Boom and the New Family Ideal

Between the mid-1940s and 1957, the peak year of the mid-twentieth century's baby boom, the United States saw an unprecedented increase, of nearly 50 percent, in the birthrate. The generally steady economic growth encouraged couples to marry at younger ages than their counterparts of the 1930s; during the early 1950s, nearly one-half of all brides were still teenagers. Postwar families were having more children sooner and in closer succession than ever before in the nation's recent history. This upsurge in births seemed especially striking when measured against the relatively low rates of the 1930s. Between 1940 and 1960, the birthrate for third children doubled and that for fourth children tripled. In contrast to the trend in the 1980s, the average family size was larger for middle- and upper-income families than for those with relatively low incomes. In 1955, a survey revealed that 40 percent of middle-income white women considered four children the ideal family size.

Sheer numbers made these baby boomers extraordinary and provided them with a vague generational identity. Certainly, the baby-boom generation strained social resources. Everywhere people turned, children seemed to be spilling out of existing facilities. They needed immense quantities of diapers, toys, schools, teachers, and jobs. And as they inexorably grew older, they constituted a huge population "bulge" that placed new pressures on public institutions; by the 1990s, social planners worried about how they might adapt the supply of retirement housing and the Social Security system to the demands of now-aging baby boomers.

During the 1950s itself, the baby boom became closely associated with a new ideal of family life. Although people steeped in nostalgia often identify the white, middle-class family of the 1950s as "traditional," social historians always emphasize its uniqueness. In particular, the postwar middle-class family seems new, rather than traditional, in terms of the domestic burdens and expectations assigned to both mothers and fathers.

Advice manuals and magazines placed special responsibilities for the care of home and children on mothers. Despite the wider availability of "labor-saving devices," such as washers and power vacuums, the amount of time women spent on housework actually *increased* during the 1950s. But fathers were also expected to participate in the creation of the new home life. Just as women's magazines featured recipes and redecorating ideas for mothers, men's magazines such as *Popular Mechanics* emphasized how fathers could make their home workshops the busy centers of cottage-based do-it-yourself enterprises. While Mom was sewing the new draperies, Dad could be building their plywood valences.

Both parents were expected to contribute, ideally in collaboration, to making the home the key element in their children's social and moral development. In 1954, the women's magazine *McCall's* coined the term *togetherness* as a shorthand description for this new family ideal. According to one survey of middle-class couples, most respondents claimed that they had sacrificed nothing by marrying and listed children and security among the things they had gained. More than ever before in American history, family life moved to the center of American popular culture. Especially after the advent of television, the family home became the place in which both parents amused and entertained, as well as reared and nurtured, their children. According to one approach, advanced by guides like *The Family Fun Book* and *Planning Your Home for Play*, the ideal home would become a kind of good-time family clubhouse.

A whole array of political and social institutions supported the material dimensions of family life. Following in the footsteps of William Levitt, who opened his first Levittown home on Long Island in 1947, giant development companies and smaller builders rushed into the home-construction business. The national government encouraged the postwar home-buying spree—especially through the Federal Housing Administration (FHA) program begun during the 1930s and the Veterans Administration (VA) subsidies established for veterans of World War II and the Korean conflict—by reducing the amount of money required for a down payment to less than 10 percent of the purchase price and by guaranteeing relatively low-interest (2 or 3 percent), long-term (thirty-year) mortgages. The housing shortage of the immediate postwar period soon seemed a distant memory; couples suddenly discovered that it was cheaper to buy their own homes than to rent apartments or houses. In the twenty-year period after 1940, the number of families owning their own homes increased by 50 percent; by 1960, fully one-fourth of the U.S. housing stock had been built during the previous decade.

While the government-supported housing industry was providing middle-income families with homes of their own, other financial institutions were helping to furnish their dwellings. Purchasing consumer goods on credit was not, of course, a postwar invention, but the 1950s did see an unprecedented surge in installment buying. Finance agencies, charge accounts, and credit cards allowed home owners to stock up on appliances, furniture, and decorative items of all kinds. Although the amount of a family's income that was spent on food and clothing rose rather modestly during the late 1940s and 1950s, outlays for appliances and furnishings rose by nearly 250 percent.

Although economic prosperity certainly contributed to the baby boom, broad cultural attitudes about the importance of marriage, children, and family life ultimately sanctified the new postwar arrangements.

Suburbia

Home buying and family building became particularly identified with suburbia. The population of central cities increased by about 8 percent during the decade, whereas surrounding suburban areas grew by nearly 50 percent. Not surprisingly, then, 85 percent of the housing built in the 1940s and 1950s was located in suburban areas.

Home planners hailed suburbia's new "ranch style" as the ideal habitat for consumer-oriented families. In contrast to the boxlike bungalow, which had dominated building styles during the first third of the twentieth century, or even the Cape Cod featured in the first Levittown developments, the ranch house suggested the openness and the adaptability associated with the expansiveness of postwar family life. The kitchen, for instance, which had been tucked away as the wife's special place at the rear of the old bungalow, generally served as both the point of entry and the center of family life in the ranch

Giant suburban shopping malls followed the suburbanization of the 1950s and continued to spur even greater urban sprawl in subsequent decades. *Source:* Tacoma Public Library Neg. TPL400.

house. Home planners still expected women to do most of the cooking, but the kitchen was no longer exclusively her domain; often configured so that it "flowed" into other parts of the house, the kitchen was also expected to serve as a family gathering place.

Proponents of the ranch style touted its other contributions to family life. In 1946, *Tomorrow's House: A Complete Guide for the Home-Builder* called for a new household space, the "family room." This room would provide an area "within which the members of a family will be better equipped to enjoy each other on the basis of mutual respect" and affection. And in line with the idea that the home should become a family clubhouse, some kind of recreation room as well as a play room for children provided other spaces for the new life-styles that the middle-class family of the postwar era was urged to embrace.

Suburban living promised contentment. The predominantly white, middle-class residents all aspired to economic success, and although preoccupation with status often bred rivalries, a shared value system also brought a sense of comfort and community. Conformity seemed a balm for rootlessness and a cushion against the anxiety of change. But every glimpse of suburban happiness had its darker side of unforeseen problems. Burgeoning residential sections often overcrowded existing facilities, creating the congestion that residents had hoped to escape. Payments for mortgages, autos, and consumer goods sometimes brought new financial worries, and the mounting personal indebtedness among Americans alarmed many economists. Distances to work grew longer and longer; those who commuted in comfortable private cars contributed to clogged freeways and polluted air.

Suburban life easily lent itself to caricature and derision. The folk singer Malvina Reynolds later labeled suburban homes "little boxes made of ticky-tacky" and jabbed at the conformity of men who all "drink their martinis dry" and of children who all "go to summer camp and then to the university." In the 1960s Andy Warhol made the slickly packaged consumer culture associated with suburbia a subject of pop art, creating still-life portraits of monotonous rows of Campbell's soup cans. Upper-class critics of suburbia snorted at its bad taste—the lack of greenery (except for the spindly tree per lot that FHA mortgages required); the cheap construction; the clutter of too many autos, tricycles, lawn mowers, and children. Low-income people and non-whites, trapped in decaying inner cities, also attacked the suburbs, envying the comparative space and quiet while resenting the drain of tax revenue to outlying areas. Suburbia, however, with its popularization of "California-style" houses and informal, family-oriented life-styles, exemplified the 1950s for increasing numbers of middle-class families.

Women's Work and Domesticity

Although the baby boom and the new suburban ethic helped create a climate of opinion that emphasized the home as a woman's proper place, the number of women employed outside the home rose substantially after the late 1940s. By 1960 over one-third of the women of working age were employed, and nearly one-third of all wives worked. Historically, a large percentage of women from working-class families and women of color had always participated in the paid labor force; for women from these groups employment trends of the 1950s represented little change. But for a growing number of middle-class families, the extra income contributed by a wife often provided the essential key to attaining middle-class status. The rising consumption and apparent prosperity of the 1950s rested, in part, on the growing number of women in the paid labor force.

Women's work had important distinguishing characteristics during the 1950s. Jobs were often part time, held after the age of thirty-five or forty, when children were no longer at home during the day, and not career-oriented. Furthermore, employment for women was generally low paid, on the theory that a woman's income was always a secondary one, providing niceties, but not necessities, for a family. The greatest job opportunities, associated with structural changes in the economy as a whole, were in occupations that came to be designated specifically as women's work: clerical and secretarial jobs, teaching, and certain sectors of retail sales. Although women attended college in unprecedented numbers, few received graduate degrees, and employment of women in prestigious professions actually dropped. Women's employment, while becoming widespread, retained the stigma of low pay and low status.

During the 1950s popular culture glorified the role of mother and homemaker, but recent studies suggest that this mass produced imagery was not as one-dimensional as the feminist author Betty Friedan claimed in her path-breaking book, *The Feminine Mystique* (1963). Magazines of the period, including those primarily aimed at female readers, regularly featured laudatory stories about women who held jobs outside the home or who served as public officials. Women were often urged, in the popular press, to take a more active role in public affairs. Similarly, in their coverage of home life, the popular

This 1958 display, in a department store window, presented a tableau of the ideal suburban family. It links the latest consumer goods—including home movie cameras and backyard barbecue equipment—with advice on "How to Keep a Man." *Source:* Norton and Peel Collection, Minnesota Historical Society.

media sympathetically discussed the problems that wives and mothers encountered, including the burdens of housework and the frustrations of childrearing.

Throughout the 1950s, though, the prevailing social imagery invariably placed special emphasis upon the importance—and the rewards—of female domesticity. Psychologists, educators, journalists, and advertisers continued to assume that home and childrearing provided a "natural" sphere and function for women, though not for men. Although the idea of separate gender spheres was tempered by praise for women who also worked outside their homes, the old ideal of female domesticity emerged in fresh garb during the 1950s. Psychologists tended to diagnose signs of women's discontent in the 1950s as a failure to adjust to "natural" passive and subordinate roles. Popular magazines featured articles that equated happiness with mediocrity: A *Good Housekeeping* column advised that a woman with a grade-point average of C was "more likely to succeed" than a woman of great intelligence because she had a greater chance for a lasting marriage and a family. If a woman showed concern about issues related to equal rights or feminism, such an interest very likely reflected some deep-seated neurosis or social maladjustment.

Women's educational institutions mirrored the emphasis on the importance of marriage and family. College presidents and campus speakers urged an education that prepared women to marry and serve the nation by raising virtuous, industrious sons and dutiful, domesticated daughters. A national poll in 1957 reported that 80 percent of the respondents believed that people who chose not to marry were sick and immoral.

Images of domesticity in the 1950s became inextricably linked to women's roles as consumers. Under the influence of the rapidly expanding advertising industry, the word *housewife* less frequently evoked sewing and baking and became closely associated with shopping. Advertisers geared their appeals to women, even for expensive, durable goods. *Better Homes and Gardens*, a women's magazine (edited by men) with a circulation of millions, exemplified the trend. Advertisements took up far more than half the space, and the remaining pages contained tips on how to consume efficiently and "scientifically"—how to plan quick meals, determine which washing machine to buy, keep a family budget, and so on. Both the ads and the articles often emphasized saving money, but even these pieces were, in fact, designed to stimulate consumer tastes and teach about new products. The popular women's magazines of the 1950s, always projecting a white, middle-class life-style as the universal norm, both reflected and reinforced the unity between domesticity and consumption.

Along with "scientific" housekeeping came an emphasis on "scientific" childbearing and child rearing. Before World War II the majority of births did not take place in hospitals; in the postwar era, more and more women had their children in hospitals, attended by male physicians using a variety of painkilling methods. As childbearing became more impersonal and institutionalized sales of commercial baby food also soared and women shifted in massive numbers from breast-feeding to bottle-feeding. In child-rearing practices, outside expertise was also exalted. Dr. Benjamin Spock's *Baby and Child Care* rivaled the Bible in sales and stood next to it as a guide to appropriate conduct in most middle-class homes. Although Spock cautioned mothers against becoming too tied to their children, he nonetheless implied that full-time motherhood was the most desirable role for women and was essential to a child's physical and emotional health.

Although the dominant media often portrayed feminist activism as outmoded and deviant, some women associated with the strong prewar women's rights movements continued to address women's issues. Members of the National Woman's Party consistently lobbied Congress on behalf of an Equal Rights Amendment throughout the 1950s. Groundbreaking studies in women's history appeared with the publication of Mary Beard's *Woman as Force in History* (1946) and Eleanor Flexner's *Century of Struggle* (1959). Zora Neale Hurston continued her studies on African-American women. And the sociologist Mirra Komarovsky published her classic work on behalf of gender equality, *Women in the Modern World* (1953). These and similar efforts laid a basis for a revitalized women's movement in the late 1960s.

Organization Men and Women

Despite the new family ideal, large corporate organizations dominated the lives of many suburban men during the 1950s. The person whom William H. Whyte described in *The Organization Man* (1956) established his primary

Hat n' Boots Gas. Such examples of oversized and commercialized art disgusted some critics, but others found them an appropriate reflection of a society that loved large-scale, ambitious undertakings. *Source:* Robert Peterson.

roots not in a particular town or region but within a corporate structure. The business corporation provided the society in which he defined himself and gauged his status. He did, of course, withdraw from the corporate world to his home and family each day, but this retreat occupied only a few evening hours. Sociological studies revealed that success as a husband and father and occupational advancement often varied inversely. Home and office were separate and competing spheres, and the organization often won out as the primary frame of reference.

The economic growth and occupational mobility of the 1950s reinforced corporate loyalty. A young executive with dedication was almost sure to rise. But advancement often meant moving around the country at the company's behest. "We never make a man move," one company president explained. "Of course, he kills his career if he doesn't. But we never make him do it." Geographic mobility only strengthened the bond between employee and company, for it hindered development of strong ties to a local community and brought the organization right into the family circle as a most important decisionmaker. Popular culture of the 1950s was replete with the theme of organizational loyalty.

The relationship of women to the large business organization was quite different. Especially to young women, corporate life seemed to promise excitement and independence. But during the 1950s most corporations generally hired women for positions in the secretarial ghetto, where pay was low and a woman remained a "girl" no matter what her age. For most organization women, love for boss or for business did not transcend dollars and cents, and many women rapidly deserted secretarial jobs for domestic life. This rapid turnover of women in corporations bolstered the myth that they were poor risks at any level in the business hierarchy. Organization "girls" were entrapped in a vicious circle of low pay, rapid turnover, and discrimination.

The wives of most corporate employees were also organization women, deriving income and even status from their husbands' jobs. A wife's identity often came through her husband, and the model corporate wife was supposed to feel devotion to the business world that she seldom saw. But this obligation of loyalty, together with the husband's unfamiliarity with his spouse's domestic routine, drove subtle wedges between married couples. *The Man in the Gray Flannel Suit,* an extremely popular book and movie in the mid-1950's, explored the tensions between corporate and family life.

Sexual Politics

In the postwar period there were efforts, only partially successful, to combat challenges to older, strict ideas about sexuality. For heterosexual relationships, outright repression seemed increasingly anachronistic, and the guardians of morality increasingly adopted new, very subtle strategies for containing sexuality. With wedding bells tolling at an earlier age for most people and with divorce rates falling, marriage seemed the perfect place in which to control sexuality, especially for women. With so many teenagers marrying during the 1940s and 1950s, the public schools and other institutions of socialization emphasized the dire consequences of premartial sex, especially to young women, at a time when most states prohibited both birth control and abortions. The perilous potential of uncontained sexuality among women was even compared to the destructive effects of uncontrolled atomic energy. Women who flaunted their sexuality became typed as "bombshells," and the brief bathing suit introduced in the 1940s became popularly known as the "bikini," after the site of an atomic explosion. The foreign-policy crusades of the cold war period, in other words, found a domestic counterpart in the battle to contain sexuality.

At the same time, moral guardians supplemented dire warnings about promiscuity with cautious support for new teenage rituals that might help to channel sexual energies. High school administrators sponsored clubs, sock-hops, and other social events as a means of gaining influence, if not control, over the leisure activities of teenagers. Similarly, they required classes in "health education," and a growing bevy of "experts" on postadolescent sexuality endorsed the practice of "going steady." This relatively new turn in heterosocial relationships, in which high-schoolers (and even junior high students) were expected to pair off in couples, could be seen as the first step to a monogamous marriage. Going steady became popularized in such teen anthems as The Five Satins' *"To the Aisle"* and Rick Nelson's *"I Believe"* (*You're Going Steady with Nobody Else but Me*). Commercial entrepreneurs supported this effort by offering a wide variety of rings, pins, bracelets, and other trinkets that could serve as signs of a "steady" relationship.

In the case of homosexuality, however, older forms of repression remained. The 1940s and 1950s represented, in some ways, a period of liberation for homosexuals. The familiarity of military life during World War II provided new opportunities for single-sex relationships, and postwar urbanization allowed homosexuals to gather, away from the glare of small-town scrutiny, in a growing urban subculture. Whereas most large cities had a number of bars catering to gay men, lesbians generally preferred to seek companionship through more private "friendship networks." Nevertheless, the results were the same: a growing sense of individual and group identity among homosexuals.

The issue of homosexuality gained considerable visibility when Dr. Alfred Kinsey first published his studies, in 1948 and 1953, on sexual behavior in the United States. Kinsey's research, conducted at the University of Indiana, suggested that people with "homosexual histories" could be found "in every age group, in every social level, in every conceivable occupation," and in virtually every part of the country. Kinsey's findings, on the one hand, helped to empower homosexuals by suggesting that homosexuality was not limited to the fringes of society. On the other hand, the idea that homosexuality could be anywhere increased the fears of people who were already opposed to homosexual life-styles.

Homosexuality became, as did communism and juvenile delinquency, another of those "diseases" that could rally the forces of containment. Anticommunist even worried that homosexual crusaders, if not already inclined toward communism because of their own "alien" life-styles, could prove particularly susceptible to blackmail by Soviet agents. In 1953, the Eisenhower administration endorsed this theory with an executive order that prohibited homosexuals from holding government jobs. And in another parallel with anticommunism, such blacklisting at the national level energized local "purity crusaders." Police departments and district attorneys could claim greater legitimacy when unleashing their own antihomosexual campaigns.

The wider issue of sexual revolution—sexual relations outside a heterosexual marriage—became increasingly visible during the 1950s in a number of ways. The *Kinsey Reports*, based on thousands of interviews with white informants, suggested that people were engaging in a wider range of sexual practices, more often, and with more partners than anyone had ever thought. Despite almost antiseptic prose, Kinsey's studies on the sexual behavior of men and women became best-sellers and their data widely popularized. The era's dominant emphasis on monogamous relationships, within the idealized nuclear family that was featured on network television, clearly existed alongside powerful centrifugal forces.

The greatest popularizer of the sexual revolution was not the scholarly Dr. Kinsey, however, but the flamboyant (or pathetically juvenile, according to his critics) Hugh Hefner. During the late 1940s and early 1950s, laws aimed at sexually explicit publications had been facing greater scrutiny from the courts; the First Amendment to the Constitution, civil libertarians argued, prevented government censors from writing their own sexual standards into law. Although legal definitions of what was obscene or pornographic remained uncertain, there was still too much liberalization for traditionalists but just enough for magazine entrepreneurs like Hefner. In December 1953, Hefner published the first edition of *Playboy*, heralded as "entertainment for men," expanding the boundaries of First Amendment protection for sexually oriented literature.

Playboy offered more than pictures of unclothed young women and articles by respected popular writers; Hefner used the publication to expound his philosophy of a "liberated" life-style based on mass consumption and sexual experimentation. The *Playboy* philosophy, as Hefner expounded it throughout the 1950s, also stressed liberation, for men, from all of the restraints associated with marriage; the nuclear family was a trap that ensnared males and robbed them of money that could be spent on hi-fi equipment, sports cars, and attractive young women. *Playboy's* philosophy, according to the social historian Barbara Ehrenreich, was part of a larger male revolt against the prevalent image of a husband-dominated home in which the man earned most of the family's income and the woman presided over its consumption and child rearing.

MASS COMMERCIAL CULTURE

After World War II, people could choose from an ever-expanding array of cultural and entertainment products aimed at a mass consumer audience. With blue-collar workers enjoying larger take-home paychecks, while suffering from increasing regimentation in their workplaces, leisure and cultural markets expanded significantly. Meanwhile, the general postwar affluence, in which the majority of people did share, made the entertainment business more profitable than ever before. By 1950, consumers were spending twice as much money on entertainment as on rent; total expenditures equaled one-seventh of the GNP.

Travel and Sports

The travel industry grew tremendously after World War II. To those who could afford the price, travel agencies marketed package tours to Europe. In only two weeks travelers could absorb the culture of the Old World—from Paris, to Brussels, to Geneva, to Rome, to Vienna, to Hamburg, and finally to London. For those who lacked the money to visit Europe (or who had already toured the Continent), the United States provided its own vacation spots. New motels, their quality certified by motor clubs or franchise owners, began to replace the old, independent tourist cabins. When affluent travelers reached Southern California, Las Vegas, or Miami Beach, they found luxury resort complexes that offered expensive nightclubs for adults, professional recreation directors for children, and deluxe kennels for family pets.

After the reduced schedules of the war years, sports promotions regained, and then surpassed, their earlier pace. Promoters welcomed back the young people who had served in the armed forces, abandoning the lesser talents and fading veterans who had performed during World War II. Although all levels of professional baseball revived, the late 1940s and early 1950s proved to be the last hurrah for baseball's minor leagues. Before the full impact of competition from network television, many cities and smaller towns eagerly supported their own professional baseball teams. And with only sixteen major-league clubs, there was a surplus of good players to stock the minor leagues. Until the late 1960s African-Americans complained, with much justification, that only outstanding athletes such as Jackie Robinson could play in the newly integrated majors; white ballplayers generally received preference for jobs such as second-string catcher or reserve infielder. Even talented white players found themselves tied to a monopolistic business system in which major-league teams owned vast numbers of players whom they could freely transfer from team to team and from league to league.

Yet in the patriotic spirit of the cold war, baseball served as a symbol of the openness and equality of American society. Sportswriters, following in the star-struck tradition of their calling, still lavished praise on the game, celebrating it as an integral part of the American way. One prominent writer-broadcaster, Bill Stern, invented uplifting stories about the national pastime. A dying Abraham Lincoln, Stern once solemnly claimed, had told an aide to "keep baseball going; the country needs it."

Professional boxing, plagued by hints of fixed fights and underworld domination, lacked baseball's hallowed reputation but attracted large audiences in the postwar period. Massive promotions for world championships and small neighborhood fight clubs all made money during the late 1940s and early 1950s. Joe Louis, the symbol of sports as an avenue of opportunity for African-American men, finally concluded his long reign as heavyweight champion; between 1943 and 1951 the flamboyant Sugar Ray Robinson lost only one of nearly a hundred bouts and won general acclaim as the greatest fighter, "pound for pound," of all time; and a stocky Italian-American from Massachusetts, Rocky Marciano, battered forty-nine opponents before retiring in 1955 as the undefeated heavyweight champion. Professional boxing quickly became a staple of network television: During the early 1950s, the networks carried four nationally televised prime-time main events every week.

Professional wrestling and Roller Derby, pseudosports that dated back to the 1930s, also reached prime-time television. Carefully contrived and prescripted, professional wrestling (as distinguished from the amateur sport) offered familiar morality plays: Stereotyped villains, often posing as Germans or "Japs," abused long-suffering heroes until some dramatic reversal sealed the bullies' fates. Justice—and the American way—ultimately triumphed. But a variety of different gambits and a flexible catalog of "rules" allowed promoters to vary scenarios and lure fans to the next big card. Only Roller Derby, with two teams of skaters careening around a banked, wooden track, offered a comparable blend of mayhem and ritualistic symbolism. According to Roller Derby's publicity, "two [recent] impacts have hit the American public—the atom bomb and the Roller Derby—and it appears the latter will have the most permanent effect."

Roller Derby soon faded from prime time into a minor oddity, but most other sports, at all levels, continued to thrive in the postwar era. Bowling, golf, and tennis attracted growing crowds to professional tournaments and matches, and millions of amateurs took to the lanes, links, and courts. Hockey and basketball, established as professional sports primarily in the Northeast, slowly gained national audiences, and professional basketball achieved needed continuity with the formation of the National Basketball Association in the years between 1946 and 1949. Football remained the premier sport on college campuses, and the professional version also made great strides in the postwar years; the Cleveland Browns, Detroit Lions, and Los Angeles Rams became the dominant powers during the early 1950s in a revamped National Football League.

Motion Pictures

While the sports industry was attracting new fans, Hollywood was struggling to retain its mass audience. Between 1945 and 1948, weekly attendance at motion picture theaters averaged around 90 million people; but by 1953, this audience had been nearly cut in half, to an average of 46 million weekly viewers. Although conventional wisdom blamed television for the decline, many different forces were responsible. In 1949, for example, the major studios settled a long-standing lawsuit, which had been brought by the federal government, and agreed to end their traditional practice of owning motion picture theaters. By producing, distributing, *and* showing films, the government had argued, Hollywood enjoyed an entertainment monopoly. Forced to sell existing theaters and prohibited from building new ones, Hollywood lost a valuable source of revenue. More important, and more broadly, the disappearance of Hollywood's mass audience can be traced to the veritable leisure explosion of the 1950s. People were spending money on a variety of recreational and leisure activities, including gardening, golfing, and home projects.

In response, Hollywood made a number of efforts to lure viewers back to half-empty theaters. First, the major studios drastically cut the number of pictures they produced, and the classic B film, which had served since the 1930s as the second half of nearly every theater's double feature, became an early casualty of the new motion picture environment. In 1953–1954, for example, the major studios released their last B western—the genre that had turned cinema cowpokes like Gene Autry, Roy Rogers, and Dale Evans into national heroes.

While western stars and other B-film stalwarts such as Ronald Reagan were galloping over to television, Hollywood executives tried to redirect the savings gained from ending the production of B movies. One strategy was to target specific audiences, such as the fans of *film noir*, with motion pictures that were carefully tailored to their interests. Director Billy Wilder's *film noir*, *Sunset Boulevard* (1950), bade a cynical goodbye to the old Hollywood. It begins with a corpse floating in a Beverly Hills swimming pool, and this dead man, formally a second-rate screenwriter, narrates the remainder of the story. A middle-aged silent film star, played by Gloria Swanson, lives under the illusion that she will triumphantly return to the silver screen in a biblical epic. A call from her old studio turns out to be merely a request to use her antique automobile, and she drifts even deeper into a fantasy world. The final scenes reveal that the actress has killed the screenwriter and gone completely mad. *Sunset Boulevard* suggests that mid-century Hollywood, like the middle-aged actress, was living on illusions while madly searching for successful artistic formulas that might revive its former glories.

Increasingly, though, Hollywood tried to recapture its mass audience with big-budget blockbusters that could provide the kind of "quality entertainment" unavailable on television. Biblical epics such as *The Ten Commandments* (1956) and films based on classic novels such as *Around the World in 80 Days* (1956) became film staples of the 1950s and early 1960s.

In addition, Hollywood began to introduce new ways to see films. In 1953, the industry introduced 3-D films, hoping to attract viewers with the illusion of a three-dimensional picture and with on-screen projectiles that seemed to hurtle toward the audience. The flimsy 3-D glasses proved a serious handicap, and this craze quickly passed. Although it would also, in time, become a novelty, the drive-in theater proved much more important to the 1950s than 3-D. In 1947 there had been fewer than 600 drive-ins in the country; by the end of the 1950s, there were nearly 5,000. Primarily aimed at the family audience, drive-ins revived the double feature—and even the triple bill—while offering snack bars, playgrounds for children, and even laundry facilities. Finally, during the 1950s, Hollywood unveiled a wider screen for all theaters, and processes like CinemaScope, VistaVision, and Panavision quickly came to dominate. The old square screen was becoming a relic of the past, as Hollywood was introducing even grander ways of seeing its new blockbuster films including Todd-AO (for such movies as *Around the World in 80 Days*) and Cinerama (for such movies as *This Is Cinerama*).

During the 1950s, Hollywood became entangled in the kinds of political issues affecting the nation at large. A number of filmmakers, for example, used the silver screen to stump for postwar, anticommunist culture. Some of the efforts were one-dimensional jeremiads on the evils of communism, but other films delivered their messages more subtly. In *On the Waterfront* (1954), screenwriter Budd Schulberg and director Elia Kazan, Hollywood liberals who had cooperated with anticommunist investigative committees, glorified the brave individual who informed on those who threatened the democratic process. Filled with Christian imagery, *On the Waterfront* featured Marlon

Brando, the biker hero of *The Wild One*, as a former prizefighter who testifies against corrupt labor union bosses. Critics of red-baiting denounced the film for simplifying complex moral and political issues, while cold war liberals and moderates praised its portrayal of the democratic promise. Gaining no less than eight Academy Awards, *On the Waterfront* became a controversial symbol of Hollywood's uneasy relationship with larger political forces.

Hollywood also offered movies that broke away from mainstream political and artistic formulas. A few offbeat films featuring no great stars and eschewing glamour appeared during the 1950s. Adapted from a successful television production, *Marty* told the simple story of a Bronx butcher, who falls in love with a woman who considered herself plain and unexciting. After the decline of McCarthyism several films treated controversial social issues. *Paths of Glory* indicted military leaders for their values and portrayed war as anything but a glorious enterprise. Shot in black and white, *Paths of Glory* did poorly at the box office but gained much critical acclaim for its youthful director, Stanley Kubrick. Racial tension provided the backdrop for several films, the most popular being *The Defiant Ones*, a chain-gang story in which interracial brotherhood triumphs over bigotry. Although the film would seem trite and overly cautious to many later viewers, Stanley Kramer's production appeared at a time when racial prejudice was still considered a dangerous subject in Hollywood.

During the 1950s a prominent school of film criticism, popular in both the United States and France, praised those Hollywood directors who could surmount the restraints of the industry and use their films to make personal statements. These *auteur* critics generally concentrated on so-called lesser films, finding much to admire in the work of directors like Budd Boettcher, Orson Welles, Anthony Mann, and Samuel Fuller. Always controversial, the *auteur* approach gained considerable power among critics when the giant Hollywood film factories began to break down in the 1960s and individual directors tried to wield greater control over their cinematic products.

Television

While the motion picture industry was struggling, television was thriving. In 1945, only a few people had ever seen a television set; by 1957, the United States claimed 40 million sets, and most cities boasted several local stations, including one for each of the major national networks. Research suggested that the larger the household size, the more likely it was to have at least one TV set.

Industry executives aggressively pushed family images. Many popular shows featured those now legendary TV families—the Andersons, the Cleavers, the Ricardos—and their never-ending familial conflicts, such as the now classic tussles between Wally and Theodore (Beaver) Cleaver. So that everyone could better watch Ward and June Cleaver save the day, TV executives urged viewers to convert their living rooms into centers of family—and TV—culture. One TV advertisement from the 1950s advised parents that their children needed the tube "for their morale as much as they need fresh air and sunshine for their health."

The movement of television into the American home did become an important part of the popular culture of the 1950s. Picture tubes were growing larger, up to 21 inches, and manufacturers were placing them inside finely finished wooden cabinets—"handcrafted and handrubbed," proclaimed the advertisements—that were designed to complement the decor of nearly any home. A piece of furniture, as well as an electronic instrument, the television was supposed to signify the growing affluence of middle-class families. Moreover, the set itself was only one of the new products that television spawned. To allow families to watch an evening's programming without interruption, manufacturers introduced the TV tray and the frozen TV dinner as alternatives to the dining-room table and the kitchen-prepared meal. Similarly, television spurred the invention of another classic piece of household furniture, the recliner chair; according to most advertisements, this nearly horizontal TV command post was generally reserved for Dad. At the same time, to supplement the frozen TV dinner, food processors marketed an increasing variety of easily unwrapped TV snacks that could help viewers sustain themselves during the networks' prime-time broadcasting hours. Although the 1960s would see the introduction of less expensive and less bulky TV sets that could be deployed to nearly every room in the house, television viewing during the 1950s generally revolved around a large, cabineted set, a kind of electronic hearth that was designed to attract the entire family to its warm (though still black-and-white) glow.

Advertising, of course, was the fuel that carried "free" television into millions of homes. As had been the case in network radio, some early TV shows even bore the names of their sponsors—the "Colgate Comedy Hour," the "General Electric Theater," or "Hallmark Hall of Fame." More commonly, in contrast to the later practice by which networks would sell brief commercial spots to different advertisers, a single sponsor would often underwrite an entire series of shows, as Texaco did with television's first smash hit, "The Milton Berle Show." This arrangement obviously gave sponsors considerable leverage over program content. Sponsors consistently urged story lines and imagery that showed people working their way up the ladder of success by buying more and better products.

Consequently, many TV programs, as well as the commercials that sustained them, stressed the glories of mass consumption. A familiar theme in early TV situation comedies, for example, found working-class families trying to move from older, Depression-era values of thrift and careful saving to postwar consumerism. Story lines on shows such as "The Life of Riley," which focused on a working-class family in Los Angeles, or "The Goldbergs," which featured a Jewish family in New York City, suggested that the road to happiness could be paved by the purchase of consumer goods and leisure-time activities rather than by faithfulness to ethnic rituals and traditions. Nonwhite ethnics were almost invisible except on "Amos 'n Andy," a show that angered many African-Americans and eventually frightened away corporate sponsors because of its stereotyped representations.

By the mid-1950s, network programmers were eliminating working-class, ethnic sitcoms altogether in favor of shows that featured upper-middle-class families who were clearly part of the culture of mass consumption. "The Adventures of Ozzie and Harriet," for instance, came to television with "The Goldbergs" but lasted into the 1960s; still a cable-TV staple in the 1990s, Ozzie and Harriet's "adventures" included frequent shopping forays, extensive leisure time, and even a live-in rock star, their son Rick Nelson.

Television touched politics as well as cultural values. During the 1952 presidential campaign, Richard Nixon used television to defend his beleaguered reputation and to salvage his political career. Two years later, the televised Army-McCarthy hearings helped bring down Wisconsin Senator Joe McCarthy. And toward the end of the 1950s, John Kennedy's media image aided his drive for the 1960 Democratic presidential nomination.

At a time of important social and cultural change in the United States, then, television was coming to replace movies and radio as the primary medium for representing everyday life and transmitting cultural and political values across generations. Moreover, the small tube not only carried its pictures into people's homes but also seemed to have the capacity, much more than the motion picture screen or radio set ever could, of providing representations that sometimes looked more real than the actual events themselves.

The rigged quiz shows of the 1950s came to symbolize most of what seemed so disturbing about TV culture. Once staples of prime-time programming, quiz shows offered tests of knowledge that paralleled professional wrestling's simulated tests of strength and power. Fearing the uncertainties of unrigged contests, quiz-show producers found they could transform unknown contestants into instant (and cheaply paid) celebrities simply by giving them answers in advance. In the most celebrated case, a Columbia University professor, who had thrilled more than 50 million TV viewers week after week by answering questions on virtually every subject, admitted that his entire performance had been rehearsed. Producers provided the answers and hints for making his replies as dramatic—and, therefore, as "real"—as possible. Critics who were already deriding the daily fare offered on the "boob tube" gained new ammunition from the quiz-show scandals.

Rock around the Clock: The Popular Culture of Youth

Accompanying the rise of television, the 1940s and 1950s saw the emergence of a distinctive youth culture. In recent years, revisionist histories have stressed that social and cultural trends among postwar youths always varied according to race, class, ethnicity, gender, and geography. In this view, a variety of different *subcultures*, produced by heterogeneous groups of young people, rather than a single, monolithic youth *culture*, characterized the 1950s. The leisure activities and peer-created rituals of working-class youths and of young people of color differed from those of white suburbanites, a fact that claims about a common teen experience can too quickly pass over.

Similarly, the so-called youth culture of the 1950s displayed significant gender divisions. Although advertisers chased after the discretionary income of all teenagers—by 1960, according to one estimate, teenagers were spending $10 billion a year on products targeted specially at them—young women were a special consumer group. Even more so than for young men, physical appearance became a woman's crucial asset in the new youth culture. Young women of the 1950s, it was estimated, devoted nearly one-fourth of their total expenditures to cosmetics and other beauty products. At the same time that they were hearing warnings about the dangers of uncontrolled sexuality, they were also surrounded by images—whether in Barbie dolls or in the latest bevy of Hollywood starlets—that celebrated the slim-waisted, big-breasted ideal dominating media representations during the 1950s. Young women, in other words, not only confronted a set of conflicting expectations about sexuality, summed up in the phrase "naughty but nice," but also encountered expectations of beauty that only a very few could hope to achieve. In contrast to the popular TV show of the 1970s, which depicted the 1950s as a series of "Happy Days," historian Wini Breines entitled her 1992 memoir–social history *Young, White, and Miserable.*

Yet, even while noting all the differences, including those grounded in race and gender, it still seems possible to discern a nationwide, leisure-oriented youth culture. A complex set of peer-oriented cultural practices, this youth culture primarily centered on the mass consumption of relatively standardized consumer goods and mass-mediated images. As early as 1944, a new magazine appeared and aimed (in its own words) at giving teenagers "a sense of identity, of purpose, of belonging." Not coincidently, this perennial drugstore favorite, *Seventeen,* also gave teenage women a sparkling, constantly updated array of consumer products and mass-consumption life-styles. Within a few years, as postwar economic growth and the baby boom took hold, a new set of specialists played it both ways: Monitoring the burgeoning teenage consumer market, they consulted with companies about what to produce and, at the same time, advised teens about what they might consume.

Another group of specialists looked after the nonconsumer behavior of young people. During the early postwar years, explaining the problem of juvenile delinquency became a growth industry. After surveying juvenile unrest, the award-winning journalist Harrison Salisbury concluded that delinquency stretched from the nation's worst slums to its most affluent suburbs. In an age of increasing world tensions, this "shook-up generation"—a song written for Elvis Presley, "I'm All Shook Up," parodied Salisbury's title—even constituted "a matter of national security," Salisbury (with apparent seriousness) concluded.

After the juvenile delinquency scare of the late 1940s and 1950s had passed, criminologists generally agreed that there had been no startling upsurge in youthful deviance, a finding that makes the postwar concerns about the issue all the more puzzling. Why were so many people convinced that postwar youths were getting out of control?

A common theory focused on changes in the nation's culture: Worries about juvenile delinquency, in many different analyses, went hand in hand with concern about the impact of postwar mass culture. Images of juvenile delinquents filled mass culture. Movies such as *The Wild One*, featuring Marlon Brando, and *Rebel Without a Cause*, which rocketed James Dean to posthumous stardom, indicated that Hollywood might attract a new youthful audience; but the sympathetic portrayal of rebellious youths in these films also threatened to cause studios problems with already-angry critics of youth and with "experts" on juvenile delinquency. Officially marketed by Hollywood as explorations of juvenile delinquency, the films seemed to their detractors more likely to serve as guidebooks for future rebels.

Comic books were another cultural product that allegedly provided lessons in juvenile delinquency. Between the end of World War II and 1953, according to one study, the comic book industry marketed a billion books every year. This flood tide did include familiar characters from other media, including Bugs Bunny, Donald Duck, and various detective and western heroes; but it also contained new comic book genres that featured stories of crime, horror, and exaggerated violence. In addition to offending genteel standards, such comics became linked to violence among troubled and rebellious youths. In one of the widely cited examples of gruesome comic art, ghouls played baseball with various parts of a dissected human body.

Arriving at about the time that concern over comics was waning, rock-and-roll music raised deeper and longer-lasting concerns. To those who considered Frank Sinatra as animated as pop music stars should ever get—and even to those who were embracing avant garde trends in postwar jazz—rock appeared to be merely gratuitous noise, wild "jungle" sounds that set young people into frenzied, new dance crazes. Moreover, the sexual innuendos in many songs seemed yet another dangerous incitement to misbehavior. And the fact that rock grew out of rhythm-and-blues, a musical style popularized by urban African-Americans, alerted social conservatives to the possibility of some plot, perhaps by subversive communists, to sway young people toward integration.

Rock-and-roll thus had to grow up, as ragtime had done at the turn of the century, outside the major channels for producing and distributing popular music. Many rock artists, such as Chuck Berry and Carl Perkins, wrote their own material, and young producers, such as Sam Phillips of Sun Records in Memphis and the Chess brothers in Chicago, began to market what the major labels hesitated even to record. During the mid-1950s, Phillips unveiled the now legendary figures of early rockabilly—Perkins, Johnny Cash, Jerry Lee Lewis, and of course Elvis Presley. The Chess brothers, who had been featuring rhythm-and-blues artists such as Muddy Waters, introduced rock-and-roll pioneers like Berry and Bo Diddley in the mid-1950s. In other parts of the country, other small producers were also experimenting, releasing songs by both black and white artists that smashed old categories of popular music. Musical purists might break all this down into new pigeonholes—such as Chicago rhythm-and-blues and West Texas country rock—but millions of young people knew it simply as rock. Although established radio stations and prominent radio personalities steered clear of the new sound, smaller stations and younger DJs hitched their fortunes to rock. The most prominent early rock-

and-roll DJ, Alan Freed, soon found himself atop a burgeoning musical empire, a kingdom that collapsed when the federal government prosecuted him
for payola—accepting bribes to promote certain records.

Freed's place was soon taken by Dick Clark, host of a popular television
show, "American Bandstand." Clark's program gave the emerging rock and
dance culture a national audience, but many purists also accused Clark of selling out. Believing that the unruliness of the new music had to be tamed, Clark
pushed for cleaner lyrics and mass-produced a new generation of singers,
such as Frankie Avalon and Fabian, who offered something of a compromise
between the wildness of a Jerry Lee Lewis and the blandness of a Perry Como.
Rock soon lost its roughness, its regional identity, and its spontaneity. (Clark,
for example, insisted that all artists appearing on "American Bandstand" lip-
synch their songs, a requirement that masked the ineptitude of a Fabian and
squelched the improvisations of a Chuck Berry.) By the late 1950s the major
record companies were absorbing rock, merging it into the mainstream of
popular music.

Like rock-and-roll, automobiles became a special passion of the middle-
class youth culture. Automobiles—especially the increasingly common second
car—made young people mobile and provided status symbols, entertainment,
and makeshift bedrooms. They provided transportation to teenage gatherings
out of parents' sight and gave the freedom of privacy. This was an age of
souped-up hot rods, of dual exhaust systems, of raked bodies, of rolled and
pleated interiors. For many young men, the transformation of one of Detroit's
stereotyped products into a special personal creation may have represented a
subtle, though tangible, revolt against the mass-produced world of their parents. Although only a small proportion of men actually owned such a creation, the "Kandy-Kolored Tangerine-Flake Streamline Baby," to use writer
Tom Wolfe's phrase, was the envy of the teenage scene.

The youth culture thrived, especially in the suburbs, where the general
affluence trickled down from parents to children. Sales of the new 45-rpm
records and long-playing albums exploded, and a collection of the latest hits
became an important teen status symbol. Other items also tempted teenagers
to spend money: record players, the latest in penny loafers or saddle shoes,
the charm bracelets displaying pictures of rock idols. The youth generation of
the 1950s was a peculiar amalgam: In its crass commercialism and unabashed
materialism it mirrored, even caricatured, the rest of society; in its hedonism
and stylistic iconoclasm it set itself decisively apart from the 1950s and anticipated the 1960s.

The Postwar Debate over Mass Culture

The association of comics, rock music, and hot rods with rebellious
young people gave a special urgency to discussions about mass culture. Invok-
ing the disease metaphors, which were prominent in so many other postwar
discussions, critics portrayed mass culture as a cancerous invader that threatened to overwhelm the nation's cultural immune system. The violence in

comic books was said to eat into young minds and produce juvenile delin-quents. Some social psychologists hypothesized that the simplicity of any comic book (or TV) story, violent or not, hindered young people's emotional development by teaching them to ignore complexities and conditioning them to expect quick, simple solutions to all of their problems. Pressure groups urged Congress to ban comic books or, at a minimum, impose censorship over their contents. Quickly responding, the comic book industry established its own regulatory code, a step that eliminated the more controversial offer-ings from the store racks and drove publishers like EC Comics into retire-ment. (The people behind EC's offbeat brand of culture quickly regrouped and produced the long-running satirical classic, *MAD* magazine.)

The passing of the great comic book scare and the taming of rock music hardly ended the larger debate over postwar mass culture. Elite critics found most of what millions of people liked to read, hear, and see as beneath contempt.

One line of criticism focused on the issue of taste. Mass culture seemed just another example of how a mass production and mass consumption econ-omy ignored issues of quality. In contrast to works of high culture, mass-marketed books and TV programs made no effort to deepen understanding about the nature of life and beauty. Cultural products aimed at the millions seemed more like chewing gum than real art: They were to be consumed as rapidly as possible and then discarded. And unlike true folk culture—what critics identified as authentic art produced by ordinary people from their communal traditions—popular culture was stamped out by hack writers and mediocre image-makers, people only concerned with meeting their quota of marketable stuff. By its very existence, mass culture represented an affront to everything noble and uplifting in the realm of culture.

Mass-marketed culture, to these critics, acted like an intellectual cancer. Even talented writers and artists succumbed to the allure of easy money, aban-doning difficult projects in favor of producing easily marketable junk; conse-quently, consumer tastes became too vulgarized even to recognize good art. Mass culture thus carried the seeds of intellectual decay: High and folk cul-tures could eventually be totally destroyed or, at best, reduced to some grotesque mutation such as a mindless middlebrow culture. Worse still, as mass culture proliferated, the ability of consumers to discriminate good from bad could become so eroded that they could fail to recognize the ways in which mass culture manipulated their desires and opinions. Especially in the view of writers who had fled Nazi Germany in the 1930s, mass culture pro-vided the basis by which a native totalitarian movement could brainwash the innocent masses.

Not every student of mass culture sounded such bleak notes. Gilbert Seldes, a long-time partisan of the popular arts, insisted that most of what was now being offered to the public was only getting better, and he chided main-stream critics for their elitism. Although lacking Seldes's enthusiasm for the cultural products themselves, others shared his skepticism of theories that me-chanically traced all manner of cultural and social problems to mass culture.

Robert Warshow, for example, decided that his own son's taste for EC Comics was hardly a serious problem. His boy was a "fan," not an "addict." Some sociologists even argued that the new popular culture could help people, especially children and adolescents, adjust to the demands of a complex society. The popular children's book *Tootle the Train,* for example, showed young people the need to "stay on the tracks" and adjust to community expectations of proper behavior.

Perhaps the most buoyant theorist of mass culture, especially television, was Marshall McLuhan. He predicted that television would eventually homogenize and standardize global culture, just as it was already doing with North American culture. McLuhan foresaw a "global village" in which peoples of previously distinct cultures could experience a common bond of sensory awareness simply by abandoning themselves to the "cool medium" of television. Initially hailed as one of the twentieth century's foremost visionaries, McLuhan saw his reputation plummet as subsequent media theorists recognized that television could not, as McLuhan implied, become an independent technological force or be analyzed apart from social-economic-political contexts.

Reinterpreting the Mass Culture Debate

McLuhan's successors, drawn from a generation who had been raised on postwar consumer culture, tried to anchor their own analyses in more specific contexts. By the 1980s, younger academics and journalists came to see postwar intellectuals' contempt for mass culture as a historical phenomenon to be explained rather than a cultural judgment to be endorsed. Prominent postwar intellectuals feared that mass culture, with its new sources of inspiration and its eclectic creativity, threatened their own cultural authority, which was rooted in the mastery of traditional works of high culture. And the fact that the new mass culture drew on sources outside the traditions of the educated, white middle class—such as the music of urban African-Americans, Mexican-Americans, and southern whites—only underscores the elitism and cultural blinders of cold war intellectuals. The music of Elvis Presley and Chuck Berry, which blended white and black sounds, crossed racial boundaries and became a kind of cultural civil rights movement. Even though 1950s rock-and-roll invariably reinforced subordinate images of women's roles, in both the lyrics of the songs and the performances of its male stars, it also displayed a healthy skepticism about many other social truths and traditional sources of cultural authority.

Other examples of postwar commercial culture also came to find a more favorable reception among cultural observers. Television, its recent defenders point out, contributed to a vibrant, quickly changing postwar culture. It extended the careers of popular vaudeville stars—including George Burns and Gracie Allen, Groucho Marx, and Milton Berle—and developed or refined newer forms of mass culture, including the sitcom ("I Love Lucy"), the police drama ("Dragnet"), and the psychological western ("Gunsmoke"). Even professional wrestling and Roller Derby have recently attracted scholarly attention; both spectacles, recent studies argue, provided working-class heroes for blue-collar audiences and offered more opportunities for participation by women than most of the "real" sports. In a similar way, other works of mass culture, even quickly written romance novels, one cultural anthropologist suggests, could provide women with sources of information and lead them to question, at least in tentative ways, the hierarchical, male-dominated structures that shaped daily lives in the 1950s. The mere act of sitting down to read a novel for pleasure, for example, represented a small revolt against the home-front ethic that a woman-and-mother's work was never done. The automatic contempt for mass commercial culture, the position championed by the literary elite of the 1940s and 1950s, no longer dominates either contemporary cultural criticism or the writing of postwar cultural history.

RACE, ETHNICITY, AND URBAN ISSUES

As middle-class city dwellers moved to the suburbs, many people from rural areas arrived to replace them. These new migrants were usually not white and not middle class. For them, the 1950s did not bring ebullient affluence; their small economic gains came only against a background of oppressive discrimination and entrapment in decaying central cities.

African-Americans

Black people from the rural South came to northern cities during World War II in search of jobs in war-related industries. But even though employment possibilities increased, the overall quality of life remained low. With the nation's resources being poured into national defense, little money remained for housing programs. In Detroit's new black ghetto, for example, one investigator reported that an aging, converted one-family dwelling might hold over a hundred people, one family to a room. But overcrowding, discrimination, and harassment by whites did not curb the postwar flow of blacks into urban areas.

The northern migration advanced the economic position of African-Americans. Between 1947 and 1952 the median income of nonwhite families rose from $1,614 to $2,338, and the gap between black and white narrowed slightly. In 1940, 80 percent of all black workers were employed in unskilled jobs; by 1950 the figure had dropped to 63 percent. Similarly, the life expectancy of blacks advanced from 53.1 years in 1940 to 61.7 in 1953 (compared with 64.2 to 69.6 for whites). Throughout the 1950s, the expanding economy and favorable job market helped maintain the economic gains that the war had initially stimulated.

During the Eisenhower years almost every area of southern society still had segregated facilities for blacks and whites. Segregation extended to public transportation, rest rooms, drinking fountains, even parking lots and cemeteries. Often required by law and always demanded by custom, these separate, but rarely equal, facilities reminded blacks of the inferior status assigned to them by white society. The National Association for the Advancement of Colored People (NAACP) had financed a series of legal challenges during the Truman years, and their success in *Brown* v. *Board of Education* (1954) marked the most important victory.

In *Brown*, all nine Supreme Court justices agreed that legally sanctioned segregation of public schools violated the equal protection clause of the Fourteenth Amendment. In a simple, straightforward opinion, Chief Justice Earl Warren argued that separate schools were "inherently unequal" and deprived black children of equal educational opportunities. But one court decision, by itself, could not produce a revolution in race relations. Bowing to political pressures and pleas by educators, the Supreme Court later ruled that school desegregation need not be immediate; it should proceed "with all deliberate speed." Ten years after the *Brown* decision only about 1 percent of black children in the South attended desegregated schools.

Resistance to desegregation hardened after the *Brown* case. Most white southerners protested this "invasion of states' rights"; some denounced the ruling as part of a communist plot to destroy "the white race"; many pledged massive resistance to school integration. The Ku Klux Klan revived, and a new organization, the White Citizens Council, became a powerful force in many areas. Not all members of the KKK and Citizens Council endorsed violent resistance, but some did use force against blacks who "didn't know their place." In 1954 a crowd of whites murdered a young black man, Emmet Till, for allegedly whistling at a white woman. ·

Southerners also used legal and political strategems to delay changes in race relations. In 1957, 101 members of Congress signed the Southern Manifesto, a protest against "federal usurpation" of states' rights, and southern senators employed the filibuster to block civil rights legislation. A segregationist image was essential to political survival in many southern states; after a moderate young lawyer, George C. Wallace, lost badly to a segregationist, he announced that he would never be "outnigraed again."

The most spectacular example of official resistance came in 1957 when Arkansas Governor Orval Faubus defied a federal court order to desegregate Little Rock High School and used the national guard to keep black children out of the building. With national authority openly challenged, the Eisenhower administration could not avoid the issue. Although never a firm supporter of school desegregation, Eisenhower placed the Arkansas National Guard under federal control, augmented it with regular army troops, and enforced the court order. The following year Arkansas officials tried to block desegregation through the courts. Meeting in emergency session, the Supreme Court rejected Arkansas's claim that the state need not obey national court orders and buried once again the states' rights argument. After the Little Rock incident the Supreme Court declared unconstitutional the evasive tactics of closing down public schools and gerrymandering school districts, and it pressed southern school districts for realistic desegregation plans.

Desegregation of public facilities in the South gained the support of influential liberals. Fighting a war against Nazi racism and crusading against atheistic communism had made American liberals more sensitive to injustices at home. The success of American institutions, they argued, required a greater commitment to racial justice. Policymakers, competing with the Soviets for the goodwill of Third World nations, found it difficult to explain away discrimination against nonwhites in the United States. When diplomats from the new African states experienced segregation firsthand, the whole system of Jim Crow became highly embarrassing to the people who directed the nation's foreign policy. Many religious leaders and scientists also lent their prestige to the civil rights cause.

At the same time, the migration of northern-based corporations and industries to the southern states was producing important socioeconomic, and ultimately cultural, changes: In many ways the South was becoming more like the North. To a new generation of white southern leaders, this process of northernization made old patterns of racial domination, such as Jim Crow and political exclusion, seem anachronistic. This new group of white southern liberals lacked a deep-seated commitment to segregation and wanted to change settled ways.

The introduction of new industries and new technologies also affected black southerners. With the rise of white-owned agribusinesses patterned on northern models and the use of new agricultural techniques, the largely rural, southern black population came under severe pressure. Old living patterns were disrupted: Slowly at first and then at a much more rapid rate, blacks found themselves pushed off the land. Many moved to cities within the South or to urban areas in the northern states. During the 1940s and 1950s, it should be recalled, more than 3 million blacks left the South. This disruption helped to break old deferential patterns and to encourage a new spirit of militancy among younger blacks. By the mid-1950s white leaders found it impossible to ignore black demands, for within the black community new leaders and new organizations were spearheading the fight for equality.

The Montgomery bus boycott of 1956–1957 provided an impetus for community action against Jim Crow. It began when Rosa Parks, a seamstress who had been involved in the local NAACP chapter, was arrested for refusing to surrender her bus seat to a white man. Very quickly, African-American leaders rallied on her behalf and organized a boycott of all municipal transit, refusing to ride until facilities were desegregated. Lasting for more than a year, the Montgomery boycott ended in a victory for antidiscrimination forces and brought to prominence a young Baptist minister, Martin Luther King, Jr.

Raised and educated in Atlanta, and earning a doctorate at Boston University before moving back to the South, Dr. King quickly gained recognition as a charismatic presence and a skilled strategist. Casting himself as a moderate, he nevertheless went beyond the courtroom tactics of the NAACP and the calm lobbying of the Urban League. He was still in his twenties when he helped to organize the Montgomery boycott. King's tactics of nonviolent civil disobedience and economic pressure soon became the civil rights movement's primary weapons. Citing the success of Mahatma Gandhi's passive resistance in India, King preached the importance of laying one's body on the line and of loving one's enemy. "If we are arrested every day . . . if we are trampled over every day, don't ever let anyone pull you so low as to hate them. We must use the weapon of love." In 1957 King and other black ministers formed the Southern Christian Leadership Conference (SCLC), which became the most active civil rights organization in the South.

King and the SCLC worked primarily through African-American churches and drew their heaviest support from middle-class blacks. The son of a prominent Atlanta minister, King spoke in the measured cadence of the black preacher, the person who traditionally led the black community, but he also had the oratorical power to move white audiences and touch their consciences with his message of Christian love. Whether he sought the role or not, King became the symbolic leader of the nation's entire black population. Such a position gained him the enmity of angry whites and, eventually, of more militant black activists.

Puerto Ricans

Thousands of Puerto Ricans moved to New York City in the decade after World War II, transforming that city's ethnic makeup. New York's Puerto Rican community grew by over half a million in twenty years, from 70,000 in 1940 to 613,000 in 1960. A variety of circumstances contributed to this massive migration. Throughout the 1940s Puerto Ricans had experienced increased contact with the U.S. mainland through mass media, advertisements, and military life (65,000 Puerto Ricans served in the armed forces during World War II). Especially to younger Puerto Ricans, life in the United States seemed alluring. New York's unemployment rate was lower than Puerto Rico's, and its social services seemed superior. The administration of Luis Muñoz Marin in Puerto Rico encouraged the trend, hoping to raise Puerto Rico's per capita income by reducing the island's population. Comparatively inexpensive air service between San Juan and New York, begun in 1945, facilitated movement. In addition, U.S. businesses encouraged migration; Puerto Ricans could find work in agriculture and in the garment trades. Once a sizable Puerto Rican community existed in New York, it generated its own growth through a high birthrate and the additional migration of friends and relatives.

The Puerto Rican community laid down roots in East Harlem and then in other neighborhoods throughout the five boroughs of New York City. Studies showed that the newcomers generally had a higher level of education and job skills than the Puerto Ricans who remained behind, but their Spanish language and close ties with the island left them outside the mainstream of city life. During the 1950s many Puerto Ricans could obtain only the lowest-paying jobs, and few entered New York City politics. Puerto Ricans suffered the fate of many groups that lacked economic power and political muscle: discrimination, deteriorating schools, overcrowded housing, and indifference to their problems. Every year around 30,000 people returned to the island, but New York City's Puerto Rican population still continued to grow rapidly throughout the 1950s and 1960s.

Mexican-Americans

New immigration from Mexico and the attraction of urban jobs brought to southwestern cities another Spanish-speaking population: Mexican-Americans (Chicanos). Before World War II Chicanos, like blacks, had lived primarily in rural areas, but by 1960, 80 percent resided in cities. According to the 1960 census, over half a million Mexican-Americans lived in the Los Angeles-Long Beach area. Large Spanish-speaking neighborhoods (barrios) also existed in El Paso, Phoenix, and other southwestern cities; and northern industrial centers such as Chicago, Detroit, Kansas City, and Denver attracted growing numbers of Mexican-Americans.

City life and the favorable job market of the 1950s raised the overall living standards of Mexican-Americans, but racial prejudice still kept a lid on opportunity and advancement. Discrimination, coupled with the ethnic awareness that grew in city barrios, produced racial tensions between Chicanos and white Anglos.

Despite widespread racial prejudice, the U.S. government welcomed additional Mexican migrants under the *bracero* (farm-worker) program. The executive agreement between the United States and Mexico that started the bracero program in 1942 was part of an effort to add workers during World War II. But under pressure from large agricultural enterprises, Congress continued to authorize migration of farm laborers long after the war. Throughout the 1950s the number of incoming Mexican workers climbed each year, reaching a peak of almost 1 million in 1959 alone. Mexican migrants provided cheap, unorganized labor to harvest seasonal crops from Texas to Montana, and growers profited enormously. By the early 1960s, however, the rising unemployment rate among Americans, combined with anti-Mexican prejudice, convinced Congress to discontinue the bracero program. Over the protests of large growers but to the satisfaction of labor unions, which feared competition from cheap labor, the bracero program ended in 1965, although illegal immigration continued.

From the New Deal of the 1930s through the 1950s, leaders in Mexican-American communities sought to promote equality in legal rights and integration into the political mainstream. Proud of their Mexican origins and cultural traditions, they envisioned fitting into a pluralist society in which cultural differences could be maintained while barriers of discrimination eroded. Gaining strength from the broader civil rights movement of the 1950s, middle-class organizations such as the League of United Latin American Citizens (LULAC) and the Unity League forced desegregation of some public facilities and schools, worked against discrimination in housing and employment, and helped elect the first local Mexican-American officeholders in the Southwest. Political mobilization of Mexican-Americans in El Paso, Texas, who made up one-half of that city's total population, swept Raymond L. Telles into office in 1957 as the first Mexican-American mayor. In the same period, the more militant working-class organization, ANMA, backed drives for labor union organizing and protested the mass deportation of Mexicans under the McCarran Act before the group became a casualty of FBI surveillance and harassment. The limited gains and gradualist strategies of the 1940s and 1950s, however, seemed scarcely to dent the structures of socioeconomic disadvantage.

American Indians

American Indians also moved to urban areas during and after World War II. Army life and lucrative industrial jobs initially attracted Indians away from reservations, and the federal government's policies during the 1950s substantially increased movement to the cities. The policy of the Eisenhower administration, as passed by Congress in 1953, called for the government to end Indians' "status as wards of the United States, and grant them all of the rights and privileges pertaining to American citizenship." The plan sought to terminate dependence on the national government, to liquidate the reservation system, and to permit states to assume legal jurisdiction over Indians. The first bills of termination, applying to tribes who supposedly no longer needed a special relationship with the federal government, passed Congress in 1954. By 1968 more than 100 Indian groups had been terminated.

While pursuing termination, the government also set up a Voluntary Relocation Program (later called the Employment Assistance Program) to coax more Indians into urban areas. Begun in 1952, this program helped Indians move to one of ten cities with field relocation offices and paid living expenses until the first wages were received. Within about a decade, more than 60,000 (approximately 1 of every 8) Indians had migrated from reservations to urban centers.

Termination and relocation greatly disrupted Indian life. Some terminated tribes, now subject to state tax requirements, fell on hard times. Others sold tribal lands to private developers. Indians who moved to the cities sometimes found the transition from a semicommunal, rural existence to the isolation of urban life very difficult. Federal officials had claimed that termination and relocation would assimilate Indians into the American mainstream and end federal outlays to support them, but assimilation proved more complicated than a geographical move. The Bureau of Indian Affairs estimated that 35 percent of all relocated Indians eventually returned to the reservations, but other studies suggested that about 75 percent would probably have returned had the reservations offered more job opportunities. By 1967, nearly half of the American Indian population lived in relocation cities.

Few Indians favored the federal policy of termination and relocation, and protests against the breakup of reservations and the destruction of Indian culture mounted. Although the Eisenhower administration never abandoned the goal of termination, officials promised not to force it on unwilling tribes. By the 1960 presidential campaign, termination was so discredited that both the Democratic and Republican parties repudiated it. During the 1960s the government revised the policy and attempted to provide new economic opportunities on reservations rather than to force Indians to leave. (Even so, the Northern Ponca underwent termination between 1962 and 1966.)

Urban Life

Although the term *urban crisis* did not become a cliché until the 1960s, severe tensions and strains were already evident during the 1950s. The construction of new office buildings and highways, the reduction of the number of substandard housing units, and a decrease in population density gave some evidence of urban growth. In addition, the diversity of urban life allowed people to cite vastly different information about the American city. Obviously, problems such as pollution, racial conflict, and crime did vary from city to city, but local stories increasingly appeared to be variations on a general trend. By 1960 almost every large city confronted serious problems that seemed beyond the capacity of established urban institutions.

Most cities were paying the price for more than a century of largely uncontrolled development. Despite the advent of planning and zoning commissions during the early twentieth century, the private decisions of business leaders exerted the greatest influence on the direction and pace of urban change. The needs of business enterprises largely determined what land would be used, how it would be developed, and what groups would pay the highest social costs.

The nation's urban population grew tremendously during the late 1940s and throughout the 1950s. Sprawling across the landscape, urban areas became more fragmented than ever before. After studying cities along the eastern seaboard during the 1950s, a French geographer called this new form of social organization the "megalopolis." "We must abandon the idea of the city as a tightly settled and organized unit in which people, activities, and riches are crowded into a very small area clearly separate from its nonurban surroundings," wrote Jean Gottman. A city would spread out "far and wide around its original nucleus" until it melted into the suburban neighborhoods of other cities.

This geographical expansion exacerbated urban problems. Larger metropolitan areas made coherent centralized administration difficult, and any decentralized arrangement left less affluent areas saddled with poor schools, inadequate public services, and too little money to address social problems. Urban sprawl made some people feel like transients rather than members of a community. As long as more affluent urbanites could commute from their jobs to their homes in suburbia, they would hesitate to commit themselves or their tax dollars to projects that aimed at tackling urban problems.

Ironically, many attempts to meet urban needs seemed only to accelerate fragmentation. Significant federal aid for construction of low-cost housing rarely reached central cities during the 1950s. Even the modest goal of 810,000 public-housing units by 1955, the target of the Housing Act of 1949, was not achieved until the end of the 1960s. In fact, the Housing Act established another program—urban renewal—that actually reduced the number of dwellings available to low-income people. In theory, urban renewal would allow local governments to use federal funds to clear out old and dilapidated buildings and to replace them with new public-housing units or with other projects, including almost anything from new cultural complexes to concrete parking garages. In practice, the Eisenhower administration allowed urban planners and private developers to evade the responsibility of replacing or increasing the supply of living units.

New York's Robert Moses, a person who held no elective office but who came to dominate building and urban planning in the nation's largest city, epitomized the postwar approach to urban issues. Moses ridiculed critics of his grandiose schemes. "When you operate in an overbuilt metropolis, you have to hack your way with a meat ax," he once explained. Flaunting his power as City Parks Commissioner and City Construction Coordinator, Moses taunted opponents that he was "just going to keep on building. You do the best you can to stop it." Moving low-income people as if they were disposable commodities, Moses held fast to his vision of urban progress. For those who "like things as they are," Moses offered this advice: "Keep moving further away. [New York] is a big state, and there are other states . . . go to the Rockies." And even though most of New York City's postwar residents owned no automobiles, Moses cut through, around, and even above the city with expensive freeway projects.

The vast networks of multilane expressways, in New York and elsewhere, brought paradoxical changes to urban life. The new freeways allowed people to travel to work in the privacy of their automobiles rather than on public transportation and enabled affluent commuters to live even farther from decaying urban centers. In addition to accelerating urban sprawl, freeways created other problems. The new concrete conveyors accelerated the decay of existing mass transit facilities and worked against construction of new ones. The stream of cars creeping to and from the central cities also increased air pollution without noticeably speeding the pace of urban commuting. Finally, the new expressways destroyed even more old buildings and further contributed to the fragmentation of urban life.

By the 1960s urban problems seemed of growing concern. During the presidential campaign of 1960 both Richard Nixon and John F. Kennedy pledged their support for creation of a new cabinet-level office to coordinate federal assistance to urban areas.

The Invisible Poor

Despite urban deterioration, the people who congregated in central-city neighborhoods were often better off than those who remained in rural areas. During the 1950s great agribusiness combinations mechanized operations and engulfed more land. By 1954, 12 percent of the farm operators made nearly 60 percent of total agricultural sales, and this imbalance continued to grow. Unemployment accompanied this agricultural revolution; severe rural poverty became a major, if often unnoticed, problem. Throughout the rural Midwest in the 1950s, many young people left their family farms rather than try to compete with large agricultural enterprises. A million and a half people abandoned unproductive patches of land in Appalachia. The many old people who remained were those least able to cope with mechanization and changing markets. Whether a person was an African-American tenant farmer in Georgia, an American Indian on an isolated reservation, a white farmer in the hills of Appalachia, or a Mexican-American migrant worker, poverty often dominated his or her life.

Although growing affluence and comfort characterized the postwar years for most Americans, inequalities remained. The medium of television made middle-class comforts highly visible to the poor, yet poverty and degradation grew more invisible to the affluent. Suburbanites in fast-moving automobiles skirted the slums and rarely penetrated the pockets of rural poverty. A gap grew between the aspirations of the lower sectors and the social consciousness of the affluent. Bitterness mounted in the central city as complacency spread through the suburbs.

In 1960, John F. Kennedy promised to "get this country moving again" and to revive the old liberal-Democratic approach to social problems. But for the decade of the 1950s, Dwight Eisenhower's desire to limit social welfare programs and the size of government prevailed. Later, when the nation had moved in directions that liberals could neither foresee nor control, more than a few people would look back to the Eisenhower years with a touch of nostalgia. What often becomes forgotten, however, is that the real 1950s, though perhaps more placid than the immediate postwar period, still exhibited tensions and strains that could not always be soothed by the official gospel of affluence and affability. This was especially true in foreign affairs, where the United States struggled to preside as the "protector of the free world."

SUGGESTIONS FOR FURTHER READING

Charles Alexander, *Holding the Line* (1975), is an older introduction to the Eisenhower years, and the early portions of Martin P. Wattenberg, *The Decline of American Political Parties, 1952–1980* (1984), set the political background. These can be updated with Chester Pach, Jr., and Elmo Richardson, *The Presidency of Dwight D. Eisenhower* (rev. ed., 1993), and the relevant chapters of Gary Reichard, *Politics as Usual: The Age of Truman and Eisenhower* (1988), and Alonso Hamby, *Liberalism and Its Challengers* (1992). Stephen Ambrose's two-volume study, *Eisenhower* (1983, 1984), will probably remain the standard source for years; but Fred Greenstein's *The Hidden-Hand Presidency* (1982); Herbert J. Parmet, *Eisenhower and the American Crusades* (1972); Robert F. Burk, *Dwight David Eisenhower* (1986); and William B. Pickett, *Dwight David Eisenhower and American Power* (1993), should also be consulted. Ike's own memoirs, *Mandate for Change* and *Waging Peace* (1963, 1965), are worthwhile. Specialized studies include Gary Reichard, *The Reaffirmation of Republicanism* (1975); Burton J. Kaufman, *The Oil Cartel Case* (1978); Mark Rose, *Interstate: Express Highway Politics* (1979); Robert F. Burk, *The Eisenhower Administration* and *Civil Rights* (1984); Duane Tanabaum, *The Bricker Amendment: A Test of Eisenhower's Political Leadership* (1989); R. Alton Lee, *Eisenhower and Landrum-Griffin: A Study in Labor-Management Politics* (1990); and Jeff Broadwater, *Eisenhower and the Anti-Communist Crusade* (1992).

The baby boom is the focus of Richard A. Easterlin, *Birth and Fortune* (1980), and Landon Y. Jones, *Great Expectations* (1980). See also the relevant chapters of John Modell, *Into One's Own: From Youth to Adulthood in the United States, 1920–1975* (1989). On women's issues, see the final chapters of Susan Strasser, *Never Done* (1982); Ruth Schwartz Cowen, *More Work for Mother: The Ironies of Household Technology from the Open Hearth to the Microwave* (1985); Alice Kessler-Harris, *Out to Work: A History of Wage-earning Women in the United States* (1982); Jacqueline Jones, *Labor of Love, Labor of Sorrow: Black Women, Work and the Family, from Slavery to the Present* (1985); Paula Giddings, *When and Where I Enter* (1985); and Sara Evans, *Born for Liberty* (1989). General surveys that focus more directly on this specific period include Eugenia Kaledin, *Mothers and More* (1984); Leila Rupp and Vera Taylor, *Survival in the Doldrums* (1987); and Cynthia Harrison, *On Account of Sex: The Politics of Women's Issues, 1945–68* (1988).

Family and gender issues are nicely tied to cold war culture in Elaine May's *Homeward Bound* (1989) and in Stephanie Coontz, *The Way We Never Were: American Families and the Nostalgia Trip* (1992). Barbara Ehrenreich, *The Hearts of Men* (1983), relates women's issues to her theory of a male revolt during the 1950s. On issues related to sexuality, see the relevant chapters of John D'Emilio, *Sexual Politics, Sexual Communities: The Making of a Homosexual Minority in the United States, 1940–1970* (1983); Paul Robinson, *The Modernization of Sex* (1976); John D'Emilio and Estelle B. Freedman, *Intimate Matters* (1988); Wini Breines, *Young, White, and Miserable: Growing Up Female in the Fifties* (1992); Rickie Sillinger, *Wake Up Little Susie: Single Pregnancy and Race Before Roe v. Wade* (1993); Graham McCann, *Rebel Males: Clift, Brando and Dean* (1993); and Joanne Meyerowitz, *Not June Cleaver: Women and Gender in Postwar America* (1993).

On suburban and urban issues, see Robert J. Caro, *The Power Broker* (1974), a fascinating study of the machinations of New York City's Robert Moses; Joel Schwartz, *The New York Approach: Robert Moses, Urban Liberals, and Redevelopment of the Inner City* (1993); Mark Gelfand, *A Nation of Cities* (1975); Kenneth Fox, *Metropolitan America: Urban Life and Urban Policy in the United States* (1990); Herbert Gans, *The Levittowners* (2nd ed., 1982); Robert B. Fairbanks and Kathleen Underwood, *Essays on Sunbelt Cities and Recent Urban America* (1989); Jon C. Teaford, *The Rough Road to Renaissance: Urban Revitalization in America, 1940–85* (1990); and Larry Bennett, *Fragments of Cities: The New American Downtowns and Neighborhoods* (1990). See also the relevant chapters of Kenneth T. Jackson, *The Crabgrass Frontier* (1985).

For overviews of postwar mass culture, see Andrew Ross, *No Respect* (1989), and James L. Baughman, *The Republic of Mass Culture* (1992). The debates over mass culture in the 1950s can be sampled in Bernard Rosenberg and David Manning White, *Mass Culture* (1957) and *Mass Culture Revisited*

(1971). James Gilbert, *A Cycle of Outrage* (1986), critiques this debate and relates it to an emerging youth culture. On sports, see Randy Roberts and James S. Olson, *Winning Is the Only Thing: Sports in America Since 1945* (1989). Different views of Hollywood's role emerge from Peter Biskind, *Seeing Is Believing* (1984); Jackie Byars, *All That Hollywood Allows: Re-reading Gender in the 1950s Melodrama* (1991); Robert Ray, *A Certain Tendency in the Hollywood Cinema* (1985); Dana Polan, *Power and Paranoia: History, Narrative, and the American Cinema, 1940–1950* (1986); Mary Doane, *The Desire to Desire: The Woman's Film of the 1940s* (1987); J. P. Tellotte, *Voices in the Dark: The Narrative Patterns of Film Noir* (1989); Frank Krutnik, *In a Lonely Street* (1991); Brian Neve, *Film and Politics in America* (1992); Eric Smoodin, *Animating Culture* (1993); and Robert J. Corber, *In the Name of National Security: Hitchcock, Homophobia, and the Political Construction of Gender in Postwar America* (1993).

On television, see David Marc, *Demographic Vistas* (1984); William Boddy, *Fifties Television* (1990); Patricia Mellencamp, ed., *The Logics of Television* (1990); Mary Ann Watson, *The Expanding Vista: Television in the Kennedy Years* (1990); Cecelia Tichi, *The Electronic Hearth* (1991); Lynn Spigel and Denise Mann, eds., *Private Screenings* (1992); and Glenn C. Altschuler and David I. Grossvogel, *Changing Channels* (1992). For an overview of recent, critical approaches to TV texts, see the various essays in Robert C. Allen, ed., *Channels of Discourse, Reassembled* (rev. ed., 1992). On music, see Greil Marcus, *Mystery Train* (3rd ed., 1990); Charley Gillet's *Sound of the City* (rev. ed., 1984); Ed Ward, Geoffrey Stokes, and Ken Tucker, *Rock of Ages: The Rolling Stone History of Rock & Roll* (1986); and Nelson George, *The Death of Rhythm and Blues* (1988). On the diversity of the youth culture, see William Graebner, *Coming of Age in Buffalo: Youth and Authority in the Postwar Era* (1989).

On social issues, see Michael Harrington's classic, *The Other America* (1962), and his later work, *The New American Poverty* (1984); James T. Patterson, *America's Struggle Against Poverty, 1900–1980* (1981); Doug McAdam, *Political Process and the Development of Black Insurgency, 1930–1970* (1982); Harvard Sitkoff, *The Struggle for Black Equality* (1983); Larry Burt, *Tribalism in Crisis* (1982); Tony Freyer, *The Little Rock Crisis* (1984); Manuel Alers-Montalvo, *The Puerto Rican Migrants of New York* (1985); David Garrow, *Bearing the Cross: Martin Luther King, Jr., and the Southern Christian Leadership Conference* (1986); the relevant chapters of Earl Black and Merle Black, *Politics and Society in the South* (1987); Jack Bloom, *Class, Race, and the Civil Rights Movement: The Political Economy of Southern Racism* (1987); David Garrow, ed., *The Montgomery Bus Boycott and the Women Who Started It: The Memoir of Jo Ann Gibson Robinson* (1987); Joseph P. Fitzpatrick, *Puerto Rican Americans: The Meaning of Migration to the Mainland* (2nd ed., 1987); Taylor Branch, *Parting the Waters: America in the King Years, 1954–1963* (1988); Steven J. Whitfield, *A Death in the Delta: The Story of Emmett Till* (1988); Herbert Haines, *Black Radicals and the Civil Rights Mainstream, 1954–1970* (1989); Mario Garcia, *A History of Mexican-Americans: 1930–1960* (1989); Ricardo Romo, *East Los Angeles: History of a Barrio* (1989); Nancy J. Weiss, *Whitney M. Young, Jr., and The Struggle for Civil Rights* (1989); the relevant chapters of Ronald Takaki, *Strangers from a Different Shore: A History of*

Asian-Americans (1989); Henry Hampton, ed., *Voices of Freedom: An Oral History of the Civil Rights Movement* (1990); Robert Weisbrot, *American Crusade: A History of the Civil Rights Movement* (1990); Armstead L. Robinson and Patricia Sullivan, eds., *New Directions in Civil Rights Studies* (1991); the relevant chapters of Jacqueline Jones, *The Dispossessed* (1992); Vicki Crawford, Jacqueline Anne Rouse, and Barbara Woods, eds., *Women in the Civil Rights Movement* (1990); David L. Chappell, *Inside Agitators: White Southerners in the Civil Rights Movement* (1993); Mark V. Tushnet, *Making Civil Rights Law: Thurgood Marshall and the Supreme Court, 1936–1961* (1993); and James F. Findlay, Jr., *Church People in the Struggle* (1993).

4

Protector
of the
Free World

REPUBLICAN FOREIGN POLICIES

President Dwight Eisenhower's personal style contrasted with that of his flamboyant predecessors. For years he had reconciled diverse opinions into consensus, first as commander of the world's greatest amphibious invasion, the D-day attack against occupied France; then as president of Columbia University; and from 1950 to 1952 as leader of NATO's (North Atlantic Treaty Organization) vast military apparatus in Europe. Distrustful of expansive government and its potential for public waste, Ike championed conservative economic principles and scrutinized defense expenditures carefully. This general enjoyed quiet games of golf and, unlike "give 'em hell, Harry Truman," vowed to "wage peace."

John Foster Dulles, the austere corporation lawyer who became secretary of state, helped chart Eisenhower's foreign policy. A fervent anticommunist, he extended the position of the 1952 Republican platform that condemned Truman's containment policy as "negative, futile, and immoral" by stridently calling for a psychological and political offensive to roll back communism. Dulles saw himself, one biographer wrote, "as the chess master of the free world, daily engaged in a mortal contest against a monolithic adversary."

The New Look

How could the Eisenhower administration reconcile a suspicion of large government with its rhetorical commitment to an open-ended struggle against anything perceived as socialist or communist? The cost-conscious president, his secretary of state, and Pentagon generals recast America's strategic doctrines into a "New Look" stressing the deterrent of massive retaliation. They believed that modern technology could increase American military power while reducing its cost: Secretary of Defense Charles Wilson quipped that nuclear weaponry provided "more bang for the buck." Nuclear bombs, together with sophisticated delivery systems, could protect the United States from attack since no nation would risk second-strike reprisal.

Determined to stake out the boundaries of the "free world" as broadly as possible, Dulles also dramatically expanded the nation's collective-security arrangements. He spent months traveling around the world, signing up allies. A succession of bilateral defense pacts with Taiwan, Korea, and Japan extended America's nuclear umbrella to the shores of China. Even more grandiose schemes shored up Britain's weakness east of Suez. The Southeast Asia Treaty Organization (SEATO) of 1954 linked Australia, the Philippines, Thailand, and Pakistan with the United States, Britain, and France. The next year Washington sponsored England's Central Treaty Organization (CENTO) with Turkey, Iraq, Iran, and Pakistan. Turkey tied CENTO with NATO; Pakistan connected SEATO with CENTO. Although these multilateral covenants remained weak, in theory they pledged that an attack against one member, either by overt aggression or, as Dulles put it, "by internal subversion," would bring all into consultation to decide common action. Eisenhower, already skeptical about the military value of large American army reserves, thought that local forces, financed partly from Washington and linked to a network of alliances controlled by the United States, could contain regional threats and prevent them from escalating into nuclear cataclysm. Although designed to decrease America's obligations, regional pacts could also increase them by involving the United States in local disputes.

The New Look stressed atomic weaponry, but it also brought other tools into what Republicans viewed as a global struggle: an increase in overseas bases; a larger commitment to foreign military aid; employment of economic assistance programs to accomplish political goals; more aggressive use of techniques of psychological warfare (such as Radio Free Europe); and a stepped-up program of covert action, run by the Central Intelligence Agency (CIA), to subvert unfriendly governments. The Eisenhower administration talked about limited government, but historians now recognize how thoroughly it expanded and employed new techniques, discretely controlled by the executive branch, of conducting foreign policy. Use of economic, psychological, and covert diplomacy—all fairly hidden from public view or scrutiny—sharply distinguished Eisenhower's foreign policy from prewar patterns and significantly shaped future capabilities. More and more, the U.S. "defense" posture against communism looked like a global offensive, Ike's "limited" government like a budding leviathan.

Korea

Armistice negotiations with the North Koreans and the Chinese had broken down in October 1952, largely because of a complicated impasse over the issue of prisoners of war. The communists demanded that the usual international practice of returning all POWs to their homeland be observed. The United States, however, insisted on voluntary repatriation. Since many enemy soldiers wanted to stay in South Korea, this formula meant that the South could gain, and the North lose, as many as 50,000 trained soldiers. Stalemate also continued on the battlefield.

True to his campaign promise, Eisenhower toured the front in November 1952 and then, with Dulles, orchestrated an exercise in New Look diplomacy. Nuclear weapons might be used to terminate the conflict if negotiations failed. The president wired General Mark Clark, the UN commander, that the United States might "carry on the war in new ways never yet tried" if the communists remained intransigent. Dulles dispatched more specific warnings through third parties: America might drop atomic bombs.

Before the United States took such a fateful step, however, negotiations resumed, and both sides quickly initiated armistice terms. Korea was to stay divided, as before the war; neutral powers were to tackle POW repatriation (an issue eventually settled according to the voluntary formula). On July 27, 1953, a truce—not a peace treaty—ended a war that had killed over 2 million Asians, mostly civilians, and 33,000 Americans.

The Korean War sharply focused the nature of U.S. policy during the 1950s. To American policymakers of the time—and many subsequent historians—it represented a clear case of communist expansionism: aggression across an international boundary to take over a free state. In this view, expansionism was successfully contained by a strong military response topped off by an atomic threat. The Korean War seemed to exemplify the cold war premises of NSC 68 and to require a rapid buildup of American military strength and nonmilitary leverage.

Yet this version of the war speaks more about the mentality of the 1950s than about Korean realities. Korea was a deeply divided society—factionalized between right and left and divided since 1946 by an arbitrary border that cut across lines of ethnicity, religion, and political allegiance. The governments of both North and South were deeply committed to reunification of the country and both were, simultaneously, attempting to consolidate their control. Within this fragmented society, the cast of characters simply did not match the cold war morality play. Kim Il Sung was a communist dictator but acted largely on his own, not as an agent of Soviet expansionism. And Syngman Rhee was poorly cast as a defender of democracy. The South seethed with discontent against his autocratic rule; indeed, the civil turmoil in the South may have convinced Kim Il Sung that the time had come to make a bid for unification. After gaining U.S. support for his own ambitions, of course, Rhee had little reason to reorient his regime in a more popular direction. Portrayed by the United States as a defender of freedom—because he was anticommunist—Rhee could continue to block needed reforms, imprison dissenters, and expand his tyranny.

Korea was consistent with a predominant trend in Eisenhower's overall foreign policy toward the Third World: the support for conservative, often autocratic dictators as the only presumed alternative to a supposedly monolithic communist menace.

Summitry

Although New Look calculations about the Soviet Union assumed an international communist conspiracy led by a Stalinist police state, Soviet communism, in fact, began to mellow after the mid-1950s. On March 5, 1953, the Soviet dictator Joseph Stalin died, and his tyranny partially withered. Stalin's theories had proved wrong: World war had revived liberal capitalism, not doomed it. The troika that replaced Stalin—Foreign Minister Vyacheslav Molotov; Defense Minister Nikolai Bulganin; and Nikita Khrushchev, first secretary of the Communist party—went along with Premier George Malenkov's plan to ease tensions with the United States. Within three years Khrushchev had triumphed over the others, and the Soviet people, tired of fear and poverty, enthusiastically responded to his promises of peaceful coexistence and more consumer goods. After Khrushchev denounced Stalin's "Gestapo tactics" in 1956, Russians dreamed of less regimentation, less sacrifice.

This new direction in Soviet policy not only substituted competition for confrontation but also reduced the dangers of massive retaliation. The Soviet Union reduced its armed forces from 4 million to less than 3 million by the mid-1950s. Though primarily an effort to shift economic priorities toward consumer industries, the unilateral gesture did seem to contradict Dulles' hard-line premises. It also calmed European fears of Soviet power. Increasingly, Eisenhower became interested in refashioning America's relationship with the Soviet Union, perhaps by easing the nuclear arms race. During the halcyon months of the Russian thaw, English leaders had urged a conference of heads of state to settle European problems, particularly German reunification. The idea of a summit meeting intrigued Eisenhower, despite Dulles's pessimistic admonitions. Summitry offered not only an alternative to grim crusades but also a new forum for long-stalled disarmament negotiations.

In July 1955 the president traveled to Geneva, where he met with his counterparts from the Big Four: Premier Bulganin and First Secretary Khrushchev, Prime Minister Anthony Eden of Britain, and Premier Edgar Faure of France. The drama of face-to-face sessions obscured otherwise desultory talks about Germany's future and East-West cultural exchanges. Then Eisenhower submitted a plan for disarmament. The United States and the Soviet Union would exchange blueprints of all military installations and permit reconnaissance flights over each other's territory. The proposal had little chance for practical success because the Soviets were deeply and historically suspicious of opening their territory to Western scrutiny, but "open skies" did represent a propaganda victory for the United States. More important, it inaugurated "the spirit of Geneva": Leaders in the two blocs had moderated their intractable rhetoric, and cultural exchanges accelerated.

The dangers of radioactive fallout from atomic tests spurred further efforts toward accommodation. In mid-1958 the Russians unilaterally suspended nuclear testing, presumably to probe American intentions while converting more of their economy to consumer production. Britain and the

United States followed later that year, finally responding to growing evidence that atmospheric tests represented a severe health hazard. The movement toward a test ban showed that in the mutual danger of the atomic age there could lie some mutual interests as well.

In the same spirit of summitry, leaders of both nations embarked on personal diplomacy. In the fall of 1959 Khrushchev visited the United States for twelve days. He addressed the United Nations, talked to Iowa farmers, and watched Hollywood stars. Then premier and president conferred privately at Camp David, a mountain retreat in Maryland. Though achieving nothing concrete, the "spirit of Camp David" further moderated rancor in both countries. The leaders also launched much-publicized goodwill trips elsewhere. Eisenhower went to Europe, the Middle East, Latin America, and the Far East, though anti-American riots protesting a bilateral defense treaty forced him to cancel a trip to Japan. Khrushchev appeared in Western Europe, Afghanistan, and India.

In early 1960 Khrushchev called for another summit meeting, this time in Paris to deal with issues of German reunification and nuclear armament. On May 1, 1960, however, the Soviets shot down an American U-2 spy plane over their territory. Khrushchev trumpeted Russia's injury, demanding both an apology and an end to such spy flights. Eisenhower knew that Khrushchev would use the Paris meeting to embarrass the West. The summit collapsed.

The summitry of the Eisenhower years did not narrow fundamental disagreements nor provide diplomatic breakthroughs. Its essence lay less in substance than in media-attracting pageantry and in the display of cold war rituals for home consumption on both sides. Still, the cold war was created by people in power, and it had to be ameliorated by people in power. The gains from face-to-face conversations, though small, seemed worthwhile.

Challenges to Superpower Dominance

Even as Soviet–American tensions eased, discontent spread within the alliance systems of both superpowers. The New Look, based on America's strategic superiority, inspired resentment against American dominance. Russia's thaw spread throughout its Eastern European empire, creating unrest—even outright rebellion. Aligned nations in both blocs rejected crucial parts of their overlords' prescriptions for the future.

Of all its crisscrossed security pacts, America's alliance with Western Europe was the oldest and strongest, but tensions nonetheless mounted. Washington had strongly urged an integrated NATO force armed with conventional weapons. A joint effort would force Europe to finance a larger portion of its defense, increase pressure against the Soviet Union, and rope German power into a regional enterprise. Dulles advocated creation of a European Defense Community (EDC), but many Europeans, particularly the French, opposed its transnational approach and its lack of nuclear weapons. In response, Dulles ruminated at a press conference about "an agonizing reappraisal" of America's relations with Europe if EDC was not supported.

Dulles's tactics only angered politicians in France and England, who asserted national defense to be the province of their own parliaments, not of foreign leaders. Specialization—an American nuclear force paired with conventional European armies—would continue Europe's second-class status in the NATO alliance. Would the United States risk nuclear war, and thus its own destruction, to save Western Europe? Conversely, might not Washington and Moscow pull back from direct superpower confrontation after mushroom clouds rose over Paris and, say, Warsaw? When the French National Assembly finally refused to ratify the EDC treaty on August 30, 1954, most Europeans happily approved. Britain and France accelerated their own plans for nuclear armament.

Nowhere were superpower hopes for mastery wrecked more consistently than in the Middle East. There nationalism and charismatic leaders defined the contours of change. In Egypt, for example, military leaders destroyed King Farouk's corrupt monarchy in a 1952 coup, intending to modernize the country and escape Britain's economic domination. Two years later a "colonels' revolt" gave Gamal Abdel Nasser near dictatorial power. The new president dreamed of making Egypt the chief military power in the Middle East so that he could lead Arab nationalism. Popular resentment at Israeli statehood and English control over much of the Middle East's political life encouraged rearmament programs; "positive neutralism" garnered money and technological aid from both East and West. Nasser's successes soon enraptured Arabs but alienated Britain and frightened Israel. Then, after an Israeli raid into Egypt's Gaza Strip, Nasser signed an agreement to buy advanced weapons from Czechoslovakia. Angry with this threat to the Western-dominated status quo, Dulles withdrew American support for loans for the construction of Egypt's Aswan Dam, a huge project designed to improve harvests along the Nile River and provide hydroelectric power for Egypt's developing industries. Nasser then seized the Suez Canal on July 25, 1956, assuming that its duties could finance the dam's construction.

Britain, France, and Israel resolved to act. Israelis saw the Suez crisis as a pretext for preventive war; Europeans hoped to destroy Arab nationalism in the Middle East. French premier Guy Mollet also reckoned that a militant response would shore up his foundering coalition government. Then, too, a blow at Nasser would discourage Arab rebels in Algeria, where France was attempting to suppress an anticolonial guerrilla movement. Meanwhile, the British had created their own domino theory: Nasser was a Hitlerian figure who, if unopposed, would unite the Arab world and confiscate Britain's most valuable investments. When Eisenhower cleverly ducked the Suez crisis during his 1956 presidential campaign, the British Foreign Office chose to interpret his obscure statements as a negative endorsement of their intervention in the Middle East. The United States, they thought, could not abandon its closest ally once military operations began. On October 29, 1956, Israel attacked Egypt, and several days later Anglo-French forces retook the Suez Canal.

The war ended quickly, partly because Egypt's armies proved surprisingly inept but largely because of superpower reactions. The United States angrily reasserted its leadership of the Atlantic community. Opposed to "any aggression by any nation," Eisenhower threatened to support cutting oil shipments to the invaders and to destroy the English pound by opposing renewal of British loans from the International Monetary Fund. Unencumbered by alliances with former colonial powers, the Russians condemned Britain and France more forcefully. Mollet and British Prime Minister Eden could only acquiesce in a Canadian-American plan for UN troops to police the Sinai Peninsula.

The affair severely damaged America's prestige in most parts of the world. Egyptians did not forget that the "American peace" had stationed foreign soldiers in their country but not in Israel, the aggressor. The Suez crisis of 1956 interjected Russia into Egyptian affairs, especially after the Soviets took over financing the Aswan Dam, and ensured Nasser's leadership of the Arab world. Washington's criticism had also alienated the Europeans. Suez convinced most French people that Washington had sacrificed their national interest, and the French government became the more determined to chart an independent course. The British were stunned but unwilling to give up their "special relationship" with the United States.

Strains within the Western alliance over nuclear policy and the Suez crisis coincided with a similar restiveness within the Soviet bloc. After World War II, Stalin had backed pro-Soviet regimes throughout Eastern Europe. These satellites embarked on industrial programs designed to complement Soviet reconstruction. Never content with Stalinist tactics and the distortion of national economic needs, some Eastern Europeans challenged these local regimes once the Soviet thaw began. Yet how much liberalization would Moscow's new rulers allow? In June 1956 over 15,000 factory workers rioted at Poznan in Poland. Their three-day rebellion set off a popular upsurge of support for Wladyslaw Gomulka, a former minister removed by Stalin when he publicly opposed collectivization and advocated national development regardless of Soviet orders. After complicated maneuvers with Poland's old guard and Moscow's politburo, revisionists forced Moscow to accept the unorthodox Gomulka. Events had caught Soviet leaders off guard, but their recognition of Gomulka seemed to indicate the feasibility of economic reform that did not threaten the integrity of the Soviet bloc.

Misunderstanding this cue, Hungarians reached for true political independence a few months later. Emboldened by Poland's success and by its own suffering from the same Stalinist exploitation, a huge crowd demonstrated on October 23. Students and workers, intellectuals, and housewives paraded for hours, demanding the return of Imre Nagy, like Gomulka a former minister disgraced for his liberal views. Nagy formed a new government, but strikes and unrest continued. Protests against subservience to the Soviet Union turned into armed rebellion in the countryside and within days paralyzed the capital as well. Misled by broadcasts from America's CIA-financed Radio Free Europe, the revolutionaries hoped for U.S. assistance. Nagy pledged free elections and a multiparty system. "No nation," he declared, "can intervene in our internal affairs." The lure of independence and Dulles's talk of "liberating captive peoples" betrayed the Hungarians into tragic illusions. As violence continued, the Russians sent a huge army into Hungary and crushed the Hungarian revolt. Moscow would not tolerate neutrality on its strategic borders and benefited from the simultaneous British and French action against Egypt. At the same time, however, the Kremlin learned that it could not assume passive subservience in Eastern Europe.

THE THIRD WORLD AND THE COLD WAR

During the 1950s the focus of international affairs shifted toward Asia, Africa, and Latin America, where charismatic leaders often pursued economic self-determination and control over national resources as well as political independence. As nationalism swept the Third World, most leaders sought to steer between Russian and Yankee, avoiding an exclusive, neocolonialist reliance on either. The Soviets argued that the Russian revolution, directed by centralized planning, was more relevant than the American to the twentieth-century problems of industrialization. Through such an appeal, the Soviets tried to build ties to anticolonial movements and to support state-directed development. United States policymakers under Eisenhower, by contrast, looked suspiciously on centralized planning and often equated economic nationalism, even liberal social reform, with communism. Under Eisenhower, the battle against communism became broad and vague and often did not take into account the appeal of nationalist rhetoric and programs.

Vietnam

America's most perplexing involvement in Third World politics came in Southeast Asia, particularly Vietnam. French colonialism had dominated Indochina for eighty years, but Japan's initial victories over the area in 1940 unseated French rule and galvanized a coterie of nationalist intellectuals into a movement for postwar independence. Ho Chi Minh, a Marxist scholar dedicated to spreading the class struggle to his country of peasants, assumed leadership of the Viet Minh, a popular front of several revolutionary parties. As Japanese power collapsed at the end of World War II, Ho declared Vietnam's independence (on September 2, 1945) and hoped that he could attract support from the United States, whose leaders were then urging decolonization. Although his provisional government wanted to negotiate, France almost immediately launched a war of reconquest. Ho and an exceptionally skillful general, Vo Nguyen Giap, countered with guerrilla tactics, seeking to avoid defeat in the field while winning the people over to their nationalist-communist cause. Financed heavily by Washington, French armies struggled against the forces led by Ho for control of Vietnam for nine years.

In 1954 the French had to accept defeat. Giap surrounded 25,000 French troops at a frontier outpost, Dien Bien Phu, while a constant artillery barrage cut off French reinforcements. The Viet Minh slowly advanced, using a complicated system of tunnels and munitions backpacked into the mountains by thousands of peasants. As the French public watched the sure strangulation of its army, the government under Pierre Mendes-France pledged to end the war, even if that meant leaving Vietnam to nationalist-communists under Ho Chi Minh. The French prepared for a peace conference in Geneva.

American policymakers were divided in their response. Shocked that yet another area might "go communist," John Foster Dulles and some Pentagon figures—notably Admiral Arthur W. Radford, chair of the Joint Chiefs of Staff—proposed an air strike against Giap's army. Some even discussed sending American troops to revitalize the French war effort or the use of atomic weaponry. Eisenhower did not want to "lose" Indochina so soon after the Chinese debacle, but he was aware of America's limited power in so remote a place and worried about the federal budget. Congressional leaders refused to authorize intervention unless the United States first secured foreign support, and Britain quickly refused. After the army outlined cost and manpower estimates, Eisenhower concluded that intervention was impossible. Chief of Staff General Matthew Ridgway predicted that a million men, huge draft quotas, and enormous destruction might win this political-guerrilla war, but he thought that even then most Vietnamese would probably still support the Viet Minh.

Meanwhile, peace negotiations at the Geneva Conference reached a conclusion. France wished only to get out of the war. The Russians and the Chinese urged Ho Chi Minh to accept a compromise. France granted Vietnam, Laos, and Cambodia full independence, though none of the new states could join foreign alliances or permit foreign soldiers on its soil. French troops were to regroup in Vietnam south of the seventeenth parallel, communist forces north of it. A nationwide election to be held within two years was to provide a single government for the reunified country. This solution—a graceful exit for the defeated French and a neutralized Indochina in exchange for the possibility of an electoral victory in communist Vietnam—satisfied almost everyone concerned.

Everyone, that is, except American policymakers. They saw a way to "save" at least some of Vietnam, though it required unilateral action. The secretary of state, not a party to the Geneva accords, announced instead that the United States considered North and South Vietnam two separate entities. The State Department hurriedly completed plans for SEATO and gratuitously extended its coverage to South Vietnam, Cambodia, and Laos. After Bao Dai, the Vietnamese emperor who had served the French, stepped down in 1955, the Eisenhower administration pledged vast amounts of economic aid to his pro-Western successor, Ngo Dinh Diem. Diem, with American backing, called off the scheduled national elections in which a communist victory appeared certain. The Republican administration updated an old doctrine, long applied to Europe, to justify these expedient maneuvers: the domino theory. If South Vietnam "fell," Thailand would be next, then the rest of Indochina, and perhaps even India or Australia. If the West stood firm now, as Britain and France should have stood up to Hitler in 1939, the communist advance would falter. Policymakers desired a democracy in Southeast Asia that could conveniently serve as an example for the Third World. But the connection between Washington and Saigon quickly became so one-sided that South Vietnam became more colony than sovereign state. Dependency reinforced the necessity for ever-increasing U.S. intervention.

Throughout the rest of the 1950s, Republicans richly supplied South Vietnam's pro-West Premier Diem with economic aid, military supplies, and diplomatic protection. The results at first seemed to vindicate their gamble that a limited commitment might not only stave off another communist victory but also build a capitalist model for the Third World. Between 1954 and 1957 South Vietnam ended wartime economic controls, initiated reconstruction, and began industrial development. Diem redistributed land confiscated from French landlords to peasants in the Mekong River delta. His steadily improving army brought order in Sagon and forced allegiance from the semi-feudal religious sects in the countryside. But Diem could never really cement the nation together, and his Catholicism alienated the predominately Buddhist population. To ensure at least the appearance of popular support, Diem replaced local officials with his loyalists. A much touted "population relocation" program degenerated into political purges. Land reform ultimately benefited a new kind of absentee owner, the Saigonese bureaucrat. Corruption diluted American aid, so that little of it helped villagers trapped in the war-ravaged countryside or refugees hounded into inflation-ridden cities. Diem retreated more and more into a contracting circle of family members and army generals. The regime's growing isolation and dependence on the United States frightened nationalists.

To protest such abuses, a coalition of anti-Diem intellectuals, nationalists, harassed politicians, and Viet Minh communists organized the National Liberation Front (NLF) in 1960. Its platform promised return to village rule, immediate land ownership for the peasants, and a coalition cabinet in Saigon. Discontent in the countryside propelled many recruits into the NLF's makeshift army, which communist cadres soon dominated, partly because of their experience during the earlier guerrilla struggle against France. The NLF championed the communal traditions of the village rather than the alien dictatorship in Saigon, which relied on Americans.

The ensuing communist-led war for national liberation set in motion a dangerous spiral of escalation. The renewal of serious fighting panicked Washington into supplying Diem with billions of dollars and a growing corps of American advisers—nine hundred by 1960. In response, Hanoi aided the insurgents, training recruits in the North. Then, after a five-year plan had made their country the most heavily industrialized state in Southeast Asia by 1959, the North Vietnamese shipped large amounts of war material south along the Ho Chi Minh Trail. Although this primitive line of communications depended as much on human backs as on gasoline engines, it permitted the NLF to make great progress despite America's reinforcements. Shielded behind popular resentments, raiders could strike almost anywhere. Their opponents could only counter by garrisoning the entire country. Thus the cycle of Saigon corruption and communist rebellion led to American reinforcement and then to more aid from Hanoi.

Washington tried to break this chain by asking Diem to reform his regime. But the premier cared little about generating local popularity as long as he could rely on Americans to support him. Despite American dissatisfaction with Diem, he seemed the only practical alternative to the NLF. The more isolated Diem became, the more American support he needed; yet the more aid he received, the more corrupt and unpopular he became. Americans began to experience, if only dimly to perceive, the frustration and the long-run dangers of building foreign alliances on client relationships.

Partly because of larger problems elsewhere, the Republicans avoided final answers in their Vietnamese policy. The secretary of state blurted out during a press conference that "the free world would intervene in Indochina rather than let the situation deteriorate." Once involved, Dulles thought, American's prestige required victory. But the president demurred. A charter member of the Never Again Club—a group of generals who, after their experiences in Korea, resolutely opposed another land war in Asia—Eisenhower flatly contradicted his chief adviser on foreign affairs. "I can conceive of no greater tragedy," he said "than for the United States to become engaged in all-out war in Indochina."

Intervention: Iran, Guatemala, Lebanon, Cuba

Vietnam was only one area of concern in America's global anticommunist crusade. In the Middle East and Latin America, as in Southeast Asia, the decline of European dominance and the rise of local nationalism forced the United States into difficult policy decisions. In these areas, Eisenhower's extensive new foreign policy apparatus—encompassing a mix of economic pressure and covert action as well as well as conventional military strength—was tested and refined.

In Iran, American economic interests had always been small; Britain held tightly to its petroleum monopoly in that oil-rich land. But in 1951 Iranian Prime Minister Mohammed Mossadegh nationalized Britain's Anglo-Iranian Oil Company. The State Department feared that the precedent of nationalization might ultimately affect America's own holdings in Saudi Arabia or elsewhere and thereby damage the free world economy. The CIA, which had previously received explicit orders to make the protection of American-owned supplies of raw materials one of its prime duties, went to work organizing and financing opposition to Mossadegh. Kermit Roosevelt, the grand-nephew of Theodore, orchestrated one of the CIA's most stunning "successes." In a swift operation in 1953, CIA agents brought crowds into the streets, forced Mossadegh out of office, and reinstalled their friend Shah Reza Pahlevi. Under the terms of a renegotiated oil contract American companies came out holding 40 percent of the Iranian oil concession previously held by British Petroleum, and the shah launched a "modernization" program closely wedded to American corporate interests.

Events in Iran enabled the major oil companies to convince the Eisenhower administration to drop a large antitrust suit against them. In 1953 Eisenhower told his attorney general that because the giant oil companies supplied an essential commodity to the free world, the enforcement of antitrust laws "may be deemed secondary to the national security interest." Iran's attempted nationalization thus proved timely and doubly beneficial to the American-dominated international oil cartel, a cartel that—at that time— controlled the world price of oil.

Success in Iran encouraged the Eisenhower administration to expand its use of the CIA. Headed by John Foster Dulles's brother Allen, the CIA escalated the use of subversion as a tactic against foreign enemies. It became clear that Ike's New Look extended toward the Soviet Union but that in the Third World covert action seemed the best substitute for outright military involvement.

Guatemala loomed as the next test of what the CIA could accomplish with covert operations. Guatemalan President Jacobo Arbenz, who had been legally elected on a reform platform, challenged the United Fruit Company's long-standing dominance in his country by threatening to nationalize lands that the company had allowed to remain idle and unproductive. And as in Iran, American business interests and government policymakers easily confused nationalistic reform with communism. Dulles, himself closely connected with the fruit company, saw Guatemala as one more battle in the global struggle to contain communism; and Eisenhower, who knew little about Latin America, accepted Dulles's oversimplification and incorrectly perceived Arbenz as controlled by communists. Ike authorized and the CIA carried out a covert 1954 operation that included economic strangulation; psychological warfare; and the funding of a pro-U.S., conservative armed force to carry out a coup. Under these pressures the Arbenz government collapsed, and an oppressive dictatorship friendly to the U.S. government and to United Fruit entrenched itself.

However, U.S.-backed repression only aggravated social hatreds in Guatemala and elsewhere. During Richard Nixon's goodwill tour of Latin America in 1958, for example, thousands of Venezuelans mobbed the vice-president's car in Caracas, upsetting Cadillac limousines and illusions of inter-American friendship. In response, Eisenhower supported creation of the Inter-American Development Bank, and the State Department stopped awarding medals to dictator allies and shifted its praises to such liberal reformers as Venezuela's Rómulo Betancourt. But only the image changed. American economic policies and military aid continued, in the name of anticommunism, to strengthen oligarchs and their military allies against rising popular demands for economic and political reforms.

As another part of its effort to contain communist influence, the Eisenhower administration tried to frame a general doctrine that would extend American security interests into the Middle East, a region still reeling from the aftershocks of the Suez crisis and the Iranian coup. After weeks of dickering during the spring of 1957, Congress authorized the president to defend countries in the Middle East "against overt armed aggression from any nation controlled by international communism." This new Eisenhower Doctrine hardly fit with the political realities of the area, in which older imperial tensions, regional and religious distrust, and the rise of fervent nationalism shaped events more than did superpower contests. But the Eisenhower Doctrine, like the Truman Doctrine before it, forced complex events into simple molds and made it easy to label any local challenge to American interests as communist aggression.

During the summer of 1958, when rioting broke out in the small country of Lebanon, the doctrine had its first test. Lebanon's government blamed the riots on saboteurs from the newly organized United Arab Republic (Egypt and Syria), but animosity between Christian and Moslem, city and countryside, Nasserites and moderates had long before turned the tiny land into a tinderbox. After nationalists in Iraq murdered King Faisal and his premier, Nuri el-Said. Iraq's new anti-Western leaders renounced ties with Washington and made overtures to the UAR. As violence in the Middle East accelerated, the established elements in Lebanon and Jordan asked the United States and Britain to stabilize the situation. Both powers quickly complied, anxious to check Nasserism and protect their dangerously exposed oil pipelines. Over 14,000 marines eventually waded ashore on Lebanese beaches in an intervention notable for its bloodlessness and short-range success. American troops set up a new, strongly anti-Nasser government in Beirut, and in Jordan the British restored King Hussein's control over Jordan's army.

Despite its apparent success, the Anglo-American intrusion provoked new fears of Western imperialism. The Eisenhower Doctrine may ultimately have pushed some Arab nationalists toward Moscow. Other Arabs began to turn away from the United States, not because they were procommunist, but because they suspected American motives.

American policy did not contain revolution everywhere. In fact, a leftist revolt succeeded in a place long considered a secure outpost of America's informal empire—Cuba. In 1959 a guerrilla leader, Fidel Castro, converted his mountaintop rebellion into a social revolution that not only deposed Cuba's dictator, Fulgencio Batista, but also ended the island's dependence on the United States. The Cuban revolution at first attracted sympathy from many Americans. The rich sugar crop had benefited foreigners and Cuba's upper class, whereas the working population had suffered low wages and miserable living conditions. Batista's regime had grown notoriously corrupt. The prospect of honest government, social justice, and land redistribution provided support for the bearded, thirty-two-year-old Castro, like Nasser a charismatic leader. Initially welcomed by many Americans as an alternative to the repressive Batista, Castro soon encountered hostility as he tried to reduce his country's economic dependence on the United States. After a disagreement with some American companies, Castro nationalized their holdings; Eisenhower retaliated by curtailing the amount of Cuban sugar the United States would import; Castro stepped up nationalization and turned toward the Soviet Union for aid. By the time the spiral of deteriorating relations ended, Castro had nationalized over a billion dollars worth of Yankee assets, taken deadly reprisals against thousands as "enemies of the people," and frightened most of the Cuban upper-middle class into exile in Florida. During a visit to the United States, Castro appealed to America's racial minorities to follow his example. Later he joined hands with Khrushchev at the United Nations and declared himself a communist.

The Eisenhower administration moved methodically to drive Castro from power. Eisenhower ended American imports of Cuban sugar, which had maintained the island's prices above world market levels. Under great pressure from Washington, the Organization of American States expelled Cuba, thus cutting off all aid to Castro's regime from the OAS. These heavy-handed measures only forced Castro further to rely on the Soviets. Anxious to take advantage of America's lost position and, no doubt, to check domestic critics, Khrushchev bought up Cuba's sugar crop in 1960 at an inflated price. CIA operatives began training a Cuban invasion force in Guatemala and plotting various kinds of sabotage against Castro's regime, but threats of American intervention only justified a further swing to the left by Castro. Attempted containment in the Caribbean, no less than in the Middle East, produced nationalist reactions often hostile to American goals.

REEVALUATION

On October 4, 1957, the Soviet Union orbited the first space satellite, *Sputnik I;* a month later *Sputnik II,* which weighed over 1,300 pounds and carried a live dog, spent several days in space. The accuracy and large payload of the Russian rockets caused alarm throughout America because of the potential military implications. Most high officials recognized that America's manned bombers far outclassed Soviet defense systems. Though spectacular, Sputnik in no concrete way threatened the safety of the United States. Still, it proved to be a powerful symbol: Coming amid a recession, it ended America's easy confidence in its technological ascendance and created new, often exaggerated fears of Soviet strength.

A sense of vulnerability pervaded American life. The *Sputnik* satellites frightened the Pentagon into deploying intermediate-range rockets in Britain, Turkey, and Italy. The Defense Department also channeled more and more money into research-and-development programs. Long restive about New Look economies, some military leaders publicly worried about the emphasis on bombers and carrier-based fighters. General Maxwell Taylor, army chief of staff, argued for "armament in depth" so that the United States could fight "low-level, conventional battles" if nuclear stalemate produced "brushfire wars on the periphery of the free world." Sensing a political advantage, many liberal Democrats saw more military spending as a means to stimulate the postwar economy. Defense intellectuals, gathered into research institutes by governments and universities, explained that atomic armaments required constant technological innovation to keep pace with scientific discoveries. The Korean War had spawned an industry dependent on arms contracts. Research-and-development money produced ever-more complicated weapons. Powerful interests in such politically important areas as Long Island, Texas, and Southern California pressed to increase lucrative defense production.

This combination of American generals, Democratic politicians, defense intellectuals, and enterprising business leaders coalesced into a powerful group that lobbied for more and more armaments. Eisenhower's immense prestige and his skepticism about Pentagon claims temporarily quieted the clamor. But opponents of the New Look wondered whether Eisenhower's economies had not misled the country. Gradually, the idea spread that the United States suffered a missile gap vis-à-vis the Soviet Union, a false analysis that John F. Kennedy nonetheless used as an election slogan against the Republicans in the election of 1960.

Eisenhower left the presidency a discouraged man. He confided to Kennedy that "foreign affairs are in a mess" and warned the American people of "a burgeoning military-industrial complex." Eisenhower tried to be cost-conscious and to pursue peace, but he also launched an open-ended ideological crusade to refashion the world into a mold compatible with U.S. interests and greatly expanded the government's foreign-policy capabilities and techniques.

The more the Republicans tried to control world events during the 1950s, the more events seemed out of control. Massive retaliation did not guarantee security but instead fueled an arm's race. A chain of anticommunist military alliances, the proliferation of bases abroad, and the growing role of the CIA entangled the United States in local complexities around the globe. Prosperity and some mellowing in the Soviet Union diverted Western Europeans from the cold war and slowly ended their dependence on Washington. The expansive rhetoric and international complexities of the 1950s heightened Americans' insecurities and set the stage for burgeoning defense spending and even more ambitious cold war crusading in the early 1960s.

SUGGESTIONS FOR FURTHER READING

Robert Divine, *Eisenhower and the Cold War* (1981), and Blanche Wiessen Cook, *The Declassified Eisenhower* (1981), offer differing interpretations. See also Joann P. Kreig, ed., *Dwight D. Eisenhower: Soldier, President and Statesman* (1987), and H. W. Brands, *Cold Warriors: Eisenhower's Generation and American Foreign Policy* (1988).

The emphasis on covert operations may be seen in several general studies of the CIA: John Ranelagh, *The Agency* (1986); John Prados, *Presidents' Secret Wars* (1986); William Blum, *The CIA: A Forgotten History* (1986); Robin Winks, *Cloak and Gown: Scholars in the American Secret War, 1939–1961* (1987); Rhodi Jeffreys-Jones, *The CIA and American Democracy* (1989); and Loch K. Johnson, *America's Secret Power: The CIA in a Democratic Society* (1989).

More specialized works on the Eisenhower era include Douglas Kinnard, *President Eisenhower and Strategy Management: A Study in Defense Politics* (1977); Robert Divine, *Blowing in the Wind: The Nuclear Test-Ban Debate* (1978); Stephen Ambrose, *Ike's Spies* (1981); Stephen Schlesinger and Steven Kinzer, *Bitter Fruit* (1981); Richard H. Immerman, *The CIA in Guatemala* (1982); Burton F. Kaufman, *Trade and Aid: Eisenhower's Foreign Economic Policy* (1982); Richard E. Welch, Jr., *Response to Revolution: The United States and the Cuban Revolution,*

1959–1961 (1985); Michael R. Beschloss, *Mayday: Eisenhower, Khrushchev, and the U-2 Affair* (1986); Richard A. Melanson and David Mayers, eds., *Reevaluating Eisenhower: American Foreign Policy in the Fifties* (1987); Stephen G. Rabe, *Eisenhower and Latin America: The Foreign Policy of Anticommunism* (1988); Richard G. Hewlett and Jack M. Holl, *Atoms for Peace and War, 1953–1961: Eisenhower and the Atomic Energy Commission* (1989); William Rogers Louis, ed., *Suez, 1956: The Crisis and Its Consequences* (1989); James Arnold, *The First Domino: Eisenhower, the Military, and America's Intervention in Vietnam* (1991); Diane B. Kunz, *The Economic Diplomacy of the Suez Crisis* (1991); David W. Lesch, *Syria and the United States: Eisenhower's Cold War Policy in the Middle East* (1993); Isaac Alteras, *Eisenhower and Israel* (1993); Robert A. Divine, *The Sputnik Challenge* (1993); and Thomas G. Paterson, *Contesting Castro* (1994).

On Eisenhower's controversial secretary of state, see Townshend Hoopes, *The Devil and John Foster Dulles* (1973); Ronald Pruessen, *John Foster Dulles* (1982); Mark Toulouse, *The Transformation of John Foster Dulles* (1985); and Richard Immerman, ed., *John Foster Dulles and the Diplomacy of the Cold War* (1989).

On the deepening U.S. involvement in Vietnam during the 1950s, see the opening chapters of George Herring, *America's Longest War* (1986); Andrew J. Rotter, *The Path to Vietnam* (1987); Lloyd C. Gardner, *Approaching Vietnam: From World War II Through Dien Bien Phu* (1988); and Melanie Billings-Yun, *Decision Against War: Eisenhower and Dien Bien Phu* (1988). For works on the Korean War, see the Suggestions for Further Reading at the end of Chapter One.

The 1950s were a period of intense debate over the direction of U.S. foreign policy. Some of the contemporary viewpoints may be found in Henry Kissinger, *Nuclear Weapons and Foreign Policy* (1957); Walt W. Rostow, *The United States in the World Arena* (1960); Maxwell Taylor, *An Uncertain Trumpet* (1960); and Robert Strausz-Hupe et al., *Protracted Conflict* (1961).

Memoirs include George B. Kistiakowsky, *A Scientist at the White House* (1976); Henry Cabot Lodge, Jr., *As It Was* (1976); and George F. Kennan, *Sketches from a Life* (1989).

5

The Liberal Promise: JFK and LBJ

THE PRESIDENT WE HARDLY KNEW

A 1973 best-seller by one of John F. Kennedy's former aides lamented, *Johnny We Hardly Knew Ye.* The title was revealing. The Kennedy administration was always shrouded in legend, and books by Kennedy's associates helped the myths grow larger. Only recently have historians begun to peek through the clouds of adulation that surrounded the thirty-fifth president.

Few fathers groom their children to be president, but wealthy Joseph P. Kennedy wanted one of his sons to gain the nation's highest office. When his oldest boy died during World War II, his other war-hero son picked up the family colors. John Kennedy had attended an elite prep school and then graduated from Harvard, all while refining his social graces and developing a tough-minded view of public affairs. He displayed an intolerance for those who did not share his pragmatic approach. People who could not say what they had to say quickly, who moralized or digressed, irritated John Kennedy. How could people who took so long to make up their minds do great things? Kennedy surrounded himself with bright, ambitious young people who shared his distaste for sentimentality. The public Kennedy—idealistic, inspirational, and sometimes emotional—was very different from the calculating, private politician from Boston.

Kennedy's narrow victory over Richard Nixon in 1960 capped a rather unimpressive political career. In 1946 JFK won election to the House of Representatives and six years later ousted a distinguished scion of the Boston aristocracy, Henry Cabot Lodge, Jr., from the U.S. Senate. Kennedy considered the slow-moving, tradition-bound Senate undemanding and often boring. He usually supported generous expenditures for social-welfare programs and championed a strong anticommunist foreign policy, but he sponsored no important legislative measures. During these years he married Jacqueline Bouvier, who proved to be an important political asset, and he wrote a prize-winning book—*Profiles in Courage*. Between 1956 and 1960 Kennedy took full advantage of the new age of jet travel, courting the Democratic party hierarchy and accumulating political debts that he could cash in during the 1960 presidential campaign. He and his close associates (the Irish mafia, some called them) put together a smooth-running organization that included pollster Louis Harris, speech writer Theodore Sorensen, the two younger Kennedy brothers, and a coterie of Harvard intellectuals.

The Election of 1960

The energetic Kennedy dominated the presidential campaign of 1960. As a politician he did few new things; he simply did the old ones better than other candidates. His speeches covered the standard postwar themes—the cold war with the Soviet Union, economic growth at home, and sacrifice for country—but they were cleverly phrased and, after some speaking lessons, effectively delivered. Kennedy's operatives employed old-fashioned arm twisting, and they generally knew just how much leverage to use and exactly where to apply it. Unlike Adlai Stevenson, who had let the Democratic convention choose his running mate in 1956, JFK made a highly political choice: Senate Majority Leader Lyndon Baines Johnson of Texas. Even Kennedy's much-discussed charisma was not a new phenomenon; throughout the 1950s political observers had analyzed the charisma of Dwight Eisenhower. But Kennedy's most distinctive qualities—his youth, good looks, and energy—did contrast his political image with that of the much older, more deliberate Eisenhower.

The Republican candidate, Eisenhower's vice-president Richard Nixon, counterposed his supposed maturity and experience against Kennedy's rather insubstantial political record. The tactic backfired in the widely heralded TV debates: Television made the sharp-featured Nixon appear old and tired, whereas it accentuated Kennedy's best qualities. The harsh lights highlighted Nixon's famous five o'clock shadow, reminding viewers of "Tricky Dick," "the man you wouldn't buy a used car from." Most important, Kennedy's confident manner during the first debate undercut Nixon's claim about his opponent's immaturity. And though Nixon scrupulously avoided any hint of anti-Catholicism during the campaign, some of his supporters did not. Catholic voters at that time tended to be Democrats anyway, and JFK piled up large Catholic majorities in several key states. The election of 1960 was still very close: Kennedy won by only 120,000 popular votes, and small shifts in several large states would have made Nixon president. The unexpectedly narrow victory probably increased Kennedy's political caution.

Camelot: The New Frontier

Although Kennedy could hardly claim a popular mandate, his publicists quickly built an imposing image for his administration—the New Frontier, the energetic successor to the New Deal and the Fair Deal. First, JFK assembled his version of Franklin Roosevelt's brain trust. He appointed his brother and campaign manager, Robert Kennedy, attorney general; Robert McNamara, president of Ford Motor Company, became secretary of defense; Harvard's McGeorge Bundy assumed the important role of national security adviser to the president; and Dean Rusk, head of the Ford Foundation, got the coveted position of secretary of state. Even the secondary jobs claimed top individuals. (Henry Kissinger found himself outgunned in such fierce competition and took over Bundy's courses at Harvard, awaiting an administration that would better appreciate his talents.) Vice-President Johnson left the first cabinet meeting dazzled by the intellect that Kennedy had assembled. "You should have seen all those men," he told his old political mentor, House Speaker Sam Rayburn. "Well, Lyndon, you may be right and they may be every bit as intelligent as you say," replied Rayburn, "but I'd feel a whole lot better about them if just one of them had run for sheriff once."

The Kennedy White House advertised itself as a center of art and culture. Jacqueline Kennedy, a well-educated woman who spoke several languages, became the special guardian of culture. She invited artists such as cellist Pablo Casals to perform at the White House, redecorated the old mansion, and then conducted a tour of it for millions of TV viewers. The Kennedy parties were lavish productions in the grand style; I. F. Stone, the dissenting journalist, complained that the atmosphere resembled that of "a reigning monarch's court." Such a comparison probably did not disturb Kennedyphiles. Many of the president's followers reveled in the reputation of the Kennedy White House as a modern-day Camelot.

In addition to intellect and style, the New Frontier emphasized toughness. John Kennedy's inaugural address boasted that he and his advisers were all young men "born in this century, tempered by war, disciplined by a hard and bitter peace." Facing the challenges of a dangerous world, they could not afford to appear soft. In defending his space program, for example, JFK bragged that Americans would accept the challenges of space "not because they are easy but because they are hard." The Kennedy team displayed its toughness during impromptu touch football games; here the president's brother Robert gained a reputation as a hard-nosed scrapper who had no room for losers. After Floyd Patterson lost his heavyweight boxing title, the attorney general quickly removed the ex-champ's picture from his office.

All the Kennedy people bragged of their ability to handle any foreign or domestic crisis, and they seemed almost anxious to find one. In 1962 Kennedy massed the full power of the national government to combat a price increase by U.S. Steel and several other large firms. JFK denounced the companies as unpatriotic, contrasting their actions with the sacrifices of military officers who were already dying in Vietnam and of reservists who had been called up to meet a feared confrontation with the Soviet Union in Berlin. The president coupled his verbal assaults with a massive legal offensive. The Justice Department sought evidence of price fixing, FBI agents started to investigate possible illegal activities by steel corporations, the Federal Trade Commission threatened to look into the same questions, and administration sources even hinted

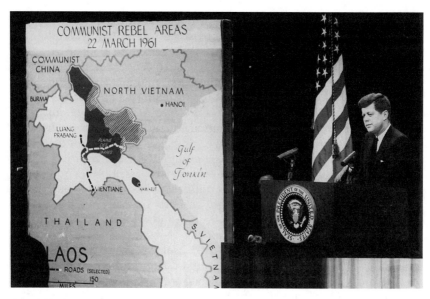

John F. Kennedy's Press Conference, 1961. Breaking with the practice of his predecessors, JFK held frequent press conferences. But he never completely revealed his administration's policies in Indo-China. *Source:* National Archives.

at antitrust actions to break up the steel giants. At the same time, the Defense Department refused to buy from companies that raised prices, and Kennedy aides pressured corporate friends to resist the lead of U.S. Steel. Confronted by this counterattack, Big Steel retreated and rolled back prices. Throughout the short skirmish the president viewed the controversy as an extension of foreign affairs, stating that price increases threatened national security. It was the type of problem, he claimed, that required crisis management.

The president's critics viewed the situation differently. Business representatives predictably denounced Kennedy for using "police state" tactics, but even some foes of large corporations expressed concern. A young law professor, Charles Reich (who would later gain fame as author of *The Greening of America*), argued that it was "dangerously wrong for an angry president to loose his terrible arsenal of power for the purposes of intimidation and coercing private companies and citizens." Other observers contended that Kennedy's actions reflected a dangerous crisis mentality and indicated a lack of consistent domestic policies. Within a year the steel firms raised prices twice, and the Kennedy administration did nothing.

Although JFK was more interested in foreign policy than in domestic affairs, he announced general goals for his New Frontier at home. The new Democratic administration revived many of Harry Truman's old Fair Deal proposals: federal aid to education, a national health program, and expansion of other welfare-state spending programs. Kennedy never saw educational or health programs or Medicare pass Congress, but he could take some credit for several less spectacular measures. Congress extended Social Security coverage to more American workers, covered more people by federal wage standards, raised the minimum wage to $1.25 an hour, appropriated nearly $5 billion for public housing, established the manpower training program, and passed an area redevelopment act for West Virginia and other impoverished areas in Appalachia. These measures reflected JFK's preference for moderate, gradual reforms and his political caution.

Kennedy also helped revive activism related to women's rights by appointing a Presidential Commission on the Status of Women, headed by Eleanor Roosevelt. The commission's report, issued in 1963, documented the discrimination in employment, the legal inequality, and the paucity of social services such as child care that kept women in subordinate status. The resultant Equal Pay Act of 1963 made it illegal for employers to compensate men and women at different rates of pay for the same job. Although this legislation did not significantly raise the economic status of working women—most of whom were employed in job categories that included few men—the issue of economic inequality had at least been made a public issue. The commission's work spurred state governments to undertake similar studies and helped galvanize a new generation of activists on behalf of women's rights.

In addition to updating the Fair Deal's social-welfare programs, the Kennedy administration tried to redefine the techniques of Truman's liberal economists. In his first state-of-the-union address, JFK promised that the sluggish economy would soon show both a prompt recovery and long-range growth. Kennedy, of course, blamed the country's economic problems on the Eisenhower administration. The GNP had risen too slowly during the late 1950s, whereas the unemployment rate had climbed to around 6 percent. Although Kennedy shared Eisenhower's limited background in economics— JFK had received a C in his introductory economics course at Harvard—he gathered a distinguished group of economic advisers, including John Kenneth Galbraith of Harvard and Walter Heller of the University of Minnesota. According to these advocates of the "new economics," the national government could use its power over federal expenditures and its controls over monetary policy to promote economic growth and to fine-tune the economy.

The Kennedy administration adopted a number of strategies for stimulating economic growth and creating new jobs. Increased government spending pumped vital funds into the economy and brightened the general economic picture. In 1962 the White House persuaded Congress to give businesses a 7 percent tax credit for investments in new machinery and plants. At the same time, the administration granted one of business's key requests—the readjustment of depreciation schedules for corporate taxes. This action encouraged purchases of new equipment by allowing businesses to write off assets more quickly. Taken together, the investment tax credit and the revised depreciation schedules reduced business taxes and theoretically increased corporate spending by about $2.5 billion; the total tax cut amounted to almost 12 percent.

Although the economy picked up considerably, many liberal economists called for further steps to boost production and employment. John Kenneth

Galbraith, who had become ambassador to India, continued to urge massive government expenditures for social-welfare programs. Kennedy rejected this approach but did consider further tax cuts. A cut in tax revenues would increase the federal deficit; it would also, however, expand purchasing power for both consumers and businesses. Heller, who became head of the Council of Economic Advisers, and Paul Samuelson, an influential economist at MIT (Massachusetts Institute of Technology), were among those who urged an immediate tax reduction to ward off a possible recession. But advocates of a balanced federal budget, particularly Treasury Secretary C. Douglas Dillon and Federal Reserve Chairman William McChesney Martin, rejected this example of the new economics, and Kennedy finally shelved the proposal for 1962. The following year, however, the administration unveiled a comprehensive revenue bill that did include a $10 billion tax cut and tax reforms.

Kennedy's carefully calculated approach to social and economic problems reflected his basic assumptions about the new role of liberal government. The "old sweeping issues have largely disappeared," he told Yale's graduating class in 1962. Basic domestic problems were now "more subtle and less simple": how to manage a complex economy; how to ensure increasing productivity and rising prosperity for all citizens. The "sophisticated and technical questions involved in keeping a great economic machinery moving ahead" required "technical answers—not political answers." Rational bureaucrats, the cool technicians who could manage complex institutions, held the keys to effective government. Although his brief tenure in office tempered some of his early optimism, John Kennedy died confident that his view of government remained correct and that Camelot's bright young people could solve most problems.

Assassination

On November 22, 1963, the presidential motorcade was winding its way past unexpectedly friendly crowds in Dallas when a volley of shots—some claimed three, others four or five—raked Kennedy's open-topped limousine. Texas Governor John Connally was seriously wounded, and one shot ripped away the top of Kennedy's head. Within an hour doctors at Parkland Hospital pronounced the president dead; the thousand days of Camelot were over. Aboard *Air Force One*, Vice-President Lyndon Baines Johnson took the oath of office as the new chief executive.

News of the president's death stunned the nation. For two days people watched an elaborate televised memorial. Pictures of Kennedy's coffin, his riderless horse, and his grieving family clashed with scenes from Kennedy's past. Images of a vibrant JFK—sailing off Cape Cod, laughing with his children, or facing down the Russians—made his death seem even more tragic. The Kennedy mystique grew.

The television spectacle also began to raise doubts about the cause of death. Within hours after the assassination, Dallas police officials announced the capture of Lee Harvey Oswald. A former marine who had lived in the Soviet Union for a short time, Oswald steadfastly proclaimed his innocence. On Sunday, November 24, while Dallas police were transferring Oswald to a new jail, millions of TV viewers witnessed the assassination of Kennedy's alleged assassin. A local nightclub operator with ties to organized crime, Jack Ruby, fatally shot Oswald at close range in the Dallas police station.

Oswald's bizarre death raised further doubts about his guilt. Was he part of a larger conspiracy? Was Kennedy's death somehow tied to pro- or anti-Castro forces? Was Ruby a hit man sent to silence Oswald? Were the Dallas police or the CIA or the FBI part of some plot? Wanting to squelch such rumors quickly, President Johnson persuaded Chief Justice Earl Warren to head an official inquiry. After a ten-month investigation, the Warren Commission named Oswald the lone assassin and rejected evidence of any broader plot. Conspiracy buffs, however, were already offering an amazing variety of scenarios, and the Warren Commission Report merely gave them twenty-six volumes of evidence to piece through. More sober critics of the commission pointed out serious flaws in the hastily researched and sloppily documented report. Despite an intensive "sell" campaign conducted by the Johnson administration and the mass media, many Americans dismissed the Warren Commission's version of what had happened in Dallas. Proponents of a conspiracy theory received some vindication when, in 1979, a special committee of the House of Representatives concluded, on the basis of new evidence, that JFK had "probably" fallen victim to some kind of plot, possibly involving organized crime figures. But the committee could offer little evidence about the details of the alleged conspiracy.

The controversy over Kennedy's death, which never receded from popular memory, revived following the release of Oliver Stone's *JFK* in 1991. Recounting the story of Jim Garrison, who had tried unsuccessfully to prosecute an alleged conspiracy while a district attorney in New Orleans during the mid-1960s, Stone's docudrama merged contemporary film footage, including Abraham Zapruda's famous home movie of Kennedy's motorcade encountering a hail of gunfire, with Hollywood recreations of events of November 22, 1963. Moreover, *JFK* supplemented the cast of bizarre characters who had become involved in Garrison's failed prosecution with a fictional governmental official who claimed that the responsibility for Kennedy's assassination extended into the highest levels of power in the government. Although defenders of the Warren Commission's findings tried to refurbish the argument for a lone assassin, often resorting to computer-generated recreations of Kennedy's final moments in Dallas, Stone's film deepened skepticism about the alleged role of Lee Harvey Oswald. More than twenty-five years after Kennedy's death, critics of the Warren Commission charged, too much evidence remained hidden from independent scrutiny. As a result, governmental agencies, including the CIA, promised to speed the process of declassifying secret documents, and a blue-ribbon commission was charged with overseeing the release of evidence about the death of John F. Kennedy.

THE GREAT SOCIETY

LBJ

When in 1901 Teddy Roosevelt succeeded an earlier slain president, William McKinley, a conservative Republican expressed fears about "that damn cowboy"; sixty-two years later, many liberal Democrats felt much the same way about Lyndon Baines Johnson. Except for being a rich Democrat, LBJ had little in common with the cool, urbane Kennedy. Unlike JFK, Johnson loved the Senate, and during the 1950s he had dominated that body as its majority leader. Kennedy always remembered how, as a senator, he had to beg Lyndon Johnson for favors. But despite years in Washington, Johnson never lost the earthy exuberance of "a good old boy from the ranch." (In his early White House days, Johnson showed a homemade film of deer mating and contributed his own ribald sound track.) A self-made entrepreneur, Johnson often was haunted by the hint of scandal. Critics snickered about "landslide Lyndon's" suspicious eighty-six-vote triumph in the 1948 senatorial primary, about his close association with convicted influence peddler Bobby Baker, and about his questionable financial dealings throughout the Southwest. Johnson came to Washington as an ambitious young politician attracted to Roosevelt's New Deal; he left as a former president and a multimillionaire. To some people LBJ looked too much like Jay Gatsby in a Stetson hat.

Johnson constantly worried about his public image. People would not give him "a fair shake as president," he often complained, "because I am a southerner." But Johnson realized that his problems lay deeper. "Why don't people like me?" he asked visitors to the White House. One elderly caller, who felt that his advanced years protected him, replied honestly: "Because, Mr. President, you are not a very likeable man." Defensive about his provincial roots in southwest Texas and perhaps still burdened by the conflicting childhood demands of his tough, hard-drinking father and his refined, intellectual mother, Johnson seemed to require constant reassurance. He also demanded unswerving loyalty from his subordinates. Among those who worked for Johnson, no one wanted to be the bearer of bad news. He often flew into sudden rages, publicly berating staff members or arbitrarily summoning them at all hours of the night. He appeared to need the LBJ brand on everything. (His wife inherited the name Lady Bird, but LBJ christened his daughters Lynda Bird and Lucy Baines and even called his dog Little Beagle.) White House employees whom he suspected of disloyalty dropped from favor, and only a few aides, such as Walt Rostow and Dean Rusk, stayed until the end of Johnson's presidency. A critical reporter might receive the "Johnson treatment"—a private audience during which Johnson conducted a nonstop monologue on his own glories. A big man, the president liked to get close to his listeners, overwhelming them by sheer size.

Johnson smoothly handled the transition from the Kennedy administration, but after 1964 he watched his popularity decline steadily. He often blamed the media for what became known as his "credibility gap." Stories about Johnson's pettiness, vanity, and duplicity colored people's perception of him. Most reporters had genuinely liked Kennedy and had sometimes pigeonholed unfavorable stories about his policies and personal life. But Johnson, like Richard Nixon after him, considered himself the target of unfair reporting by journalists who compared Johnson unfavorably with the still untarnished image of JFK as well as with the vigorous reality of the Kennedy family. John Kennedy's youngest brother, Edward, represented Massachusetts in the Senate, and in 1964 Robert Kennedy overcame charges of being a carpetbagger to win election to the Senate from New York. The Kennedys only thinly veiled their distaste for Johnson, and many reporters expressed more sympathy for Camelot-in-exile—the intellectuals and politicians who swarmed around Bobby's home at Hickory Hill and the Kennedy family compound on Cape Cod—than for Johnson's entourage.

Toward the end of his presidency, as controversy over the Vietnam War obsessed both the president and the press, many people forgot Johnson's domestic accomplishments and positive qualities. He could take much credit for the Great Society legislation passed between 1964 and 1968, and even most critics conceded his sincere commitment to social and racial justice. For all his faults, Johnson was an intelligent, complex, sensitive person. The American people, particularly the opinion-making elites, probably misunderstood Johnson as much as he misunderstood them. He was, according to one observer of his last years, a tortured man who was torn between his fervent, populist hopes and his meaner, less noble impulses.

The Johnson Program

Lyndon Johnson moved to fulfill JFK's promise of promoting rapid economic growth. Aided by a reduction in taxes (the Tax Act of 1964, of course, was originally a Kennedy proposal) and by increased federal spending (particularly for the expanding war in Southeast Asia), the economy built on gains begun under Kennedy. Between 1960 and 1964 the gross national product increased by 24 percent while corporate profits went up by 57 percent; the next year the GNP climbed by almost 7 percent and corporate profits by 20 percent; and by 1965 the nation reached what most economists considered full employment, an unemployment rate less than 4 percent. The boom lasted throughout Johnson's second term: Unemployment never exceeded 4 percent, and the GNP expanded at a rate of almost 5 percent a year. The median family income, measured in constant dollars, increased from $8,543 in 1963 to $10,768 in 1969.

Not everyone was impressed by the Kennedy-Johnson boom. Some economists warned that the expansion was too rapid and that the Johnson administration was ignoring the threat of inflation. Others argued that LBJ's economic wizardry was largely a fraud. Truman's old economic adviser Leon Keyserling contended that the Tax Act of 1964, which came out of Congress without most of its original reforms, primarily assisted the wealthy. According to Keyserling's calculations, the average taxpayer in the $10,000 income bracket received only a 3.5 percent increase in disposable income; in contrast, the taxpayer who earned $100,000 enjoyed a boost of 16.5 percent; and the very wealthy, those in the $200,000 category, got a 31.1 percent windfall. Keyserling charged that the nation's basic economic problem remained an inequitable distribution of income. Radical economists concurred. Citing the tremendous rise in corporate profits during the Kennedy-Johnson years, they noted that large corporations were the primary beneficiaries of the high-growth policies of the new economics.

Lyndon Johnson, who sincerely wanted to be "president of all the people," saw the situation differently. Of course, large businesses would benefit from economic expansion, but so would middle-income workers and budding entrepreneurs. Moreover, galloping prosperity enabled the country to advance beyond the limited goals of Truman and Kennedy and extend greater assistance to the very poor in the best LBJ style—with great breast-beating and with promises of much government money. Buoyed by his early successes and the economic boom, LBJ claimed "a broad, deep and genuine consensus among most groups within our diverse society" on behalf of his programs.

If only everyone would "sit down and reason together," they could realize the Great Society. Speaking in the spring of 1964 before an outdoor crowd of almost 100,000 people, LBJ heralded the coming of a society "where the meaning of our lives matches the marvelous products of our labor . . . a place where men are more concerned with the quality of their goals than the quantity of their goods." Even Kennedy's speechwriters might have blushed at this rhetoric, but JFK could never approach the carload of legislative measures that LBJ rolled through Congress in 1964 and 1965.

In the wake of Kennedy's death and LBJ's own landslide triumph over Republican Barry Goldwater in 1964, Johnson broke a congressional stalemate that dated back many years. Never in recent memory had Congress done so much so quickly. When Johnson left Washington in 1969 his cabinet gave him a plaque commemorating the more than two hundred "landmark laws" passed during his administration. During LBJ's first full year as president, Congress approved the Tax Act of 1964, a new civil rights law, federally sponsored recreation programs, funds for urban mass transit, and the Economic Opportunity Act (the measure that signaled the beginning of Johnson's War on Poverty). And this was merely the preclude to the Great Society programs that Johnson took to the nation in the 1964 presidential race.

The Johnson Landslide

The Republicans graciously handed Johnson the 1964 election. Militant conservatives, most of whom lived in the rim states from southern California to Florida or in isolated enclaves in the Middle West, gained control of the GOP. Wanting to offer the nation "a choice, not an echo," they nominated Senator Barry Goldwater of Arizona for president. The hero of militant conservatives, Goldwater soon acquired a reputation among liberals and moderates as an injudicious extremist. During a series of bitter primary campaigns, some of his overzealous supporters reinforced this image by vehemently attacking more liberal Republicans, particularly New York's Nelson Rockefeller. When Rockefeller rose to address the GOP's 1964 convention, Goldwaterites in the galleries shouted him down. Goldwater's acceptance speech only increased doubts about his candidacy. "Extremism in the defense of liberty," he challenged his critics, "is no vice. . . . Moderation in the pursuit of justice is no virtue."

Goldwater ran squarely against Johnson's brand of liberalism. Ever since the New Deal, Republican candidates had ritualistically denounced the central government in Washington, but Goldwater really seemed to mean it. His strategists—highly disciplined professionals who had studied JFK's campaign techniques—hoped that a militantly conservative campaign would bring millions of alienated people to the polls and attract a backlash vote from whites who were frightened by the antidiscrimination movement. A Goldwater administration, the senator from Arizona appeared to say, would sweep away all the baneful welfare programs established since the New Deal: agricultural subsidies, prolabor union legislation, civil rights measures, and all the other "socialistic" laws. "I will give you back your freedom," he promised. On several occasions he even hinted at making Social Security voluntary, a position that Democrats falsely translated into the charge that Goldwater planned to abolish the entire system. At the same time, missile-rattling statements about taking care of the USSR and gaining a quick victory in Vietnam enabled Democrats to paint Goldwater as a trigger-happy Neanderthal.

With the moderate center of the electorate deserting the Republican party, Johnson and his running mate, Senator Hubert Humphrey of Minnesota, recorded a landslide victory. The Democratic presidential ticket gathered 61.3 percent of the popular ballots and the electoral votes of all but six states. At the same time, Democrats gained thirty-nine seats in the House of Representatives and more than five hundred new seats in state legislatures across the country. Johnson celebrated his "politics of consensus," and some nervous Republicans even feared that the "Goldwater caper" might destroy the GOP.

The Great Society and the War on Poverty

After his smashing victory, LBJ pushed more Great Society measures through the new Eighty-ninth Congress. Medicare and Medicaid programs fulfilled Harry Truman's goal of some type of government-sponsored health care for people over sixty-five and for those with low incomes. Two other long-debated measures, the Elementary and Secondary Education Act and the Higher Education Act, extended federal funds to schools at all levels of the educational hierarchy. The Voting Rights Act of 1965 eliminated barriers against black voters in the South: It suspended literacy tests and authorized federal inspectors in areas where the attorney general suspected chicanery in voting procedures. To deal with urban decay, Congress passed the Housing Act of 1965, which created the new Department of Housing and Urban Development

(HUD), and the Demonstration Cites and Metropolitan Development Act of 1966, which provided federal money for local model city projects. Prodded by advocates of automobile safety, Congress passed several bills dealing with highway and traffic safety. One measure, the Motor Vehicle Safety Act (1966), inaugurated federal safety standards for the auto industry and established a uniform grading system for tire manufacturers. As in the case of urban problems, Congress also created a new cabinet department—that of transportation—and gave its secretary the job of coordinating all the new programs. Finally, Congress passed a number of "minor" pieces of legislation such as a new immigration act, which admitted newcomers primarily on the basis of their economic skills rather than their national origin, and the Truth in Packaging Act, which provided consumers with some protection against deceptive advertising.

Most people readily accepted these programs, measures once labeled "socialistic," as integral parts of an expanded welfare state. Controversies still erupted over details—how much Medicare patients should pay from their own pockets, or how quickly automakers should comply with safety standards—but few people disagreed with the purpose of Great Society laws. Much to LBJ's displeasure the loudest complaints came from social activists who charged that the programs required only minimal sacrifices from wealthy, corporate groups and provided too little assistance for needy citizens. Consumer advocates, for example, claimed that auto manufacturers blocked truly effective safety laws while using the cost of minimal improvements as an excuse to raise their prices. And despite all Johnson's promises, basic needs such as better mass transportation systems and effective urban housing programs remained only dreams.

In addition to expanding the New Deal–Fair Deal welfare state, Johnson launched a crusade of his own—elimination and prevention of poverty. Because of their material abundance, middle-class Americans had largely forgotten that one-fourth to one-fifth of the population, mostly whites, still lived in substandard housing and subsisted on inadequate diets. Michael Harrington's *The Other America* helped spark concern for this issue, and Johnson declared his own War on Poverty. At first glance, the array of programs seemed impressive: federal funds for public-works projects, particularly new highways in Appalachia; a Job Corps to train young people who lacked marketable skills; Work-Study, a program to supplement the incomes of college students; Volunteers in Service to America (VISTA), which would send young volunteers into low-income areas; and Head Start, a program designed to provide compensatory education for preschoolers from disadvantaged families. Although these measures went far beyond any previous national efforts, even the programs' supporters conceded their traditionalist approach. In providing federal money and another federal agency (the Office of Economic Opportunity, or OEO), the Great Society was still borrowing the techniques of the New and Fair Deals.

One part of the War on Poverty, the Community Action Program (CAP), did represent a significant change in federal policy. Under Title II of the Economic Opportunity Act, Congress authorized funds for local groups—either private nonprofit or public organizations—that developed innovative, grass-roots programs. Sounding a theme that Richard Nixon and Ronald Reagan would later adapt to their own purposes, President Johnson argued that CAP rested on "the fact that local citizens best understand their own problems and know best how to deal with these problems." At first, many people praised CAP as an attempt to check the extension of federal power into local affairs. Many people looked forward to being able to use federal funds to plan their own social and economic agenda.

The War on Poverty brought Lyndon Johnson—or low-income people—few clear-cut victories. Many Republicans and blue-collar Democrats denounced the poverty program for giving money to those allegedly too lazy to help themselves. ("Yeah, I helped the War on Poverty," went one lame joke of the mid-1960s. "I threw a hand grenade at a bum.") Actually much of the available money went to OEO's white-collar bureaucrats or into expensive equipment. After their stints in public service, some antipoverty workers established consulting firms that received government contracts to provide "expert" advice. Early in the fight, some social critics declared that the "poverty-industrial" complex was a far bigger winner than those people who were supposed to receive assistance.

The widely heralded CAP also produced mixed results. Established welfare agencies and local political leaders opposed grants of funds to new community groups. When some of the CAP organizations espoused militant demands, such as redistribution of wealth and political power, OEO's bureaucrats quickly sided with the vested interests and against low-income people themselves. Even radicals, after all, could hardly expect the establishment to finance its own overthrow. In time, OEO placed more emphasis on prepackaged programs from Washington, such as Head Start, community beautification projects, and legal aid, and employed local CAP groups as administrators rather than innovators.

Though Lyndon Johnson would not admit it, the nation simply could not wage both a war in Vietnam and one against economic inequality at home without increased taxes. As a result of Johnson's determination not to raise taxes, the entire nation soon faced a rising rate of inflation, and low-income people saw funding for social programs slowly level off. Federal expenditures for social programs, measured in proportion to the country's GNP, did increase between 1965 and 1975, but the sums appropriated never matched those LBJ had once projected or those needed to change social conditions.

More than thirty years after Johnson sounded his battle cry, historians and students of public policy continue to disagree about the exact results—and the larger meaning—of the Great Society. Defenders of its basic premises heralded its successes. They insisted that its goals were realistic, that its programs were managed with reasonable efficiency, that they provided tangible benefits to recipients, and that the Great Society itself demonstrated the untapped potential of welfare liberalism. For example, within two decades, voting rights laws guaranteed that blacks, 90 percent of whom were effectively disenfranchised in 1965, could cast ballots, including ones for the more than 6,000 black officeholders. Medicaid provided minimal health care for low-income people, and Medicare offered coverage, albeit incomplete, for the elderly. Twenty years after the Great Society began, studies by the Census Bureau found more than 15 percent of all households in the country receiving benefits from Johnson-era programs.

Beginning in the late 1970s, when conservative political and intellectual winds were sweeping over American life, Johnson's Great Society began to attract even harsher criticism than it had received during the 1960s. In his much-discussed book, *Losing Ground* (1984), for example, the conservative social scientist Charles Murray argued that the massive government programs begun during Johnson's presidency not only had failed to help low-income people but also had actually caused widespread social decay. Enticed by higher welfare payments, for example, many low-income people, Murray charged, saw little need to marry, settle down, and pursue permanent employment. A life on government assistance seemed a viable alternative. Thus the Great Society, according to this interpretation, was both ineffective and socially pernicious.

Moreover, according to Murray, the Great Society programs, by stimulating inflation and by converting potential investment capital into nonproductive government spending, had killed off the economic growth of the postwar years. Had healthy economic structures not been undermined by ill-conceived social spending, virtually everyone could have gained middle-class lifestyles. Embellished in various ways, this conservative thesis, which gained wide currency in both the media and academic institutions during the 1980s, saw the Great Society, at best, as an ignoble failure and, at worst, as the precipitant for the nation's ongoing economic problems.

Analysts who challenged this conservative thesis drew very different pictures of the Great Society's legacy. They rejected, for example, the conservative claim that low-income people actually preferred welfare to meaningful employment. Moreover, they argued, expenditures on Great Society programs never approached the massive levels claimed by the conservative thesis. Appropriations for OEO, the centerpiece of the War on Poverty, never amounted to more than $2 billion per year.

Yet despite the fact that actual levels of funding never matched Johnson's extravagant promises, the Great Society was a landmark in social policymaking. It marked the first significant commitment to federal spending for social welfare since the 1930s. Between 1964 and 1976, federal spending for social-welfare programs increased from 5 percent of GNP to 11 percent. As a result, by the early 1970s, many low-income people could at least hope to receive services, including medical care and legal advice, that more affluent Americans simply took for granted. Although the Great Society never fulfilled Johnson's grandiose goals, it inaugurated more than a decade of significantly increased social spending that improved the everyday lives of millions of Americans.

Finally, it might be reemphasized, Johnson never intended a radical assault on entrenched wealth or economic inequality. Emphasizing their goal of creating new economic opportunities, architects of the Great Society opposed any serious talk of redistributing income or political power. Their solution to what they themselves conceded was economic injustice remained essentially the same as Truman's: use the existing political machinery to promote economic expansion and try to target a portion of the new growth for social projects. The promise of an ever-growing economic pie could postpone, as it had in the 1940s, discussions about what proportion of the whole should go to each citizen.

With the national government fighting a lengthy war overseas and a battle against inflation at home, an antipoverty program predicated on an ever-expanding economy and on steadily increasing expenditures for social welfare could not run its charted course. Some gains were made, as even the program's severest critics allowed. Yet even the Great Society's most enthusiastic supporters had to concede that the government's own figures on income distribution and various independent studies on the distribution of individual and family wealth showed that the gap between the rich and the poor narrowed very little during the 1960s. Johnson's program did not change the basic socioeconomic structure, nor was it intended to do so. But neither did the Great Society reach its stated goal—to deal seriously with the problems of economic inequality and social injustice.

The Warren Court and Liberal Reform

The Supreme Court also discovered the difficulties of effecting social change from above. Chief Justice Earl Warren, appointed by Dwight Eisenhower in 1953, and his "activist" colleagues believed that they could forecast the path of social progress and hasten the coming of justice and equality. The result was a flood of landmark decisions during the years of the Warren Court.

Even before Johnson became president, controversy surrounded the Supreme Court and Chief Justice Warren. The famous desegregation decision, *Brown* v. *Board of Education* (1954), angered segregationists throughout the country. In a series of decisions handed down in 1956 and 1957, a divided Court also protected the free-speech rights of alleged communists. Anticommunist crusaders denounced the Court, and the ultrareactionary John Birch Society erected billboards that demanded "IMPEACH EARL WARREN." And when the Court appeared to reverse itself on free-speech issues in the later 1950s, civil libertarians criticized the justices, particularly Felix Frankfurter, for allegedly caving in to popular pressures. Because of internal divisions and external pressures, the Warren Court established no clear pattern on civil liberties during the chief justice's first years on the bench.

During the 1960s, however, the liberal activists gained ascendancy. Led by Chief Justice Warren and two veteran justices, William O. Douglas and

Hugo Black, the Court began to require state and local governments to conform to the guarantees of the national Bill of Rights. The activists recognized, for example, that effective legal protection remained largely a matter of one's income and social standing. Wealthy people could afford good lawyers and thereby gain valuable legal protection. Low-income people rarely employed attorneys, and they faced powerful government institutions with inadequate knowledge of their rights. In *Gideon* v. *Wainwright* (1963) the Court held that states must furnish indigents with lawyers in felony cases. Such decisions expressed the court's commitment to a single standard of due process and to the principle of equality before the law.

In addition, the Warren Court attempted to align constitutional law with the larger political assumptions of New Deal-Fair Deal liberalism. Beginning with *Baker* v. *Carr* (1962), a majority of justices held that the way that most states laid out electoral districts deprived urban voters of equal protection. *Baker* v. *Carr's* "one man, one vote" rule aimed at correcting situations in which rural districts with comparatively few people had the same number of political representatives as populous urban districts. Hoping to encourage more vigorous scrutiny of public officials, the Court made it more difficult for politicians to sue their critics for libel (*The New York Times* v. *Sullivan*, 1964). In a series of highly controversial decisions, the majority declared that Bible reading and prayer in public schools violated the First Amendment's prohibition against the establishment of religion. Earl Warren was declaring God himself unconstitutional, grumbled conservatives. Their mood remained sour when the same Court struck down laws against obscenity. Despite all the criticism, however, the Court seemed to have consolidated its new position by the mid-1960s. The Kennedy-Johnson appointees—particularly Arthur Goldberg; Abe Fortas; and the court's first black justice, Thurgood Marshall—offset the increasing conservatism of Justice Black and appeared to ensure an activist, liberal majority for years to come.

Then, after 1966, the liberal majority collapsed. One of the Court's own decisions did much of the damage. In *Miranda* v. *Arizona* (1966) the Court held that once a police investigation focused on a particular suspect, the authorities had to inform the defendant that he or she could remain silent, have a lawyer present during questioning, and request a free attorney provided by the state. More than any other decision, *Miranda* united the Court's critics around one emotional issue. It coincided with rising fear of crime in the streets, and people blamed the Warren Court for handcuffing the police. Although criminologists easily demonstrated that such charges were without foundation, popular criticism and pressure from within the legal establishment increased. Congress considered legislation to overturn the *Miranda* decision, and politicians such as George Wallace and Richard Nixon promised to appoint new justices who would "interpret the Constitution strictly." (This meant, of course, judges who favored *less* strict protection of individual liberties and who opposed the political assumptions of the Warren majority.)

Amid all this controversy, Chief Justice Warren announced his impending retirement. President Johnson wanted to replace Warren with his old friend Abe Fortas and then appoint another crony, Homer Thornberry, to the Court. Anticipating a Nixon victory in the 1968 election, Republicans and many conservative southern Democrats tried to block Johnson's plan. Their job became easy when *Life* magazine uncovered what appeared to be evidence of official misconduct by Justice Fortas. Johnson had to withdraw his nomination, and Fortas eventually resigned in disgrace. Newly elected President Nixon thus gained two vacancies on the Court—the chief justice's post (which went to Warren Burger) and Fortas's old seat (which was ultimately filled by another Minnesotan, Harry Blackmun).

Even before the demise of the activist majority, however, legal scholars were beginning to question the impact of the Warren Court's decisions. Obviously the Court had eliminated some gross inequities in the American legal system and had established stricter standards for law enforcement officials. But it lacked the means—as it always had and always will—to enforce its ruling to the letter. Police departments could effectively evade the *Miranda* decision; publicly appointed lawyers often acted more as agents of the prosecutor's office than as representatives of their clients; and local pressures often made broad principles superfluous.

In an even more fundamental sense, decisions by judicial activists were not always effective tools for social engineering. New interpretations of the law of libel, for example, could not make every journalist into a vigorous crusader for the public interest, and reapportionment of state legislatures would not automatically produce more effective bodies. On the most explosive public issue of the late 1960s the Court took no position at all: It avoided ruling directly on cases that challenged the legality of the undeclared war in Vietnam. And though the Warren Court played a vital role in the early movement for legal and political equality, the justices had no independent power to effect the sweeping social and economic changes that militants came to demand. When the black revolution turned away from legal issues involving official discrimination during the Johnson presidency, the judiciary could play only a limited role.

CIVIL RIGHTS TO BLACK POWER

Civil Rights: The Kennedy Years

Several other groups joined forces with Martin Luther King's SCLC in the early 1960s. The Congress of Racial Equality (CORE) had employed nonviolent civil disobedience as early as the 1940s; led by James Farmer and later by Floyd McKissick, it became more active during the early 1960s. Another group, the Student Nonviolent Coordinating Committee (SNCC), evolved from demonstrations in North Carolina during the winter of 1960. Black college students, polite and neatly dressed, unsuccessfully tried to eat at a dime-store lunch counter. Braving hostile whites—who tossed lighted cigarettes, dumped ketchup, and threw punches—the young blacks remained seated, patiently waiting for service. The sit-in movement quickly spread to other kinds of public facilities as thousands of young activists, both white and black, joined the protests. In April 1960 a group of these students formed SNCC and accepted Dr. King's approach—nonviolent protest. Some of the early freedom songs expressed their optimism:

Freedom's Comin' and It Won't Be Long
We took a trip on a Greyhound bus,
Freedom's comin' and it won't be long
To fight segregation, this we must
Freedom's comin' and it won't be long.

Violence in 'bama didn't stop our cause. . . .
Federal marshals come enforce the laws. . . .

On to Mississippi with speed we go . . . .
Blue-shirted policemen meet us at the door. . . .

Judge say local custom shall prevail. . . .
We say "no" and we land in jail. . . .

The election of John Kennedy in 1960 seemed to offer hope of greater support of the civil rights movement from Washington. During his campaign JFK criticized the Eisenhower administration's reluctant support of integration and promised a new frontier for African-Americans. Once in office, he appointed a number of prominent blacks to federal positions, filed more desegregation suits than his predecessor, and supported a new civil rights act. (The previous civil rights laws of 1957 and 1960 had dealt primarily with voting rights; Kennedy supported a measure that would ban discrimination in public accommodations and give the attorney general authority to file school desegregation suits.)

Kennedy's political caution, however, influenced his racial policies. During the campaign he had denounced Eisenhower's refusal to issue an executive order ending discrimination in housing—Ike could do it with "a stroke of the pen," claimed Kennedy—but he delayed his own order for two years. Desiring good relations with southern Democrats, Kennedy often deferred to them on patronage questions, appointing several outright racists to the federal bench. (One Mississippi judge referred to black civil rights workers as "monkeys" and consistently demeaned African-American defendants.)

Kennedy also refused to cross J. Edgar Hoover, allowing the FBI leader considerable leeway to set his own rules in civil rights cases. In effect, this meant that Hoover, no friend of civil rights groups, would do as little as possible to help African-Americans and to jeopardize his close relationship with segregationist law officers in the South. Without thorough background investigations by the FBI, the Justice Department often lacked evidence to prosecute cases of alleged discrimination. Meanwhile, Hoover steadily stepped up his bureau's surveillance on African-American groups and leaders, with

Martin Luther King, Jr., becoming the increasing focus of the director's attention. Hoover pondered how he might neutralize the civil rights movement, and the FBI slowly mounted a campaign of wiretaps, surveillance, and harassment that eventually touched every aspect of the movement, especially the personal and political life of Dr. King.

Dramatic events in the Deep South, more than symbolic and bureaucratic moves in Washington, however, determined the pace of change. In 1961, young activists from CORE and SNCC defied the racial segregation laws for interstate buses and southern terminals. Angered by these "freedom riders," segregationists used iron bars, clubs, and finally explosives against the nonviolent activists. Increasing racist violence finally forced the government to respond: Attorney General Robert Kennedy dispatched his Justice Department troubleshooters and a corps of federal marshals to protect the freedom riders. He also asked the Interstate Commerce Commission to end segregation in interstate facilities, a request that the ICC honored in the fall of 1961. The use of federal personnel to protect the freedom riders established a pattern, and the following year President Kennedy reinforced the marshals with United States Army troops to quell the violence that followed the enrollment of a black student at the University of Mississippi. Kennedy's actions probably prevented bloodshed on other campuses—two people died during disorders at Ole Miss—and a confrontation at the University of Alabama in 1963 ended differently. After symbolically "standing in the schoolhouse door," Governor George Wallace—who had championed "segregation now and forever"—stepped aside and watched Justice Department officials integrate the university without serious incident.

In the spring of 1963 the focus of integration efforts shifted from southern college campuses to the streets of Birmingham, Alabama. The drive to desegregate public facilities in this industrial center marked an important turning point in the struggle for racial equality. Police violence escalated into savagery. Police Commissioner Eugene "Bull" Connor, who fit perfectly the northern stereotype of a redneck southern law officer, turned fire hoses and dogs on black demonstrators, including small children. Club-swinging police rounded up thousands of protestors and threw them into makeshift lockups. White vigilantes unleashed a terror campaign that culminated in the bombing of a black church; four children at Sunday school died in the blast.

Covered extensively in the media, the events in Birmingham had a significant impact. Appalled by the violence, liberal opinion in the North and in Congress swung behind new civil rights legislation. Ultimately, then, the police and segregationist violence in Birmingham rebounded against Bull Connor and his allies. Equally as important, the militancy of Birmingham's young blacks gave a new urgency to liberal efforts, in both Alabama and Washington, to calm racial conflict. Seeking to avoid further violence and bloodshed, leaders of Birmingham's white business community compromised: Three thousand imprisoned demonstrators were released, and the city's white leadership agreed to begin desegregation efforts. In Washington, John Kennedy told the nation that the "rising tide of discontent that threatens the public safety" could not be calmed by "repressive police action"; it was time, he urged, for Congress to act. He would press it, he pledged, to enact a strong civil rights program.

Calm returned to Birmingham, but the events there presaged important changes in racial politics. Some people in crowded urban neighborhoods had never really accepted the rhetoric of nonviolence, and many young blacks voiced displeasure with King's stated philosophy. On the one hand, Birmingham began the long period of urban violence that transformed both the black movement and its white supporters. On the other hand, Birmingham also brought a subtle change in the strategies of King and the SCLC. He and his associates recognized that any violent white response ultimately rebounded to their benefit. Although members of the SCLC never admitted it, their organization turned increasingly toward "nonviolent provocation," a strategy designed to exploit coverage by the media and to use racist violence in the cause of civil rights. The SCLC relied on this approach during its 1965 crusade in Selma, Alabama, a voter registration drive that helped push Congress to enact the Voting Rights Act of that year.

But in August 1963, the violence that lay ahead remained hidden beneath a glow of optimism and a temporary spirit of cooperation that climaxed in a march on Washington. Most northern newspapers and magazines praised the neat appearance, politeness, and commitment of the estimated 200,000 marchers. The unity within the movement also seemed exemplary: Young activists from SNCC shared the platform with the NAACP and the Urban League as well as with white church and labor leaders. And just when the August sun threatened to wilt the marchers, Martin Luther King revived their spirits with his stirring "I Have a Dream" speech. A carefully structured series of images, the address confirmed King's reputation as the movement's greatest spellbinder. With the formalities completed, civil rights leaders adjourned to the White House for a coffee hour with the Kennedys.

The Civil Rights Act of 1964: End of an Era

Even though civil rights leaders had recognized JFK's limitations, his death seemed a great blow to their movement; it brought a southerner with an even more ambivalent record into the White House. But Lyndon Johnson quickly dispelled doubts about his commitment when he helped push a stronger version of Kennedy's civil rights bill through Congress in 1964.

The Civil Rights Act of 1964 outlawed racial, religious, and sexual discrimination in private businesses that served the general public—such as restaurants and gas stations—and in public facilities such as swimming pools. It also authorized the executive branch to withhold federal grants or contracts from institutions that discriminated against nonwhites and empowered the attorney general to file school desegregation suits at his initiative. To safeguard voting rights, the law contained a section that established a sixth-grade education as the basic requirement for literacy. This provision, it was hoped, would end "literacy" tests. (A white voting inspector in Alabama once rejected a black applicant because his literacy test contained "an error in spilling.") The

March on Washington, 1963. The peaceful mood and optimistic spirit of August 1963 would not survive the turbulent 1960s.
Source: National Archives.

Civil Rights Act of 1964 changed the pattern of race relations. It demanded no less than destruction of a settled way of life in the South, a system of racial discrimination that had evolved after the formal end of slavery in 1865. According to the act, blacks could now sleep in any motel, eat in any restaurant, or sit anywhere on any bus. Important as these legal changes were, however, they required no basic alteration in the nation's socioeconomic structure or in the distribution of political power.

By 1964 many blacks were seeking more than equal access to public accommodations and government facilities; the battles of the 1950s and early 1960s had raised the stakes. Black militants demanded monetary compensation for the years of discrimination, immediate economic assistance, and greater political power. Such things, white politicians argued, were clearly impossible; it had taken much bloodshed and political skill even to obtain the act of 1964. But young activists rejected arguments based on what older black leaders and white politicians considered possible. Some charged that civil rights leaders with selling out. After the troubles in Birmingham, white philanthropists, perhaps worried about violence moving northward or perhaps sincerely moved by the rightness of the cause, pledged almost a million dollars to the leading civil rights organizations. Militants denounced this as a payoff and Kennedy's civil rights program as tokenism. During the march on Washington, John Lewis, the youthful head of SNCC, had been forced to rewrite his fiery address. Lewis had intended to criticize the Kennedy civil rights bill— "What is there in this bill to ensure the equality of a maid who earns $5 a week in the home of a family whose income is $100,000 a year?"—and to condemn "the cheap political leaders who build their careers on immoral compromises and ally themselves with open forms of political, economic, and social exploitation." To preserve the harmony of the day, Lewis agreed to soften his speech, but others did not attend the march or temper their words. One person who had not even been invited asked, "Who ever heard of angry revolutionists all harmonizing 'We Shall Overcome Some Day' while tripping and swaying along arm-in-arm with the very people they were supposed to be revolting against?" The young man was Malcom X, an eloquent advocate for political militancy and black pride.

A series of disturbing events in 1964 and 1965 made nonviolence and peaceful political appeals less attractive to some activists. In Mississippi three civil rights workers—Andrew Goodman, James Cheney, and Michael Schwerner—were brutally murdered; Cheney, the only black among the three, was apparently beaten to death with steel chains. That same year an interracial group risked their lives to organize the Mississippi Freedom Democratic Party (FDP), only to watch white liberals join with southern segregationists to deny the FDP formal recognition at the Democratic National Convention. And during the Freedom Summer of 1964—a SNCC-sponsored campaign to register voters and establish "freedom schools" throughout the South—racial tensions within the movement itself increased. Blacks frequently ridiculed "paternalistic" whites and "fly-by-night freedom fighters who were bossing everybody around." Sexual relationships among the young civil rights workers, especially those between black men and white women, quickly added gender and racial conflicts to the list of problems with which those committed to the Freedom Summer had to deal. As SNCC and other interracial organizations tried to limp along, testing the viability of nonviolence in the South, African-Americans in some northern cities expressed their grievances and frustrations in very different ways.

The Ghettos Explode

Less than three weeks after President Johnson signed the Civil Rights Act of 1964, violence broke out in several northern cities. Immediately recognizing that some politicians would use this violence to cripple his civil rights and Great Society programs, Johnson enlisted the aid of J. Edgar Hoover in orchestrating a report that blamed economic and racial discrimination, rather than some subversive plot, for the outbreaks.

Although Johnson's theory implied that further Great Society spending would calm northern cities, a second violence-filled summer followed the first. In August 1965, a clash between a white highway patrol officer and an African-American motorist touched off four days of violence in the Los Angeles neighborhood of Watts. Thirty-four people lost their lives; property losses, from fires and looting, reached more than $20 million; and the National Guard patrolled the streets of Los Angeles. According to one administration official, the president "just wouldn't accept it. He refused to look at the cables from Los Angeles" that described the escalating conflagration.

Several more years of urban disorders followed the outbreak in Watts. The worst was 1967, with trouble in 128 cities and major clashes in Newark and Detroit. In Detroit, regular army units assisted police and the National Guard; at least 43 people died; and fires and looting left permanent scars on Detroit's black neighborhoods. In all the confrontations, the vast majority of people killed were African-Americans, and property damage remained largely confined to their communities. Investigations revealed indiscriminate shooting by authorities and even a few incidents of outright murder by white police officers. In addition to burned-out buildings and escalating tensions in black neighborhoods, these long, hot summers produced growing unease among white liberals. Johnson himself was reported to have asked, "How is it possible after all that we've accomplished? . . . Is the world topsy-turvy?" Certainly, he had a point; the trouble had come during a period of at least some progress in fighting racial discrimination. What could explain the violence?

Official explanations tried to steer between right-wing theories of a grand revolutionary conspiracy and left-wing claims of an incipient popular revolution against white exploitation. Investigating the Watts disorder, the McCone Commission (headed by former CIA Director John McCone) propounded a "rotten apple" or "riff-raff" interpretation. A small group of troublemakers, the McCone Report concluded, had precipitated the trouble and fueled the violence. The "riots" were not legitimate protests against substantive grievances but "formless, quite senseless, all but hopeless" outbursts of looting and burning—"engaged in by a few but bringing great distress to all." The commission theorized that most of these "rotten apples" had recently migrated from the rural South and had not yet adjusted to urban life. Though it refused to call Watts a ghetto (because it contained mostly single-family dwellings and fairly wide streets) or to concede a serious issue of police brutality, the commission did see these problems. Watts had inadequate mass transit, poor educational facilities, and a small number of poorly trained police. Suggesting that the situation required no fundamental social or economic changes, the report called for greater job opportunities near Watts, more money for education, and "better understanding" between police and citizens. Throughout the report, McCone and the other commissioners viewed greater respect for the law enforcement system as the major issue.

More critical investigators quickly challenged the McCone Commission. They considered the disorders to be political protests rather than formless riots. The violence in Watts, they claimed, involved a sizable portion of the community, not simply a few misfits. The protesters, in fact, had lived in Watts for some time, usually held low-paying jobs, and possessed the best education that the neighborhood schools could provide. Disputing the idea that the violence had been senseless, critical researchers argued that protesters had tried to avoid black-owned businesses and had concentrated on white firms that were considered dishonest. Much of the housing in Watts was dilapidated, many businesses exploited black customers and employees, and police brutality was an everyday occurrence. These writers concluded that the violence grew out of deep-seated, legitimate grievances.

This dispute between "riot" and "protest" theorists involved more than a semantic difference. The riot view sought the quick suppression of such disorders and pointed to the need for gradual changes *within* the existing system; the protest position implied the legitimacy of the violence and supported the need for more sweeping social and economic changes. Equally as important, the riot view tended to see the problem as one between good people and bad people. The protest theory pointed to a deep-seated socioeconomic and racial crisis.

As disorders continued, official explanations changed very little. The most extensive government investigation, done in 1968 by President Johnson's National Advisory Commission on Civil Disorders (commonly called the Kerner Commission), rejected evidence that suggested fundamental problems with the political system. In the end, the commissioners did identify white racism as part of the trouble, but not before they had fired 120 staff members who wanted stronger language and had suppressed the staff's radical report, "The Harvest of American Racism." The commissioners' own document recommended a moderate, two-pronged approach: increased social-welfare expenditures and more effective use of force to suppress disturbances. The last solution, greater force, proved more acceptable to most white politicians, and Congress voted additional funds to beef up local law enforcement agencies and to train the National Guard in more efficient riot control. Saddled with burgeoning expenditures for the Vietnam War, the president filed away the commission's other recommendations. Johnson, like most other national leaders, ultimately preferred to ignore the broader implications of the commission's report.

Black Power

Meanwhile, some African-American leaders were already citing white intransigence as justification for rejecting integration—the traditional goal of the civil rights movement. An established separatist group, the Black Muslims, suddenly gained prominence in the early 1960s. The Muslims preached the superiority of black people and black institutions, predicted eventual collapse for the decadent white society, planned the creation of separate black areas in the United States, and stressed the necessity for hard work and self-discipline. The sect gained converts during the 1950s, including Malcolm Little, a self-educated man with a keen intellect. Rejecting his "Christian slave name," Malcolm X became Muslim leader Elijah Muhammad's top aide and his most eloquent spokesperson. Malcolm's fiery oratory and the conversion of the heavyweight boxing champion Cassius Clay (who became Muhammad Ali) gained the Muslims national attention.

Malcolm X anticipated and helped to inspire the militant Black Power movement of the late 1960s. He questioned the value of nonviolence in a culture filled with hate and ridiculed the possibility of integration. Malcolm X re-fused to denounce violence, at least when used in self-defense, and he dismissed civil rights leaders as "professional beggars" who were constantly seeking handouts from powerful white leaders. The only viable solution for white racism, he preached, was a complete separation of the formally enslaved people from their white masters. This kind of rhetoric, especially his exhortation for community self-defense "by any means necessary," frightened both black and white liberals, who condemned Malcolm X as a racist and a demagogue. Meanwhile, though, his appeal and power base within African-American communities began to grow, and his emotional speaking engagements attracted ever-larger crowds.

At the same time, Malcolm X began his own search for new ideas to bring about political and racial change. He broke from Elijah Muhuammad and the Black Muslims and formed his own Organization of Afro-American Unity. Although he remained interested in political and economic issues and even made tentative moves toward alliances with white progressives, Malcolm X came to place special emphasis on African-American culture. If black people were to organize for social and economic change, they first needed to recapture their heritage as African-Americans and to "launch a cultural revolution to unbrainwash an entire people." Although Malcolm X was assassinated in 1965, allegedly by old enemies from his days with the Black Muslims, his emphasis on reinvigorating African-American culture and on cultivating a strong sense of individual self-identity was to live on. Younger activists eagerly read his *Autobiography* and listened to his record albums, especially *Message to the Grass Roots*. According to one of the architects of the later Black Power movement, "Black history began with Malcolm X."

By 1965, racial politics in the United States were in a state of flux; the forward march of the civil rights movement toward legal and constitutional change seemed stalled. Racist resistance to the Civil Rights Act of 1964 and the new Voting Rights Act of 1965 produced further bloodshed; to some blacks, the urban disorders in the North suggested the possibility that violence might bring more concessions than nonviolent civil disobedience. In May 1966, SNCC, still officially committed to integration, urged blacks "to begin building independent political, economic, and cultural institutions that they will control and use as instruments of social change in this country." Later that summer SNCC joined other civil rights groups, including the SCLC and CORE, in a protest march through Mississippi, an effort that only widened divisions within the civil rights movement. Stokely Carmichael, SNCC's new head, took the spotlight away from Martin Luther King, who was often absent. Carmichael vowed that he would never go to jail peacefully again and declared that "every courthouse in Mississippi ought to be burned down to get rid of the dirt." In the most publicized event of the march, he coined the movement's new slogan: Black Power!

The people in SNCC and CORE had tried nonviolence and cooperation with whites, and they believed that these tactics had failed. Integration, wrote Stokely Carmichael, "reinforces among both black and white, the idea that 'white' is automatically better and 'black' is by definition inferior." The search for political and legal equality, the basis of the civil rights movement, now seemed less important than economic power. Black people, it was argued, had to gain control of their communities and expel the "white power structure"—the "dishonest" businesspeople, the "rent-gouging" landlords, and the "crooked" politicians. Along with economic independence, young activists promoted black pride. Since many whites would always see blacks as inferior, they contended, black people must forge a cultural identity based on their own heritage. As a means of stimulating black pride and cultural nationalism, militants demanded community control of neighborhood schools and, where this was not immediately possible, black studies courses taught and administered by African-Americans.

There were many variations on the themes of black power and black nationalism. Some people, identifying with dark-skinned peoples in the postcolonial countries, viewed African-Americans as colonized people subject to the domination of alien white masters. Others adopted a Marxist framework, seeing blacks as the most exploited group in an exploitative capitalist society. Violent revolution, a few extremists even suggested, offered the best means of redressing grievances. But even most activists warned against open confrontations with the overwhelming firepower of white America and sought to build bases of local support before pressing the movement for peaceful but significant social change.

The history of the Black Panthers, an organization that attracted the media spotlight in the late 1960s, revealed the tensions generated by debates over black power and black nationalism. Formed in Oakland, California, the Panthers gained attention primarily through a shootout with Oakland police and through the success of Eldridge Cleaver's book, *Soul on Ice*. Outfitted in paramilitary garb, the Panthers frightened many people, and law enforcement officials denounced the group as a grave threat to American society. Panther leaders Huey Newton (who was convicted of killing a police officer during the Oakland shootout) and Bobby Seale urged "self-defense groups that are dedicated to defending our black community against racist oppression and brutality." The Panthers also demanded a guaranteed income for all citizens, exemption of blacks from military service, government funds for cooperative housing facilities, reparation payments "as retribution for slave labor and mass murder of black people," release of all black prisoners "because they have not received a fair and impartial trial," and use of all-black juries to try black defendants. Such demands borrowed from black nationalist ideas, but they also owed much to a curious blend of Marxism and the rhetoric of American constitutional law. (Huey Newton always carried a stack of law books in his car.) The Panthers found it difficult to articulate a transformational strategy: Should they ally with white activists or should they avoid ties with nonblacks and go it alone? The Panthers finally did seek ties with both white and black radicals, a course that helped to divide the party's members.

The Civil Rights Act of 1968, the last major civil rights measure, indicated the ambivalent response of white politicians toward such militancy. Title VIII of the law prohibited discrimination in the advertising, financing, sale, or rental of most homes and charged the executive branch with acting "affirmatively" to achieve integrated housing. Together with state open-housing laws, the act pointed toward integration of the largely white suburbs. If coupled with generous funding for inner-city projects, it also promised better urban housing for low-income families of color. The urban violence of the 1960s did, therefore, produce some positive responses, in the form of congressional legislation and bureaucratic attention, from the political system.

However, in the act of 1968 the majority of whites in Congress also indicated their fear of black militancy. At the insistence of Strom Thurmond of South Carolina, Congress made it a crime to use the facilities of interstate commerce "to organize, promote, encourage, participate in, or carry on a riot; or to commit any act of violence in furtherance of a riot." In approving this seemingly vague provision, most members of Congress knew exactly what they wanted: a federal law that would stop the activities of black power advocates such as H. Rap Brown of SNCC. This so-called "Rap Brown section" gave national authorities a catchall statute to halt the travels and organizing efforts of radicals.

The Black Power movement articulated powerful, new themes. Most African-Americans, according to public-opinion polls, still supported the goals of the civil rights movement—integration, equality of opportunity, and equal rights. At his death in 1968, Martin Luther King, Jr., remained the preeminent black leader. At the same time, though, the growing white backlash against the civil rights movement and the positive messages of the Black Power crusade helped to change the African-American agenda.

In a sense, there seemed no fundamental conflict between integration and the renewed ethnic pride. Black politicians, gaining crucial votes from white progressives and other people of color, built on their own power base within black communities and won elective office in a number of cities during the late 1960s and early 1970s. At the same time, the average income of black families rose, and the gap between the yearly income figures for whites and for blacks began to narrow. African-Americans who had skills and educational credentials found it easier than ever before to purse the integrationist dream that King had sketched in his famous speech of 1963.

In another sense, though, the new spirit of racial pride and self-identity helped to produce vibrant cultural movements that challenged the liberal-integrationist ethic that had shaped the early civil rights movement. Although the more radical political goals of the Black Power movement were not realized, many of its cultural initiatives did take root. The African-American rennaissance of the 1960s extended from the angry verses of the Last Poets to the sweet soul music of Sam Cooke, from the multifaceted Black Arts movement to the macho posturing of singer James Brown, from the precisely crafted sounds of Miles Davis to the contradictory imagery of "blaxploitation" films like *Superfly* and *Foxy Brown*. It became increasingly clear that there was not simply *a* black *culture*—and, indeed, there never had been merely one—but many different African-American *cultures*. Black feminists, for example, were finding their own voices and denouncing not only racism but also the sexism that they found embedded in both white and black cultures. They were unwilling to allow black men alone to define racial struggles in ways that papered over gender divisions and that relegated African-American women to becoming black June Cleavers.

The transition from civil rights to black power had a significant impact on all parts of American society and culture. Between 1954, when the Supreme Court struck down legal segregation, and 1968, when King was gunned down in Memphis, the crusade against racial discrimination helped to transform the entire nation. Although the first civil rights battles focused on African-Americans and segregation in the South, the struggle soon expanded. Many liberal and progressive whites were forced to reexamine their own ideas, especially when racial politics moved into the North and when the focus shifted from racial segregation by law to more subtle, less identifiable forms of discrimination. At the same time, other ethnic groups began to emulate African-Americans and their desire to confront the effects of discrimination. Very quickly, there were many different antidiscrimination movements, all searching for legal equality and for cultural and political empowerment.

Finally, for most African-Americans themselves, the struggle for civil rights and against discrimination proved transforming. The new emphasis on self-identity, group pride, and cultural representations helped to change the nature of the issues—for African-Americans and for the entire nation. The early civil rights movement attempted to lift the burdens of legalized racism and to open up the political process to black voters. Although legal and political battles remained to be fought, the Black Power movement introduced new concerns about cultural empowerment. The cultural issues first raised in the 1960s were to become even more important in the decades to come. Indeed, in an age in which images from the 1960s could be reproduced for mass distribution, as in the "Eyes on the Prize" TV series, or recreated in docudrama form, as in Spike Lee's *Malcolm X*, the power of cultural representations, past as well as present, would increasingly help to shape the complex politics of race.

The Kennedy and Johnson years brought important social-welfare legislation, several civil rights laws, and scores of liberal Supreme Court decisions. But the liberal promise of the early 1960s slowly faded as conventional political remedies, carefully drafted legislation, and soundly reasoned court opinions seemed to address only some of the riddles of social policy and racial politics. At the same time, problems in foreign affairs, largely the result of Kennedy's and Johnson's efforts to hold on to earlier cold war policies in the face of important international changes, also helped to diminish the promise of the early 1960s and demonstrate, often tragically, the perils confronting a nation whose leaders unwisely thought their power was almost unlimited.

SUGGESTIONS FOR FURTHER READING

The best study of the problems of liberalism in the 1960s is Allen J. Matusow, *The Unraveling of America* (1984), but see also the relevant chapters of Alonso Hamby, *Liberalism and Its Challengers* (1992). Garry Wills, *Nixon Ago-*

nistes (rev. ed., 1980) and *The Kennedy Imprisonment* (1983), offers critical viewpoints, as does Thomas C. Reeves, *A Question of Character: A Life of John F. Kennedy* (1991). More favorable, though not uncritical, is David Burner, *John F. Kennedy and a New Generation* (1988). James N. Giglio's *The Presidency of John F. Kennedy* (1991) provides a reliable overview. For more detail, see Herbert J. Parmet's two volumes—*Jack* (1980) and *JFK* (1983). Finally, there are many sympathetic accounts of Kennedy's presidency by close associates; by far the best is Arthur Schlesinger, Jr., *A Thousand Days* (1965).

Events surrounding Kennedy's death have attracted almost as much attention as his life. Edward Jay Epstein's two studies, *Inquest* (1963) and *Legend* (1978), are the best of the older accounts that reject the Warren Commission's version of the assassination. Michael J. Kurtz, *The Crime of the Century* (1982), tries to offer historical grounding, and Barbie Zelizer, *Covering the Body* (1992), is a superb cultural study. Recent theories of the assassination itself include Henry Hurt, *Reasonable Doubt* (1988); John H. Davis, *Mafia Kingfish: Carlos Marcello and the Assassination of John F. Kennedy* (1989); and Peter Dale Scott, *Deep Politics and the Death of JFK* (1993), all of which are critical of the Warren Commission's conclusions. But also see two attempts to rehabilitate its general conclusions in David Belin, *Final Disclosure* (1989), and Gerald L. Posner, *Case Closed* (1993).

Specific aspects of the Kennedy administration may be explored in Grant McConnell, *Steel and the Presidency—1962* (1963); Jim F. Health, *John Kennedy and the Business Community* (1969); Victor Navasky, *Kennedy Justice* (1971); Carl M. Brauer, *John F. Kennedy and the Second Reconstruction* (1977); and James Tobin and Murray Weidenbaum, eds., *Two Revolutions in Economic Policy: The First Economic Reports of Presidents Kennedy and Reagan* (1988).

In addition to general studies on the civil rights movement cited at the end of Chapter Three, the following studies are also recommended: Howard Zinn, *SNCC* (1965); Elliot Rudwick and August Meier, *CORE* (1972); David Garrow, *Protest at Selma* (1980); William Chafe, *Civilities and Civil Rights* (1980); Clayborne Carson, *In Struggle* (1981); Elizabeth Jacoway and David R. Colburn, *Southern Businessmen and Desegregation* (1982); Steven Lawson, *In Pursuit of Power* (1985); Doug McAdam, *Freedom Summer* (1988); Emily Stoper, *The Student Non-violent Coordinating Committee: The Growth of Radicalism in a Civil Rights Organization* (1989); David Garrow, ed., *Birmingham, Alabama, 1956–1963: The Black Struggle for Civil Rights* (1989); John Walton Cotman, *Birmingham, JFK, and the Civil Rights Act of 1963* (1989); Kenneth O'Reilly, *Racial Matters: The FBI's Secret Files on Black America, 1960–72* (1989); Stewart Burns, *Social Movements of the 1960s: Searching for Democracy* (1990); Raymond S. Franklin, *Shadows of Race* (1991); Richard A. Couto, *Ain't Gonna Let Nobody Turn Me Round* (1991); John T. McCartney, *Black Power Ideologies* (1992); Mark Stern, *Calculating Visions: Kennedy, Johnson, and Civil Rights* (1992); William L. Van Deburg, *New Day in Babylon: The Black Power Movement and American Culture, 1965–1975* (1992); and Eric R. Burner, *And Gently He Shall Lead Them: Robert Parris Moses and Civil Rights in Mississippi* (1994).

Many of the works cited on gender and family issues at the end of Chapter Three are also relevant here. In addition, see Susan M. Hartman, *From Margin to Mainstream: American Women in Politics Since 1960* (1989), and the relevant chapters of Linda Gordon, ed., *Women Welfare and the State* (1990).

On Lyndon Johnson, see Paul K. Conkin, *Big Daddy from the Perdaneles* (1986); Robert Caro, *The Path to Power* (1982) and *Means of Ascent* (1990); Robert J. Dallek, *Lone Star Rising: Lyndon Johnson and His Times, 1908–1960* (1991); and Paul R. Henggeler, *In His Steps: Lyndon Johnson and the Kennedy Mystique* (1991). Vaughn Davis Bornet, *The Presidency of Lyndon Baines Johnson* (1983) is relatively sympathetic, and Doris Kearns's *Lyndon Johnson and the American Dream* (1976) remains worthwhile. Robert A. Divine, *The Johnson Years, Volume Three: LBJ at Home and Abroad* (1993) is valuable. Joseph A. Califano, Jr., *The Triumph and Tragedy of Lyndon Johnson* (1991) is a recent memoir.

On the Great Society and the War on Poverty, begin with the critical assessment in Matusow, *The Unraveling of America*. A much more positive view is *The Promise of Greatness* (1976) by Sar Levitan and Robert Taggert. John E. Schwarz, *America's Hidden Success* (rev. ed., 1988), is equally upbeat. The most influential analysis of Great Society liberalism from the right has been Charles Murray's *Losing Ground* (1984); for views of the Great Society from the left, see, for example, William P. Ryan, *Equality* (1982), and Richard Cloward and Francis Fox Piven, *Poor People's Movements* (1978). Marvin E. Gettleman and David Mermelstein, eds., *The Great Society Reader* (1965), remains a useful documentary collection. More recent studies include the relevant chapters of Christopher Jencks, *Rethinking Social Policy* (1992), and Martha F. Davis, *Brutal Need: Lawyers and the Welfare Rights Movement* (1994).

On the Warren Court and liberal reform, see the unabridged edition of Bernard Schwartz, *Super Chief* (1983); G. Edward White, *Earl Warren* (1982); and the relevant parts of Mark Tushnet, *Red, White and Blue: A Critical Analysis of Constitutional Law* (1988), and of Samuel Walker, *In Defense of American Liberties: A History of the ACLU* (1990). See also Neil McFeeley, *Appointment of Judges: The Johnson Presidency* (1987); the relevant chapters of Melvin I. Urofsky, *The Continuity of Change: The Supreme Court and Individual Liberties, 1953–1986* (1991); and Tinsley E. Yarbrough, *John Marshall Harlan: Great Dissenter of the Warren Court* (1992).

6

The Perils of Power: Foreign Policy in the 1960s

KENNEDY'S FOREIGN POLICIES

New Programs

John F. Kennedy's New Frontier asserted a new activism into the cold war. In the presidential campaign of 1960, Kennedy charged that the Eisenhower-Nixon team had created a dangerous missile gap between the United States and the Soviet Union and had not worked vigorously to eliminate Castro. (Neither charge was true.) Once in the White House, Kennedy waged the cold war in a determined way and with a great variety of techniques. He promised that his foreign policy would provide a "flexible response": It would challenge communism on every level, from atomic weaponry to "counterinsurgency units" to economic pressure to enlarged covert capabilities.

General Maxwell Taylor, army chief of staff, told Kennedy, "We must show the Russians that wars of national liberation are not cheap, safe, and disavowable but costly, dangerous, and doomed to failure." Believing that ground combat was relevant, even in the era of atomic brinkmanship, Taylor and his staff sketched a heady new mission for the army: "nation building." Highly trained elite forces would teach local troops the techniques of counterinsurgency against guerrilla fighters and instruct them in twentieth-century technology and liberal democracy. Air cavalry and special units such as the Green Berets were to ensure that the Third World would be stable and friendly to the United States. For Kennedy even more than for Dulles, the front lines of the cold war were everywhere, and Capitol Hill enthusiastically funded Taylor's experiments.

Others in the new administration stressed using America's wealth to pro- mote development. In a fervor of can-do activism, these individuals talked about short-circuiting the poverty and sense of helplessness that they felt fueled communist appeals in the underdeveloped world. Ironically, while Kennedy found it difficult to secure congressional approval for reform at home, Congress authorized new departures in foreign aid, such as the Al- liance for Progress and the Peace Corps. The Alliance for Progress, the New Frontier advocates calculated, would thwart radicalism in Latin America and encourage moderate, reformist leaders while breaking oligarchic or anti- American regimes. This "ten-year plan for the Americas" was signed at Punta del Este, Uruguay, in August 1961 by all nations of the Western Hemisphere except Canada and Cuba. The United States promised new credits and private investment that over the next decade would finance social programs, such as health care, housing, and education; boost local rates of growth by 2.5 percent annually; and encourage industrial diversification and land reform. The Agency for International Development (AID), operating on a smaller scale in all Third World areas, also promoted anticommunist modernization.

An even more imaginative program, the Peace Corps sent volunteers to willing nations throughout the world. Functioning primarily in rural areas, it worked to improve health, education, and economic efficiency. Director R. Sargent Shriver expected no dramatic results, only "cumulative years of goodwill among the common folk." By 1963 volunteers were working in over forty countries as teachers, crop specialists, and construction supervisors.

The Alliance for Progress became a disaster because reform stalled and expectations outran growth. Latin America grew more debt-ridden and even more dependent on U.S.-based multinationals. The Peace Corps also came under attack from some who suspected its motives; Bolivia, for example, ex- pelled volunteers. But both programs reflected the New Frontier's confidence in its ability to shape the world in its own image.

Cuba

Events in Cuba made an activist foreign policy not only feasible but al- most mandatory. The Eisenhower administration had given the green light to a CIA project to invade Cuba with a small force of anti-Castro expatriates, and Kennedy decided to follow through on his predecessor's plan. The dis- gruntled population of Cuba, America's spies predicted, would welcome these rebels as liberators. On April 17, 1961, two days after CIA mercenaries had at- tacked Cuba's air bases with B-26 bombers, approximately 1,400 Cuban exiles waded ashore at the Bay of Pigs. Local peasants ignored the unlikely army, most of them pro-Batista urbanites, and Castro's forces soon surrounded them. Though some in the State Department urged full-scale intervention, Kennedy reluctantly accepted the fact of disaster. "Victory has a hundred fa- thers," he said, "but defeat is an orphan." The Bay of Pigs fiasco only tight- ened Castro's control in Cuba, reinforced his dependence on the Soviet Union, and loosed yet another round of Yankeephobia throughout most of

Latin America. The debacle also raised Kennedy's anxiety about being perceived as weak-willed and thus increased his determination to "get tough" in future showdowns.

Before Washington officials could recover from this setback, another confrontation loomed. Perhaps hoping to gain easy concessions from an inexperienced president at an informal summit meeting in Vienna in June 1961, Khrushchev hinted at war unless NATO abandoned West Berlin. If the United States did not agree, the premier explained, he could secure the same result by signing a separate peace with his East German ally Walter Ulbricht. Determined to uphold America's credibility, Kennedy mobilized the National Guard, accelerated arms production, and tripled draft calls. Khrushchev blustered about "thermonuclear holocaust" but acted much more cautiously. Barbed wire and then a wall of cement blocks sealed off West Berlin from the rest of East Germany, ending an embarrassing flow of defectors to the West (some 3 million since 1945) and cutting off a black market in goods and currencies. Kennedy gracefully accepted this compromise, realizing the substance of victory.

Stung by rebukes from domestic critics for his poor showing, Khrushchev quickly looked for a major strategic victory. Frightened of America's aggressiveness, Castro asked the Soviet Union for military hardware, and Khrushchev replied with large shipments of sophisticated weapons, including missiles armed with atomic warheads. Kennedy responded with a week of crisis diplomacy. In a televised address on October 22, 1962, he vowed, "The United States will not compromise its safety," and ordered the Strategic Air Command to full alert. Two days later the navy quarantined the island, its destroyers ready to turn away any Soviet merchant ships carrying missiles. But Kennedy also began searching for compromise: If the Soviet Union removed its weapons, the United States would not attack Cuba again. While public prodding continued—UN Ambassador Adlai Stevenson urged the Soviets "to save the peace"—complicated secret messages between the Kremlin and the White House soon confirmed Kennedy's offer. Amid headlines warning of imminent nuclear war, Khrushchev ordered Soviet ships to return home, and the missiles began to be dismantled. Castro's Cuba continued to be harassed by CIA plots to destabilize the regime, but superpower confrontation there was over.

The Cuban missile crisis highlighted the perils of cold war diplomacy. The swiftness of nuclear escalation frightened both sides; mutual blackmail, if miscalculated, could easily get out of control. Then, too, both powers had other concerns. In late 1962 China overran Tibet and ostentatiously began atomic tests near the Soviet border. Mao Zedong openly challenged Moscow for leadership of the Communist bloc. The Americans looked toward Vietnam, experimenting with counterinsurgency, nation building, and the other tactics of flexible response. Superpower rhetoric mellowed: Khrushchev talked of "peaceful coexistence," and Kennedy called for "mutual tolerance." During the summer of 1963 the two countries set up a "hot line," a direct telephone link between their capitals. And on July 25, 1963, America, Britain, and the Soviet Union initialed a nuclear test-ban treaty that ended all except underground atomic explosions. (Soviet fears that on-site inspections might reveal too much about its industrial potential made a total ban impossible.) Such gestures did little to ease rivalry between the two superpowers, but they did indicate a mutual desire to avoid nuclear confrontation.

If Cuba daily reminded Washington officials of cold war dangers, peaceful coexistence allowed them to act elsewhere in the Third World. And most Americans, proud of their ingenuity, did not easily recognize limits to what was possible. Surely, with such riches, such power, such determination, the United States could build nations in the Third World like itself: prosperous, democratic, and anticommunist. Nurtured by this self-confident, activist atmosphere in the Kennedy administration, the American role in Vietnam fatefully expanded.

STRUGGLE IN VIETNAM

Hoping to sharpen the nation's credibility while pushing back a communist liberation movement, the Kennedy administration tested its new flexible approach in Southeast Asia. Diem still blocked reform, despite pressure from American ambassadors. Nonetheless, the Democrats undertook a military defeat of the National Liberation Front (NLF). Billions of dollars, tons of sophisticated weapons, and 16,000 American support and combat troops inundated the Vietnamese countryside by 1963. At first, the communist effort wavered, seemingly justifying the Pentagon's tactics. But then Hanoi increased its aid to the insurgents, and Kennedy widened the American intervention to include a covert war against North Vietnam. More discouraging, Diem's regime came apart at the seams. Limitless treasure from Washington brought jolting corruption to Saigon. The scramble for loot hindered normal operations of state. Land reform collapsed.

In May 1963, the Catholic archbishop forbade the carrying of Buddhist flags, and Diem's anti-Buddhist persecution grew strong throughout the provinces. Now, forced either to abandon some religious practices or to face charges of treason, Buddhists organized massive demonstrations, which culminated on June 16, 1963, when a priest martyred himself by setting fire to his gasoline-soaked robes. As if finally convinced of Diem's turpitude, city people paraded in the streets and prayed at pagodas for his downfall. For nearly two months the regime waited for animosities to abate, but more self-immolations and the growing violence of student strikes convinced Diem and his brother, Ngo Dinh Nhu, that only strong measures could restore order. On August 21, detachments from American-trained special-forces units attacked Buddhist sanctuaries in Saigon, Hue, and most provincial capitals. This repression, coupled with political arrests, prompted another, even more violent, cycle of protests and autocratic response. Intellectuals and the urban middle class abandoned the Diem regime, which was now consumed in self-destruction.

No one in Washington knew what to do. One obvious reaction was to excise the cancer: Diem must go. The internal chaos of his regime enervated the war effort against the communists and mocked hopes for a democratic example for the Third World. Religious persecution bothered Americans, including the president, himself a Catholic. During the fall of 1963 several Vietnamese generals suggested plans for a coup to the American ambassador, Henry Cabot Lodge. They received the encouraging reply that Washington would not intervene in "an internal matter." The CIA also began to work toward Diem's replacement. In October the Kennedy administration unexpectedly canceled the commercial-import program that financed Diem's government and publicly disavowed the rest of his family. Reassured that Washington would support Diem's ouster, the generals wheeled into action, and on November 1st Vietnamese battalions near Saigon captured administrative centers and surrounded Diem's palace. The man whom Americans had vainly tried to turn into the George Washington of Vietnam died that night, murdered while trying to escape from his country.

American Goals and Vietnamese Realities

That same month an era also ended in the United States. On November 22, 1963, President Kennedy died in Dallas, Texas, victim of an assassination. Anxious to maintain continuity, Lyndon Johnson did not challenge the growing involvement in Vietnam, and White House advisers put forth new variations on cold war themes. The United States must repel communist aggression now or face repeated nibbling elsewhere. If Washington faltered, many Third World leaders might question America's ability, even its willingness, to protect their countries against subversion. The Soviet Union must understand Yankee determination to contain communism. Walt Whitman Rostow, a top adviser on foreign affairs, speculated that American pressure in Vietnam would divert Chinese attention away from the Pacific and toward central Asia, thus aggravating the Sino-Soviet split. Vietnamese problems therefore became absorbed into global strategy: A Pentagon expert explained in 1968 that repelling communist aggression in Asia was "only 10 percent" of America's purpose; the war was being fought primarily to reassure allies that the U.S. would keep its commitments.

Seeking larger goals, bureaucrats lost sight of their tool, Vietnam, still a very traditional peasant society. For centuries, ritual emperors had symbolized universal order for thousands of economically self-sufficient villages. Individuals molded themselves into a historical process that emphasized continuity with the past, not progress toward a different future. The Vietnamese valued harmony, unanimity, and adherence to legitimate authority as a means of ensuring the day-to-day functioning of society and its primary institution, the village. French colonialism had ripped away the emperor's "mandate of Heaven"—popular confidence in his right to rule—and warped the agrarian economy. The new masters demanded surplus, not self-sufficiency, and herded Vietnamese together on rice or rubber plantations. Saigon and Hanoi became parasitic pleasure spas for these *colons* and their upper-class mandarin supporters. Although ethnocentric French teachers tried for decades to "civilize" the population, they educated only a class of intellectuals, who were thereby alienated from the rest of the people. Despite such changes, the villages' agrarianism remained the basis for both society and ethics.

The first Indochinese war, followed by Diem's ruthless centralism, aggravated the rural-urban split, the tension between old and new, familiar and foreign. Westerners preached development, whereas the National Liberation Front extolled the communal basis of life in Vietnamese villages. Red cadres talked of traditional ways and enacted land reforms immediately. Rulers in Saigon tried to impose forms of democracy, but peasants feared Saigon as a hostile place with novel, disruptive ideas.

Americans never realized how hard it would be for their revolution from above to compete with the NLF restoration from below. In one sense, however, President Johnson had few, if any, options. Only a strong American presence could stave off internal collapse in South Vietnam, now without a leader or even a government. The new president's advisers did not readily abandon old rationales. Johnson accepted their theories about credibility as much as he had earlier theories about dominoes: "The United States must take a strong stand," he said, "or else no one will believe our promises." After a month-long inspection tour, Secretary of Defense Robert S. McNamara and Chief of Staff Maxwell Taylor had reported on October 2, 1963, that the United States could probably begin pulling out its troops by early 1964. The opposite occurred.

A Vigorous Beginning, 1964–1965

America began the second Indochinese war during the winter of 1964–1965, responding to growing chaos in South Vietnam. A revolving door of military juntas undermined the anticommunist effort on the battlefield and aggravated Diem's legacy of corruption and malaise. The NLF rapidly filled the political vacuum in the countryside, appealing to many Vietnamese frustrated by years of indecisive warfare. By the middle of 1964 the NLF, always supported by military aid from Hanoi, had begun preparations for a major assault on provincial capitals. Considerably frightened at this prospect, Pentagon officials drew up plans for an air war against North Vietnam. No other option seemed feasible, short of an embarrassing disengagement or total war. But escalation required legal, if not moral, justification. The White House drafted a congressional resolution authorizing air attacks and waited for an opportunity.

It came almost too quickly. In early August a confrontation developed in the Gulf of Tonkin. The U.S. spy ship *Maddox* violated Hanoi's self-proclaimed 12-mile territorial sea limit. Assuming that the destroyer was part of a larger operation, North Vietnam ordered several PT boats into the area and several volleys were exchanged. Two days later the *Maddox* and another destroyer, the

C. Turner Joy, returned to the Gulf of Tonkin. In the midst of a storm on the night of August 4, anxious naval captains and malfunctioning sonar equipment reported an attack. By afternoon the commander of the *Maddox* wired that there had been no visual sighting and that freak weather effects may have explained the sonar and radar signals. But the Johnson administration sought an excuse for retaliation and chose to believe the first reports of an attack.

Denouncing "unprovoked aggression" during a nationally televised speech, President Johnson ordered reprisal raids against North Vietnamese naval bases. The temporary feeling of crisis prompted Congress to pass the so-called Gulf of Tonkin resolution. Its open-ended phraseology authorized Johnson "to take all necessary measures" to repulse communist advances. Unaware of the dubious nature of Hanoi's attacks and, like the chief executive himself, ill informed about Vietnamese complexities, the Senate adopted the

South Vietnam and Cambodia

de facto declaration of war, eighty-eight to two. Only Senators Wayne Morse and Ernest Gruening voted against this potentially unlimited commitment.

During his 1964 presidential campaign, Johnson had presented himself as a peace candidate, firmly rejecting prescriptions from critics, such as former air force Chief of Staff Curtis Lemay, for "bombing Hanoi back into the Stone Age." After the 1964 presidential election, however, U.S. officials launched a sustained air assault. Pentagon bureaucrats argued that the Saigon clique could not reform itself as long as insurgency continued. Guerrilla attacks would go on as long as North Vietnam supplied them. Bombing strikes against the North and elite counterinsurgency operations in the South would defeat this war of national liberation, Washington's best and brightest told one another, and restore America's global credibility. But analysis could not alter reality. Anger and discontent with the Saigon regime, together with carefully cultivated affinities between Vietnamese communism and Vietnamese traditionalism, fueled the NLF's success.

More and more, the problem of Vietnam preoccupied Washington's planners. The treadmill of escalation continued. It seemed reasonable: Just a little more aid, just a few more soldiers would break the rebellion. Victory always seemed so close. Johnson himself believed that a steady, predictable escalation would avoid intervention by China or Russia and at the same time convince the NLF and Hanoi that they would not win.

Determination Becomes Self-delusion, 1965–1967

The war slowly intensified. Sustained bombing of North Vietnam began on February 15, 1965, ostensibly in reprisal for an NLF mortar attack against a Marine Corps base at Pleiku. That spring, American combat troops began to aid Vietnamese army units under fire. Johnson authorized the first search-and-destroy missions—independent sweeps involving large numbers of GIs—in June 1965, several miles northwest of Saigon. Most military experts guessed that victory required a ten-to-one numerical advantage over NLF–North Vietnamese troops. But the enemy, then recruiting the bulk of their troops within South Vietnam itself, at this ratio more than matched Pentagon escalations.

Against a backdrop of Johnsonian rhetoric about "winning the hearts and minds of the Vietnamese people," a plethora of bureaucrats crisscrossed the countryside with experiments. AID officials ostensibly brought health care and modern agricultural techniques. Combat units built hospitals, schools, orphanages. Government programs assured farmers of high prices for their crops but low prices for consumers. The junta in Saigon periodically deployed urban volunteers to counteract the work of communist cadres. Such nation building, however, barely touched communist strength in rural areas. By 1967 frustrated officials adopted still another device for rural pacification: the strategic-hamlet program. To protect villagers from NLF attack and ensure their loyalties to Saigon, American soldiers garrisoned many rural towns, often erecting makeshift forts. Herded into barbed-wire enclosures, living under American machine guns, the peasants were expected to continue their agrarian way of life. Such concentration camps did achieve their military purpose, but they alienated farmers, now isolated from land and tradition.

Bewildered and angered by the failure of their good intentions, Americans came to rely on more direct and even savage tactics. Computer printouts in Washington explained that improved "kill ratios" were needed. Bombs, artillery, and rifles could kill so many enemy soldiers that eventually the NLF and North Vietnamese could not replace them, given their relatively small population base. If such thinking skirted genocide, the nature of guerrilla war made it almost inevitable. The NLF did not wear uniforms. Taking Mao Zedong's advice, insurgents "swam like fishes in a sea of people" and fought a war of stealth: ambush, booby trap, sabotage, and quick mortar barrage.

To many American soldiers, both enthusiastic volunteers and scared draftees, the war became one against the Vietnamese themselves. Search-and-destroy missions created a misconception that "body count" alone mattered. Some officers, realizing that careers depended on numbers, lied to superiors about enemy dead; GIs tortured NLF suspects, matching the tactics of their foe. The U.S. command in Saigon charted free-fire zones, huge areas in which helicopter gunships strafed anything alive. Chemicals defoliated the earth, and bombers pulverized North Vietnam's industry and South Vietnam's farms. Some devices may have limited communist freedom of movement, but they also destroyed American prestige. In a traditional society whose members valued their ties to ancestral lands and to village communities, terror, free-fire zones, and wholesale murder steadily discredited the American cause.

The Americans miscalculated badly, but few admitted it. Middle-level civilians and field officers reported what higher officials in Saigon wanted to hear, not the actuality of stagnation. America's ambassadors and generals further refined the stylized ritual: We are winning the war, they wired Washington, but send us more money, more men. For many in the administration, tough-mindedness became not a style but an end. A militant stand ensured approval as a "realistic appraisal," and giving assurance of victory garnered points in bureaucratic infighting. Having shoehorned the conflict into America's global strategy, Johnson isolated himself completely from Vietnamese realities and vowed that "I will not be the first president to lose a war."

Neither Diplomacy nor Reform

Unrealistic calculations scuttled opportunities for compromise. Johnson and his advisers used diplomacy either to justify further escalation or to attempt to secure an American victory. When U Thant, secretary-general of the United Nations, suggested in July 1964 that the Geneva Conference reconvene, Johnson righteously refused: "We do not believe in conferences called to ratify terror." But nine months later, the war firmly escalated, the president told an audience at Johns Hopkins University that the United States would discuss peace. He even offered American capital to rebuild "a peaceful Southeast Asia," almost a bribe for surcease. Yet his continued demand for a noncommunist regime in Saigon was unrealistic, tantamount to a Hanoi-NLF capitulation. The enemy routinely rejected such transparent efforts to achieve at the bargaining table what American soldiers had not won in the field. Every rebuff, the president chided his critics, proved communist perfidy.

Johnson used diplomacy more for warmaking than for peacemaking. During a thirty-seven-day period in December 1965 and January 1966, he halted the Rolling Thunder bombing raids against North Vietnam and ostentatiously sponsored a far-flung peace initiative. His closest friends applauded his cleverness. The air war had not materially impaired Hanoi's war production, and few military targets remained. Ho Chi Minh had simply decentralized, then camouflaged his industry in the countryside. Although Ho responded to Johnson's pause with hints about a coalition or neutralist government for South Vietnam, Johnson rejected further talks. Instead he pointed to enemy "truculence" and unleashed a new air war, this one directed against Hanoi's supply routes through Indochinese mountains and jungles. At the same time Johnson vigorously escalated the ground war. Troop levels jumped from 150,000 in February 1966 to 550,000 at their peak in 1968. For nearly twenty-four months, America saved South Vietnam from communism by systematically destroying its land and people.

Washington bureaucrats also tried to reform Saigon's government. Absorbed in its coups and intrigues but assured of American money, the military junta became not only dictatorial but also useless. Johnson summoned the two most recently installed generals, Nguyen Van Thieu and Nyguyen Cao Ky, to a meeting in Honolulu in February 1966. He extracted promises from the quiet Thieu and the more flamboyant Ky that they would redistribute land, end corruption, and rule more liberally. Like Kennedy before him, the president had few levers to enforce the glib assurances from Vietnamese leaders. Thieu and Ky were elected president and vice-president by suspiciously lopsided victories in 1967 after a "constitutional convention," but they "postponed" reforms and ruled through fiat and secret police. This facade of democracy in Saigon only aggravated discontent in the countryside.

The ugliness of brutal, unending war in Vietnam began to repulse many American citizens. A growing protest movement questioned the country's purposes. Although he had guided the Gulf of Tonkin resolution through the Senate, J. William Fulbright lashed out against what he called "the arrogance of power." "Power," the head of the Foreign Relations Committee observed, "tends to confuse itself with virtue." Many thought dangerous the Pentagon's sense of omnipotence and the president's voluble self-righteousness. Perhaps America could not reshape other societies. More and more people expressed their moral distaste for the Vietnam adventure. Months of generally peaceful protest marches culminated in October 1967 in a giant three-day rally in Washington, D.C. The mushrooming antiwar movement deprived Johnson of part of his natural constituency among liberal Democrats. More ominous, the protests polarized American society into "hawks" or "doves"—those who favored pursuing victory or a compromise peace.

Tet and the President's Discontent, 1968

The year 1968 became a turning point. Many people already doubted whether the United States could ever win in Vietnam at any reasonable cost, but a majority of Americans still believed in the cause. Walt Rostow told reporters that captured documents showed a communist collapse to be "imminent," and, indeed, the NLF was becoming exhausted and desperate. Then in late January 1968, during celebrations for Tet, Vietnam's lunar new year, NLF guerrillas and North Vietnamese armies coordinated a massive attack against Saigon and Hue, the imperial capital of Vietnam, and also against nine provincial capitals. The insurgents overran much of Cholon, the Chinese section of Saigon, and even penetrated the American embassy, killing several guards. In Hue the rebels executed a reign of terror against their political opponents. The attacks on regional cities had the greatest military repercussions. To restore control, General William Westmoreland had to shift troops from northern South Vietnam and from rural areas to take and then garrison places like Tay Ninh, Quang Tri, Pleiku, and other towns. Communist cadres quickly infiltrated the now unprotected countryside.

The U.S. command saw silver in the lining of the Tet offensive cloud. The NLF had overextended itself, exhausting months of supplies in an unsuccessful effort to end the war. "The enemy is on the ropes," Westmoreland said.

In 1964 Lyndon Johnson was widely celebrated as a political genius; by 1968, largely as a result of the Vietnam War, and the growing protests against it, his popularity and his political reputation were in eclipse. *Source:* National Archives.

"Tet was his last gasp." If only he had 200,000 more men, the American commander promised, he would crush the rural insurgency "once and for all." But several civilian advisers had for months counseled diplomatic compromise. McNamara recommended a coalition government for South Vietnam and then resigned. George Ball, the under secretary of state, repeatedly pointed out the folly of shooting a people into allegiance and had already resigned; the CIA for years had counseled against the effort. But Johnson had, until now, listened more to his generals, demanding only good news and then relying on their promises. After the Tet offensive, the president asked an old friend and much-respected confidant of Democratic presidents, Clark Clifford, to chart a fresh course. As the new secretary of defense, Clifford soon discovered that the military numbers game was relatively straightforward. To send 200,000 men to Southeast Asia and still protect American commitments elsewhere, the president would have to call up the army reserves or triple already high draft quotas. Only new taxes and wide-ranging controls on an overheated economy could ensure war production at a reasonable cost and temper an accelerating inflation. Senators privately told their former majority leader what many citizens knew instinctively: The country would reject such steps toward mobilization for war. Despite the fact that Tet had been a major military setback for the NLF, Clifford urged Johnson to negotiate.

Events, not advice, finally shoved the president toward diplomacy. The Tet offensive had convinced many in Vietnam that the war could never end until the United States left. "Before the Americans came," an old man told a reporter in Saigon, "my home was on the land of my ancestors and my family was honorable. Now I live off my daughter's earnings as a hooch-girl." Morale cracked in the U.S. Army. Helicopter pilots refused to fly during their last four weeks "in country." Some units sought escape in drugs or "fragging"—surreptitious assaults on their own officers. Others lost all restraint, as at My Lai, where American soldiers bayoneted children, women, and old men, apparently without thought or guilt. Both Vietnamese society and the army were coming apart under the strain of a stalemated war.

Amid the pressures for peace, Johnson gradually lost control of his party. Senator Eugene J. McCarthy, an outspoken Democratic critic of Pentagon policy, nearly won New Hampshire's presidential primary, and Robert F. Kennedy announced his candidacy and pledged to stop the conflict. And the president, a great campaigner, could not defend himself publicly on the hustings: The Secret Service considered the security risk too great. Trapped in the White House, losing both the presidential nomination and popular respect, Johnson brooded about his nemesis, Vietnam. Finally, on March 31, 1968, Johnson told a nationwide TV audience that he had rejected Westmoreland's request for more troops. American escalation would stop. To signal his good intentions and lure Hanoi to the bargaining table, he halted bombing north of the nineteenth parallel. Then, almost as a postscript, Johnson announced that he would not run for reelection.

Yet the level of violence within South Vietnam actually increased. Thieu promised to conscript another 135,000 men, a figure that together with more

Americans already in training camps would almost fulfill Westmoreland's request. Proscribed from attacking the North, American pilots intensified the air war in the South. The president was still attempting to "negotiate from strength." Moreover, he intentionally omitted any reference to a coalition government. Johnson still sought an American peace, a noncommunist South Vietnam.

Ho Chi Minh, wanting to ensure the bombing halt, took up Johnson's offer for talks, and in private American and Vietnamese negotiators gradually worked out a practical arrangement that reflected battlefield realities. America would end all bombing if North Vietnam agreed "by its silence" not to escalate support for the NLF. Both sides might then consider possible coalition governments for South Vietnam. In this compromise, however, Johnson had not reckoned with his obstreperous ally in Saigon. Thieu thought that the Republican candidate could arrange better terms: "I will win the peace," Richard Nixon had vowed. So Saigon obstructed multilateral talks with the NLF, thus scuttling the compromise. Johnson stayed the bombing anyway, but he could not guarantee Saigon's good faith. If he cut off American aid, the communists would win by default. Thieu could always discipline Washington with threats that he would quit and thereby bring on chaos. Nixon's victory pleased Thieu immensely, but the new president required time to formulate specific policies. Diplomats marked time by haggling over the shape of the bargaining table. By the beginning of 1969, the Republicans faced an extraordinarily difficult situation: stalemated war, ungovernable allies, and domestic impatience with half measures.

VIETNAM FALLOUT

Washington's fixation with Southeast Asia distorted U.S. foreign policy. The war in Vietnam simultaneously pleased and worried the Soviets. America's burgeoning armies flanked their Chinese rival while it consumed capitalist treasure. Yankee search-and-destroy missions in the Mekong Delta freed the Soviets for attempts to expand their influence in the Middle East. Yet Johnson's very willingness to use force convinced Khrushchev's successors, Leonid Brezhnev and Aleksei Kosygin, that the Americans respected only military strength. Many Soviet scientists worried about the implications of NASA's (National Aeronautics and Space Administration) mammoth space rockets and plans for orbiting platforms. The Soviets stepped up production of their most sophisticated missile, the SS-9, and accelerated atomic stockpiling. Unable to match this buildup weapon for weapon, given Vietnam's huge drain on available resources, the United States intensified the technology of nuclear war, developing Multiple Independent Reentry Vehicles (MIRVs), which vastly increased the payload of a single rocket, and "smart bombs," which guided themselves to their target through electronic devices.

But neither power wanted to let cold war rivalry escalate beyond its control. During June 1967 Johnson and Kosygin conferred privately at Glassboro

State College in New Jersey. Worried that the enormous success of Israel's just completed Six-Day War might somehow bring on a Soviet-American clash, each promised to respect his rival's vital interests in the crucial Middle East region. Rather than jeopardize the Nuclear Nonproliferation Treaty, finally signed in early 1969, Washington reacted mildly to Moscow's brutal repression of Czechoslovakian reform efforts in 1968. Such tradeoffs symbolized, once again, the high priority both nations placed on avoiding atomic war.

Though consistently proclaimed as a crusade to reassure its allies, America's adventure in Southeast Asia further fragmented the Atlantic alliance. Western Europe's accelerating prosperity—itself a reflection of American spending overseas—eroded its sense of dependency. Arguments over strategy vitiated traditional comradeship. Determined to build a national nuclear force and, more grandiosely, to break out of "sterile bipolarity," Charles de Gaulle took France out of the NATO alliance, though he did not relinquish its protection. Many West Germans, hoping to build better relations with their neighbors, chafed at Washington's rigid anticommunism. Even the "special relationship" between Great Britain and the United States withered a bit. As economic obsolescence shoved the English toward the Common Market, they realized more and more their junior membership in the "atomic club." Prime ministers and many other Britons opposed America's policy in Vietnam. If Johnson felt somehow betrayed, England, no less than the rest of NATO, worried that its powerful protector had lost a sense of proportion. The United States seemed so drained by Vietnam that it could hardly attend to other pressing problems (its balance of international payments, for example). Vietnam became the most visible wedge that drove the Atlantic community apart, Europe's regional interests clashing with America's global visions.

Throughout the Third World the conflict in Southeast Asia resuscitated old devices in American diplomacy. Determined to create an Asian consensus for his policy, Johnson did not challenge oppressive regimes in the Philippines and South Korea as long as they supported the American effort in Vietnam. Both countries sent troops to Vietnam. American money once again supported a military oligarchy in Indonesia after General Suharto ousted the increasingly pro-Chinese Sukarno in 1965. During the late 1960s, then, the United States forced everyone into roles as pro–United States or procommunist, ignoring throughout Asia, as in Vietnam, both nationalism and indigenous cultures.

Such attitudes reverberated in policies toward Latin America. Once again Washington honored dictators. In 1964 in Brazil, for example, a cabal of generals supported by the United States toppled the populist Joao Goulart, who was showing growing interest in the nationalization of foreign businesses. Panicked by fears of "another Cuba," Johnson even resorted to military intervention in the Caribbean. In the Dominican Republic, a right-wing coup had ousted the constitutionally elected reformist government of Juan Bosch. But when Bosch's supporters attempted to regain control, American representatives on the island reported that communists had infiltrated Bosch's movement and requested Johnson to send the marines. Some 20,000 troops landed in mid-1965, and despite the quickly discovered inaccuracy of American reports, Johnson left the troops there until September 1966, when carefully supervised elections installed another pro-American leader, Joaquin Balaguer, as president. American gunboat diplomacy and alliances with dictators complemented a geyser of private investment by American corporations looking to Latin America for a quick profit but demanding political stability.

Preoccupied with Vietnam, Johnson either ignored change elsewhere or woodenly enforced the status quo. In this way the Southeast Asian war blinded America to the future, distorting its foreign policies and pushing others into a ready-made mold. The tensions could not be checked for long, but Johnson contained them for the moment.

Johnson's Legacy

If complex, the Democrats' legacy was not unmanageable. Peace talks in Paris provided a continuing structure for negotiation, but Johnson (and his successor) still hoped to win. South Vietnamese troops, presumably more motivated than America's dispirited soldiers, and sophisticated firepower, American leaders hoped, could "Vietnamize" the war while winning it. However plausible in the short run, such tactics could not remedy the flaw of American involvement. More years would pass before the nation's leaders abandoned this goal. By then, Johnson's war had become Nixon's war.

Most people did not immediately recognize another casualty of war—American socioeconomic stability. To pay for the most expensive war in the country's history, the White House loosed an inflation at home and a dollar crisis abroad that developed their own momentum. By the 1970s America's wealth and self-confidence had visibly atrophied. The adventure in Vietnam, far from protecting American institutions from foreign dangers, helped to bring them under increasing attack both from domestic critics and from external forces.

SUGGESTIONS FOR FURTHER READING

Many of the general studies listed in *Suggestions for Further Reading* in Chapter One—such as McCormick, LaFeber, and Ambrose—are relevant for the 1960s. In addition, see Richard J. Barnet, *Intervention and Revolution* (rev. ed., 1972); Thomas G. Paterson, ed., *Kennedy's Quest for Victory* (1989); Bernard Firestone and Robert C. Vogt, eds., *Lyndon Baines Johnson and the Uses of Power* (1989); David W. Levy, *The Debate Over Vietnam* (1991); and David L. Di Leo, *George Ball, Vietnam, and the Rethinking of Containment* (1991).

On specific issues, see Graham Allison, *Essence of Decision* (1971), on the missile crisis; Warren Cohen, *Dean Rusk* (1980); Henry Jackson, *From Congo to Soweto: United States Foreign Policy toward Africa Since 1960* (1982); Walter A. McDougal, *The Heavens and the Earth: A Political History of the Space Age* (1985); Richard D. Mahoney, *JFK: Ordeal in Africa* (1983); Glen Seaborg, *Stemming the Tide: Arms Control in the Johnson Years* (1987); Jane Stromseth, *The Origins of*

Flexible Response (1988); Trumbell Higgins, *The Perfect Failure: Kennedy, Eisenhower, and the CIA at the Bay of Pigs* (1989); Bruce Palmer, Jr., *Intervention in the Caribbean: The Dominican Crisis of 1965* (1989); Dino A. Brugoni, *Eyeball to Eyeball: The Inside Story of the Cuban Missile Crisis* (1991); Michael R. Beschloss, *The Crisis Years: Kennedy and Khrushchev, 1960–1963* (1991); and Richard B. Parker, *The Politics of Miscalculation in the Middle East* (1993).

Much of the scholarly debate, like most of the contemporary debate during the 1960s, has focused on Vietnam. In addition to volumes listed earlier—such as George Herring's *America's Longest War* (1986)—the following are good places to begin: William Appleman Williams et al., *America in Vietnam* (1985), a very valuable set of documents; Leslie Gelb and Richard K. Betts, *The Irony of Vietnam* (1978); Paul Joseph, *Cracks in the Empire* (1981); Larry Berman, *Planning a Tragedy* (1982); the relevant chapters of Lawrence Wittner, *Rebels Against War: The American Peace Movement, 1933–1983* (1984); Bruce Palmer, Jr., *The 25-Year War* (1985); William Conrad Gibbons, *The United States Government and the Vietnam War: Executive and Legislative Roles and Relationships* (1986); R. B. Smith, *An International History of the Vietnam War* (2 vols., 1985, 1987); Gabriel Kolko, *Anatomy of a War* (1986); Melvin Small, *Johnson, Nixon, and the Doves* (1988); Larry Berman, *Lyndon Johnson's War: The Road to Stalemate in Vietnam* (1989); John P. Burke and Fred Greenstein, *How Presidents Test Reality: Decisions on Vietnam, 1954 and 1965* (1989); Mark Clodfelter, *The Limits of Air Power: The American Bombing of North Vietnam* (1989); Marilyn Young and Jon Livingston, *The Vietnam War: How the United States Intervened in the History of Southeast Asia* (1990); David Levy, *The Debate Over Vietnam* (1991); James J. Wirtz, *The Tet Offensive* (1991); Ronald Spector, *After Tet: The Bloodiest Year in Vietnam* (1992); Noam Chomsky, *Rethinking Camelot: JFK, the Vietnam War, and U.S. Political Culture* (1993); and David M. Barrett, *Uncertain Warriors: Lyndon Johnson and His Vietnam Advisors* (1993).

For cultural views of the war, see Loren Bartiz, *Backfire: A History of How American Culture Led Us Into Vietnam and Made Us Fight the Way We Did* (1985); Susan Jeffords, *The Remasculinization of America* (1989); John Carlos Rowe and Rick Berg, eds., *The Vietnam War and American Culture* (1991); Linda Dittmar and Gene Michaud, eds., *From Hanoi to Hollywood: The Vietnam War in American Film* (1990); and Michael Gregg, ed., *Inventing Vietnam: The War in Film and Television* (1991). Kathleen Turner, *Lyndon Johnson's Dual War* (1985), looks at LBJ's problems with the press.

7

The Years of Protest and the Search for Empowerment in the 1960s and Early 1970s

THE YOUTH MOVEMENT AND THE SEARCH FOR A NEW POLITICS, 1963–1968

For more than two decades, people have been debating the meaning of the dissenting movements of the 1960s and early 1970s. During recent years, for example, some former activists have dismissed their old antiestablishment ideas and activities as the dangerous fantasies of youth. In stark contrast, many others reject confessions or apologies. Still committed to the dissenting spirit of the years of protest, they insist that the old insurgent agenda remains relevant to the problems of the 1990s. But even people espousing these polar positions, as well as those who have views that fall somewhere in between, agree on one point: The outpouring of dissent during the 1960s and early 1970s represented one of the central themes in postwar history.

The Revolt of Youth

Young people's enthusiasm for John Kennedy led supporters of the New Frontier to expect that the 1960s would be a decade of nearly steady liberal reform. But even before Kennedy's death, some young people were expressing disillusionment with JFK's gradualism and with liberalism itself, and they were calling for a new youth movement. *Youth movement* is an imprecise term for a loose collection of very diverse groups with very different styles of political and cultural dissent. Members of the New Left concentrated on finding political solutions for what they considered liberalism's failures; they believed that radical action by youthful community activists could bring significant social change and "power to the people." In contrast, cultural radicals displayed little interest in traditional political concerns; devotees of the counterculture advocated altered forms of social consciousness and a revolution in values as the best antidotes for what they saw as the sterility and repressiveness of post-war society.

Radicals never discovered how to alter dramatically the direction of post-war society. The New Left did gain allies and make headway on specific issues—especially opposition to America's involvement in Vietnam—but radical politics sometimes tailed off into ineffectual gestures and, on a few occasions, random acts of violence. Cultural radicals also left an ambiguous legacy. Many young people adopted the outward symbols of cultural revolt, such as drugs and faded blue jeans, but most retained a desire to one day settle down within the existing social and economic structure. Some aspects of the cultural liberation, such as the desire for self-gratification, proved perfectly compatible with the ethos of a mass consumption society. Moreover, both political and cultural protests became captives of the mass media. Film, television, and the popular press helped to contain and then trivialize the youth movement.

Still, the youth movement touched nearly every area of life. By challenging the dominant political and cultural values of the 1950s, it exerted a significant impact on the nation and widened opportunities for diversity and dissent. Especially for women of all races and for all people of color, the cultural and political insurgency that began in the 1960s helped to emphasize that the political was personal and the personal was political. This understanding contributed to a diverse and activist political culture.

The potpourri of sources from which disaffected young people sought insight and inspiration underscored the diversity of this new radicalism. Unlike the "old left" of the 1920s and 1930s, which looked primarily to Marxism, radicals of the 1960s sampled a variety of social theories. Beat writers, Eastern mystics, academic mavericks, and the civil rights movement helped provide the youth movement's eclectic intellectual base.

Radicals of the 1950s

The middle-class protesters of the 1960s were still opening their school day by saluting the flag when the Beat writers of the 1950s were already dismissing the United States as an "air-conditioned nightmare." Jack Kerouac's novel *On the Road* (1957) glorified the drifter, the rebel who resisted the temptation to conform. The poems of Allen Ginsberg denounced materialism and middle-class morality and celebrated the satisfaction of marijuana, Eastern mystical religions, and homosexual love. In their best works, Beat poets such as Ginsberg and Gary Snyder displayed a free-flowing style that challenged restrictive cultural forms. Part hipster and part huckster, Ginsberg kept alive the spirit of the Beat movement, becoming a revered elder-in-residence to new generations of young radicals.

While the Beats condemned postwar cultural values, the sociologist C. Wright Mills concentrated on the postwar political system. He cultivated his image as a maverick outsider, wearing a motorcycle jacket and riding a Harley Davidson. He also rejected the dispassionate, carefully nuanced stance of cold war academics in favor of politically committed, rhetoric-filled analysis. Mills helped to popularize theories that became the New Left's central tenets: that an undemocratic power elite dominated American society; that liberalism had lost its social consciousness and become an ideology of the status quo; that most liberal intellectuals merely offered rationalizations for an unjust society. An activist as well as a scholar, Mills visited Cuba and wrote a short book praising Fidel Castro's social experiments. After his death in 1962, Mills became one of the youth movement's most revered saints.

The critique of American liberalism received philosophical development in the works of Herbert Marcuse. A German-born Marxist, Marcuse attacked the sophisticated technology and economic prosperity that liberals praised so highly. The United States, according to Marcuse, was a quasi-totalitarian "technocracy." Real power lay with the technocrats—the experts in government, business, science, and other dominant institutions, who defined social policies and national priorities. In such a one-dimensional society, a technological imperative prevailed. The mass production, mass consumption economic system satisfied only "false" needs—mass-produced gadgets that provided no real sense of happiness or personal fulfillment. Disaffected young people borrowed from Marcuse and his many popularizers. Terms such as *false consciousness* and *technocracy* became parts of the radical vocabulary. The liberal "good guys"—including the people who ran the big universities and the big government in Washington—became technocratic villains. At best, liberalism seemed to be a new form of conservatism; at worst, it seemed to be a kind of suave totalitarianism that dominated people with mass-mediated images and popular illusions rather than with guns and concentration camps.

Paul Goodman, another radical social critic, claimed that liberal institutions actually repressed young Americans, especially males. In *Growing Up Absurd* (1960), Goodman argued that educational institutions stifled healthy natural instincts and subtly indoctrinated young people with the values of a badly flawed culture. Order and regularity, he claimed, took precedence over spontaneity and creativity; memorization of meaningless data became more important than critical thought; the interests of teachers and administrators outweighed the needs of students. Goodman extended his anarchist critique, contending that large bureaucracies run by technocratic experts were coming to dominate life in the United States. He did not see technology as an uncontrollable demon, as did some of his younger disciples; the problem, he argued, lay in the way that centralized institutions misapplied technology to social situations.

Experiences in the civil rights movement also propelled many young radicals, white as well as African-American, toward an open break with liberalism. Civil rights leaders relied on youthful volunteers for time-consuming, labor-intensive jobs: preparing leaflets, running copying machines, and canvassing neighborhoods. In time, the ways in which these tasks were divided along gender lines would encourage many women to embrace a new feminism; but initially, these activities brought young people together in a common cause. Often traveling long distances and sleeping in makeshift accommodations, civil rights workers discovered a sense of community that seemed missing elsewhere in the United States. As one woman later wrote, the civil rights movement to her "was everything: home and family, food and work, love and a reason to live." In such a community atmosphere, many young people found personal fulfillment in a crusade that they expected would change the entire society.

Seeking immediate solutions, civil rights workers inevitably confronted hostile or cautious political leaders. Segregationists in Alabama and Georgia would make no concessions, and liberal politicians stressed the need to move slowly and to avoid sudden changes in race relations. On many occasions southern crowds beat up civil rights workers while FBI agents simply looked on and took notes. After confronting the racial hatred of Oxford, Mississippi, or Cicero, Illinois, many young activists charged that liberals offered Band-Aid solutions for deep national wounds. Segregation and racism, young civil rights workers charged, were evils that no decent society would tolerate.

Beyond Liberalism and Toward a New Left

Not all young people protested, and the new radicals constituted only a minority of those between eighteen and twenty-five. Others remained true to the liberal spirit of John Kennedy, voting for Lyndon Johnson and going off to fight a war for "democracy and freedom" in Vietnam. Many young people bitterly resented long-haired "hippie" protestors, and they embraced the consumer products and the nine-to-five jobs scorned by the radicals. Talk of a generation gap obscured equally large fissures within the youth generation itself. It also ignored the small, yet significant, group of older radicals who joined the protest movement. But the young dissenters seemed to overshadow their peers; certainly they dominated the media and the political debates in the 1960s. Critical of the direction of society and convinced that they could find alternatives, the youthful rebels became the symbols of their entire generation.

What distinguished the young radicals from others of their age? Drawing on several studies of college students, psychologist Kenneth Keniston argued that the rebels were "psychological adults" but "sociological adolescents." Contrary to conventional wisdom, Keniston found that protesters tended to be excellent students, usually in the humanities, who suffered no great psychological difficulties. But as the products of affluent or solidly middle-class homes, they could postpone a decision to settle into permanent social roles. Instead of having to choose an established career path, they could adopt a less conventional role—that of social activist and agitator for political change. The fact that many believed their parents shared many of their ideals, but were forced to compromise them in their day-to-day lives, only intensified their own desire to remain free from settled, adult routines.

To the young dissenters, liberalism's failures seemed more important than its admitted successes. Postwar America did enjoy greater material affluence, but at a price: Most jobs seemed boring, life lacked adventure and excitement, racial discrimination oppressed millions of people, and personal relationships seemed artificial. The cool, rational world of John Kennedy appeared to lack genuine feeling and to substitute rhetoric for meaningful social change. In contrast, a stance of opposition seemed to offer hope for immediate personal fulfillment as well as the chance for basic social change. Through a commitment to radicalism young people could instantly complete Paul Simon's "dangling conversations" or explore Bob Dylan's "smoke rings of the mind."

At various universities—especially the University of Wisconsin at Madison, the University of California at Berkeley, and the University of Michigan—dissident students tried to link "radical scholarship" and social activism. The "scholarly dispassion" of their professors seemed to justify a repressive status quo. In contrast, radical graduate students came to see themselves as prototypes for a new breed of college teacher: They would awaken campus life and revitalize radical thought. Other university students took more direct action. In the San Francisco Bay area, activists from Berkeley joined older activists and staged well-publicized protests against the HUAC, capital punishment, and racial discrimination. Young people were also active in the South, helping miners fight the large coal companies in Hazard County, Kentucky, and working for civil rights organizations.

Students for a Democratic Society (SDS) epitomized the early New Left. SDS's Port Huron Statement of 1962 pleaded for a dramatically new social and political system in which people "shared in those social decisions determining the quality and direction" of their lives. As an alternative to the liberal political order—which "frustrates democracy by confusing the individual citizen, paralyzing policy discussion, and consolidating the irresponsible power of military and business interests"—SDS espoused "participatory democracy." A true participatory democracy, the Port Huron Statement argued, would be "governed by two central aims: that the individual share in those social decisions determining the quality and direction of his life; that society be organized to encourage independence in men and provide the means for their common participation." Still, the manifesto of 1962 remained essentially a leftist-liberal document. It sounded no call for revolution and endorsed specific political programs only slightly to the left of the Fair Deal–New Frontier agenda.

SDS's leaders initially viewed community organizing as the first step toward participatory democracy. Low-income people fell victim to better-organized elites, SDS argued, because they could not exert political pressure commensurate with their numbers. SDS branched out from the college campuses and launched grass-roots programs. In cities such as Newark, New

Jersey, it mounted drives against urban renewal and in support of better housing, more jobs, and school lunch programs. The first members of SDS displayed a missionary zeal. While the cultural radical was smoking dope, they bragged that they were turned on to political organizing. But they quickly discovered the difficulties of organizing low-income people, especially by a group of affluent young whites committed to participatory democracy. Inexperience in organizing, impatience with endless rounds of face-to-face meetings, and doubts about their initial visions of participatory democracy all led most SDS members to abandon the community projects. Seeking a more congenial environment and switching to the issue that seemed most pressing—the Vietnam War—SDS moved back to the college campus, the center of the youth revolt of the 1960s.

Campus Protests

The most publicized campus protest occurred at the University of California at Berkeley in the fall of 1964. When university officials tried to limit political activity by radical students, protesters charged the administration with bowing to pressures from right-wing business leaders and destroying free speech. As protests against restrictions on speech escalated, mass rallies, takeovers of university buildings, and raids by local police highlighted the Berkeley student revolt. A number of campus groups, not all of whom represented New Left factions, joined under the banner of the Free Speech Movement (FSM). Thus, the earliest protests represented more of an attack on the paternalistic, bureaucratic routine of Berkeley than a revolt against the entire university structure. In early December 1964 student protesters began wearing IBM cards as name tags; militants soon called a campus-wide strike. Student leaders claimed that almost three-quarters of the student body—and a sizable portion of the faculty—supported their three-day walkout.

The FSM also expressed cultural and political impulses that transcended campus life. To some, these seemed trivial. A young New Yorker who had drifted West, just to "check out the scene," arrived with a simple protest sign—FUCK. (Some people claimed that this really stood for Freedom Under Clark Kerr, the president of the university.) His example inspired a group of imitators, the "word mongers," and allowed the FSM to be identified by its opponents as the Filthy Speech Movement. But the FSM also represented much deeper concerns and personal commitments. As one of the movement's leaders put it, there were times when the social-political machinery "makes you so sick at heart . . . [that] you can't even tacitly take part. And you've got to put your bodies upon the gears and upon the wheels, upon the levers, upon the apparatus, and you've got to make it stop." By the spring of 1965, many of the campus issues that had precipitated the first student protests had faded, replaced by larger concerns, especially the war in Vietnam.

Berkeley provided a scenario that repeated itself on many large college campuses. Increasingly, the tone and the aims of the protesters grew more militant. In banding together to fight college administrators and their outside supporters—a student observer of the 1968 disturbances at Columbia called them "the biggies"—young people often discovered a new sense of community. As the civil rights workers in Mississippi had done earlier, though, they also developed a kind of garrison mentality, viewing themselves as victims of a faceless power structure.

The modern "multiversity" provided a perfect target. Big universities displayed what radicals considered the major sins of modern liberalism: emphasis on competitiveness, reliance on bureaucratic structures, restrictions on personal life-styles, and the belief that bigger inevitably meant better. Even many nonradicals shared some of these concerns. Sensitive young students, many of whom had been reared in families that stressed openness and concern for individual feelings, complained that large, impersonal lectures and haphazard discussion sections exemplified the multiversity's assembly-line approach to education. Many students complained about being faceless numbers, subject to the whims of giant computers and faceless bureaucrats. Even the University of California's liberal president, Clark Kerr, saw himself as the administrator of a large "benevolent bureaucracy," a huge enterprise that produced knowledge instead of consumer goods. "The university and segments of industry are becoming more alike," Kerr had observed in 1960.

Finally, most students resented what they considered invasions of their personal freedoms. Women, even those who were of legal age, had to observe dress codes and dorm hours on most college campuses during the early 1960s; men at many state universities were required to take two years of military training; and administrators routinely censored student publications. Dissidents began to demand that universities abandon or relax restrictions on personal conduct, reduce the number of required courses, and offer educational programs "relevant" to mid–twentieth-century society.

When student muckrakers examined the multiversity's social role, they found additional grievances. Professors conducted classified research for the Defense Department; Harvard chemists, not Dow Chemical, had developed napalm. Seeking space for expansion, many universities spread into neighboring areas and pushed out the residents. Some private universities, radicals also discovered, owned inner-city properties and qualified as genuine slum landlords. To make the indictment complete, big universities rarely admitted students of color; when they did, recruitment efforts centered on talented athletes and a few academic superstars. Viewed from within, the multiversity seemed to offer mind-numbing courses and senseless regimentation. Seen as part of liberal society, it appeared implicated in war and racism.

Student and faculty pressures brought significant changes and a few strategic retreats by the old guard. Most colleges relaxed life-style restrictions, abolished compulsory military instruction, adjusted curriculum requirements, made special efforts to recruit students of color, and established ethnic studies programs. Some professors encouraged social activism by permitting students to substitute outside projects for more traditional assignments. Many campuses came to serve as staging areas for demonstrations, and large groups of nonstudents provided additional troops for campus demonstrations and swelled the ranks of the "student" opposition. A radicalized university, activists began to hope, would be an important tool for changing the larger society.

The protests against growing U.S. involvement in the Vietnam War demonstrated the value as well as the limitations of the university in radical politics. The crusade against the war did not begin on the campuses, but dissent there gave the antiwar movement influential forums. Early in 1965, when President Johnson mounted his all-out bombing campaign against North Vietnam, antiwar activists organized a nationwide series of teach-ins, meetings at which supporters and opponents of LBJ's policies debated before largely student audiences. Initially, some protestors hoped that the teach-ins might eventually change policies. But by 1966 most militant opponents of the war were charging that teach-ins only wasted precious time. Although they continued sporadically through the 1960s—and even into the 1970s on some campuses— the antiwar movement began to desert the lecture platforms for the streets.

Antiwar demonstrations borrowed from both the tactics of the civil rights movement and the techniques of the teach-in. Beginning with a mass march, demonstrations invariably concluded with a series of speeches and musical entertainment. Organizers hoped that large numbers of people in the streets would dramatize the strength of the youth movement, increase radical consciousness, and force Washington to change its policies. Thus, each new march had to outdo the last; organizers struggled to attract more people and to devise new strategems for lampooning the liberal establishment. During the October 1967 march on Washington, a group of what the *East Village Other* called "witches, warlocks, holymen, seers, prophets, mystics, saints, sorcerers, shamans, troubadours, minstrels, bards, roadmen and madmen" tried to exorcise the Pentagon, hurling "mighty words of white light against the demon-controlled structure." Alas, the five-sided bastion of the military-industrial complex hardly budged, and the war in Vietnam continued.

The politics of organizing such demonstrations helped cover up deeper differences over goals and tactics. Negotiations with political leaders, police chiefs, rock entrepreneurs, and portable-toilet vendors sometimes seemed as complex as the conduct of the war itself. For many people, marches and demonstrations served much the same function as religious revival meetings: The faithful assembled, felt their spirits renewed, and then went back home to prepare for the next gathering. And by attracting tens and then hundreds of thousands of people to a single demonstration, antiwar leaders could reassure themselves that all was going well. Even a fraction of a percentage of the baby-boom generation, when assembled in one spot, made a good-sized crowd, and a sprinkling of older people raised hopes that the movement was edging outside its core youth market.

What was the impact of these mass demonstrations and marches? Critics have claimed that they actually rebounded against the antiwar forces by daring the combative President Johnson to hang tough and to conduct more of the war in secret. Others, though, have argued that the techniques did help end the war. Although policymakers publicly denied that they took any notice of the mass protests, the gatherings undoubtedly helped to convert some former hawks and embolden doves. Moreover, they made it more difficult for Johnson to claim any consensus for his war policies and, once the secret portions of his policies became public knowledge, to mount any bold escalations. Whatever their precise impact, mass demonstrations remained a central part of the new politics.

Radical Youth Culture

The vast majority of youthful protesters strongly opposed the war and felt estranged from liberal society, but many also came to lose interest in sustained political activity. In time, antipathy toward the liberal establishment extended to "peace bureaucrats" in the New Left. Cultural radicals emphasized "doing your own thing" rather than joining political organizations. San Francisco, the old haunt of many of the Beats of the 1950s, once again became a mecca for a group of cultural dissidents that came to be called the hippies.

In the mid-1960s the Haight-Ashbury neighborhood of San Francisco became famous, or notorious, as the focus of cultural revolution. "Hip" people from all over the country flocked there, hoping to enjoy the "laid-back" lifestyles of the "age of Aquarius." Soon, the media highlighted the comings and goings of the hippies. Many young people were intrigued by communal living arrangements, liberated views on sex, experimentation with drugs, and the electrified sound of folk-rock music. Hippies celebrated their emancipation from "hang-ups" such as work and clothing fashions. Attired in America's castoffs, including old military uniforms, the new rebels espoused philosophies that stressed mystical experiences and universal love.

Most devotees of the counterculture showed little interest in political questions or new political organizations. Following the Beat writers of the 1950s some began to study Eastern faiths such as Zen and Taoism; others eclectically sampled psychedelic drugs; many simply relied on slogans. "Make love, not war" and "Flower power" became familiar parts of the hippie litany. Sociologists eagerly studied hippie culture, pop journalists such as Tom Wolfe breathlessly covered it, and middle-class vacationers made a quick bus tour of Haight-Ashbury an essential part of their visit to San Francisco.

But Haight-Ashbury soon became something other than a quaint haven for flower children. San Francisco's political establishment declared war on "this hippie thing," and many patrol officers ruthlessly searched for drugs and often harassed any unkempt young person. At the same time, the Haight faced an invasion of petty criminals, drifters who saw the hippies as easy prey. The community also developed internal divisions; "hip entrepreneurs" took control of Haight-Ashbury's economic life, and phony "weekend hippies" invaded the area. Dope became big business, and pushers began to peddle stronger and stronger chemicals. The wiser "heads" warned about the dangers—"Speed kills," proclaimed posters—but the naive became hooked on hard drugs or experienced bad "trips" on powerful hallucinogens. A few died from overdoses. A handbill printed in August 1967 expressed the growing disillusionment with Haight-Ashbury:

The trouble is that the hip shopkeepers probably believe their own bullshit lies. They believe that dope is the answer and neither know nor care what the question is.

Have you been raped? Take acid and everything will be groovy. Are you cold, sleeping in doorways at night? Take acid and discover your inner warmth. Are you hungry? Take acid and transcend these mundane needs.

You can't afford acid? Pardon me, I think I hear somebody calling me.

Despite the rapid rise and fall of Haight-Ashbury, the counterculture grew, especially as it became closely linked to new trends in rock music. By 1966 the Beatles and the Rolling Stones were dominating rock, and Bob Dylan was augmenting his acoustic guitar with the amplified sound of folk-rock. Groups from San Francisco took the lead in exploring the new possibilities. Jerry Garcia and the Grateful Dead attracted a particularly devoted following. The Dead gradually added various kinds of light shows, and the Merry Pranksters (a group of young people attracted to the novelist Ken Kesey) laced the audience with LSD. ("Can you pass the acid test?" the Pranksters slyly asked concertgoers.) The result was acid rock and a whole new genre of drug-related, "mindblowing" sounds. Soon, something called progressive rock became a smashing success, financially as well as artistically. Although cautious programmers and disc jockeys generally excluded the new sounds from AM radio's top-40 play lists, progressive rock spawned its own medium—free-form FM radio. The popularity of San Francisco groups—particularly the Dead, Jefferson Airplane, and Big Brother and the Holding Company (featuring Janis Joplin)—rapidly spread across the country.

The union of disaffected youths, drugs, and rock music—the combination that made the Woodstock Rock Festival of 1969 briefly appear to represent the flowering of a true cultural revolution—was consummated. By the later 1960s the counterculture seemed to be a nationwide phenomenon. However, the counterculture was difficult to classify; it was variously a state of mind, a way of life, or sometimes merely a style of dress. It developed its own mass media, underground newspapers like the *Berkeley Barb* and the *Los Angeles Free Press*, even a Liberation News Service. Although few of these enterprises survived, the underground media symbolized the counterculture's broad aspirations.

Few youthful dissidents had greater aspirations, especially for media fame, than Abbie Hoffman and Jerry Rubin, the creators of the spurious Youth International Party—the Yippies. Yippie philosophy owed more to Groucho, Harpo, and Chico than to Karl Marx. The Yippie program was theater in the streets, an updated, drug-inspired vaudeville of the radical left. With the Yippies, revolution and symbolic defiance became one and the same. In one of their most famous escapades, Yippies invaded the New York Stock Exchange, hurling currency at brokers who were wildly trading their paper securities. Hoffman facetiously suggested that such theatrics would eventually produce upheaval through a mystical process he called "cultural jujitsu":

Confronted by the taunts of the Yippies in the streets and by its own innate contradictions, corporate America would hack itself to pieces. The Yippies' penchant for playing radicalism for laughs—Hoffman entitled his treatise *Revolution for the Hell of It*—and their adolescent bravado, which often took the form of media-oriented theatrics, only underscored their lack of any serious program for social change, let alone for political transformation. Rubin and Hoffman drew more support from the managers of the mass media than from members of the youth movement; but certified as hippie celebrities, they came to enjoy the visibility that more thoughtful dissidents could never obtain.

The Meanings of the Counterculture

From the very beginning, critics denounced radical youth culture as a dangerous and foolish attack on the realities of modern life. The prominent psychologist Bruno Bettelheim dismissed the outcries against technology as the babbling of "obsolete youth" in a technological age that required discipline and order. Zbigniew Brzezinski, who would later be President Carter's national security adviser, condemned the youthful protesters as "twentieth-century Luddites." Noting that most college dissidents came from the humanities rather than from the sciences or engineering, Brzezinski claimed that the rebels were blindly attacking the new learning because it threatened their power and prestige. The counterculture, Brzezinski concluded, was "the death rattle" of the historically obsolete.

Even people critical of postwar liberalism criticized the spirit of the counterculture. Writing in the 1970s, Peter Clecak saw leaders of the cultural insurgency vying with one another for the chance to be packaged and sold as media celebrities. Having been raised on the juvenile TV fare of the 1950s, he complained, the eternal adolescents of the 1960s "easily fell into the comic roles" assigned them by TV producers. The result, Clecak concluded, was the trivialization of dissent. Another critic of liberalism, the historian Christopher Lasch, drew an even broader indictment of the impact of the 1960s on the 1970s. The counterculture's infatuation with "finding oneself" and with "alternative consciousness" ultimately contributed to a "culture of narcissism"— a rootless, self-absorbed search for the latest prepackaged life-style and, more dangerously, a radically scaled-down vision of one's own connection to history and to any large community.

Many of those associated with the feminist movement, which grew rapidly in the 1970s, also showed ambivalence toward the counterculture. By breaking old conventions, the counterculture helped provide space for the renewal of feminist activism. But part of the preceding Beat movement was, as Barbara Ehrenrich has pointed out, a "male revolt" hostile to family and to women. Moreover, males dominated the radical movements of the 1960s, often viewing women as primarily secretarial or sexual servants to the cause led by males. The drug culture and the sexual revolution could sometimes victimize women in the name of liberation.

The counterculture, however, had—and still has—its defenders. The historian Theodore Roszak, who first popularized the term *counterculture*, viewed dissident young people as the vanguard of a reaction against an oppressive technological society. Saturated by misdirected technology, "technocracy's children" sought a society and a level of consciousness that allowed for beauty, mystery, feeling, and love. In *The Making of a Counter-Culture* (1969), Roszak sympathetically explored the counterculture's interest in Eastern religions, Beat writers, anarchist philosophers, and mystics of all kinds. But even he warned that the middle-class rebels would have to avoid at least two dangers: losing touch with disadvantaged people, particularly nonwhites who had never enjoyed the temptations of technology, and becoming "an amusing side show" for people who confused changes in life-styles with liberation. Indeed, more than Roszak would allow, elements within the counterculture itself displayed much the same commercial slickness and infatuation with technology, albeit in different forms, as the entrepreneurs on Madison Avenue. In time, hippie-style clothes, high-tech toys, and a more casual attitude toward sex became fashionable among many business and professional people; the hippie life-style could blend, without much difficulty, into the dominant values of an advanced industrial society.

THE POLITICS OF CONFRONTATION, 1968

Many politicians attacked "those dirty hippies" and "permissiveness." Ronald Reagan, for example, left Hollywood for good and pledged to "straighten out things at Berkeley" during his successful campaign for the governorship of California in 1966. Reagan and many other conservative politicians took an increasingly hard line against the use of drugs, condemning the growing popularity of marijuana as proof of disrespect for law and authority.

The 1968 presidential campaign expressed the complex tensions within American society and channeled them into the political arena. The electoral system, however, offered a poor forum for resolving the deep social and cultural divisions; few national contests have produced as much bitterness and political violence as the 1968 presidential campaign.

The Fall of Lyndon Johnson

Lyndon Johnson became the first casualty. After capturing more than 60 percent of the popular vote in 1964, Johnson had celebrated his "politics of consensus." Some Republicans even worried about their party's survival. But committed to his cause in Vietnam, blamed for racial conflict, and assailed by critics of his Great Society, Johnson was deserted by old supporters. Trapped in the White House by the antiwar demonstrations that followed him everywhere, Johnson spent considerable time staring at his bank of TV sets. Where had he gone wrong? Why had such a promising presidency turned into such a debacle? Johnson's standing in opinion polls steadily plummeted; his support in Congress evaporated; and dissident Democrats organized a "dump-Johnson" movement in order to do the unthinkable—deny an incumbent president his party's nomination.

At first considered hopeless, especially when Senator Robert Kennedy refused to challenge LBJ for the nomination, the dump-Johnson effort finally coalesced behind an unlikely standard-bearer, Senator Eugene McCarthy of Minnesota. An unorthodox, aloof antipolitician—detractors simply called him arrogant and lazy—McCarthy promised no great societies. "All we want is a moderate use of intelligence," McCarthy told supporters. A small army of college students rallied behind the only "peace candidate" in either major party, and when Johnson declined to campaign personally in the New Hampshire presidential primary, McCarthy's "quixotic children's crusade" dominated the TV screen. Meanwhile, the communists' Tet offensive in South Vietnam and worries about the violence at home increased doubts about Johnson's capacity to lead the nation. Although McCarthy actually won only 43 percent of the Democratic vote in New Hampshire's March 1968 primary, he ran well enough to refute claims of Johnson's invincibility within his own party. McCarthy also captured media attention for the anti-Johnson movement. (In some ways McCarthy's appeal was as much anti-Johnson as it was antiwar: When asked about their second choice as a Democratic candidate, McCarthy supporters often named Alabama's hawkish governor, George C. Wallace.)

After the New Hampshire primary, Johnson's political and personal problems only increased. Robert Kennedy quickly announced his intention to enter the race for the Democratic nomination. Facing certain defeat by McCarthy in the Wisconsin primary, a physically exhausted Johnson retired without a fight. On March 31, 1968, the president dramatically announced that he would not seek another term. About to be relieved of the responsibilities of the presidency, Johnson abandoned the Spartan routine that his heart condition required. He resumed smoking and began to eat greater quantities of rich, fried foods. Within two years he suffered a serious heart attack; within five years he was dead.

The New Politics and the Election of 1968

Hubert Humphrey, LBJ's vice-president and an unsuccessful presidential contender in 1960, enjoyed the full support of Democratic party chieftains in 1968. Labor leaders like George Meany, political bosses like Chicago Mayor Richard Daley and Texas governor John Connally, and LBJ himself all endorsed Humphrey. With this backing, Humphrey could ignore the primaries and use his political muscle to line up delegates. At first, he preached "the politics of joy," but then even Humphrey came to recognize the joyless political atmosphere of the 1968 election.

The unrelenting political violence of 1968 made a mockery of Humphrey's slogan. In April, Martin Luther King, Jr., was gunned down in Memphis, and black neighborhoods erupted in anger. Disorders rocked more than 100 cities, 36 people died, and public officials deployed more than

50,000 National Guard and federal troops. Many people refused to believe that another lone gunman, this one an escaped convict named James Earl Ray, could have killed another national leader. (In 1979 a special House committee concluded that some type of conspiracy very likely did surround King's shooting, but it provided no firm evidence, and doubts that James Earl Ray acted alone still persist.)

Eugene McCarthy and Robert Kennedy attempted to bring alienated people back into "the system." McCarthy's brand of "new politics"—a much-abused phrase that suggested no backroom deals with powerful interest groups, reliance on youthful volunteers, and straightforward political speeches—appealed to bright, politically aware college students. (Bobby Kennedy once joked that McCarthy had all the A students whereas he could attract only those who got grades of B or B–.) Shaving beards and donning skirts to "come clean for Gene," thousands of young people canvassed for their hero. Kennedy's efforts also excited young people, but many complained that his campaign smacked too much of the "old politics." Kennedy tried to make special appeals to a diverse coalition of white ethnic voters, minorities, liberals, and even George Wallace's supporters. As he vigorously stumped Indiana, reporters dubbed his campaign train the "Ruthless Cannonball."

> He has the Poles in Gary,
> The blacks will fill his hall,
> There are no ethnic problems on the Ruthless Cannonball.

While Humphrey rested on his safe cushion of nonprimary delegates, Kennedy and McCarthy tried to demonstrate their vote-getting ability. In Oregon, McCarthy became the first politician ever to defeat any Kennedy. But a Kennedy campaign was something special: an array of movie stars, musicians, athletes, university professors, and even business executives dropping everything to follow Bobby. Ignoring threats against his life, Kennedy waded into crowds wherever he went, with only a few burly friends to shield him from danger. The night of the California primary, these same supporters stood helplessly nearby as Kennedy was shot at point-blank range in the kitchen of a Los Angeles hotel. Police immediately arrested Sirhan Sirhan, a Jordanian immigrant, whom a jury later convicted of Kennedy's murder. Minutes before the shooting Kennedy had accepted congratulations for a narrow victory over McCarthy in the climactic California primary; twenty-four hours later he was dead. Although McCarthy said that he would continue to fight for the nomination, Kennedy's death took the heart out of his campaign. Humphrey had a clear path.

Meeting amid racial violence and protest in Miami (four people were killed during racial disorders there), Republicans chose a face from the past—former Vice-President Richard Nixon. Although he had lost the 1960 presidential contest and had presumably retired from politics after his defeat in the California gubernatorial race of 1962, image makers proclaimed a "new Nixon." (Early in the 1968 campaign, a critic complained that "there is no new Nixon. What we have here is the old Nixon, a little older.") The "new Nixon" suggested peaceful overtures to the Soviet Union and the People's Republic of China and pledged to give black Americans "a piece of the action in the exciting ventures of private enterprise." There were also echoes of the old Nixon. He praised the "forgotten Americans, the nonshouters, the nondemonstrators"; he suggested that Americans had been "deluged" by government welfare programs that had only "reaped . . . an ugly harvest of frustrations, violence, and failure"; and he promised that his attorney general would "open a new front against crime." The dogged campaigner, whom his fellow law students had called "Old Iron Butt," simply outlasted the field. Nominated on the first ballot, Nixon surprised the convention by selecting Spiro T. Agnew, the governor of Maryland, as his running mate.

The cry for law and order became stronger after the Democrats' Chicago convention. Mayor Richard Daley expected trouble. Several peace groups planned demonstrations, and the Yippies promised a "festival of life," an answer to what they called the Democrats' "festival of death." Abbie Hoffman talked about sending 10,000 nude Yippies wading into Lake Michigan, releasing greased pigs in Chicago's crowded Loop area, and slipping LSD into the city's water supply. Mayor Daley took Hoffman's jokes seriously, readied his police force, and had the Illinois National Guard and the United States Army standing by. "If you're going to Chicago, be sure to wear armor in your hair," warned an underground newspaper.

After several days of skirmishes between youthful protesters and the Chicago police, serious violence erupted on the night delegates nominated Humphrey as the Democratic nominee for president. Police beat demonstrators, nonprotesting bystanders, and even reporters. A special commission eventually labeled the disorders a "police riot." But many people saw events the other way: One poll claimed that nearly 60 percent of their sample blamed the demonstrators and supported the police. On the question of disorders at the convention, as well as on the war issue, Hubert Humphrey was surrounded by squabbling Democrats. He dared not openly criticize either Mayor Daley's police or the antiwar forces. Humphrey tried to pretend that his party would pull together, but his early campaign efforts belied such optimism. Antiwar hecklers confronted the underfinanced and badly advised Humphrey at every stop, and his audiences remained small and generally unenthusiastic.

George Wallace had hoped to benefit from Humphrey's troubles. Running on the American Independent ticket, the former governor of Alabama preached law and order, a slogan that his critics called code words for racism. Wallace's angry denials were, in a sense, correct. Race was only one of the social issues that Wallace hoped to exploit. In his standard address he contended that "there's not a dime's worth of difference" between the two major parties, denounced "pointy-headed bureaucrats" who "don't know how to park a bicycle straight," and predicted that "intellectual morons" and "theoreticians" were "going to get some of those liberal smiles knocked off their faces." Wallace cleverly linked distaste for big government with fears of the

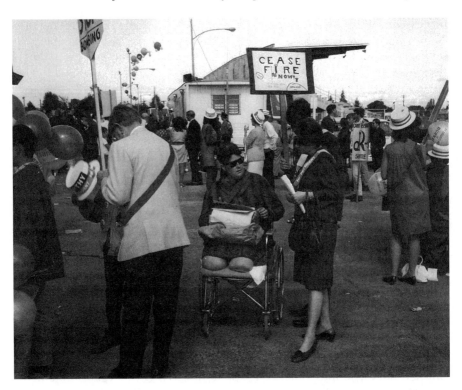

Antiwar protestors at the Washington State Democratic Convention of 1968. *Source:* Tacoma Public Library Neg. # TPL 371.

counterculture: "Our lives are being taken over by bureaucrats, and most of them have beards." As election day neared, however, many northern blue-collar workers and ethnic voters, Democrats who had been leaning toward Wallace, rejoined the ranks.

Richard Nixon won a narrow victory in November. Finally cutting loose from Johnson's Vietnam policy, Humphrey announced that he favored a bombing halt as a way of speeding up Vietnam peace talks, and several days before the election President Johnson did order a temporary cessation of air raids over North Vietnam. These steps induced some antiwar people, including Eugene McCarthy, to announce grudging support of Humphrey's candidacy. But Humphrey fell about 100,000 votes short, and Nixon captured the presidency with only about 43 percent of the popular vote. The lonely, long-distance runner, as Garry Wills called Nixon, had finally won his big race.

Although even Nixon and Humphrey had tried to identify themselves with the new politics, their nominations and the election of Ike's former vice-president demonstrated the tenacity of traditional political habits and institutions. The people most likely to cast ballots were unyoung, unpoor, unblack, and largely unsympathetic to youthful radicalism. Most voters identified the cultural rebellion with ingratitude for America's material abundance; they considered left-wing politics, with its demonstrations and direct participation, socially disruptive. People who initially wanted to cast a protest vote looked toward McCarthy, Kennedy, or even Wallace, believing that in their own unique ways, these three had broken with conventional politics. With Kennedy's death, McCarthy's virtual retirement from political life after Chicago, and Wallace's decline, many supporters of the new politics simply stayed home. Others reluctantly joined the other voters in choosing between two familiar candidates, Nixon and Humphrey who were both, in their own ways, thoroughly conventional.

Although historical movements rarely take sudden turns or end abruptly, many scholars mark 1968—a year that saw massive youth protests in Germany and France as well as in the United States—as the terminal date or an important turning point for the movement of the 1960s. In this view, the violence of 1968 and an election that came down to Humphrey against Nixon underscored the organizational limits and ultimate failure of the new politics. The "good" days of the early movement were over, a judgment found in many histories and reminiscences written by people, especially men, who had themselves been radical leaders during the early 1960s. Those commentators who lack much sympathy for any phase of the youth politics tend to see 1968 in an even worse light: After 1968, political naivete became fanaticism and cultural infantilism turned into simplistic barbarism. In one form or another, variations on these viewpoints have come to dominate discussions, especially after the flood of books that appeared in 1988–1989, marking the twentieth anniversary of 1968.

Seen in another way, though, 1968 marked neither a sudden end nor a radical turn in dissenting politics. The impulses of the 1960s never were nor could have been represented by a single movement, and a single election provides too narrow a lens through which to view the complex social and cultural changes associated with the political insurgency of the 1960s. The year 1968 included many important events, but the age of protest and confrontation was far from over.

THE VIOLENT YEARS, 1968–1972

Violence in Southeast Asia

Despite antiwar protests and Richard Nixon's talk of a peace plan, the war in Vietnam continued, even accelerated, after 1968. After a thorough review of war policy Nixon and his national security adviser, Henry Kissinger, made several crucial decisions. As quickly as possible the United States would turn the ground war over to its South Vietnamese allies and begin a gradual withdrawal of U.S. ground forces while stepping up the air war. At the same time, the United States would try to enlist Soviet help in wringing concessions from Hanoi. In July 1969 the president placed his Vietnam policy within a grander design—the so-called Nixon Doctrine—pledging that the United

States would continue giving military assistance to anticommunist governments in Asia but would have Asians, not Americans, do the fighting. The president was promising peace but still hoping for the military victory that had beguiled and eluded Kennedy and Johnson. Essentially "Vietnamization" was a formula for stepping up the war while defusing domestic dissent by ending the involvement of American draftees.

Nixon looked to Henry Kissinger rather than to his cabinet to design Vietnamization. In fact, the foreign-policymaking process was so thoroughly centralized in the White House that Secretary of State William Rogers and Secretary of Defense Melvin Laird often remained peripheral to important decisions. Kissinger, a former Harvard professor, saw world policies as a global geopolitical confrontation between Soviet and American power. America's primary duty consisted of foreclosing Soviet opportunities for expansion; conflicts anywhere in the world had to be viewed in light of how they "linked up" to the central concern of American policy. It was through his crucial concept of linkage that Kissinger justified his hopes for an early and favorable settlement in Vietnam. Kissinger hoped, he later wrote in his memoirs, to make "progress in settling the Vietnam war something of a condition for advance in areas of interest to the Soviets, such as the Middle East, trade or arms limitation."

This plan for ending the war by enticing the Soviets to pressure the North Vietnamese made at least two faulty assumptions: one, that the Soviets could easily influence Hanoi; and two, that the Soviets would be persuaded to pull their strings on America's behalf. Neither proved correct, but Kissinger continued to pursue Vietnamization.

To buy time for Vietnamization to shape South Vietnam's army into an effective force and to prepare for bringing American ground troops home, Nixon and Kissinger accelerated the conflict while still technically honoring Johnson's bombing halt over the North. They launched offensives against targets in the South and accelerated full-scale combat inside Cambodia. To mask this new escalation, the military revised the English language, calling its new offensives "accelerated pacification" and "protective reaction strikes."

In May 1970 Nixon went on television to announce that he had ordered an American-led invasion of Cambodia, technically a neutral country. In making this decision, he ignored the advice of his secretaries of state and defense and neglected to consult (or even inform) Lon Nol, America's Cambodian ally, who less than two months before had successfully overthrown the neutralist regime of Prince Norodom Sihanouk. North Vietnamese forces had been using various parts of Cambodia as staging areas, and Pentagon strategists had long pressed the White House to enter Cambodia and destroy a mythical Vietnamese guerrilla headquarters. A quick strike, it was hoped, would unsettle the enemy and capture valuable supplies.

Widening the war into Cambodia had disastrous consequences. American troops met surprisingly little resistance and found no guerrilla headquarters, but Nixon's defenders nevertheless considered the maneuver a success. The Nixon administration continued to wage a secret air war in Cambodia long after the April strike, and the heavy bombing destroyed large portions of what had been a peaceful, agricultural country, creating a large refugee population and a devastating decline in food supplies. The Khmer Rouge, the native communist guerrillas, transformed themselves from a disorganized force of 5,000 in 1970 to a fierce army of 70,000 in 1975; Lon Nol, now clearly seen as a U.S. puppet, found support only in the capital city. Subsequent American defeat and withdrawal would leave communist regimes in both Vietnam and Cambodia, realizing the domino effect the war had initially been staged to prevent.

Antiwar forces at home severely criticized the accelerating violence in Southeast Asia. Public revelations of the My Lai massacre (which had occurred in March 1968) intensified criticism of American involvement in Southeast Asia. The slowly unfolding story of My Lai told of American troops killing unarmed civilians, including women and children. After bungling an attempt at a cover-up, the army finally prosecuted several officers, but only a young lieutenant named William Calley was convicted. A member of another unit testified to similar activities by his outfit. "I used to think my company was a bad-ass one until I started seeing others," he said. "Sometimes you thought it was just my platoon, my company, that was committing atrocious acts. . . . But what we were doing was being done all over."

The Cambodian invasion of 1970 galvanized opposition to the war, especially on college campuses. Students mounted protest marches and strikes at more than four hundred schools, and some demonstrations led to violence. Many colleges abruptly ended spring semester early and simply closed their doors. The invasion of Cambodia did produce a small tide of approval in Nixon's direction—according to one poll, the percentage of people who approved of the way the president was handling his job increased by six points—but it also hardened antiwar sentiments. Most important, the incursion into Cambodia clearly stamped the conflict as "Nixon's war."

Violence at Home

Paralleling the bloodletting in Vietnam was a violent new direction in the radical movement at home. The Weathermen pledged to "bring the war home to Amerika" in order to help the National Liberation Front. This violent offshoot of SDS gained considerable attention from the media but almost no political success. Its much-publicized Four Days of Rage, a protest campaign in Chicago in 1969, proved a disaster. After smashing some windows, almost all of the helmeted protesters were overwhelmed, beaten bloody, and arrested by Mayor Daley's police.

After this, many of the prominent political radicals went underground. Some were trying to avoid arrest for previous activities. Some joined other desperate young people in a bombing campaign. Between September 1969 and June 1970 there were more than 170 bombings and attempted bombings on college campuses. An explosion at the University of Wisconsin killed a graduate student, and other campuses endured nonlethal attacks. Universities gradually adjusted to the threat of violence, and cautious scholars began keeping valuable materials and manuscripts at home. Bombers also struck off campuses, hitting such targets as the Bank of America, the Chase Manhattan Bank, and even the U.S. Congress. Three radicals blew themselves apart when their bomb factory in Greenwich Village exploded in 1970. Few of the attacks did major damage—corporation bathrooms, the easiest place to hide explosives, suffered the brunt of the onslaught—but they contributed to an increasingly ugly mood throughout the country. As a result of the bombings and other violent activities, another small group of radicals went underground; during the 1970s, 1980s, and even the 1990s, refugees from these desperate days of violence emerged and surrendered to authorities.

President Nixon and Vice-President Agnew sanctimoniously upheld the rule of law. "You see these bums, you know, blowing up the campuses," the president grumbled after students protested (in most cases nonviolently) the invasion of Cambodia. "We cannot afford to be divided or deceived by the decadent thinking of a few young people," fumed Agnew. We could, he argued, "afford to separate them from our society—with no more regret than we should feel over discarding rotten apples from a barrel."

But most of the violence came from the upholders of law and order rather than from outgunned students and radicals. In early 1968 state troopers killed three protesting black students at Orangeburg State College in South Carolina. During a 1969 confrontation at Berkeley, state police indiscriminately dropped tear gas from helicopters and fatally shot a long-haired bystander in the back. In December 1969 Chicago police stormed the Illinois headquarters of the Black Panthers and killed two people. In May 1970 white police officers opened fire on a women's dormitory at Mississippi's Jackson State College, an all-black institution; two unarmed students were killed. And in the most celebrated incident, the Ohio National Guard shot thirteen students, four of whom died, at Kent State.

A Law-and-Order Administration

Ironically for an administration in which most of the top officials ended up facing criminal charges, Nixon proclaimed a drive for "law and order." Youth and nonwhite insurgency movements were singled out as special targets. To many Americans, the young antiwar protesters seemed a band of troublemakers. After the killings at Kent State, public-opinion polls showed that most people believed that the National Guard had fired on the unarmed students in self-defense; Nixon and Agnew continued their tough talk, and Attorney General John Mitchell strengthened the Justice Department's internal security division. Moreover, the White House, the FBI, and the CIA all continued—or intensified—various illegal activities against domestic radicals.

The FBI, for example, did not limit itself to surveillance of groups espousing violence; it also worked to infiltrate and harass groups and individuals who favored significant, but peaceful, social change. In one celebrated case, the bureau circulated vicious rumors about the personal life of a prominent actress who had ties to the Black Panthers. Similarly, some of the FBI's undercover agents operated as *agent provocateurs* and actually urged violent action by protesters. Commenting on the FBI's notorious COINTELPRO operation—which extended from 1956 to 1971 and was canceled only after stolen FBI documents revealed its existence—a committee of the House of Representatives made a sweeping indictment: "Careers were ruined, friendships severed, reputations sullied, businesses bankrupted and, in some cases, lives endangered."

While conducting or condoning massive lawbreaking by the national surveillance bureaucracy, the Nixon administration was also mobilizing the legal system against dissidents. In the most celebrated political prosecution since the 1940s, the Chicago conspiracy trial of 1969, Attorney General Mitchell pressed for indictments against eight leading radicals. (Mitchell's predecessor, Ramsey Clark, had decided not to prosecute because of insufficient evidence.) The government charged the group—which included Tom Hayden, Bobby Seale, Abbie Hoffman, and Jerry Rubin—with conspiracy and with crossing state lines to encourage violence at the 1968 Democratic convention. Some of the defendants viewed the affair as a countercultural "happening" rather than a legal battle, and the defense never mounted a coherent counterattack. At the end of the trial, the judge unexpectedly cited all of the defendants for various actions in contempt of court. Concluding the sorry affair, the jury rendered a compromise verdict: It acquitted all of the defendants of the more serious conspiracy charge but convicted the most famous—including Yippies Rubin and Hoffman—of crossing state lines to incite a riot. After a lengthy appeal process, all of the defendants escaped jail, but the Chicago conspiracy trial hardly cast much credit on the American legal system.

Other such trials—including prosecutions of antiwar priests Philip and Daniel Berrigan, of Bobby Seale, and of various lesser-known radicals—produced few convictions, but they did help to label political dissidents as "criminals in the streets." Simply by filing charges, the Nixon administration and state officials encouraged public fears of the radical "menace" and increased the disarray of the left.

The Violence Wanes

Meanwhile, Richard Nixon continued to pose as the president who would listen to the "forgotten American." From 1969 to early 1972 Nixon and Agnew warned "middle Americans" that New Left "hooligans," aided and abetted by "radical liberals" in the Democratic party, threatened the country's stability. Agnew assailed the "biased liberal" media, which "slandered" the president; the "nattering nabobs of negativism," who scorned traditional American values; the "curled-lip boys in the eastern ivory towers," who thumbed their noses at ordinary people; and renegade professionals such as Dr. Benjamin Spock, who encouraged the "growing spirit of permissiveness."

Still, the Republicans made few gains in the 1970 elections. The GOP did add a couple of Republicans to the Senate but dropped about a dozen seats in the House and lost no fewer than eleven governorships. The Democrats, though badly divided and somewhat demoralized, remained the majority party. Nixon's political strategists consequently abandoned grand theories about "an emerging Republican majority" and began to plan a 1972 campaign that divorced the president, as much as possible, from the rest of the Republican ticket. Nixon's image-makers left all the invective to a slightly more subdued Agnew, planned more subtle campaign tactics for 1972, and accentuated the president's role in foreign affairs.

The passions of the 1960s slowly seeped from domestic politics. By beginning to reduce U.S. ground forces in Vietnam, promising to end the military draft, and helping to lower the voting age to eighteen, the Nixon administration removed three highly emotional issues from the political agenda. Although many other questions remained, especially the conflict in Southeast Asia itself, they no longer brought massive numbers of people into the streets.

Youth-oriented politics, for example, lost its prominent position in the mass media. Seeking new sources of inspiration and fresh recruits, a few reckless radicals saw prison inmates as the new vanguard of revolution. This desperate turn—toward the most powerless group in the country, and one heavily infiltrated by police informers—proved suicidal. In 1973, a tiny group of white radicals joined with an escaped African-American prisoner to form the Symbionese Liberation Army, or SLA. The kidnapping of Patricia Hearst, daughter of a prominent newspaper publisher, instantly converted members of the SLA into celebrities; finally, in the spring of 1974, six members of the group were killed in a shoot-out with the Los Angeles police, which was carried live on television. Patty Hearst was freed but later stood trial for complicity with her SLA captors.

Although a few other young people, claiming inspiration from the 1960s, dabbled in similarly suicidal activities, the vast majority of social activists adopted new, nonviolent strategies in the early 1970s. Having discovered no magical shortcuts to social transformation, some drifted away from all movements; but while the ups and downs of Richard Nixon dominated the national political stage during the early 1970s, many other activists worked quietly, outside of the media's gaze, for significant social change.

THE SEARCH FOR POWER, 1968–1976

Although the Nixon administration's constant fears were undoubtedly overstated, dissent did spread widely throughout American society. In the early 1970s a number of different groups were demanding empowerment. Few achieved stunning victories, but they all laid the groundwork for what they expected would be new gains in the future.

African-American Politics

After the collapse of the Black Power movement, African-American politics moved in many different directions. Following Martin Luther King's murder, SCLC lost prestige, especially when its Poor People's March of 1968 proved a complete disaster. Dr. King's unfinished project, this "march ... more than a single-day event: It sought to make an interracial group of poor people an ongoing presence in Washington and to lobby Congress and the Nixon administration for new social legislation. But its tent encampment became waterlogged in torrential spring rains, and the inhabitants split into squabbling factions. Nixon's administration expelled the few remaining activists, bringing a dismal end to the era of mass civil rights demonstrations.

Taking a different tack, a broad coalition of African-American activists formed the National Black Political Assembly in 1972. More than 10,000 people met in Gary, Indiana, to hammer out a "Black Agenda." A militant statement that upset integrationists, it charged that the "crises we face as black people . . . are the natural end-product of a society built on the twin foundations of white racism and white capitalism." Within months, deep fissures developed within the Black Political Assembly as Marxists tilted with liberals, integrationists with cultural nationalists. And while these activists debated theories of cultural and political change, the African-American historian Manning Marable has argued, the mass of workers, students, and the unemployed lost interest in this bold effort to create a nationwide political structure for African-Americans.

Nonetheless, African-American politics changed significantly. The continued migration of people to northern cities (together with the flight of many whites) ensured the election of greater numbers of African-American political leaders. In 1955, for instance, only a couple of districts of New York City and Chicago sent black representatives to Congress; by 1972, fifteen African-Americans held seats in the House of Representatives. A number of cities—including Cleveland, Gary, and Newark—elected African-American mayors, and several northern states, especially Michigan and New York, claimed growing numbers of black officials at all levels of government.

But new African-American officeholders brought only minor policy changes. Cities with black-elected officials also generally had large (and largely poor) African-American populations; their urban problems certainly involved, but also transcended, racial issues. African-American politicians, no more than their white predecessors, were not miracle workers. And they faced, once in power, a particularly difficult problem: Should they target the majority of new programs directly for low-income neighborhoods or should they work with local whites and thereby gain access to public and private funds for rebuilding the entire urban infrastructure? Skillful (or lucky) African-American politicians, such as Coleman Young in Detroit, seemed able to satisfy conflicting pressures, but others (such as Kenneth Gibson in Newark) found themselves ensnarled in the competing demands.

The efforts of African-American politicians to reach out to powerful interest groups to obtain private and public funds for general urban projects did not always satisfy the specific desires of their black constituency. In Detroit, for example, leaders from poor black neighborhoods charged that Mayor Coleman Young (elected in 1973) catered to the corporate and political elites' desire to rebuild the Motor City's business center while generally ignoring the plight of Detroit's poorest black residents. Young countered that Detroit's citizens desperately needed a viable business environment and that his policies addressed the needs of the entire population. In local communities, cynicism about all politicians, black as well as white, set in. Despite a voter registration movement, for example, the percentage of northern blacks who bothered to register and to vote actually declined between 1964 and 1972.

Meanwhile, the Nixon administration moved cautiously and obliquely on racial questions. Gaining only five of every one hundred votes cast by African-Americans in 1968 and doing no better in 1972, Nixon had the bulk of his political capital invested elsewhere. Although he took a strong stand against school busing, even appearing on national television in 1972 to seek a moratorium on this method of achieving integration, he generally followed a more circumspect course on racial issues. Daniel Patrick Moynihan urged "benign neglect"—a policy of scaling down the level of promises as a means of generating less frustration among African-Americans over the slow pace of change.

Moynihan's proposal, whatever its merit as a public-policy position, did represent a shrewd appraisal of the nation's ambiguous record on racial progress. Change on both the economic and the political fronts was occurring, but the immediate results were seldom dramatic. Aided by favorable rulings from the Supreme Court and by pressure from Democratic holdovers in the Department of Health, Education and Welfare (HEW), a number of young blacks were finding greater educational and economic opportunities. A majority of the Supreme Court gradually moved beyond a narrow reading of *Brown v. Board of Education* and held that the Constitution demanded schools to be "racially mixed." Although the Court did not apply this principle in every case, its new rulings generally required considerable busing of children from their old neighborhood school districts to other schools in order to provide "racial balance."

Officials in HEW, citing the small numbers of nonwhites and women in the professions, began to press graduate and professional schools to take "affirmative action" and recruit a student body that was not overwhelmingly white and male. College-educated blacks stood to gain from such pressure, but many universities hesitated to overemphasize their affirmative action programs, which were often denounced for establishing quotas and for denigrating merit. Working-class blacks encountered more obstacles, especially from labor unions whose largely white memberships considered the government's efforts to increase minority employment a direct attack on their traditional seniority systems. In 1970, for example, only 3.3 percent of the nation's sheet-metal workers and 1.7 percent of its tool and die makers were black.

The Nixon administration was the most active on economic issues. It promised to help find better jobs for African-Americans who already possessed marketable skills and to promote more opportunities for "black capitalists." Some gains were made. The number of banks owned by African-Americans, for example, more than doubled between 1970 and 1975; a similar expansion occurred in the small-business sector, especially with mom and pop stores. The administration did urge graduate and professional schools to take affirmative action and recruit student bodies that contained more minorities, especially African-Americans. Citing gains such as these, Attorney General John Mitchell advised African-Americans to "watch what we do, not what we say."

But many critics denounced what the Nixon administration did as well as what it said. The NAACP accused the administration of adopting racist policies to attract the "white backlash" vote; the head of the U.S. Civil Rights Commission denounced its reluctance to enforce existing civil rights measures; and Leon Panetta, head of the Civil Rights Division in HEW, resigned in protest over Nixon's opposition to school busing as a means of integrating public schools.

In many areas, Nixon's record did look bad. The administration did little to help register African-American voters in the South; its promises to push integration of federal housing programs went almost nowhere; and it even failed to provide adequate funding for its own project, black capitalism. On a broader front, the gap between black and white incomes, which had narrowed in the late 1960s, grew wider during the 1970s.

Meanwhile, the Voting Rights Act of 1965 (renewed in 1970) and pressure from black groups gradually produced some tangible results in the South. In the election of 1970 more than 100 black candidates gained office in the South; by the end of that year more than 700 black people held political office in the southern states. At the same time, black voters gained more leverage in contests involving only white candidates. Openly seeking the support of blacks, many white candidates moderated their stands on racial issues.

Such gains, however, did not automatically bring significant changes to the South. In many heavily black counties and towns, black candidates still failed to gain office. More important, even the triumph of black politicians could not solve long-standing social and economic problems. Changing the skin color of mayors and county officials did not rejuvenate those rural areas plagued with limited resources and antiquated public services. Even the most energetic black officials often found it difficult to run all the bureaucratic roadblocks and obtain state or federal funds for their communities.

Mexican-American Militancy

Although the Black Power movement captured the most media attention, other ethnic groups also displayed new cultural pride and growing political militancy. Mexican-Americans, living principally in the Southwest and in northern communities close to migrant farming jobs, grew in numbers and began to assert their political power.

During the 1960s the average Mexican-American child had only a seventh-grade education; nearly nine of every ten dropped out of Texas high schools before graduation. Many young people had to leave school to help support their families. As one teacher put it, "Our kids don't drop out; they are pushed out by poverty." The tradition of maintaining a Spanish-based culture and the proximity of Mexican cultural institutions also stigmatized Mexican-Americans. In some California school districts students could be expelled for speaking Spanish, even on the playground. Bilingualism, a quality highly valued among middle-class white children, often became a badge of inferiority for Mexican-Americans. Standing on the edge of two cultures, some Mexican-Americans suffered all of the consequences of marginality: low wages, political powerlessness, inadequate housing, and limited access to services.

By the late 1960s, a new generation of young leaders, impatient with the legal and political strategies of the 1950s, launched militant mass movements designed to lift the people's economic status and to create a positive cultural identity. Some demanded more aggressive mobilization on behalf of political and economic goals; others advocated separation from the dominant society.

César Chávez launched a drive to raise wages among Mexican-American farm workers. Chávez, who had grown up in California migrant camps during the late 1930s, recalled his family's first grape-picking job: "Each payday the contractor said he couldn't pay us because the winery hadn't paid him yet. At the end of the seventh week we went to the contractor's house and it was empty—he owed us for seven week's pay. . . . We were desperate." Chávez never forgot his people's poverty, and when the federal government's *bracero* (farm worker) program ended in 1964 he began to unionize workers in the grape fields. With the source of new, cheap labor from Mexico diminished, unionization had a chance. The outlook grew even brighter when Chávez's United Farm Workers Union (UFW) attracted support from the powerful American Federation of Labor. During the grape pickers' strike in Delano, California, in 1965, Walter Reuther of the United Auto Workers joined Chávez on the picket lines, carrying a sign reading HUELGA ("STRIKE") and reminiscing about his own organizing fights during the 1930s. Robert Kennedy also visited the scene and became the UFW's most influential political supporter. But the growers held out, always finding enough hungry and jobless people to replace the strikers. Finally, Chávez adopted the technique that would make him famous—the nationwide boycott. Dramatizing his personal commitment, he went on a lengthy fast, an act that damaged his frail health.

Chávez's appeal to boycott California grapes captured widespread sympathy among liberals and radicals during the mid-1960s. For over a year, millions of Americans refused to buy grapes (the army bought them in great quantities to send to Vietnam, however), and growers finally signed with the UFW. Chávez, always a favorite of the media, became the first Mexican-American to appear on the cover of *Time* magazine, and many reporters hailed him as a Spanish-speaking Martin Luther King. When lettuce growers signed what Chávez considered "sweetheart contracts" with the Teamsters Union, he appealed to Americans to boycott lettuce. By the early 1970s, however, the novelty of boycotts had worn off, and Chávez's victories grew fewer and fewer.

While Chávez worked to improve economic conditions among field workers, a militant Chicano student movement demanded and promoted educational change. In East Los Angeles in 1968, 10,000 high school students participated in a "Blow Out," a strike dramatizing racism in education. Similar student strikes spread throughout the Southwest. On college campuses, radicalized students successfully formed Chicano studies programs at some universities and made new contributions to Mexican-American history and literature. *El Grito* and *Aztlan*, the first national Chicano studies journals, and Quinto Sol Publications, the first independent Mexican-American publishing house, provided sympathetic forums for new Chicano writers and scholars.

Student militancy fed new political movements. A charismatic minister in New Mexico, Reies Lopez Tijerina, attempted to organize a separatist movement and reopen the Mexican-American War of 1846–1848. His organization, the Federal Alliance of Land Grants, reclaimed southwestern land, water, and grazing rights that whites had usurped over the previous hundred years. In 1967 he declared the area an independent republic. Guerrilla bands supporting Tijerina formed in northern New Mexico in the late 1960s and seized control of a portion of Kit Carson National Forest. When authorities arrested some of his followers, other disciples of Tijerina raided the courthouse in Tierra Amarilla to free them. The desperate action, which killed one deputy, catapulted Tijerina into the national news and caused widespread fear among Anglos in the area. Rumors swept New Mexico that Cuban-trained guerrillas were hiding in the mountains, and the National Guard patrolled the area for a time.

José Angel Gutiérrez's political party, La Raza Unida, directed dissent into politics. In 1970 La Raza captured a majority of seats on the school board in Crystal City, Texas, and began to remold the educational system according to the needs of the Spanish-speaking population. Soon La Raza gained control of all other political offices in Crystal City and turned the town into a showcase of Chicano government, hoping to spread the party's popularity into barrios throughout the Southwest. Throughout the decade, Chicanos, like African-Americans, made substantial gains in political officeholding.

Despite the rising level of Chicano militancy, officials on the national level devoted little serious attention to the problems of Mexican-Americans. In 1969 Senator Joseph Montoya of New Mexico introduced a bill to extend the life of the President's Inter-Agency Committee on Mexican-American Affairs, a group that studied Chicano problems. The bill passed the Senate and went to the House, where it was lost. After months of delay searchers finally found the bill, misfiled in the Foreign Affairs Committee. The movements led by Chávez, Tijerina, and La Raza declined rather rapidly, weakened by both internal division and external repression, including FBI surveillance, infiltration, and mass arrests.

Still, the political militancy and cultural pride of those years helped nurture major political gains for Mexican-Americans in the future: By 1994, some 3,360 Latino officials held elected office, mostly in areas where the militant Chicano movements of the late 1960s had been strongest.

American Indian Militancy

"Red power" did not really break into the national news until a cold November morning in 1969, when a group of militant Native Americans seized

Alcatraz Island in San Francisco Bay. Hundreds of supporters soon joined them, demanding that the government convert the island into an Indian cultural center and appropriate funds for a Thunderbird University. Few white people took the Indians' proposals seriously. For many Indians, nevertheless, the occupation had a symbolic significance. It was an important step in the effort to create a pan-Indian cultural consciousness. The Indians on Alcatraz represented tribes throughout the United States, and Alcatraz provided a particularly appropriate symbol: Its uninhabitable buildings, bad water and sanitation, and certain unemployment resembled conditions on many Indian reservations.

The vast majority of Indians missed out on the affluence of postwar America. Two-and-a-half decades after World War II, the per capita income of Indians was 60 percent less than that of whites, Indian life expectancy was only forty-seven years, half of all Indian children never completed high school, and the unemployment rate for Indians was 40 percent (on most reservations it exceeded 50 percent). But statistics told only a small part of what it meant to be a native of America. Discrimination against Indians was everywhere. La Nada Means, one of the original occupiers of Alcatraz, remembered the "meanness of the small towns around the reservation. Blackfoot, Pocatello— they all had signs in the store windows to keep Indians out. . . . There were Indian stalls in the public bathrooms; Indians weren't served in a lot of the restaurants; and we just naturally all sat in the balcony of the theaters." What were the effects of such treatment? "It becomes part of the way you look at yourself," she explained.

After Alcatraz, Indian activists became even more militant. Ojibwas in the Minnesota–St. Paul area organized the American Indian Movement (AIM). In 1973 two AIM leaders, Russell Means and Dennis Banks, began protesting the disparity in law enforcement for Indians and whites. In Custer, South Dakota, officials charged a white with second-degree manslaughter for fatally stabbing an Indian, whereas in nearby Rapid City an Indian accused of killing a white woman was held without bail for murder. Means and Banks led protests in both cities, and AIM eventually seized a trading post at Wounded Knee, South Dakota, where the Seventh Cavalry had crushed in the 1890s the last substantial pan-Indian resistance movement. AIM leaders believed that this small community on the Pine Ridge Reservation offered an appropriate place for launching a cultural-political revival.

AIM's bold tactics split the Indian community at Pine Ridge. Some condemned AIM's members as outside agitators who brought physical destruction to an Indian town and repudiated Indian ways by attacking tribal elders. Others, including many older traditionalists, sympathized with AIM's opposition to tribal leaders, criticizing them for corruption and for a cozy relationship with the Bureau of Indian Affairs.

Federal marshals finally cleared Wounded Knee, but AIM then shifted its focus into the courts. Indicted on various counts, Banks and Means began a spectacular trial in St. Paul, first trying to have U.S. treaties with Indians (which, they contended, the government had systematically violated) admitted into evidence on their behalf. After a nine-month trial the presiding judge dismissed the indictments and charged the government prosecutors with serious misconduct. By the mid-1970s other Indians throughout the country were launching legal challenges and threatening direct action to redress grievances. Although these tactics did not gain support from the entire Indian community, this militancy had a far-reaching impact. It promoted a new pride in Indian culture, a fresh concern with preserving an ancient heritage, and a stronger determination to use the courts to make whites live up to past promises.

A New Women's Movement

A new women's movement became an increasingly important part of the social ferment of the 1960s and 1970s. Public rhetoric of the 1950s had emphasized domestic roles for women. In 1955 Adlai Stevenson, the two-time Democratic candidate for president, told graduates of a prominent women's college that their job in politics should be to use the "humble role of housewife" to influence their husbands and sons. Eminent male psychologists of the era warned that mental disorders could result from a woman's failure to accept passive, "feminine" characteristics, and they portrayed those who advocated broadening acceptable social roles for women as maladjusted and neurotic. Popular magazines and programs for women also emphasized channeling self-expression in so-called "natural" directions—toward cooking, child rearing, and interior decorating.

During the 1960s, however, the ideology of domesticity increasingly clashed with women's experiences and, eventually, with a growing feminist consciousness. The number of women working outside the home rose dramatically; a growing percentage of young women remained single much longer than had their sisters during the 1950s; divorce rates increased; the number of female-headed households grew; women, especially African-American women, played significant roles in the early civil rights movement; and the birth-control pill contributed to changes in sexual relationships.

In 1963 Betty Friedan published *The Feminine Mystique,* an influential critique of the sex-role conditioning that Friedan believed channeled women into positions of inferiority. From dolls and dainty ruffles through teenage dating conventions to myths of married bliss as a happy dependent, women were confined within a mystique that prevented them from developing their full potential as human beings. According to Friedan, women should be able to move beyond the domestic sphere without suffering social stigma and should have options for self-fulfillment equal to those accorded to men. Friedan's book touched a nerve, particularly among white middle-class women whose lives were most bound by postwar expectations of domesticity.

Organizing followed. In 1966 Friedan and other women founded the National Organization for Women (NOW). Modeled on civil rights organizations, NOW campaigned against institutions that practiced sex discrimination, lobbied for child-care centers, and publicized women's causes through the media. NOW created local chapters and eventually adopted, from other feminist groups, the idea of "consciousness raising." Consciousness-raising sessions encouraged small groups of women to vent grievances; to question prevailing constructions of gender; and perhaps most important, to explore the larger political dimensions of their own personal lives. Consciousness raising, feminists hoped, would enable women to examine social arrangements and draw the collective strength needed to make changes in society and in their everyday lives.

The Civil Rights Act of 1964, enacted mainly to assist the struggle for racial equality, offered a new legal tool for women, and women's organizations lobbied hard for its passage. The act prohibited discrimination on the basis of sex as well as on race; some southern representatives had pushed for a provision on sexual equality, hoping that this might diminish the bill's chances for passage. Using this new Civil Rights Act, women's groups attacked a host of discriminatory practices. Newspapers could no longer run want ads that distinguished between men's and women's work, and the federal government's requirement of equal pay for equal work was strengthened. By the late 1960s, the government mandated that corporations or institutions receiving federal funds adopt nondiscriminatory hiring practices and, in the early 1970s, pressed for affirmative action as a means to recruit more women and minority-group applications into those schools or jobs in which there were smaller percentages of women than in the larger population.

The antiwar and New Left movements of the late 1960s also contributed to a new brand of radical feminism. Both movements developed sociopolitical critiques that fed the growing feminist consciousness. Moreover, in organizing against racial injustice and the Vietnam War, women realized their own second-class status, even within supposedly radical movements. Men generally monopolized the podia and the media spotlights, relegating women to lesser roles. In the Black Power movement, militancy sometimes intertwined with assertions of male dominance; within organizations such as SDS, the white male leadership initially saw little contradiction in expecting women to accept secondary roles. While participating in movements committed to social change, many women came to realize, for the first time, the extent of gender discrimination. As a result, struggles for women's liberation developed within older insurgency movements: Chicana groups coalesced within the Farm Worker's movement in the West; African-American women expressed and organized around an ethic of "black feminism"; white women also discovered that "sisterhood is powerful."

By the early 1970s, feminism became a broad, but by no means unified, movement; class, race, and ethnicity divided women even as gender united them. Consisting largely of middle-class professional women, NOW sought legal equality through the legislatures and the courts. Political radicals—such as Jane Alpert, who became a fugitive from justice after getting caught up in several bombing incidents—attacked the same capitalist system in which members of NOW wanted to work. Cultural radicals assailed marriage, a social arrangement that they considered inherently sexist and exploitative. A new generation of African-American writers, including Alice Walker and Toni

Morrison, gave voice to the traditions of black women. And groups of women from all racial and ethnic backgrounds built new institutions to serve needs that male-dominated structures had long ignored: rape-crisis centers, battered-women's shelters, women's health collectives, women's studies programs in colleges and universities, and support groups for clerical workers combating sexual harassment in the workplace. New periodicals such as *MS* and more scholarly journals such as *Feminist Studies* (1972) and *Signs* (1975) provided forums for feminist ideas.

As feminism expanded its base, counter-organizations of women who recoiled against "women's lib" also began to appear. Resenting implications that they were ignorant, useless, and exploited, some housewives rallied around older values. These women claimed that motherhood and devotion to their husbands should continue to be the hallmarks of true femininity.

One of the most bitter battles pitting women against women came over the long-proposed Equal Rights Amendment (ERA) to the Constitution. The amendment, granting equal rights specifically to women, passed Congress in early 1972 and was quickly ratified by more than half of the states. But the necessary approval from three-quarters of the states did not come, and the amendment's progress stalled. NOW lobbied intensely on its behalf, but vigorous opposition from people such as archconservative Phyllis Schlafly and organizations such as the Christian Crusade more than counterbalanced NOW's efforts. Opponents charged not only that the amendment would undermine the stability of the traditional family but also that its effect on alimony, protective labor laws, and eligibility for military service would positively harm women themselves. In response to such arguments and to the growing identification between the political right and antifeminism, the Republican party reversed a position it had held for the past forty years and dropped support of the ERA from its 1980 platform. The ERA was never ratified.

Abortion became an even more controversial issue. In *Roe* v. *Wade* (1973), the Supreme Court upheld a pregnant Texas woman's claim that her state's criminal abortion law abridged her personal privacy by denying her the right to seek a medically safe abortion. After this decision, abortions could be legally and more safely obtained by most women during the first trimester of pregnancy. But people who supported a woman's right to make her own reproductive choices quickly realized that *Roe* v. *Wade* was an ambiguous victory. Most immediately, it fueled a powerful backlash in the form of the "right-to-life" crusade.

The right-to-life movement—which drew much of its support from traditionalist Catholics, fundamentalist Protestants, and ultraconservative political groups—denounced abortion as legalized murder and championed the "rights of the unborn." Calling their crusade "profamily," it bitterly condemned many social changes of the 1960s and 1970s, especially those related to achieving greater gender equality. Abortion rights advocates countercharged that antiabortion activists usually ignored most other questions involving family or right-to-life issues. A powerful element in the New Right coalitions that were emerging in the 1970s, prolife groups often favored a militaristic foreign policy and the death penalty, and they generally opposed so-cial programs, such as subsidized child care and sex education, that might offer alternatives to abortion. As public debates became more acrimonious, politicians found that abortion could overshadow all other issues, even in local elections. The right-to-life crusade, like that against ratification of the ERA, gained strength throughout the 1970s.

By mid-decade, women's roles were clearly undergoing significant changes. Women working outside the home became the norm, and gender barriers were toppled in nearly every occupation and profession. However, not all changes were positive. Greater employment opportunities by no means brought equality at the pay window: The median income for women who worked full time was less than 60 percent of the median income for men. (The disparity actually grew larger during the 1960s and 1970s; the ratio had been 63 percent in 1956.) In addition, most men continued to expect certain supposedly male prerogatives. On the average, for example, husbands of working wives did only about one-fourth of all work around the house, creat-ing a "double day" for women who were employed outside the home. Changes in gender roles also seemed to bring a dangerous antifemale backlash; do-mestic violence against women appeared on the rise (or as feminist con-sciousness grew, this crime was more often reported to public authorities); rates of divorce also increased, a trend that often meant a drastically reduced living standard for newly single women. Similarly, with large numbers of un-married women trapped in low-paying jobs or on welfare, some analysts high-lighted "the feminization of poverty" as one of the major legacies of the 1970s.

Still, the late 1960s and the 1970s did see major social changes for women. On college campuses, faculty and administrators became more sensi-tive than ever before to practices and attitudes considered sexist. The Girl Scouts developed a new concern for female autonomy. There was growing admission of women into the ministry of mainline Protestant churches, and gender integration of previously all-male bastions such as Rotary Clubs and Chambers of Commerce. Although much remained to be done, even in the area of defining basic goals, the everyday lives of millions of women were becoming fundamentally different from those of their mothers only a generation earlier.

The "Unmeltable Ethnics"

During the 1960s the crusades linked to gender and race tended to dominate the discussion of social problems by the media and by academi-cians. By the early 1970s, however, it became evident that other people began to demand empowerment as well. Spokespeople for white ethnic groups com-plained that liberal reformers were too anxious to advance others, especially African-Americans, at their expense. Despite optimistic theories about the emergence of a "postindustrial" society and despite many years of faith in the fabled melting pot, ethnicity remained an important part of daily life.

In some ways the assertiveness of white ethnic groups represented a complicated response to the black movement. These groups, like proponents of black pride, extolled the traditional values of their cultures and emphasized the deep significance of the old country to them and to their children. The melting pot had only singed the people whom Michael Novak, a Catholic philosopher of Slovak background, called the "unmeltable ethnics." Efforts at Americanization had never extended into the private realm, into the close-knit, family-oriented communities of the white ethnics. As a result, large numbers of ethnic families devoted much of their leisure time to social and cultural activities that expressed pride in their Old World pasts. Thus, the new ethnicity was an old phenomenon; the novelty came in the greater pride and the increased self-confidence with which younger Polish-Americans, Slovak-Americans, and other "unmelted ethnics" defended their cultural heritage and their present way of life.

The new directions in the black movement also had much to do with the surfacing of the new ethnicity in the late 1960s and early 1970s. Deeply rooted in clearly identified neighborhoods, many members of white ethnic groups felt threatened by the influx of black newcomers, many of them from the South, into northern industrial cities. Many ethnics also felt challenged when people of color pushed for greater employment opportunities. They regarded hard-won union seniority systems, for example, as forms of social insurance and were not ready to sacrifice them for affirmative action. Their resentment only increased when they were called barriers to social progress.

The ethnic awakening, though, represented more than a white backlash. Although there were many points of conflict between blacks and white ethnics, there were also, as the 1970s would reveal, equally important common interests. Poor schools, decaying transit facilities, inflation, and other problems affected most urbanites. Even more important, the new assertiveness among blacks and the unmelted ethnics could be traced back to the high-tech, corporate-dominated society that the United States had become. There was a recognition by many white ethnic and African-American leaders that dominant elites had long ignored their interests and their cultures.

Despite generally rising real wages, for example, workers felt that they were not doing as well as they should be. The small increase in real income, for example, never quite covered all the new expenses. Moreover, working-class families complained that their neighborhoods had been destroyed by urban-renewal projects, their streets overrun by criminals, their savings and paychecks undermined by inflation, their take-home pay cut by rising taxes, and their sons shipped to Vietnam. In 1968 an urban worker with two children, according to figures from the Bureau of Labor Statistics, needed almost $10,000 a year to live at "a moderate but adequate standard of living." Yet even well-paid workers made less than $8,000. Only through the miracle of installment buying and the growing number of working women, who provided families with a second paycheck, could most families maintain middle-class status; in 1969 the nation's total installment debt reached almost $90 billion.

The tremendous popular response to the television version of Alex Haley's *Roots* and to the film *Rocky* (1976) suggested the depth of dissatisfaction. Haley's tale about the tenacity of the black family experience was not exactly the story of Polish-American or Irish-American roots. Yet the dominant theme *was* the same: the search for links to the past and a sense of stability in a time of change. If African-Americans found their special heroes in Haley's characters, many white ethnics found theirs in *Rocky*. Never patronizing the working-class culture of Philadelphia's Italian-American neighborhoods, the popular motion picture—as opposed to its formulaic sequels—depicted the ethnic's version of the American dream: a decent place to live; a life of understandable scale; and above all, respect for one's own accomplishments.

THE YEARS OF PROTEST, 1963–1976: AN AMBIGUOUS LEGACY

The years of protest, which had begun during the 1960s, continued into the next decade. Even after Nixon's 1968 election, significant social change still seemed possible; indeed, sometimes, as one believer in the promise of the 1960s later recalled, it appeared that "everything was possible."

By the mid-1970s, however, the new politics of the 1960s and many of the insurgent movements no longer provided the driving forces in American political culture. Once so hopeful of rapid, almost instantaneous change, many veterans of the various movements seemed worn down from too many battles. The more radical ones always had to consider the danger—a very real one, as members of the Black Panthers and the American Indian Movement found out—of government actions, both legal and illegal, against them and their friends. Writing after the deaths of two black students, killed during protests at Southern University in 1973, the black poet June Jordan confessed

> *I'm tired*
> *and you're tired*
> *and everybody's goddam tired*
> *tired*
> *students tired*
> *Liberals tired*
> *Revolutionaries tired. . . .* *

Moreover, the search for power and the struggles for change produced fragmentation as well as community. As feminists and black activists discovered, new strategies and tactics could lead to confrontations not only with defenders of the status quo but also with both liberals, who still supported gradualist social change, and "sisters" and "brothers" who disagreed about where to take the next steps toward some significantly different future. The gap between what insurgents believed needed to be done and what could be accomplished rarely seemed to be closing.

*Reprinted by permission.

But the sense of exhaustion, deep as it ran among veterans of the movements, proved to be only one of the legacies from the years of protest. Looking back, we can see other broad themes emerge.

First, most of the various movements seeking greater power and social change left important legacies. Civil rights laws, abolition of the military draft, withdrawal of U.S. troops from Vietnam, less restrictive drug laws, and changes in college curricula and social life were only some of the more immediate changes traceable to the movements started in the 1960s. If one takes a longer view of their impact, the insurgents created the basis for ongoing activity by feminist groups, advocates of gay and lesbian rights, environmental groups, community-based self-help organizations, and a variety of other organizations and impulses that took their original inspiration from the years of protest.

A second legacy of the years from 1963 to 1976 was the gradual exhaustion of the welfare-state liberalism of the Fair Deal, the New Frontier, and the Great Society. The search for empowerment by people who felt postwar liberals had done too little, too slowly, contributed to welfare-liberalism's decay. In this sense, the years of protest cost centrist liberals like LBJ much of what they had expected would be their natural constituency among those young people and people of color who came to identify welfare liberalism with a corrupt status quo. In another sense, when liberals tried to move cautiously leftward, hoping to catch up with at least some of the various movements, they risked losing many people who justifiably feared that they would shoulder the tax burden for larger welfare-state programs. Both radicals and liberals, argued Richard Nixon, had lost touch with the nation's "real majority." Many of those to the right and those to the left of welfare liberalism agreed: It represented an outdated approach to social and economic problems.

Thus, another legacy of the years of protest gradually emerged: a new conservative movement, symbolized by Ronald Reagan and his attacks on the welfare state. The years of protest threw up all kinds of unusual political figures, most of whom enjoyed instant media attention and then suffered almost equally rapid obscurity. Most political pundits predicted a similarly brief career for Ronald Reagan, who emerged in 1964, during Barry Goldwater's presidential campaign. Despite the conventional wisdom, heard from 1965 until 1980, that "Reagan is too old," he capitalized on resentment against radicals and against the liberal welfare state to become almost the only prominent political figure from the years of protest to thrive during the 1980s. Reagan's curious career says a great deal about the ambiguous legacy of the years of protest.

SUGGESTIONS FOR FURTHER READING

The literature on the opposition movements of the 1960s and 1970s is already immense—and of widely varying quality. Several classics of the 1960s are good places to begin: Philip Slater, *The Pursuit of Loneliness* (rev. ed., 1976); Theodore Roszak, *The Making of a Counter Culture* (1969) and *Where the Wasteland Ends* (1972); and Charles Reich, *The Greening of America* (1970). Sohnya

Sayres et al., *The 60s Without Apology* (1984), and Clair Albert and Stewart Albert, *The Sixties Papers* (1984), remain useful anthologies, which can be supplemented by Barbara Tischler, ed., *Sights on the Sixties* (1992). David Chalmers, *And the Crooked Place Made Straight: The Struggle for Social Change in the 1960s* (1991), is a more recent overview. See also Timothy Miller, *The Hippies and American Values* (1991).

Milton Viorst, *Fire in the Streets* (1981), brings to life the personal stories of some of the leading cultural radicals, and Marty Jezer, *Abbie Hoffman: American Rebel* (1992), looks at the Yippie celebrity. On opposition to the war, see Thomas Powers, *The War at Home* (1973); Nancy Zaroulis and Gerald Sullivan, *Who Spoke Up?* (1984); Charles De Benedetti, *An American Ordeal: The Anti-war Movement of the Vietnam Era* (1990); Melvin Small and William D. Hoover, eds., *Give Peace a Chance* (1992); Kenneth J. Heineman, *Campus Wars: The Peace Movement at American State Universities in the Vietnam Era* (1993); Amy Swerdlow, *Women Strike for Peace: Traditional Motherhood and Radical Politics in the 1960s* (1993); and Tom Wells, *The War Within* (1993).

Todd Gitlin indicts the media for speeding the fall of opposition efforts in *The Whole World Is Watching* (1980). Maurice Isserman, *If I Had a Hammer* (1987), looks at the conflict between the old and new lefts. Wini Breines, *Community and Organization in the New Left, 1962–1968* (1982), and Peter B. Levy, *The New Left and Labor in the 1960s* (1993), are important studies on New Left politics. Government surveillance of radical cultural and political figures is the subject of James Kirkpatrick Davis, *Spying on Americans* (1992).

The diversity of the counterculture is evident after considering Tom Wolfe, *The Electric Kool-Aid Acid Test* (1969); Morris Dickstein, *Gates of Eden* (1977); Joan Didion, *The White Album* (1979); Charles Perry, *The Haight-Ashbury* (1985); and Sally Banes, *Greenwich Village 1963: Avant-Garde Performance and the Effervescent Body* (1993). Abe Peck covers the underground press in *Uncovering the Sixties* (1985), and Daniel Yankelovich tries to fathom changing social values in *The New Morality* (1974) and *New Rules* (1982).

During the 1980s, strong nostalgia for the early and mid-1960s began to emerge. Jim Miller, *Democracy Is in the Streets* (1987); Todd Gitlin, *The Sixties: Years of Hope, Days of Rage* (1987); Joan Morrison and Robert K. Morrison, eds., *From Camelot to Kent State: The Sixties Experience in the Words of Those Who Lived It* (1987); and Hans Konig, *Nineteen Sixty-Eight: A Personal Report* (1987), all express complex, though not uncritical, feelings of loss. In contrast, the former radicals who look back in Peter Collier and David Horowitz, eds, *Second Thoughts* (1989), have almost nothing good to say about the 1960s. Among the attempts to gain some perspective on the decade, especially the allegedly pivotal year of 1968, see Irwin Unger and Debi Unger, *Turning Point, 1968* (1988); David Caute, *The Year of the Barricades: A Journey Through 1968* (1988); David Farber, *Chicago '68* (1988); and Douglas Knight, *Streets of Dreams: The Nature and Legacy of the 1960s* (1989). On the election of 1968, see Lewis Gould, *1968: The Election that Changed America* (1993).

Sara Evans, *Personal Politics: The Roots of Women's Liberation in the Civil Rights Movement and the New Left* (1979), and Alice Echols, *Daring to Be Bad:*

Radical Feminism in America, 1967–1975 (1989), seek to trace the emergence of a new feminism out of the male-dominated ethos of the New Left and the counterculture and to suggest that 1968 did not represent a sudden end to insurgent movements. See also Blanche Linden-Ward and Carol Hurd Green, *Changing the Future: American Women in the 1960s* (1992), and Winifred D. Wandersee, *On the Move: American Women in the 1970s* (1988).

On the escalation of violence in Southeast Asia, see Seymour Hersh, *Cover-up* (1972); William Shawcross, *Sideshow* (1979); and Karl D. Jackson, *Cambodia, 1975–1978: Rendezvous with Death* (1989).

One can get a sense of the mood at home from *The Age of Paranoia* (1972), a selection of stories from *Rolling Stone*, and from Joseph Kellner and James Muneves, *The Kent State Coverup* (1980).

For a general theory of insurgency during these years, see Ira Katznelson's *City Trenches* (1981). See also Michael Reich, *Racial Inequality* (1981); Rufus Brown, Dale Rogers Marshall, and David Tebbs, *Protest Is Not Enough: The Struggle of Blacks and Hispanics for Equality in Urban Politics* (1984); Peter Mathiessen, *In the Spirit of Crazy Horse* (1983); George Lipsitz, *A Life in the Struggle: Ivory Perry and the Culture of Opposition* (1988); Barbara Epstein, *Political Protest and Cultural Revolution* (1991); and William H. Chafe, *Never Stop Running: Allard Lowenstein and the Struggle to Save American Liberalism* (1993).

The complexity of ethnic issues may be gleaned from Michael Novak, *Rise of the Unmeltable Ethnics* (1973); Richard Kirckus, *Pursuing the American Dream* (1976); Patricia Zavella, *Women's Work and Chicano Families: Cannery Workers of the Santa Clara Valley* (1987); William Julius Wilson, *The Declining Significance of Race: Blacks and Changing American Institutions* (1978) and *The Truly Disadvantaged: The Inner City, the Underclass, and Public Policy* (1987); Carlos Munoz, Jr., *Youth Identity and Power: The Chicano Movement* (1989); Jim Sleeper, *The Closet of Strangers: Liberalism and the Politics of Race in New York* (1990); Charles Pete Banner-Haley, *The Fruits of Integration: Black Middle-class Ideology and Culture, 1960–1990* (1993); and Herbert Hill and James E. Jones, Jr., eds., *Race in America* (1993).

On the continuation of the new feminist movement, see again many of the works noted at the end of Chapter Five; see also Jo Freeman, *The Politics of Women's Liberation* (1975); Linda T. Sanford, *Women and Self-esteem (1985);* Jane J. Mansbridge, *Why We Lost the ERA* (1986); Mary Francis Berry, *Why ERA Failed* (1986); Johnnetta B. Cole, ed., *All American Women: Lines that Divide, Ties that Bind* (1986); Catherine MacKinnon, *Feminism Unmodified* (1988); and Susan Staggenborg, *The Pro-choice Movement* (1991).

8

The Oversized Society: Life during the 1960s and 1970s

The 1960s ushered in a tremendous growth in the scale of American economic and social institutions. Lyndon Johnson, the extravagant Texan who dominated the middle of the 1960s, symbolized the trend: He drove too fast; he threw gargantuan barbecues; and in one well-publicized incident, he pulled his dog's ears until the puppy yelped. Restraint seemed a quality of the past. The era throbbed with raw power and extremes. American involvement in Vietnam seemed to escalate uncontrollably; both Johnson and Nixon roared at their critics; huge business conglomerates formed; rock singers grew old before they turned thirty; football replaced baseball as the national sport. The 1970 census reported that three of every ten homes had more than one TV set and that only three of a hundred had no television at all. The post office, assisted by its new zip code numbers and electronic equipment, delivered a yearly average of 400 pieces of mail to every man, woman, and child. Book publishers issued more than 35,000 titles annually, double the number put out just ten years earlier. According to one study, the average American threw away four pounds of garbage per day, and the nationwide total amounted to 150 million tons a year—enough refuse to fill three lines of garbage trucks extending from New York to Los Angeles and enough potential energy to light the United States for an entire year.

Growth did not necessarily bring satisfaction. To many people the change in the scale of life had become bewildering. Who could understand a trillion-dollar economy, trace lines of responsibility through the sprawling federal bureaucracy; or gain redress from an impersonal, computerized corporation? Summing up the misgivings of many, the journalist Kirkpatrick Sale argued in 1980 that American life had come to exceed any meaningful human scale.

THE ECONOMY: A GATHERING OF GIANTS

The Military-Industrial Complex

In his farewell speech of 1961, President Dwight D. Eisenhower warned of a permanent, government-supported weapons industry. No longer, he explained, did Americans mobilize civilian industries for war and reconvert them after the peace. Cold war pressures had kept the economy on a perpetual war footing and had created "a permanent armaments industry of vast proportions." The old general warned that "we annually spend on military security more than the net income of all United States corporations," and he feared that the military-industrial complex held the "potential for the disastrous rise of misplaced power."

The military-industrial complex grew even larger during the Vietnam War. This national defense structure consisted, at the top, of politicians, military people, business contractors, and university researchers and, at the bottom, of workers in defense industries. All of these groups were mutually dependent. Government grants for research and development constituted a significant portion of many university budgets; huge corporations, such as General Dynamics and Lockheed, depended almost exclusively on government contracts; in 1967 the salaries of nearly 3 million people came from defense-related work. If the air force wanted a new plane, Boeing Aircraft wanted a lucrative contract and the people of the Pacific Northwest wanted more jobs. Taxpayers who shouldered the bill had little control over spiraling costs, for few could evaluate the need for a new weapons system. Government was the beneficiary as well as the benefactor: Without this complex of research, industry, and manpower, policymakers could not have pursued their idea of national security, which in postwar years required large-scale and high-tech military capabilities. The Pentagon directed the largest planned economic system outside of the Soviet Union.

The end of the Vietnam War brought little decrease in military production. Profits for defense industries had become so important that the Nixon administration assiduously sought new customers abroad. During the 1970s American arms sales to foreigners boomed, providing one of the few bright spots in a dreary picture of deteriorating trade balances. There were always customers for arms—always friends, such as the Shah of Iran and the generals in Brazil, eager to beef up their military establishments. Between 1972 and 1978 the Shah purchased nearly $20 billion worth of military equipment from the United States. For America, arms sales supposedly brought two blessings—profits and the development of strongly militarized allies who could police their particular region and relieve the United States of direct involvement in the maintenance of the status quo.

The main drawback to arms sales was the rising level of violence throughout the world, as countries in Southeast Asia, the Middle East, Latin America, and finally Africa began to engage in mini–arms races. As sophisticated weaponry saturated the world, the toll of death and destruction from regional rivalries and civil war increased immeasurably. Even President Jimmy Carter, who had promised in his 1976 campaign to curtail America's role as a merchant of death and encourage human rights abroad, proved unwilling to accept the consequences of canceled contracts, reduced exports, and discontented allies. The flow of arms sales under the Carter administration continued unabated, changing not its volume but only its channels. After the Shah's ouster in 1979, for example, the huge amounts of advanced weaponry formerly sold to Iran found buyers in Israel, Egypt, and elsewhere. And in January 1980 Carter gave the go-ahead for production of America's first armament manufactured solely for export—the FX fighter plane.

Brisk military spending also continued at home. One might have expected that a period marked by the end of conflict in Vietnam and by arms limitation (SALT) talks with the Soviets would have deemphasized the arms race, but the reverse was true. Expenditures in Vietnam had delayed modernization, and the military had accumulated a backlog on its wish list. The lengthy SALT negotiations, which produced an interim agreement called SALT I in 1972 and the more comprehensive accord, SALT II in 1979, actually inflamed military rivalry as both sides hurried to develop new weapons that could be traded off for concessions from the other side.

The space program—which depended on the interrelationship of university research, government funding, and industrial production—was also a child of this new age. Shortly after the Soviet Union launched its first Sputnik satellite in 1957, Congress created the National Aeronautics and Space Administration (NASA), and in 1961 President Kennedy committed the nation to landing a man on the moon by 1970. The space program, often compared to the Manhattan Project, which developed the atomic bomb during World War II, organized scientific and technical bureaucracies into a crash effort to surpass the Soviet Union in space exploration.

Critics of the program's expense called it a moon-doggle and compared it to ancient Egypt's pyramids—a feat of much grandeur but little practicality. They pointed to the trading advances Japan was making by directing its research and development efforts into products that would do well in foreign markets. The space program, they argued, directed American specialization into channels ultimately detrimental to its balance of trade.

To counter such charges NASA stressed the spinoffs of space research for civilians, such as heart pacemakers and miniature electronic components. Space satellites brought a quiet revolution in international communications, increasing America's worldwide dominance over radio and TV transmission. NASA officials liked to compare their feats to that of Charles Lindbergh in 1927. (Lindbergh celebrated his solo flight across the Atlantic as a union of man and machine in a book entitled *We*; the original astronauts issued a ghost-written account of their adventures called *We Seven*.) But Lindy's flight rested largely on private effort and a few financial backers; the Mercury and Apollo programs, products of government-managed technology, relied on thousands of people in aerospace industries, "operation teams," and recovery forces. Even the tiny Mercury program required nearly two hundred managers.

Government research money accelerated other new developments that transformed American life. The electronics industry became a chief beneficiary of well-funded research, and most sectors of the economy entered the computer revolution during the 1960s and 1970s. Everything from police records to life-support systems in hospitals to office typewriters were plugged into computers. File cabinets eased toward obsolescence, and information managers and word processors replaced old-fashioned bureaucrats and secretaries.

Business Giants

During the 1960s, the huge infusion of government money into the economy, together with a rising level of consumer spending, brought rapid business expansion and consolidation. Growth seemed to be the key to survival, and the fastest way to expand was to merge with or purchase other firms. The growth of huge enterprises further centralized economic power. By the late 1960s the two hundred largest U.S. companies controlled 58 percent of all manufacturing assets in the nation.

New companies most often were not purchased by competitors in the same field but were absorbed by conglomerates made up of a wide variety of unrelated industries. Financial daredevils could no longer legally corner the market in any one product (horizontal monopoly) or establish control over all the steps of production in the manufacture of any one item (vertical monopoly). Conglomerates, however, minimized overall risk by diversifying their holdings. Gulf and Western and Transamerica Corporation, two of the wonder children of the 1960s, acquired companies as fast as they could find them; they owned Hollywood studios, auto parts distributorships, land development corporations, insurance companies, and sports arenas.

As American enterprise expanded at home, it also moved into other lands at a pace that astonished and alarmed many foreigners. A variety of motives led American businesses to establish operations in foreign lands: cheaper labor, lower interest rates, favorable tax laws, and proximity to new markets and raw materials. Whatever the precise constellation of motives in particular cases, the net result was an unparalleled outflow of investment dollars. IBM, for example, provided 70 percent of all computers in the noncommunist world and maintained research labs in most of the developed nations; Standard Oil of New Jersey drilled and distributed oil throughout the globe; Pepsi-Cola became a universal refreshment, admitted even into the Soviet Union.

The financial power of these multinational companies often exceeded that of the nation in which they operated. One official for the American Agency for International Development reported in the late 1960s that if the gross national products of nations were ranked with the gross annual sales of corporations, half of the top hundred would be corporations and two-thirds of these would be American-based. During the 1970s, other multinational competitors—especially Japanese companies—began to challenge Americans, but the globalization of the world economy continued to accelerate.

Rapid business growth and new technological discoveries changed the way Americans lived. Demand for natural materials, such as wood, wool, cotton, and natural rubber, declined relative to artificial substitutes—plastics, acrylic fibers, and synthetic rubber. In 1968 the quantity of synthetic fibers surpassed the output of natural fibers. All kinds of new products flooded the marketplace. During the 1960s drug and grocery stores stocked six thousand new products every year; the rate for the introduction of new items nearly doubled during the 1970s. More than half of the items stocked by supermarkets in the 1970s did not even exist in 1960, and nearly half of the products available in 1960 had been withdrawn from the marketplace a decade later. Stiff competition for the buyer's dollar often made packaging and advertising more important than a product's content. Critics of the highly competitive breakfast food industry, for example, claimed that the quality of some products was so low that the flashy packages had more nutritional value than the overprocessed grain inside. The variety of new products grew so rapidly that finding an unused brand name could be a problem. Some large companies set their computers to work providing printouts of letter combinations that sounded attractive—Exxon and Pringles were just two of the results.

Entrepreneurs devised new marketing methods. During the 1960s, independently owned, locally operated shops found their customers turning to large chain or franchise operations that offered greater volume at lower prices. What McDonald's did for hamburgers, Holiday Inn did for travel, K-Mart for retailing, and 7-Eleven for neighborhood groceries. Every city of any size had a "miracle mile" or a "strip" nearly identical to that of every other: a string of discount houses, supermarkets, and fast-food chains. Shopping became easier when the Bank of America introduced Bank America (renamed Visa). This new credit card, quickly imitated by New York banks, tempted customers to spend and borrow more and channeled large amounts of consumer purchasing through a few large banks.

During the 1970s many of the old industrial-age companies, such as automakers and steel, declined and faced retrenchment, but newer sectors boomed. Demand accelerated for consultants of all sorts, cable television became a major industry, aircraft manufacture flourished, and sporting-goods and leisure companies chalked up large gains. (In 1979 American joggers spent $400 million on running shoes and warm-up suits alone.) Perfection of the silicon chip, a tiny microprocessor that for $10 could do the work of a $100,000 computer, revolutionized electronics, opening the way for such new products as computerized cash registers and video games. Challenging supermarkets as the source for family meals, fast-food chains also continued their growth. McDonald's, always the front-runner, erected 4,000 new outlets during the 1970s.

Energy and Ecology

Galloping growth strained resources and the environment. In 1970, according to one calculation, Americans constituted less than 6 percent of the human race but used 40 percent of the resources consumed worldwide each year and produced 50 percent of the physical pollution.

Availability of cheap energy lay behind postwar economic growth. Gasoline consumption rose from 1 billion barrels in 1950 to 2.25 billion barrels in 1971; the production of electricity increased 500 percent between 1950 and 1971. By 1979 the United States was using 18.4 million barrels of oil a day, nearly half of which was imported; the United States was consuming nearly 30 percent of all the oil produced in the world.

New products were partly to blame. Aluminum, for example, an excellent substitute for steel and tin in certain cases, was dubbed "congealed electricity" because of the enormous amount of energy required to produce it. The United States processed twenty times more aluminum in 1971 than it had before World War II, and each year production figures climbed higher. Aluminum beer cans, aluminum pipe, aluminum siding, all treasured for their light weight and noncorrosiveness, contributed to the pressure on the environment.

Where would Americans find the energy required to fuel their economy in the future? The question became more urgent after the Organization of Petroleum Exporting Countries (OPEC) embargoed oil in 1973 and sent prices skyrocketing. In January 1971 the average price of a barrel of OPEC oil was $1.80; by the end of the 1970s it was $20.00 and going up.

Advocates of unrestricted domestic development of energy sources had some answers. Increased strip mining and relaxation of environmental regulations would enhance the nation's ability to use its enormous coal deposits. Accelerated oil drilling in offshore beds would bring new supplies hitherto blocked by environmental safeguards. Development of atomic power plants would increase America's energy self-sufficiency.

Environmental groups questioned many of these plans, and their organized strength grew steadily throughout the 1970s. In April 1970 environmentalists held Earth Day, a carnival extravaganza of booths and speakers designed to spawn the same kind of nationwide concerns that civil rights and antiwar causes had generated during the 1960s. Subsequently, scientists such as Barry Commoner, author of *The Closing Circle*, became popular on the college lecture circuit. Commoner warned that, beyond a certain point, damage to ecological systems was irreversible. The obsession with careless material growth, he argued, had strained the environment to the breaking point. Commoner and others popularized the word *ecology*, the natural balance necessary to sustain life on this planet, and tried to put distance between the new environmental movement and the "Don't Be a Litterbug!" and "beautification" campaigns of the past.

Toward the end of the 1970s, environmental groups increasingly focused on the issue of nuclear power. Ralph Nader and other consumer activists argued that atomic power plants presented unacceptable risks, and the "antinuke" movement received a boost from the popularity of a film about a nuclear meltdown–*The China Syndrome* (1978). And just when the power industry was laughing at the implausibility of the movie, a real-life accident in the spring of 1979 raised fears about nuclear energy to new heights.

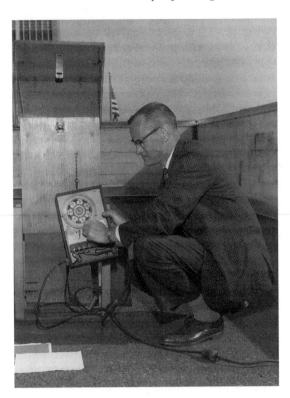

Air pollution, a major urban problem in the 1960s, prompted the passage of new federal antipollution regulations. Here, an official from the Tacoma, Washington, health department is measuring air pollution from the roof of the public library.
Source: Tacoma Public Library, Trueblood Collection #884.

A malfunction in the nuclear reactor at Three Mile Island, near Harrisburg, Pennsylvania, touched off a near disaster. Residents living near the facility evacuated their homes, and the confusion and conflicting reports during the several days of crisis ballooned public doubts about technicians' abilities to handle this deadly new technology. According to power-company supporters, the Three Mile Island accident proved that the ultimate disaster, a total meltdown, could be avoided and that even a fairly serious accident could result in no loss of life. Critics, however, pointed out the lack of established safety procedures, highlighted the escape of radiation into the surrounding atmosphere and water, and calculated the huge costs of cleanup. The official reports of a special presidential commission and of the Nuclear Regulatory Commission (NRC) came down hard on the power industry. The NRC's investigation concluded that without "fundamental changes" in the nuclear industry "similar accidents—perhaps with the potentially serious consequences that were avoided at Three Mile Island—are likely to recur." The expense of new designs, more elaborate safety procedures, and possibly even further damage suits exploded claims that nuclear energy would be cheap and safe. The all-out rush to switch to nuclear energy sources slowed and then stopped.

By the late 1970s most people agreed that they should meet the energy crisis with some sort of common action. But what? Environmentalists favored federally assisted crash programs to encourage decentralized production of power through solar, geothermal, or wind-generated systems. Ralph Nader and Barry Commoner pressed the argument that the energy debate, in fact, involved fundamental issues of economic control: It pitted decentralized, "democratic" energy sources against those that the utility and oil companies could continue to monopolize and run from a centralized facility. Supporters of the power industry, however, considered solar, geothermal, and wind power to be marginal sources at best, unable to satisfy the nation's voracious appetite for energy. They urged Washington to cut the red tape of environmental regulations and open some long-delayed offshore oil developments, and they continued to tout coal, synfuels, and atomic power.

Everyone, though, stressed conservation: Tax breaks encouraged home weatherization, utility companies advertised wise use, and the American people responded to higher prices. Consumption of crude oil fell from 7.15 million barrels in 1979 to 6.8 million in 1980. Buying habits or life-styles were not significantly scaled back, but the meteoric rise in energy use since World War II did level off.

Environmentalists and industrialists also continually clashed over the related issue of pollution. The rising material standards that people thought would enhance their comfort bore price tags—brownish skies, strangely colored rivers, drying lakes, aggravated respiratory problems, and a sharply rising cancer rate. Urban areas suffered most visibly in the 1960s; breathing New York's air for a day, one study reported, was the equivalent of smoking four packs of cigarettes. Strip mining, which had doubled during the 1960s, raised the specter of the permanent destruction of land. Business pressure groups and political conservatives tried to make environmentalism a dirty word. Affluent environmentalists, it was charged, opposed the kind of economic development that would allow middle-class Americans to maintain their present living standard and poorer citizens to improve their lives. Industrialists and their supporters emphasized two other points: Stringent regulations would put an even greater stress on America's apparently dwindling energy reserves by making it difficult to use high-pollution fuels, such as coal, and the cost of meeting tough environmental standards would make domestic industry uncompetitive with foreign enterprises. Environmentalists, they charged, were impractical; it was impossible to live in a risk-free society.

Trying to steer a course between environmental hazards and tolerable costs was the government's Environmental Protection Agency (EPA). Established in 1970, it became the government's largest regulatory body, employing 10,000 people and striving to enforce the new statutes enacted by Congress. The new environmental legislation of the 1970s aimed at limiting the use of pesticides, protecting endangered species, ensuring occupational safety, controlling strip-mining practices, and establishing maximum levels of emission of certain chemical and bacteriological pollutants into the air and water. Predictably, the EPA came under sharp attack from both industrialists and environmentalists: Industry charged it with obstructionism; environmentalists assailed its laxity. But the EPA's efforts did improve safety in the work-place, dissipated much of the urban smog of the 1960s, and cleaned up at least the surface of many of the nation's waterways.

With visible pollutants and some gross violations of nature under greater control by the late 1970s, even graver problems emerged. The higher smoke-stacks that had helped eliminate smog merely elevated pollutants, spread them over wider areas, and altered their chemical composition. The resultant acid rain, which threatened croplands throughout the country, constituted a less visible but more serious hazard than smog. Safe disposal of toxic wastes presented another significant problem. In the early 1980s people began to discover that many industries had for years haphazardly dumped toxic chemi-cal wastes. These substances, some of which were capable of promoting ge-netic defects and cancer, sometimes even became landfill for housing proj-ects, as was the case at Love Canal in upstate New York. Unlike the pollution problems of the past, those of the oversized society tended to be invisible; their toxic effects were more long term and were not immediately apparent. Any increased rate in environmentally caused cancer, for example, might take twenty years to detect. The 1970s may have been an "environmental decade" of new concern and legislation, but the environmental problems bequeathed to the 1980s seemed more complex than previous ones.

Land and Real Estate Hustlers

A great land boom that began in the mid-1960s added to environmen-talists' concerns. Huge land development corporations began subdividing tracts at an alarming rate, focusing their efforts on the sunbelt states of Florida, California, New Mexico, and Arizona but also operating in northern recreational states, such as Colorado and Maine. "Development" corporations sprang up everywhere. Some created attractive planned communities with good sanitary facilities, nearby employment opportunities, and luxurious recreation areas. But too many others simply bought large tracts of cheap land and resold it in expensive lot-sized packages. A development company in Florida, for example, purchased some swampy land for $180 an acre and quickly resold it for $640 an acre. To make this enormous profit, the company did not drain the land, build roads, plan sanitation facilities, or construct major buildings. It merely hired a high-pressure sales force, ran advertise-ments around the country, and gave the supposed community a fancy name. Word of such profits turned subdividing into a national craze, and most con-glomerate enterprises quickly created land development subsidiaries. By the early 1970s developers in California were buying 50,000 to 100,000 acres a year; subdivided land near Albuquerque, New Mexico, was slated to hold a population four times the size of Baltimore; and plots for sale in Colorado would have increased the state's population five times over. In North Car-olina, a real estate entrepreneur and a former lawyer were charged with mail fraud after allegedly trying to sell over 60,000 acres of the Great Smoky Moun-tain National Park.

During the 1970s the land boom expanded to the nation's central cities, which had declined sharply in the 1950s and 1960s. The 1970s bred near-perfect conditions for a reversal in urban fortunes. Rising gas prices mounted a frontal assault on commuting; the large baby-boom generation strained the housing market; widespread cultural nostalgia helped generate interest in the renovation of old houses; a temporary decline in the crime rate boosted the image of cities. New pollution standards made urban air bearable again, and cities also benefited from the demise of some dirty industrial-age jobs and the rise of clean service occupations. By 1980 the largest single employer in "steel city"—Pittsburgh—was not U.S. Steel but the University of Pittsburgh. Although New York City and Cleveland hit the headlines for walking the tightrope of bankruptcy in the 1970s, many more urban centers found that federal funds temporarily gave them a surplus. In 1969 few cities received more than 10 percent of their general revenue in the form of federal money; by 1980 many cities received over 50 percent in federal funds.

Such conditions produced urban revitalization in some sections of most American cities. Developers once devoted to mapping out suburban shopping centers began selling designs for urban malls. In "rescued" neighborhoods, renovators attacked any edifice with a brick facade still standing, and prices shot up as speculators quickly acquired an interest in promoting historical preservation. Condominiums attracted a generation of young professionals who wanted the advantages of home ownership without the disadvantages of single-home upkeep.

This gentrification—the return of the gentry class to the inner city—had its flip side. Revitalization was, after all, highly selective. "Old towns" of new–old cobblestone streets sprouted where architecture was interesting and sound. But the rise in rents drove the poor out of the best of their neighborhoods and left them in the worst. And where did people in need of inexpensive housing go? Moving to a more run-down neighborhood only increased the general demand for housing and mercilessly drove up prices for everyone. Speculators began to realize that even nonrenovated areas experienced a boom in prices and brought easy profits. For the poor, the inner-city renewal of the 1970s was often something to oppose and organize against. It brought not only rising prices but also physical disruption, dispersion of older communities, and a growth in homelessness. But most city officials were slow to grapple with the adverse results of gentrification; they were delighted by the new activity, and they kept joining public and private capital in new development projects that were aimed at their most affluent residents and the highly courted tourist trade.

AN OUT-SIZED CULTURE

The Publishing Industry

The book publishing industry, once the comfortable preserve of gentlemen-publishers and small booksellers, underwent considerable growth and change after 1960. In the mid-1970s, the number of bookstores in the United

States surpassed, for the first time since the early days of the cinema, the number of movie theaters, and the yearly revenues of the publishing industry outstripped those of Hollywood. Americans bought twice as many books each year as movie tickets. Although small bookstores still held their fascination, especially for browsers, most people shopped in streamlined book supermarkets. Large-scale operations, such as the spectacularly successful B. Dalton chain, dominated sales figures. Using their own computerized systems, book supermarkets stocked relatively few titles, primarily mass-market paperbacks and hardbacks from the best-seller lists, and aimed for a brisk, steady turnover. Such a sales system threatened the survival of many small bookstores and made it more difficult for readers to find shops willing to stock, or even order, volumes that lacked mass appeal.

As a consequence of the general consolidation of American business, most American publishers became subsidiaries of large corporations, often "communications groups" that included newspapers, electronic media, and records. Some publishers conceded that before making a final commitment to publish a book, they considered the author's potential charm on TV talk shows. The publisher of the best-selling *Your Erroneous Zones* recalled that he had been more enthusiastic about the TV personality of the author, Dr. Wayne Dyer, than about his book. The tie-in between book publishing and the electronic media grew even closer as the communications groups began to package expensive media products. The ultimate in commercialized art might span the entire communications spectrum: a network TV miniseries for the domestic market, a theatrical movie for distribution overseas, a record album of the sound track, and a mass-market paperback for drugstore racks and large bookstore chains.

Many veterans of the literary establishment condemned such trends. Publishing, they conceded, had never been a purely philanthropic enterprise, but never had it been so crassly commercial. The metamorphosis of the highly prestigious National Book Awards—prizes selected by prominent literary critics and by celebrated authors—into the American Book Awards—which were to be chosen by committees that included mass-market publishers and individuals from the bookstore chains—symbolized the new developments.

Similar trends toward consolidation and commercialization affected American journalism. Continuing a pattern that had been evident for more than half a century, the newspaper business became increasingly concentrated. By 1980 readers in only the largest cities could turn to competing daily papers. Whereas financial pressures forced some papers to fold, including the widely acclaimed *Chicago Daily News*, many more, especially in smaller cities, became the property of large newspaper chains. Although not all chains imposed a single editorial policy on their papers, there could be no doubt that fewer and fewer hands wielded the power of the press. Because of such concentration, critics of the media complained that journalists became too complacent; lacking competition, they also lacked incentive to dig out fresh material on local affairs. Reluctance to probe into the dark corners of municipal life, it was further charged, reflected the close, interlocking relationships between newspapers and powerful local interests.

Critics of the media also denounced celebrity journalism. Recognizing that most Americans relied on television as their primary source of information, newspapers increasingly emphasized soft features on popular culture, living styles, and prominent personalities. Celebrity journalism also spawned personality magazines, including the very successful *People*, devoted almost entirely to the rise and fall of celebrities and was distributed only at magazine counters and on supermarket racks.

Although the catchwords *consolidation* and *celebrification* accurately summarized the dominant trends in publishing in the 1960s and 1970s, there were other forces at work. Despite the growth of publishing conglomerates, many smaller houses did prosper on the fringes of the industry. Many publishers, regardless of size, remained committed to bringing out specialized works. Meanwhile, the fragmentation of cold war orthodoxies was reflected in the magazine publishing business. Many of the magazines that had sought a general, family-oriented readership—such as *Look*, the *Saturday Evening Post*, *Life*, and *Harpers*—either folded completely or underwent drastic overhauls. More specialized journals—such as the *National Review* on the political right and *The Nation* on the left—gained circulation. Even in the newspaper business, diversity survived. Most of the underground papers of the 1960s, including the famous *Berkeley Barb*, disappeared, but alternative journalism survived in the form of community-based newspapers. The going was always rough for these publications, but many journalists, especially younger ones who could not find other jobs in a glutted market, were willing to make the sacrifices. Finally, the growing amount of criticism directed at the publishing industry by media-watching publications such as the *Columbia Journalism Review* offered a healthy contrast to the smug complacency that had prevailed during the cold war era.

The Motion Picture Industry

Significant changes also affected the motion picture industry during the 1960s and 1970s. For more than four decades, filmmaking and the huge Hollywood movie factories had been synonymous. Using their sprawling back lots and deploying vast armies of contract players and stars, the major studios nourished the dreams of millions of moviegoers. Young men dueled alongside Errol Flynn or Clark Gable, and women floated through the glamorous world of Barbara Stanwyck or Lana Turner. But during the 1960s the giant studios came upon bad days. Challenged by television and victimized by urban decay, which frightened many people away from the old downtown movie palaces, Hollywood's film moguls watched box-office receipts decline steadily. Seeking to reduce production costs and to bring new realism to the screen, many filmmakers abandoned the Hollywood sets and shot on location, often outside the United States. At the same time, many of the old stars either died or retired; others, such as Rock Hudson and Elizabeth Taylor, suddenly discovered that their names alone no longer guaranteed a film's financial success.

During the late 1960s and early 1970s, filmmakers sought new audiences, especially young people, with movies that were very different from the classics of Hollywood's studio era. Consciously working against Hollywood's standard promilitary frame, Stanley Kubrick populated the national defense establishment with morons and lunatics in *Dr. Strangelove* (1963); he later explored the mystical science fiction of Arthur C. Clarke in *2001* (1968) and looked at the issues of violence and behavior modification in *A Clockwork Orange* (1972). While traditionalists denounced new films such as these, movie executives recognized that only a handful of films aimed at the old family audience still made any money. The box-office success of Dennis Hopper's *Easy Rider* (1969), a cheaply made film about two hippies who used a drug sale to finance a motorcycle trip across the southwestern United States, wove together many themes of the "new Hollywood"—social criticism, sex, and violence—and inspired a number of (much less successful) films about the counterculture, including the documentary *Woodstock* (1970). Meanwhile, African-American directors offered a series of pictures, derided by critics as "blaxploitation" films, set in violence-filled, corporate-controlled, inner-city neighborhoods, the kinds of places through which Gene Kelly had danced in films of the 1940s and 1950s.

Perhaps the most interesting series of films to span the late 1960s and the entire decade of the 1970s focused on loneliness and alienation in an oversized society of overgrown institutions and increasingly powerless individuals. Many of these films also rebelled against the old genres, the tight forms—such as the gangster movie or the western film—that had marked Hollywood's classic studio system. Robert Altman's *M*A*S*H* (1970) mocked the standard war picture, and his *McCabe and Mrs. Miller* (1968) and *Buffalo Bill and the Indians* (1976) debunked the myths on which Hollywood's western films had long been based. In *The Long Goodbye* (1973), Altman turned Philip Marlowe, the independent detective hero made famous in *film noir* of the 1940s, into a confused loser, a patsy who could not even find his own cat. Going even further, Francis Ford Coppola's *The Conversation* (1974) offered a chilling and almost despairing view of a culture based on surveillance.

Although many of these films gained more support from critics than ticket-buyers, Coppola in particular attracted huge audiences with his *Godfather* sagas, films that reworked the gangster genre while also exploring the theme of alienation. *Godfather II* (1974) presented a deeply pessimistic critique of American society and American history. The only refuge the film offers is the tightknit, patriarchal family, a place of apparent warmth and safety, lorded over by a tough but protective godfather. Inexorably, though, the godfather's business as a crime boss—which also blends into his other business and political connections—corrupts the family circle. One by one, family members fall. At the end, in the America of the 1970s, the new godfather is left alone: isolated, lonely, alienated, an outcast from both society and his own family.

Toward the end of the 1970s, this cinema of loneliness and alienation lost touch with popular tastes. Altman's only commercial success came with *M*A*S*H* at the beginning of the decade, and Coppola's ambitious plans to create his own studio collapsed from a lack of box-office hits. Challenging the cinema of loneliness was a new cycle of motion pictures from film-school graduates who had reverentially studied Hollywood's traditional myths. Steven Spielberg updated the monster genre with his blockbuster *Jaws* (1975), and George Lucas surpassed Spielberg's epic with *Star Wars* (1977), a film that owed most of its images and situations to familiar Hollywood genres—especially to the war film and the western—as well as to the graphics of video games. In contrast to previous films of the 1960s and 1970s, *Star Wars* seemed to make militarism seem fun once more.

Although some critics decried the emphasis on giant blockbusters such as *Star Wars*, a trend necessitated by rising marketing costs, film culture in many ways grew stronger than it had ever been before. Increased popular attention to film styles and themes, for example, reflected the popularization of more sophisticated types of cinematic criticism. During the 1970s most urban areas supported retrospective houses—commercial theaters that specialized in previously released classics—and theaters that emphasized foreign movies and the type of thoughtful films once dismissed as noncommercial art movies. And even as Hollywood's revenues declined in relation to those of television (or even the record and book publishing industries), more people were coming to take the motion picture itself seriously. The study of film, both Hollywood's products and documentary works, became a part of most university and many high school curricula. Journals devoted to criticism, theory, and film history proliferated as more and more people came to appreciate the subtle, complex connection between the world of the movies and everyday life.

Sports

Sports also exemplified the expansive trends in American life. There were more fans, more teams, and more TV coverage. At the beginning of the 1960s big-league baseball still dominated the sports scene, and the two major leagues expanded into new cities during the 1960s and 1970s. But despite its growth, the national pastime lost ground to other spectator sports, particularly to the faster-moving, more violent games of football, basketball (a non-contact sport only in theory), and even ice hockey. Professional football's Super Bowl replaced baseball's World Series as sports' most talked-about annual attraction. Cities competed vigorously for almost any type of professional franchise; lucrative TV contracts and generous tax write-offs made ownership of a team especially alluring to wealthy businesspeople.

Always seeking new forms of competition to sell, promoters aggressively marketed golf tournaments (women's as well as men's), imported soccer, tried (unsuccessfully) team competition in tennis, and even formed short-lived "major leagues" for slow-pitch softball and volleyball. Similarly, the growing popularity of women's sorts produced a women's professional basketball league and superstar status for women's tennis and golf. Predictions that the energy shortage was ending America's love affair with the automobile did not cool sports fans' ardor for all types of auto racing. The Indianapolis 500 rivaled the Super Bowl as sports' biggest one-day event, and President Jimmy Carter's favorite spectator sport, stock-car racing, retained its great popularity in the South.

Even professional boxing, once considered on the ropes because of the taint of fixed matches and the declining supply of "hungry" fighters, staged a vigorous comeback. The dominant figure was Muhammad Ali, the three-time heavyweight champion of the world. Ali modestly claimed that he was the best-known person on the planet, and there seemed little reason to doubt him. Certainly, he made boxing a worldwide enterprise. In 1964 he made his first title defense before a handful of people in a hockey rink in Lewiston, Maine; when he retired, he could boast that he had fought before millions of people from Malaysia to Zaire. Ali noted accurately that governments, and not simply promoters, bid for his services. His success in the ring, however, was tempered by a dramatic decline in his personal health, a condition some physicians blamed on his long career.

Sports figures remained society's special heroes. Some, like football's Jim Brown, retired in favor of full-time acting; others, such as O. J. Simpson and Joe Namath, found it more profitable to hop back and forth between stadium and sound stage. Many sports celebrities discovered that business ventures could handsomely supplement their athletic contracts. During the heady 1960s, some even challenged Colonel Sanders and McDonald's in the highly risky franchise food business, but most contented themselves with a safer course—product endorsements. After breaking Babe Ruth's lifetime home run record, Hank Aaron signed a $5 million contract with Magnavox.

Inevitably, politicians tried to tap the glamour that surrounded big-time sports celebrities. Richard Nixon assiduously cultivated his image as the nation's number-one sports fan. (He even contributed a trick play to the 1972 Super Bowl; perhaps an evil omen, the play lost 13 yards.) During presidential campaigns candidates rushed to sign up prominent athletes for their campaign squads, and a former professional football star, Jack Kemp, rivaled a former college benchwarmer, Ronald Reagan, as the hero of conservative Republicans.

Most of the professional team sports went through considerable legal turmoil during the 1960s and 1970s. Players achieved at least partial emancipation from the once dictatorial control of their owners. Professional athletes had long complained that they received a disproportionately small share of the profits, but through the 1950s the laws applying to sports stood fully on the side of capital. A new generation of athletes, armed with union advisers and spurred on by the sight of burgeoning sports revenues, changed this slant. Hockey, basketball, and football players made some gains when rival leagues began to bid for their services in the late 1960s and early 1970s, but not until the mid-1970s were their victories, and new breakthroughs by baseball players, written into law. In 1970 baseball's owners narrowly escaped defeat when the Supreme Court, after considerable internal squabbling, finally voted five to three to reject a suit challenging the national pastime's reserve clause as the basis of a form of involuntary servitude. The owners' victory was short-lived.

By 1980 other legal decisions had given athletes in all major sports the freedom to play out their options to their old team and to auction off their services as free agents in the marketplace. The result was hefty inflation in the entire salary structure of professional sports. In 1979 Nolan Ryan, owner of baseball's fastest fast ball, became a million-dollar-a-year player when he switched his allegiance from Gene Autry (the cowboy-star owner of the California Angels) to the Lone Ranger (the old cowboy hero who symbolized the home state of Ryan's new team, Houston). Although some fans grumbled—especially when highly paid players failed to deliver—most owners found that steadily rising revenues and generous tax breaks could cover the new salaries.

Sports and legal questions became intertwined with issues relating to gender. Sports critics condemned big-time sports for promoting sexism—pointing, for example, to the emphasis on female cheerleading squads that resembled Las Vegas chorus lines—and urged inclusion of more women into the world of athletics. Colleges and universities, mandated by law to achieve equality in sports activities, faced especially difficult decisions about how to finance and promote women's sports. In sports where professionalism prevailed, such as tennis and golf, the trend was unabashedly toward emulating the male model: Prize money, endorsement contracts, and media coverage for women all steadily escalated after the mid-1970s.

The growing commercialization of big-time sports, even at the collegiate level, also provoked lively debate. Traditionalists continued to defend amateur sports as character-building enterprises, and some social observers joined fans in celebrating the vicarious thrill of watching highly skilled professionals perform their special magic. Writing in a different vein, Christopher Lasch argued that the real tragedy of recent years had been the trivialization of athletic contests into debased, prepackaged spectacles often suffused with nearly criminal violence. A cult of violence was especially evident in professional hockey and boxing and wrestling.

Television

The key to the exploding popularity of sports was television. At the beginning of the 1970s professional football invaded Monday night's prime-time schedule and, to the surprise of most sports and media experts, ran away with the ratings contest. Two years later, even before a terrorist attack on Israeli athletes gave the 1972 summer Olympic Games new political significance, the Munich Olympics confirmed the drawing power of sports, including previously obscure ones such as women's gymnastics. During the 1970s, the airtime devoted to sports by the three major networks more than doubled. The reason was simple. Sports brought "good numbers"—high ratings; good numbers produced another set of happy figures—increased advertising revenues; and together, the two sets of numbers translated into greater corporate profits for ABC, CBS, and NBC. Between 1970 and 1975 the percentage of NBC's advertising take from sports nearly doubled. And higher TV revenues *from* sports inevitably meant higher payments *to* sports for the privilege of carrying events

The care and feeding of complex media equipment became part of everyday life in the "oversized society." *Source:* National and Peel Collection, Minnesota Historical Society.

on television. In 1976 the rights to telecast the Montreal Olympics cost ABC $25 million; four years later, the same network paid more than $200 million dollars more for rights to the 1984 summer games.

The symbiotic relationship between sports and television helped to solidify television's position as the most popular of the popular arts. First of all, television remained popular in terms of its ability to attract mass audiences, not only in the United States but throughout most of the world. According to a study completed in the mid-1970s, nearly half of the population ranked watching television—as opposed to watching motion pictures, reading, playing cards, talking with friends, or any other activity—as their favorite pastime. Surveys also showed that people were spending more and more time with their sets: In 1961 respondents indicated that they watched television slightly more than two hours a day; by 1974 the figure had jumped to more than three hours a day. By the time a child graduated from high school, it was estimated, he or she had spent more time with TV than with a twelve-year supply of teachers.

Network television's content was shaped by its broad-based audience. Throughout the 1950s some people had hoped that television would emphasize such programming as symphony concerts, sophisticated dramas, and in-depth news analyses. When some prominent sponsors underwrote entire shows, corporate image-makers often considered critical acclaim as important as mass audiences, if not more so. But when television changed its sponsorship base, so that the thirty-second, individually sold commercial became the key element in network programming, the number and type of people tuned to a particular show became all important to both sponsors and programmers. Few advertisers wanted to buy time on a program with small audiences or on one with a viewership made up largely of people with small disposable incomes. Television programmers came to focus more and more on the bottom line: They were in the business of attracting the largest possible segment of the American population and then reselling this audience to corporate sponsors at the highest possible rates.

Faced with the almost impossible task of predicting what a diverse audience might want to watch, network executives came to rely on a relatively small group of programmers and on tried-and-tested formulas. People who had developed and packaged one successful show gained an inside track. During the 1970s, for example, Aaron Spelling became a prolific presence in network television. Beginning with "The Mod Squad," a program about youthful crime-fighters who supposedly expressed the countercultural values of the 1960s youth generation, Spelling developed a string of crime series that ended with "Hart to Hart," a show that featured a wealthy couple who flaunted all the upscale consumer values of the late 1970s. Every one of his shows hit the top twenty-five for at least one year, and Spelling, who called his programs "mind candy," epitomized the successful television *auteur*. He offered viewers predictable plots, simplistic characters, lush scenery, and reassuring endings; he provided ABC with consistently high ratings; and he left himself with a backlist of series that could be sold for syndication outside of prime time.

Despite the increasingly narrower range of programming during the 1960s and 1970s, some shows did break familiar genres and molds. CBS's "Sixty Minutes," the first TV magazine, eventually entered the Nielsen's top-ten ranking. "The Mary Tyler Moore Show," a variety of programs by Norman Lear (including "All in the Family"), and "M*A*S*H" won plaudits for bending hackneyed TV formulas. Because of the emphasis these programs gave to character development and ensemble playing—rather than focusing on a show's headliners or weekly guest stars—viewers could find a continuity missing from most TV shows. With Hollywood's film archives almost depleted, TV executives also began to produce their own made-for-television films and longer miniseries, including the much-discussed "Roots" in 1977. Meanwhile, TV comedy broke new ground in the 1970s with "Saturday Night Live" and "SCTV," two ensemble shows that specialized in satire directed not only at political and social events but also at the TV medium itself.

By the 1970s viewers could also select a highbrow alternative to network television, though few actually did so. Public television, authorized by Congress in 1967 and expanded (with the help of corporate and foundation grants) in the 1970s, attracted only about 5 percent of the viewing audience for its most popular adult shows. (Children's programs, such as "Sesame Street" and "Mr. Rogers' Neighborhood" did considerably better.) But the Public Broadcasting System (PBS) produced considerable controversy. In 1972 Richard Nixon tried to block its appropriations because of the allegedly left-liberal bias of its public affairs offerings. Private broadcasting interests complained bitterly about the steadily increasing federal subsidies. Public television's most popular programs, critics liked to point out, were purchased from British television rather than produced by PBS' own staff. Finally, noting the large number of programs bankrolled by oil companies, some wags claimed that PBS stood for the Petroleum Broadcasting System.

Most people who touted television's potential ignored both the networks and PBS; instead, they claimed that new technologies unveiled in the 1970s seemed the best hope for innovation and greater diversity. Minicams and new videotape equipment greatly increased television's mobility and the speed with which it could send images back to viewers. The new communications satellites allowed live transmissions from most parts of the world. Introduction of cable TV systems gave millions of subscribers new options, including channels reserved for public access programming. The arrival of videocassette recorders (VCRs) allowed more affluent viewers to record programs for replay at their convenience, an important step toward breaking the tyranny of the network schedules.

Pop Music

Many pop music stars surpassed TV personalities and sports figures in popularity and wealth. Performers received huge fees for concert appearances and staggering royalties from album sales. Some of the superstars of the 1960s—Janis Joplin, Jimi Hendrix, and Jim Morrison, for example—lived at a frantic pace, spending money wildly while killing their talent and ultimately themselves with drugs and alcohol. When Morrison succumbed to a heart attack at twenty-seven, physicians reported that his internal organs resembled those of a person in his fifties. Other stars displayed more concern about their health and their financial balance sheets. Bob Dylan, the Beatles, and Mick Jagger became multimillionaires. Even the Grateful Dead, the group most closely associated with San Francisco's original hippie movement, eventually concentrated on cash flows and tax write-offs as much as on musical arrangements. In 1973 the business magazine *Forbes* estimated that at least fifty rock superstars earned between $2 million and $6 million a year. "The idea all along," explained Alice Cooper, "was to make $1 million. Otherwise the struggle wouldn't have been worth it." As one study put it, "Rock and Roll was here to pay."

In addition to obtaining great financial rewards, rock musicians finally gained serious critical attention. The success of the Beatles and Dylan helped rock music escape its juvenile image, and both rock and folk rock became widely accepted as serious forms of artistic expression. The poetic lyrics of Dylan and Paul Simon articulated the frustrated dreams of restless youth, their concern about the "sounds of silence" ("people talking without listening"), and their outrage against the persistence of social injustice. Young composers blended various types of musical styles into the rock idiom. Traditional folk music, black blues, jazz, and country-western music all influenced the progressive rock of the 1960s.

Throughout the 1960s, rock music constantly intersected with political and cultural events, offering a kind of running commentary on each new turn in the youth movement. In 1966, for instance, the Beatles released both their much-celebrated psychedelic album, *Sgt. Pepper's Lonely Heart's Club Band,* and John Lennon's "All You Need Is Love." Juxtaposed with the intense outpouring of feeling against U.S. involvement in Vietnam, violence in black ghettos, and the rising fervor of the youthful New Left, the Beatles appeared to be urging young people to take a break from politics and immerse themselves in the pleasures of the counterculture. As if in reply, Bob Dylan's *John Wesley Harding* avoided psychedelic trappings and adopted a philosophical-religious tone, with songs like "All Along the Watchtower" and "I Dreamed I Saw St. Augustine." The following year, as the political atmosphere became more explosive, the Rolling Stones issued "Street Fighting Man," a new rock anthem that expressed both anger at the political establishment and a deep ambivalence about the role of rock-and-roll millionaires in the so-called youth revolution.

The Stones' *Sympathy for the Devil* (1968) presaged the music of the 1970s, which replaced songs of community and hope with ones of individualism and decadence. In contrast to the communal spirit of the late 1960s, much of the music of the 1970s highlighted the cult of rock stars as lonely, isolated artists, people set apart from the larger community, except from those consuming communities expected to buy singles, albums, and T-shirts. Beset by personal and artistic difficulties, the preeminent symbol of the rock community, the Beatles, released their final collaborative album in 1970. By then, the high-tech, decibel-breaking sound of heavy metal contrasted vividly with folk-rock anthems of the 1960s. Designed largely for audiences of working-class males, who gathered in cavernous urban auditoriums, heavy metal seemed calculated to drown out all sense of feeling and to mimic the screeching noise of industrial society. Heavy metal groups, such as Kiss, also explored another popular theme of the 1970s-style rock: decadence. Rock artists of various persuasions became symbols of spiritual exhaustion and the single-minded pursuit of pleasure. Always alert to changing consumer trends, the Rolling Stones easily slipped from a revolutionary stance to a calculated pose of decadence.

At the same time, the entrepreneurs of pop music, seeking a cleaner image, began to distance their products from rock-and-roll. The big business of making and distributing music was returning to a kind of prerock standardization. Recording companies, which surpassed the Hollywood film industry in yearly revenues during the 1970s, emphasized expanding their incomes. Competition among record executives, who were expected to anticipate not only the next new musical fad but also the following one, encouraged corruption and discouraged innovation. The major labels, which were generally owned by giant multinational firms, were more than eager to package the latest trend, subsidizing journalistic puffs for the rock magazines and concert tours for the latest products of their hit-making machinery; they were more reluctant to underwrite significant new directions in music.

A similar situation prevailed in the radio industry. The expansion of FM stations during the 1960s and early 1970s broke the tyranny of the old top-40 playlist. Formats became freer, the range of music expanded, and local and regional artists could usually get their recordings on the air. By 1980, though, radio programming services had again narrowed the musical spectrum. Relying on sophisticated survey data, programming services carefully packaged each minute of airtime, eliminated the discretion of disk jockeys, and emphasized the music that their data said would appeal to their clients' desired audience. They ignored artists and musical styles that did not fit the program. Local talents lost out to national recording stars, and individuals on the smaller record labels lost out to artists being promoted heavily by the majors.

Corporate domination also affected African-American music. During the 1960s, James Brown became a symbol of both independent black capitalism and cultural innovation. "The hardest working man in show business," Brown broke rock and rhythm-and-blues molds to feature soul music and its later variant, funk. From the late 1960s through the mid-1970s, Aretha Franklin, with her gospel-inspired readings of soul, broke through the male-dominated genres that had epitomized rock. Brown, Franklin, and the various artists who recorded for Stax, a small record label based in the South, all tried to avoid the kind of accommodation that many African-Americans associated with the Detroit-based Motown sound. But the money that could be made from soul and from its African-American consumers eventually attracted the attention of both the Harvard Business School—which did a study for CBS in 1971—and the major record labels. By 1976, Stax had been absorbed into CBS, and other multimedia conglomerates were working to assimilate soul into various cross-over forms, such as disco.

Meanwhile, country and country-rock music, especially in the early 1970s, suddenly became a national, increasingly corporate-based phenomenon. During the 1950s and even much of the 1960s, northerners who had wanted to hear country music on their radios had to wait until evening when they could pick up high-beaming stations from the Deep South. By the 1970s, though, every metropolitan area had several country music stations, and many country artists were crossing over to the pop and rock stations. Singers such as Kris Kristofferson, Dolly Parton, and Willie Nelson (the first country artist to win a platinum record, symbolic of sales of 1 million albums) became nationwide celebrities with TV and movie careers.

The appeal of country music was difficult to explain. Some people claimed that they liked its simplicity and honesty, its stories of broken hearts and faded loves—"Your Cheatin' Heart Will Tell on You." Others seemed attracted by its nostalgic overtones, its celebration of rural life and simple virtues—"My Heroes Have Always Been Cowboys." But perhaps in the over-sized 1970s, country music's deeply rooted quality, its sense of limits, and its acceptance of failure articulated a regional idea that came home to the rest of the nation.

Give Me that Old-Time Religion/
Give Me that Big-Time Religion

During the 1950s some observers claimed that Americans were becoming an increasingly religious people. Church membership climbed steadily; President Eisenhower spread "piety along the Potomac"; and the Reverend

Norman Vincent Peale's popular *Power of Positive Thinking* seemed to carry faith and optimism to Protestants throughout the land. In 1955 the sociologist Will Herberg noted that the Judeo-Christian religious tradition was merging with American ideas to produce a consensus on deep-seated values among Protestants, Catholics, and Jews. A few skeptics warned that church attendance did not necessarily measure religious commitment and charged that churches emphasized form over substance, fund-raising over worship. But if the religious messages were vacuous, at least the sanctuaries were full. Most churchgoers seemed content with the way things were.

Churches, however, did not escape the broad turmoil of the 1960s—the bureaucratization, the splits over social issues, and the disenchantment of the young. By the end of the decade established churches had been wracked by factionalism, had lost membership, and were challenged by newer sects and evangelical movements.

During the 1960s the merger movement became almost as fashionable in religion as in business. Mainstream Protestant denominations seemed preoccupied with consolidation and centralization. Lutherans, Methodists, and Congregationalists each approved important mergers arranged by their national decision-making bodies and accepted by most local congregations. Greater centralization crept into other functions as well. More and more, national church boards set church policy, raised funds, budgeted money, and directed missionary and social efforts. The umbrella organization for Protestant churches, the National Council of Churches, revamped its structure in mid-decade to further the centralized direction of policy. But the interjection of national-level decisions into affairs of local churches often created dissension within individual congregations.

When national church bodies, which were fairly liberal politically, began to express themselves on controversial issues, such as civil rights and the war in Vietnam, factional disputes in local congregations became severe. Some people wanted their church to remain detached from social issues; others pressed for it to be even more active in protests against injustice and inhumanity. The split over the role of the church was basic, and it was bitter. According to surveys conducted by the Gallup organization, there was a marked decline in church attendance during the 1960s; this drop was most evident in the mainline denominations.

The Catholic church had to contend not only with social issues—Catholics were bitterly divided between deep-seated conservatism and the Catholic left radicalism of priests such as Daniel and Philip Berrigan—but also with the even more explosive matter of church policy. The Second Vatican Council of 1962–1965 ushered in a reformist period by substituting English for Latin in the liturgy. Subsequently, demands accelerated for greater changes. While traditionalists looked on in horror, some Catholics pressed for liberalization of rules concerning priestly celibacy, the role of women in the church, and birth control.

American Jews confronted a problem even more baffling than divisions over doctrine and social policy: how to maintain an ethnic and religious identity. Large numbers of young people failed to understand or follow Hebrew school lessons; many married gentiles. In fact, the majority of American Jews, although still identifying themselves as part of a Jewish ethnic group, belonged to no synagogue or temple. Economic success within the Jewish community and the decline of overt anti-Semitism, ironically, actually posed serious challenges for the Jewish faith.

Discontent within established churches and general social turmoil benefited new movements and faiths. Evangelical spirit swept the country, turning revivalists such as Billy Graham, Oral Roberts, and Billy James Hargis into the heads of multimillion-dollar enterprises. Although their religious organizations became huge bureaucracies relying on mass media and the latest advertising techniques, their evangelism attracted people through its appeal to personal religion and past virtues. Evangelical fundamentalism provided an anchor for many Americans who felt buffeted by change.

Some popular preachers, such as Hargis and Carl McIntire, closely linked Christianity, anticommunism, and ultra-right-wing politics. Hargis charged that equal rights for women would bring the nation to the brink of hell, and his organization carried on a well-funded campaign against feminist causes. McIntire joined Hargis in an attack on the environmentalist movement, charging it with rejecting Christianity and assisting communism.

While Hargis and McIntire occupied the far right, Oral Roberts and Billy Graham became important establishment figures. Roberts financed his own university in Oklahoma and used the school's successful basketball team as a promotional device. (During one stretch the squad lost only 19 of 134 games.) He also built a huge TV empire, which rivaled that of the acknowledged king of evangelists, Billy Graham. Still, Graham continued to be the most revered fundamentalist leader. He took his crusades around the world, preaching to crowds of over a hundred thousand people, and he became an important spiritual counselor to President Nixon, often leading prayer breakfasts at the White House. Year after year he stayed near the top of the list of most admired Americans.

During the 1960s new religious movements sprang up, particularly among the young. The Bahai faith built several breathtaking and expensive structures in the United States and gained numerous converts; members of the Hare Krishna sect, with their shaved heads and robes, appeared in larger cities; "Jesus freaks" replaced political agitators on some college campuses; the Children of God and other communal cult groups attracted middle-class youths who were willing to renounce their families and adopt a new life and loyalty. Religiosity took on other dimensions as well. Americans became fascinated with spiritualism, mysticism, and transcendental mediation. Bookstores expanded their sections on religion and the occult. Many people of all ages and political persuasions, it seemed, were seeking refuge from a bureaucratic, centralized, and oversized society.

Many of the religious trends of the 1960s continued through the 1970s. Although attendance at Catholic masses leveled off after the declines of the 1960s, mainline Protestant and Jewish congregations continued to lose members. At the same time, all of the major denominations still struggled to heal internal divisions, especially those involving the role of women in the church. By the 1970s feminists in major religions argued that women were entitled to participate more fully in nearly all phases of spiritual life. The Roman Catholic church reaffirmed its opposition to such changes—including papal bans on female priests and on artificial methods of birth control—but most Protestant denominations agreed to modify at least some patriarchal practices. The situation in Judaism was complicated by the division among the Orthodox, Conservative, and Reform movements. Although Conservative and Reform congregations changed some traditional rituals and doctrines, the Orthodox movement, the only wing of Judaism to gain members in the 1970s, held firm. Finally, the evangelical revival of the 1960s gained momentum in the 1970s. Even though mainline Protestant denominations lost members, the total number of Protestants attending church remained constant because of the growth of evangelical congregations.

The growth of evangelicalism and religious fundamentalism could be measured in watts, in dollars, and in political power—as well as in the number of people actually attending churches. Radio and TV ministries remained central forces in this surge; Billy Graham and Oral Roberts were joined by hundreds of other media preachers. Among the most prominent were Robert Schuller, who preached an updated, California version of Norman Vincent Peale's *Power of Positive Thinking*; Jerry Falwell, a family-oriented fundamentalist in the Oral Roberts mold; and dynamic, gospel-singing Jimmy Lee Swaggart, a cousin of country-rockers Jerry Lee Lewis and Mickey Gilley. In an even less traditional vein, Pat Robertson, a former corporate lawyer turned evangelist, hosted the "700 Club," a born-again Christian version of the familiar TV talk show.

Although the three TV networks refused to sell any of their prime time to religious broadcasters, the media preachers used their burgeoning bank accounts to purchase time from local stations and even to establish their own networks. Robertson's Christian Broadcasting Network (CBN) boasted of its own satellite system and of its ability to reach hundreds of stations and cable-TV systems on an around-the-clock basis. By the end of the 1970s there were more than 1,400 radio stations and 30 TV outlets that specialized in religious broadcasts.

Some of the more prominent preachers entered the political world. While many people lost faith in established institutions, especially the national government and the public school systems, evangelical and fundamentalist religious groups attracted new converts and gathered political strength. Both Pat Robertson and Jerry Falwell, for example, promised to lead their followers and the nation out of the wilderness by joining with political figures on the right. Falwell's political lobby, the Moral Majority, campaigned against homosexuals, federal involvement in education, and the Equal Rights Amendment for women. The Moral Majority also ran workshops and seminars for religious politicos and issued a morality rating for members of Congress. By the end of the 1970s an alliance between the right wing of the GOP and ultraconservative religious groups was clearly evident: The 1980 Republican platform promised to tear down the signs of an oversized government and to put the nation back on proper moral footing by, among other things, appointing as federal judges only those individuals who opposed abortion.

At the same time, the religious cults condemned by both the Moral Majority and hard-line ministers continued to flourish. These groups, like the evangelicals, seemed to gain support as a result of continued popular doubts about many social institutions. A powerful cult, the Unification church, was headed by South Korea's Sun Myung Moon, a staunch anticommunist. Using sophisticated behavior modification methods to gain followers and corporate management techniques to handle the church's growing wealth, the "Moonies" gave thousands of young people a new sense of community. Moon's church also gained the endorsement of prominent supporters, including some conservative academics who shared Moon's political outlook. His sect pushed right-wing politics, laissez-faire capitalism, and a hard-line anticommunist foreign policy. From 1969 to 1974 it funneled a considerable amount of money—much of it coming from young Moonies selling flowers—to various groups supporting Richard Nixon. Such activities finally provoked several federal investigations and a jail sentence for Moon himself.

A crusade against cults gained considerable attention when 918 members of the People's Temple died in a mass-suicide ritual in Guyana in 1978. Led by a charismatic and increasingly paranoid preacher, the Reverend Jim Jones, the People's Temple appealed to the very poor, to those who could find no secure place in the oversized society. Loosely aligned with the political left, Jones offered the promise of both religious salvation and social progress. He gained thousands of followers, especially among poor African-Americans in the San Francisco Bay area, and many of them moved with him to South America. Jones and his followers ultimately believed they could save themselves and their families only through flight—from this country and, finally, from life itself.

The Education Labyrinth

Pressure from the baby-boom generation and demands of a rapidly expanding economy initially brought enormous changes to America's educational establishment in the postwar era. Thousands of new schools had to be built and equipped, and many corporations stood ready to sell the latest in instructional devices. Under Lyndon Johnson's Great Society programs, federal funds became available for expanding and upgrading educational facilities. Almost every suburban classroom had its arsenal of audiovisual equipment and supply of "teaching packages" for exploring a particular topic or concept. Most of the new techniques sought to involve students as active participants rather than as passive listeners. In some schools, architects eliminated walls, creating an open and airy environment in which students would, it was hoped, become more expressive.

The educational revolution involved course content as well as teaching techniques. The "new math" and the "new English" substituted analysis and understanding for traditional categories and extensive memorization; the "new social studies" emphasized personal evaluation of documents and "values clarification" exercises rather than regurgitation of names and dates. Under pressure from women's organizations and minority groups, most elementary schools replaced the white, middle-class characters of Dick and Jane. At its best, the educational revolution promised to produce individuals who could think, evaluate, and make critical judgments. At their worst, changes in method outstripped changes in educational personnel, and many older teachers found themselves confused and resentful. New approaches that worked in a laboratory school did not always succeed in the average classroom. Brighter pupils easily adapted to the new math, but slower students graduated without the basic skills needed to balance a checkbook. After more than a decade of experimentation, critics of the new techniques contended that "Johnny still can't read, and he can't add, either."

Another trend of the 1960s was to offer education outside of the school system. Some parents who disliked the authoritarianism of traditional public schools sent their children to experimental "free schools." In response to criticism of education for minority children (such as Jonathan Kozol's *Death at an Early Age*), some reformers attempted to use the free-school concept in underprivileged areas. Head Start, a key Great Society program, attempted to provide educational experiences for poor and minority preschoolers so that they could enter kindergarten on a par with more privileged, middle-class children. Educational television also helped preschoolers and reached dropouts, adults, and school-aged children with educational material ranging from U.S. history to language instruction to guitar playing. Public television developed the most successful venture in children's shows—"Sesame Street." Colorful and fast-moving, "Sesame Street" had its viewers reciting numbers, letters, and difficult words (some in Spanish) before they entered kindergarten. Although "Sesame Street" captivated both parents and children, traditionalists disliked the program's flashy style and rapid visual cuts.

In many schools there were important changes in the student bodies during the 1960s. Especially in rural areas, public officials worked to consolidate small schools into better-equipped large ones. As a result, the size of educational institutions increased dramatically. In 1950 there were over 86,000 school systems in the country, averaging about 300 students each; by 1965 there were fewer than 30,000 systems, averaging 1,400 students each. Most children no longer knew all their classmates or teachers, and many students rode buses to school. The undeniable educational gains of consolidation came at the expense of nearby facilities and a feeling of community.

As long as school buses assisted consolidation of small schools they were generally welcomed as symbols of educational progress, but when courts began to order busing to fulfill another educational function—racial integration—busing became highly controversial. In the late 1960s and early 1970s, busing was the focus of discussion on civil rights questions. Using buses to achieve racial balance raised complicated social, legal, and educational problems. Many white parents opposed busing and even some minority-group parents denounced forced integration, fearing that their children would lose traditional cultural values in white-dominated schools.

The baby-boom generation also strained institutions of higher education during the 1960s. Universities contended not only with the natural population increase but also with a rising percentage of youths who chose to go to college. In 1955 only 27 percent of college-aged people attended schools; by 1965 the figure had risen to 40 percent. The flood of new students stemmed from postwar affluence, government-assistance programs, the desire of many young men to avoid the draft by staying in school, and a huge influx of young women. Graduate schools also boomed. By the mid-1960s there were about a quarter of a million full-time graduate students, three of five receiving some form of financial support. Half of all the Ph.D. degrees granted in the United States between 1861 and 1970 were earned in the 1960s. A researcher writing in 1971 accurately predicted that the graduate education and research establishment in American universities was about 30 to 50 percent larger than could be effectively used in the 1970s.

The debates of the 1960s—over the size and structure of schools, over philosophies and techniques of instruction, and over the content and the rigor of the curriculum—became more bitter and complex during the 1970s. The declining birthrate of the 1960s finally caught up with education: For the first time in several decades students were not crowding the education labyrinth. Already faced with rising costs and declining revenues, school officials responded at the primary and secondary levels by consolidating some schools and closing down others. Even without busing for racial balance, neighborhood schools would not be nearly as close to most people's homes as they had been during the 1950s and 1960s. Moreover, public schools, which had to depend on tax dollars, faced growing popular protests against higher property taxes and new school-revenue bonds. As a result, many school districts throughout the country were forced to slash educational staffs, instructional programs, and extracurricular activities. The problem was most serious in large cities, where shrinking tax bases and rapidly escalating costs added to difficulties produced by reluctant taxpayers.

But the problems of American education transcended issues of revenue and taxation. There were more subtle forces contributing to what appeared to be a growing backlash against a strong commitment to education of the young. Put simply, more and more people saw public schools, especially in urban areas, as educational and social failures. In some schools, traditional discipline problems—truancy, smoking in rest rooms, scuffles on the playground—seemed trivial when compared with the everyday reality of hard drugs and violent attacks on both teachers and students. At the same time, educational results, as measured by standardized tests, steadily dropped. Between 1966 and 1976 the average score on the verbal portion of the Scholastic Aptitude Test (SAT) dropped from 467 to 429. The hope that school integration would introduce children to a heterogeneous environment began to fade as more affluent families, minority as well as white, left for the suburbs or sent their children to private schools. The vast majority of urban public schools came to serve primarily children from poor families. In Pasadena, California, for example, more than 35 percent of white parents removed their children from public schools after court-enforced busing went into effect; nationwide, it was estimated, 40 percent of middle-class African-American parents sent their children to private schools.

Although colleges and universities also began to face the necessity of contraction, they enjoyed greater flexibility than primary and secondary schools. They, unlike the lower-level schools, could create students. Increasingly, colleges and universities sought "the nontraditional student." Foreign students and "adult scholars"—individuals (especially women) slightly or considerably older than the traditional eighteen to twenty-two age group—became obvious targets. Four-year institutions also began to compete more actively with two-year colleges for students. And, of course, colleges and universities vied with one another to attract a steady number of students from an ever-shrinking pool of high school graduates. Admissions offices became recruiting centers, relying on consultants to provide their college with an attractive image and an effective set of recruiting tools. A number of smaller colleges gave up and closed their doors.

Meanwhile, at all levels, people debated familiar, yet central, questions: What should students learn? And how should they be taught? In response to the continuation of trends begun during the late 1960s, which tried to open up new subject areas and introduce more flexible methods of instruction, a strong back-to-basics movement emerged. At the postsecondary level, traditionalists began to regroup and to seek a rollback of changes they believed were eroding "educational excellence." A movement to reinstitute requirements, to establish core curriculums (or at least core courses), and to limit the spread of programs in areas such as women's and minority studies slowly took shape. The educational debates over school curriculums would merge in the 1980s and 1990s with broader social debates over policies relating to gender and race.

SUGGESTIONS FOR FURTHER READING

Changes in the scale of social and economic institutions are analyzed from varying perspectives in W. Lloyd Warner, *The Emergent American Society* (1967); Arthur Selwyn Miller, *The Modern Corporate State* (1976); Morris Janowitz, *The Last Half-century* (1978); Christopher Lasch, *The Culture of Narcissism* (1978); Kirkpatrick Sale, *Human Scale* (1980); Theodore Lowi, *The End of Liberalism* (rev. ed., 1979); John Tirman, ed., *The Militarization of High Tech* (1984); Donald Worster, *Rivers of Empire* (1985); Louis Galambos, *The New American State: Bureaucracies and Policies Since World War II* (1987); Paul Kennedy, *The Rise and Fall of the Great Powers* (1988); Juliet B. Schor, *The Overworked American* (1991).

On social and demographic developments, see Seymour Melman, *Pentagon Capitalism* (1970); Richard J. Barnet and Ronald Muller, *Global Reach* (1974); Samuel Bowles, David M. Gordon, and Thomas Weisskopf, *Beyond the Wasteland* (1983); Charles P. Kindleberger, *Multinational Excursions* (1984); Lester Thurow, *Dangerous Currents* (1984); the relevant portions of Lewis Mandell, *The Credit Card Industry: A History* (1990); Raymond Mohl, ed., *Searching for the Sunbelt* (1990); Mike Davis, *City of Quartz: Excavating the Future in Los Angeles* (1990); and Alejandro Portes and Alex Stepick, *City on the Edge: The Transformation of Miami* (1993).

On environmental issues see Rachel Carson, *The Silent Spring* (1962); Barry Commoner, *The Closing Circle* (1971); Amory Lovins, *Soft Energy Paths* (1977); Richard J. Barnet, *The Lean Years* (1980); Michael Brown, *Laying Waste* (1980); Worster's *Rivers of Empire*; Samuel P. Hays, *Beauty, Health, and Permanence* (1987); Joseph Morone and Edward Woodhouse, *The Demise of Nuclear Energy? Lessons for Democratic Control of Technology* (1989); the relevant portions of Anna Bramwell, *Ecology in the Twentieth Century* (1989); Thomas Huffman, *Protectors of the Land and Water* (1994); and Kirkpatrick Sale, *The Green Revolution: The American Environmental Movement, 1962–1992* (1993).

On education, see the conflicting interpretations in the following: Herbert Gintis and Samuel Bowles, *Schooling in Capitalist America* (1976); Hugh Davis Graham, *Uncertain Triumph: Federalist Education Policy in the Kennedy and Johnson Years* (1984); Ira Katznelson and Margaret Weir, *Schooling for All* (1985); Lois Weis, ed., *Class, Race, and Gender in American Education* (1988); Alan Bloom, *The Closing of the American Mind* (1988); Richard M. Freeland, *Academia's Golden Age: Universities in Massachusetts, 1945–1970* (1992); and Roger L. Geiger, *Research and Relevant Knowledge: American Research Universities Since World War II* (1993).

On mass culture, see Robert Lipsyte, *Sportsworld* (1975); Geoffrey Stokes, *Star-making Machinery* (1976); Robert Venturi, Denise Scott Brown, and Steven Izenour, *Learning from Las Vegas* (rev. ed., 1977); Edwin Cady, *The Big Game* (1978); Peter Guralnick, *Lost Highways* (1979); Robert Sklar, *Prime-time America* (1980); Greil Marcus, *Mystery Train* (3rd ed., 1990); Ben Bagdikian, *The Media Monopoly* (1983); Jon Weiner, *Come Together: John Lennon and His Time* (1984); Herbert Schiller, *Who Knows? Information in the Age of the Fortune 500* (1984) and *Culture, Inc: The Corporate Takeover of American Expression* (1989); Todd Gitlin, *Inside Prime Time* (1985); Benjamin Rader, *In Its Own Image: How Television Has Transformed Sports* (1985); Helen Baehr and Gillian Dyer, eds., *Boxed In: Women and Television* (1987); John Fiske, *Television Culture* (1987); Mark Crispin Miller, *Boxed In: The Culture of TV* (1988); Robert Kolker, *Cinema of Loneliness* (rev. ed., 1988); Stuart Ewen, *All Consuming Images: The Politics of Style in Contemporary Culture* (1988); Michael Ryan and Douglas Kellner, *Camera Politica: Politics and Ideology in Contemporary Hollywood Cinema* (1988); Ethan Morden, *Medium Cool: The Movies of the 1960s* (1990); Michael Parenti, *Make-believe Media: The Politics of Entertainment* (1992); Neil Postman, *Technopoly: The Surrender of Culture to Technology* (1992); and Stephen M. Fjellman, *Vinyl Leaves: Walt Disney World and America* (1992).

On religious trends see Marshall Frady, *Billy Graham* (1979); David Harrell, *All Things Are Possible* (1974), *Oral Roberts* (1985), and *Pat Robertson* (1987); Charles Shepard, *Forgiven: The Rise and Fall of Jim Bakker and the PTL* (1989); Randall Balmer, *Mine Eyes Have Seen the Glory: A Journey Into the Evangelical Subculture of America* (1989); Garry Wills, *Under God* (1990); Bryan V. Hillis, *Can Two Walk Together Unless They Be Agreed: American Religious Schisms in the 1970s* (1991); Michael Lienesch, *Redeeming America: Piety and Politics in the New Christian Right* (1993); James Hunter, *Smile Pretty and Say Jesus: The Last Days of PTL* (1993); and R. Laurence Moore, *Selling God* (1994).

9

The Politics
of the 1970s

DOMESTIC POLITICS UNDER NIXON AND FORD

Richard Nixon promised a law-and-order administration and political calm; instead, his reckless and lawless presidency produced even more political turbulence in addition to a constitutional crisis that Nixon himself never seemed fully to understand. The president's tight circle of advisers—notably his "Berlin Wall" of John Ehrlichman and H. R. (Bob) Haldeman—shielded him from dissenting views and reinforced his worst instincts, especially a penchant for seeing politics in personal terms. Nixon seemed to enjoy tilting at political enemies, so it was not surprising that his White House would have its own "enemies list" and order illegal surveillance of people whom the president deemed "dangerous." Only after it was too late did Nixon recognize the depths of his Watergate problems.

Even after Richard Nixon's forced resignation in 1974, the nation's political culture, including popular attitudes toward public policy and government, appeared unsettled. Both of Nixon's successors in the 1970s, Gerald Ford and Jimmy Carter, came to the same realization as their ousted predecessor: The presidency, though obviously an office of great power, could not always command. Belying the idea that the nation was saddled with an imperial presidency, the chief executives of the 1970s constantly confronted the limits of their effective power. The presidency, like other political institutions, remained hamstrung by ongoing controversies about the proper role of government and by continuing struggles among institutions and individuals. The 1970s, then, did not signal the end of the political battles of the 1960s but, rather, a continuation of attempts to define the nation's role in the world and the meaning of equality at home.

Nixon's Domestic Policies

On most domestic issues, Richard Nixon provided no sustained or consistent leadership. Playing to the Republican party's right wing, the president ritualistically condemned the "welfare mess" and promised to get people off relief rolls and onto work roles. But charmed by Daniel Patrick Moynihan, a Democrat and then a professor at Harvard, Nixon presented Congress with a dramatic welfare proposal, the Family Assistance Plan, or FAP. The plan horrified conservative Republicans by proposing that the federal government guarantee every American family an annual income of $1,600. In addition, Nixon and Moynihan touted FAP as a way to eliminate many burdensome restrictions, including the provision that denied aid to low-income families with a man living in the household, and to pare down the welfare bureaucracy. Angry conservatives, wondering if Nixon had lost his sanity, grumbled at the program's potential costs, whereas liberal Democrats, who also wondered what Nixon might have in his mind, denounced FAP's $1,600 guarantee as too miserly. Meanwhile, Nixon himself never pressed vigorously for FAP's passage, and the program was blocked by a peculiar coalition of conservatives and social liberals. As one of Nixon's biographers later suggested, the idea of simply offering a plan for bold change seemed enough for the president; once Nixon was forced to steer the FAP proposal into law, he seemed to lose interest in the whole project.

Despite Nixon's tendency to walk away from domestic initiatives, his presidency saw the enactment of significant tax revision measures, consumer protection legislation, health and safety laws, and environmental regulations. Indeed, the decision to index Social Security payments to the rate of inflation, argue most students of social welfare policy, provided one of the federal government's most important anti-poverty programs; without the indexing feature of Social Security, millions of elderly people would have seen their incomes drop below what the federal government defined as the poverty line during the inflationary period of the 1970s and early 1980s. In addition, two potentially important federal agencies, the Environmental Protection Agency and the Occupational Health and Safety Administration, were created during Nixon's presidency.

Finally, expenditures for social welfare programs actually grew during Nixon's years in office. This growth was a result of the residual strength of welfare liberalism in Congress, the power of insurgent pressure groups, and Nixon's own general lack of concern for developing a coherent domestic agenda of his own. During the years between Lyndon Johnson's last budget and Nixon's 1971–1972 budget, spending for nondefense programs increased by about 46 percent.

Nixon showed the most interest in a domestic program he called the "New Federalism," part of his plan for cutting back the federal bureaucracy. The most tangible part of the proposal was "revenue sharing," a concept that paralleled a goal of the failed FAP—cutting red tape. Under revenue-sharing, the federal government would return a portion of its tax revenues, with relatively few restrictions on how these were to be spent, to state and local governments. Revenue sharing, Nixon argued, would take political power away from the bureaucrats in Washington and redistribute it, along with the money, to people at the grass roots. As with FAP, conservatives worried about the federal government, in effect, handing over its tax dollars. For their part, liberal Democrats worried that revenue-sharing funds would not redistribute power at all; instead, the money would be spent for projects, they argued, that would do little to help people who already lacked political power at the state and local levels. Ultimately, giving money to state and local governments proved more popular than giving it to people with low incomes, and Congress enacted a modified version of Nixon's revenue-sharing in 1972.

Nixon's record on domestic issues, in short, was a curious one. Despite his right-wing rhetoric and some conservative policies, particularly on civil liberties and school integration in the South, Nixon updated the broad outlines of Dwight Eisenhower's modern Republicanism. Even on social welfare issues, Nixon managed to position the Republican party to the left of the positions that Barry Goldwater had staked out in 1964.

Yet, despite initiatives such as FAP and the New Federalism, Nixon simply cared much more about foreign policy than domestic issues. And when he gazed inwardly, he generally focused on punishing his "enemies" and rewarding his "friends" rather than at actually changing the basic assumptions of the welfare state, a clear goal of Ronald Reagan when he came to Washington in 1980. In the end, Nixon appeared to believe more was to be gained—for his political ambitions, his psychological need for confrontation, or both—from battling a host of different adversaries than from tackling substantive policy issues.

Politics in a Media Age

George McGovern, a convert to the "new politics," captured the 1972 Democratic nomination for president. Working with activists who wanted to move their party dramatically leftward and capitalizing on changes in the party rules, which were enacted after the chaos at the 1968 Chicago convention, the McGovern campaign skillfully lined up delegates in the nonprimary states. Meanwhile, in those states that did hold primaries, the South Dakota senator outlasted more centrist candidates, notably Edmund Muskie and Hubert Humphrey. Overall, though, McGovern won only a handful of popular-vote primaries.

By the time Democratic delegates gathered in Miami for their 1972 convention, a number of familiar faces, including Mayor Richard Daley of Chicago, were absent. Outmaneuvered by McGovern's strategists, many Democratic regulars watched the convention on television. The Miami gathering, complained one veteran labor leader who disliked the new politics, contained too many women, too many long-haired young men, and too few cigars. McGovern easily captured the nomination on the first ballot, but a number of old-line Democrats, such as Chicago's Daley and labor's George Meany, were less than enthusiastic and gave McGovern only tepid support or left him to stumble on by himself.

And stumble he did. McGovern was soon forced to jettison his running mate, Senator Thomas Eagleton of Missouri, when it was revealed that Eagleton had undergone electric-shock treatment for nervous exhaustion. Worse, several prominent Democrats (including Edward Kennedy) declined to become Eagleton's replacement. McGovern eventually did find a partner (Sargeant Shriver, a brother-in-law of Ted Kennedy and LBJ's ambassador to France), but he could never get large numbers of voters to accept his theme of "Come Home, America." His central issue, a speedy withdrawal from Vietnam, angered those who endorsed Nixon's call for an "honorable" peace, and McGovern failed to convert his reformist stands on domestic issues into popular support. Calls for higher taxes on large inheritances and for "demogrants" of $1,000 to every citizen, for example, appeared to alienate some traditionally Democratic voters without attracting significant numbers of new supporters.

The Nixon reelection campaign, in contrast, enjoyed plenty of support, some of it in the form of illegal financial contributions from large corporations. While importuning potential donors, Nixon's "bagmen" warned of the antibusiness tone of a McGovern administration and hinted at the advantages contributors would gain from a second Nixon administration. Not even the arrest, in mid-June 1972, of the Watergate burglars—political spies with close

In the happy days of his presidency, Richard Nixon relaxes with his wife, Pat; his daughters, Julie and Tricia; and his son-in-law, David Eisenhower. In his final days, Nixon retreated into a closed circle of his family and a few close friends.
Source: National Archives.

ties to the Republican campaign and to the White House itself—could slow Nixon's reelection drive. The president's press secretary quickly dismissed this illegal entry into Democratic party headquarters, by people who had links to the CIA and FBI and who were equipped with sophisticated wiretapping equipment, as a "third-rate burglary." He was soon forced to retract this statement, but the media gave the Watergate break-in little attention during the 1972 campaign. Certainly it had no discernible effect on Nixon's or McGovern's political fortunes. The McGovern-Shriver ticket carried only one state, Massachusetts, and the District of Columbia. Richard Nixon, dismissed only six years earlier as a political has-been, captured nearly 61 percent of the popular vote and all but a handful of the electoral ballots.

Subsequent analysis confirmed what was apparent in November: The electorate perceived George McGovern as far outside the political mainstream, while Richard Nixon managed to occupy a broad centrist position, as LBJ had done against Barry Goldwater in 1964. In some ways such a view was accurate. On a number of issues McGovern did stand to the left of Fair Deal–Great Society liberalism. Yet his basic position hardly qualified as a radical one; he did not lean as far to the left in 1972 as Goldwater had to the right in 1964.

Although McGovern, like Goldwater, sometimes failed to explain his position as clearly as he might have, the mass media failed to break through the protective shield around the Committee to Re-Elect the President (CREEP). The problem was not that most members of the press secretly favored Nixon, nor was it that Nixon and his aides skillfully managed events. The basic difficulties transcended CREEP's "dirty tricks" and Madison Avenue tactics. As observers of the media noted, the rules of "objective" reporting tended to work in favor of the incumbent, who relied on traditional themes, and against his challenger, who tried to interject new issues and to attack Nixon's performance as chief of state. It seemed a revolutionary departure, for example, when NBC reported that Nixon was distorting McGovern's positions on defense expenditures, welfare policies, and changes in the tax laws. For most of the campaign, the "boys on the bus" (as *Rolling Stone's* Timothy Crouse called the press corps) reported statements by Nixon or by his press secretary at face value. Thus, McGovern "alleged" whereas the president "announced." This dominant media frame proved particularly helpful to Nixon—and damaging to McGovern—when the administration was "announcing" the impending "end" of the war in Vietnam or "denying" charges about Watergate and other alleged dirty tricks by the Nixon forces.

Most of the investigative reporting about Watergate came from a single newspaper, the *Washington Post*, and from two individuals, the *Post's* Bob Woodward and Carl Bernstein. Even these reporters, persistent as they were, uncovered little new material. In developing their stories on Watergate, they had to rely on "Deep Throat," a still-unidentified informant (or perhaps several informants) in the government bureaucracy.

Although the media may not have initially played the dramatic role pictured by journalists themselves or by the film *All the President's Men* (1974), they ultimately became a force in Watergate politics. If the press could not discover many dark secrets by itself, journalists could give widespread coverage to the taint of scandal spreading around the Nixon administration. Using information developed by federal prosecutors and relying on leaks by anti-Nixon sources in the vast federal bureaucracy, some journalists finally assumed an aggressive, adversary relationship toward the administration. For their part, Nixon and his advisers, who had been castigating the press for several years, issued vague hints about reprisals against "irresponsible" journalists.

Threats against the media represented only part of an increasingly desperate game plan being diagrammed in Nixon's Oval Office. As transcripts of tape conversations between the president and his aides later revealed, Nixon found that he could not halt, or even slow, critical stories about his administration. In the late summer of 1973 rumors of wrongdoing began to envelop Nixon's vice-president, and in October, Spiro T. Agnew pleaded no contest to charges of accepting kickbacks. With Agnew forced to resign in disgrace, Nixon chose Gerald Ford, the Republican's minority leader in the House, as his new vice-president. The man who held the office generally considered to be the most powerful in the world discovered his inability to control events or even employees of his own executive branch.

The Underside of the Nixon Administration: Leaks and Plumbers

Many of Nixon's Watergate troubles stemmed from his own fears about the reliability and loyalty of various government agencies and officials. The Watergate burglary team, it appears, first took shape from efforts to provide the White House with its own covert intelligence unit. As early as the summer of 1970, the so-called Huston Plan proposed reorganizing covert activities to improve the administration's ability to coordinate the use of wiretaps, mail covers, and "surreptitious entries" (that is, burglaries). Although Nixon secretly approved the outlines of such a plan, it alarmed the established arms of the nation's secret government, the CIA and the FBI. Claiming that the Huston Plan threatened serious violations of civil liberties, J. Edgar Hoover offered such strong resistance that the president was forced to drop the idea.

While the White House began to leak information to the press critical of the aging FBI director, it also looked for ways of restarting the Huston initiative. Top officials finally decided to use the issue of drugs as a cover for the creation of a secret strike force, controlled from the White House, that could bypass agencies allegedly "infested" with Democrats. G. Gordon Liddy, a former FBI agent, played a key part in formulating plans for a new antidrug squad in the Treasury Department. Once operational, the unit could undertake covert work against Nixon's enemies and draw on the resources of the national government. And if things went wrong, claims that the unit was fighting the drug menace could be used as a justification for its covert activities. The administration began planning a mass media crusade against drugs, and a presidential declaration of a national "heroin emergency" was slated for late June 1971. But on June 13, *The New York Times* began to publish excerpts from the Pentagon Papers, a hitherto secret history of America's involvement in Vietnam.

Enraged at the appearance of this classified report, which had been prepared by the Defense Department during the Johnson administration, Nixon's inner circle shifted their attention from drugs to security leaks. His antidrug speech was canceled, and the national heroin emergency was never declared. Instead, the administration mobilized to stop further publication of the Pentagon Papers and to plug the leaks within its own executive branch. Almost immediately, it obtained a court injunction that barred further publication of the Pentagon Papers. Responding to this unprecedented use of a prior restraint—censorship in its classic form—*The New York Times* appealed to the U.S. Supreme Court. By a vote of six to three the justices lifted the injunction, holding that the First Amendment barred prior restraints in instances such as this. Although many people, particularly in the media, celebrated this as a victory for open government, the administration was already mounting a much more extensive, and more covert, crusade for executive secrecy.

Using personnel already assembled for the antidrug crusade, the White House formed its own leak-stopping crew, the self-styled "Plumbers." The group soon included Liddy, E. Howard Hunt (a former CIA agent), and several Cuban exiles with close ties to the CIA. After it became known that Dr. Daniel Ellsberg, a former analyst for the Defense Department, bore primary responsibility for leaking the Pentagon Papers, the Plumbers began a campaign to harass and discredit him, including a burglary of the office of his psychiatrist. The secret strike team conducted similar activities against other "enemies" of the White House. This group, with the significant addition of James McCord, another former CIA operative, formed the nucleus of the group that was caught inside Democratic headquarters at the Watergate building.

Nixon's defenders have consistently contended that these kinds of activities did not start with Watergate. Indeed, careful studies relying on documents obtained under the Freedom of Information Act have shown that the development of secret government preceded the presidency of Richard Nixon. John Kennedy, for instance, took a particular interest in expanding the executive's covert capacities, both overseas and at home, and Robert Kennedy, his attorney general, gave the FBI nearly carte blanche in wiretapping and bugging operations.

The Nixon administration did, however, significantly expand the scope and purpose of covert activities. During Lyndon Johnson's second term, for example, his attorney general had moved to limit FBI wiretaps, and the number of taps declined from 233 in 1965 to only 9 in 1968. The next year, though, Nixon and his attorney general, John Mitchell, claimed that the chief executive could order wiretaps, without having to obtain a court order, on any group or individual considered a threat to national security. (In 1972 the Supreme Court held that presidents could not order, on their own authority, electronic surveillance of purely domestic organizations.) Reports on some of these taps, were forwarded not only to officials concerned with national security but also to Nixon's primary political strategist, Bob Haldeman.

Haldeman's involvement in the earliest wiretaps established the pattern that would lead to Nixon's downfall: the attempt to centralize power within the president's inner circle. As the historian Garry Wills has noted, Nixon and his close aides operated a kind of counterinsurgency presidency. Seeing themselves as lonely defenders of the American way, the Nixonites waged war against not only the New Left but also the very same establishment that the protesters often attacked—the mainstream press, J. Edgar Hoover's FBI, and even the CIA. In the end Nixon became ensnarled in his own clumsy effort to create a secret government, one that could spy on both the people in the streets and on various elites in Washington.

The same concern for centralizing control within the White House affected the conduct of foreign relations. Nixon and Henry Kissinger, his national security adviser, saw the official foreign-policy agencies—including the departments of State and Defense and the CIA—as often uninformed and as consistently unimaginative. Worse, Nixon and Kissinger believed, these branches of government were filled with individuals who would obstruct presidential initiatives or, as in the case of Daniel Ellsberg, leak sensitive and secret material to the press. As a result of their fears and their desire for greater White House power, Nixon and Kissinger began to conduct their own secret foreign policy—secret from the American people and from other government officials as well. Their decision in 1970 to begin heavy bombing of neutral Cambodia, for example, deliberately bypassed high officials in the State and Defense departments.

Nixon's Last Battle

In the end, Nixon's secret war in Cambodia—like his other attempts to bring foreign and domestic dirty tricks under the control of the White House—became public knowledge and then part of the legal case against him and members of his administration. Despite various attempts to cut off the trail of criminality—at the Watergate burglars, then at high officials in CREEP, and finally at top-ranking members of the White House staff—Nixon's pursuers pressed on. In May 1973 a special Senate committee headed by North Carolina's Sam Ervin began televised hearings into the 1972 presidential election. Ervin, who liked to call himself a simple country lawyer, quickly became a media celebrity, and his folksy image contributed to the panel's public credibility. Throughout the summer of 1973 witness after witness offered tantalizing hints about involvement by the White House in a series of unseemly campaign activities. Even Senator Howard Baker of Tennessee, a Republican loyalist, came to ask a familiar question: "What did the president know and when did he know it?" Then, in mid-July, the answer to this query suddenly had a most unlikely source of verification—Richard Milhaus Nixon himself.

"Nixon Bugged Himself!" proclaimed newspaper headlines. An obscure White House official named Alexander Butterfield revealed that Nixon had secretly taped the bulk of his presidential conversations and his phone calls. These tapes promised the "smoking gun" that Nixon's defenders had challenged his accusers to produce. The Ervin committee and the special Watergate prosecutor, Archibald Cox of Harvard Law School, immediately sought access to the tapes. Claiming an absolute executive privilege, Nixon flatly refused.

Ringed by lethal strands of audiotape, Richard Nixon struggled to survive the Watergate fight. Although some advisers urged him to destroy the tapes, Nixon tried to battle free while still clutching the damning evidence. A veteran political club fighter who trusted his ability to survive any scrap, the president bobbed and weaved and occasionally even tried to counterpunch. But his opponents had the heavier weapons. In October 1973 a desperate attempt to knock out the special Watergate prosecutor backfired: Nixon's dramatic dismissal of Archibald Cox, for his refusal to accept Nixon's formula for limited access to nine crucial tapes, only led to the resignations of Elliot Richardson and William Ruckelshaus, two of the most respected figures remaining in the Nixon administration, and to the arrival of another prosecutor, Leon Jaworski. It also forced Nixon to surrender the tapes, one of which contained an 18 1/2-minute gap that was later found to have been the result of deliberate erasing.

The "Saturday Night Massacre," as the firing of Cox was called, represented Nixon's last attempt to take the offensive. Slowly the president retreated, trying to stave off impeachment. By early 1974, after a grand jury indicted seven of his top aides, Nixon could do little more than continue his personal cover-up, hoping that his opponents would run out of energy and that he could somehow avoid being indicted by a grand jury or impeached by Congress.

Increasingly, the fight pitted a badly confused Nixon, comforted in the final days of his presidency only by his immediate family and a handful of loyal aides, against the combined power of the other branches of the national government. Nixon tried one last desperate gamble: He released his own edited version of forty-two taped conversations that were being sought by Jaworski and by the House Judiciary Committee. The bowdlerized transcripts, often sanitized by the phrase "expletive deleted," only raised new doubts about the president's honesty and his competence.

Nixon's defenders in Congress and his lawyers before the Supreme Court had no better luck than their chief. By early summer the issue was not whether the House Judiciary Committee would support Nixon's impeachment but how many Republicans would join the Democratic majority and how many articles of impeachment they would vote against the president. On the other side of Capitol Hill, the Supreme Court, which had expedited the appeal of Nixon's refusal to honor a subpoena for additional tapes, voted unanimously to reject the president's sweeping claim that tapes needed for a criminal investigation were protected by executive privilege.

At nearly the same time, the House Judiciary Committee completed its deliberations on articles of impeachment. On July 27, 1974, three days after Nixon's defeat in the Supreme Court, the committee passed, by a margin of twenty-seven to eleven, the first article of impeachment against the president. It charged Nixon with obstruction of justice for his efforts to impede the investigation of Watergate. Subsequently, the committee voted two other articles. One charged Nixon with abuse of presidential power by trying to use agencies, such as the IRS and the FBI, for partisan purposes, and the other charged him with violating his constitutional duty to enforce the law by refusing to turn over subpoenaed tapes. (Significantly, the committee rejected an article that would have cited Nixon for his secret bombing of Cambodia.)

Although Nixon promised a floor fight in the House and a last-ditch battle in the Senate, the president's shrinking entourage was working to ease him out of office. While waiting for the Supreme Court to hand down its decision on Nixon's tapes, a presidential aide finally found, in these same tapes, the elusive "smoking gun." The tape of a conversation between Nixon and Haldeman on June 23, 1972, was unequivocal: The president had plotted from the very beginning to use the CIA to halt investigation of the Watergate break-in on the spurious grounds of national security. The tape showed that the president himself had orchestrated the cover-up, had conspired to obstruct justice, and had been systematically lying about his role.

In late July and early August, aides to Nixon and to Vice-President Gerald Ford began discussing plans for terminating the Nixon administration and inaugurating a Ford presidency. Unyielding to the end, Nixon insisted that his conversation with Haldeman contained no fatal admissions. But his new chief of staff, General Alexander Haig, flatly contradicted this claim and went ahead with plans for the transition to a new presidency. Once the transcript of the June 23 meeting became public, most of Nixon's remaining supporters vanished. Finally, Richard Nixon gave up his lonely battle and surrendered. On August 9 he resigned, and Gerald Ford became the nation's first nonelected president.

Within several years, however, Richard Nixon made his final comeback. Although political figures in the United States continued to treat the former President as something of a pariah, Nixon slowly rebuilt his reputation among the general public and foreign leaders. While fighting vigorously in the courts to keep the tapes of his presidential conversations out of the hands of historians and journalists, Nixon used television appearances and numerous publications to create the image of a wise, even seerlike, elder statesperson. Meanwhile, the passage of time eliminated or mellowed many of Nixon's old critics, and a new generation of historians began to paint relatively favorable pictures of the Nixon presidency—"without Watergate," of course. After Nixon's death, during the spring of 1994, a public funeral attracted hundreds of dignitaries. Surprisingly, though, Nixon's death also helped to fuel a new round of critical commentary about the only President whose illegal activities forced his resignation from office.

Stagflation

The Watergate scandal paralyzed the national government just when complex economic problems required attention. Richard Nixon faced two alarming new economic trends—"stagflation," a concurrence of recession and inflation, and a growing deficit in the U.S. balance of payments.

Conventional economic wisdom held that inflation resulted from an overheated economy in which demand far exceeded supply; dampening demand by inducing a mild recession would thus reduce inflation. In attacking inflation early in his presidency, Nixon acquiesced to policies that, in order to slow spending, raised interest rates and brought more unemployment. The recession came. Skyrocketing interest rates nearly ended residential construction, forced businesses such as the Penn Central Railroad into bankruptcy, brought a decline in industrial production, and raised unemployment to 6 percent. Yet, contrary to expectations, prices still galloped forward. Big business and big labor continued to layer higher wages and higher costs on an economy now slumping into recession. By 1971 pundits were speaking of "Nixonomics"—a new economic condition of stagflation in which unemployment and the spiral of inflation moved upward simultaneously.

After trying these anti-inflation measures, Nixon decided that inflationary prosperity was better than an economic slowdown that might, as it had done in 1960, jeopardize his next presidential campaign. He endorsed policies to correct the recession he himself had earlier induced. After telling a startled group of journalists, "I am now a Keynesian," Nixon embraced the favorite tactic of liberal Democrats, deficit spending financed by government borrowing. This dramatic about-face prompted a TV commentator to quip, "It's a little like a Christian crusader saying 'All things considered, I think Mohammed was right!'" But antirecession spending scarcely dented unemployment, and under renewed stimulus, prices spurted ahead even faster. Measures taken against either inflation or unemployment seemed only to make the other problem more severe. Some advisers in and out of the administration began to advocate an across-the-board government-imposed freeze on wages, prices, and interest rates as the only way to hold down inflation, but Nixon shied away from "artificial controls which could only foul things up."

Worrisome foreign-trade statistics soon caused the president to change his mind once again. For eighty years the United States had exported far more than it imported, but after World War II huge military expenditures and corporate overseas investment created deficits in the balance of payments. The country paid some of this debt with gold; by 1972 America's prewar hoard of bullion had shrunk by half, to $10 billion. For the rest, foreign creditors accepted paper dollars, pleased with the stimulating effect of this large new source of capital that could be used for domestic investment. By 1970, however, the Vietnam War had brought ever-larger deficits, and inflation had crippled America's ability to sell its high-priced goods abroad. More and more paper flooded Europe's money markets, inevitably jolting prices. United States Treasury officials, hoping to avoid devaluation of the dollar—an act that would undermine its position as the preeminent international currency—quickly urged England, West Germany, and Japan to revalue their currencies upward to discourage American buying. Only the Germans complied. Then, at the end of June 1971, the Commerce Department announced a trade deficit, the first since 1890. As fears rose about the nation's solvency, speculators attacked the U.S. dollar, dumping vast amounts on world currency exchanges to avoid the losses that would result from its widely expected devaluation.

In August 1971, Nixon dramatically responded to the international monetary crisis and to the larger problems—including inflation and the new trade deficit—that fueled it. First, the United States ceased to value the dollar in terms of gold. Instead, American currency would float on the world's money exchanges, supply and demand determining its worth. Second, a 10 percent tariff surcharge was instituted, which significantly reduced imports into America. Nixon later removed the surcharge in return for obtaining new world monetary agreements. The new arrangement terminated the system of fixed monetary exchange rates established in the Bretton Woods Conference of 1944, and it reduced the dollar's position as the most privileged medium of international exchange. The dollar became just another currency whose value fluctuated. By substantially altering the system of international exchange, Nixon had given Americans more room to manipulate currency values in the fight against the trade deficit, but he had also led the United States and the world into the uncharted waters of floating exchange rates, a system that had proved perilous and destabilizing in the 1930s.

Nixon's advisers also plotted a new anti-inflation program for the domestic economy. The president froze wages and prices for ninety days, an interim measure called Phase I, while he worked on a comprehensive program to attack inflation and the trade deficit. On November 15, 1971, the White House announced its new program, Phase II. It cut government spending (slashing $5 billion from foreign aid and the federal civil service) but focused far more on stimulating business through a tax credit aimed at promoting the modernization of American enterprise. To stimulate the crucial automobile industry, Congress repealed the 7 percent excise tax on American-made cars. Such measures ensured higher profits for business and, together with the certainty that Nixon would not risk retrenchment in an election year, perked up the sluggish economy. Consumer spending increased, and public confidence rose. Meanwhile, the new Cost-of-Living Council attacked inflation by banning wage hikes of more than 5.5 percent and supposedly limiting retail price increases to 2.5 percent. Though inflation continued, especially in the uncontrolled food and farm commodity markets, public confidence improved enough for Nixon to defuse the economic issue during the 1972 campaign.

Nixon's tactics were thus to give the economy a mild stimulus while holding down inflation through government controls. The strategy lasted just long enough to aid Nixon's reelection. Once settled in his second term, Nixon replaced Phase II price ceilings with voluntary restraints. Predictably, consumer prices shot upward, compensating for the time they had been under controls. Within six months, Treasury Secretary George Shultz candidly admitted, "Phase II is a failure." So in midsummer Nixon again froze prices, this time for sixty days, while his advisers again debated alternatives. Finally, in April 1974 he again reversed course, canceling all government restraints. Nixon—now immersed in Watergate difficulties—lost interest in seeking any coherent strategy for dealing with stagflation.

The effectiveness of Nixon's mercurial economic strategies was not helped by the deadlock between the executive and congressional branches. Nixon's economic programs—especially the one to cut federal spending for social welfare—provoked growing hostility between the White House and the Democrat-controlled Congress. In 1973 the president vetoed nine major bills, even education and antipollution measures. He also calmly announced that he would impound funds, rather than spend them, if Congress overrode his decisions, an action that congressional opponents (and later the courts) condemned as unconstitutional. Growing personal hostilities and policy differences, aggravated by Watergate, brought the two branches of government into an adversarial relationship in which nothing was accomplished.

When Nixon left office, economists, like members of Congress, continued to debate what had gone wrong. Had government controls been too severe or insufficient? Should government spending have been cut to curtail inflation or increased to combat recession? Meanwhile, inflation continued at an annual rate of nearly 10 percent and unemployment hovered at just under 6 percent, a recession rate. After a five-year battle against stagflation and trade deficits, the economic situation was worse than ever, and inflation had become endemic. All of Nixon's remedies had failed, though economists and politicians differed sharply in their diagnoses of the precise reasons for their failure. All could agree that inconsistencies of approach and scatter-gun solutions had seriously aggravated the problems.

The Ford Presidency: The Wounds Remain

The failed Nixon presidency, coming so soon after the political traumas of the late 1960s, raised new doubts about the nation's political system. Although defenders of the postwar order, such as the semiofficial presidential chronicler Theodore White, saw Nixon's fall as proof that "the system worked," less sanguine observers pointed out that the Watergate battle showed the inflexibility of the constitutional system and that the affair ended only because of Nixon's telltale tapes. Moreover, might not Watergate represent only one more episode in the seamy history of America's "secret state"? In this view, Watergate grew out of a long power struggle involving several government bureaucracies and various political and economic elites opposed to the Nixon administration. Investigative reporters, for example, have suggested that Woodard and Bernstein's "Deep Throat" could have been a CIA operative who had "infiltrated" the White House and that one of the Watergate burglars, James McCord, may have deliberately sabotaged the ill-fated operation at Democratic headquarters.

For many ordinary voters Watergate appeared to be yet another example of political corruption in Washington. Although millions of people did retain their faith that the political system worked, a majority of those eligible to vote displayed considerably more cynicism. According to public-opinion polls, popular confidence in government officials had been declining throughout the 1960s, the years of Vietnam, and this slide continued both during and

President Gerald Ford, whose brief post-Watergate presidency was filled with more symbols than substance, throws out the ceremonial first pitch. *Source:* Gerald R. Ford Library.

after the Watergate period. In the presidential election of 1972, only 56 percent of those eligible to cast ballots did so; in 1976 the turnout decreased once again, this time to 54 percent.

Gerald Ford later remembered his brief presidency as a time for healing, but during the years 1974–1976 old political wounds continued to fester and new ones appeared almost daily. Popular doubts about politics were only increased—or simply confirmed—when Ford granted Nixon an unconditional pardon, an act that shielded the former president from prosecution and contributed to Ford's defeat in the 1976 presidential race. Moreover, the Ford years brought new revelations about illegal, or at least questionable, activities that had been undertaken since World War II by the FBI, by successive presidents, and by the CIA.

The CIA was already deeply divided by its involvement in Watergate politics and by serious internal power struggles, and the agency could no longer keep its own secrets. Former agents wrote best-selling exposés, and aggressive reporters exploited leaks within the agency to reveal the CIA's domestic spying operations, clear violations of the agency's mandate to operate only overseas. Ironically, Gerald Ford, who gained notoriety for his personal clumsiness—including a history of stumbling in and out of helicopters and of careening down ski slopes—ineptly blurted out the clandestine government's most explosive secret: Before a group of *New York Times* executives, Ford revealed the CIA's involvement in attempts to assassinate foreign leaders, including Cuba's

Fidel Castro. Although the *Times* itself sat on the story, Ford's gaffe soon reached reporters who were not bound by the president's claim that his remarks to the *Times* had been off the record.

Even before the story about assassination plots broke, President Ford had created a special commission, headed by his newly appointed vice-president, Nelson Rockefeller, to look into allegations of domestic spying by the CIA. In time, committees in both the House and the Senate heard testimony about a wide range of CIA "dirty tricks"—drug-testing projects on unsuspecting subjects, mail covers on private citizens, efforts to destabilize the economies of hostile nations, and several bizarre plots to murder foreign leaders. Although cynics doubted that the whole story had been told, the hearings did fuel the long process, begun by dissenting scholars and journalists during the 1960s, of rewriting the simplistic history of the cold war era. Testimony before several congressional committees, left no doubt that intelligence officials considered constitutional and legal restraints mere annoyances, paper restrictions that were to be ignored whenever it seemed convenient to do so.

Ford's greatest annoyance may have been the revelations of past misdeeds that undercut the public's faith in government. His most pressing problem, however, was the economy. Like Nixon, Ford aimed his economic remedies alternately at inflation and then recession, and they ended up producing worse cases of both.

During the first weeks of his presidency Ford targeted inflation, rather than unemployment, as the nation's most serious economic problem. The White House organized a belt-tightening campaign against rising prices that Ford called WIN (Whip Inflation Now). WIN was accompanied by buttons and ballyhoo, but its primary achievement was to nudge the country into its worst recession since the 1930s. Consumer demand dropped precipitously, especially in the crucial automobile industry, where higher sticker prices and worries about the availability of gasoline frightened off potential buyers. Triggered by large layoffs in Detroit, unemployment quickly spread. Slackening demand closed more and more factories, which in turn further reduced demand.

Faced with a jobless rate averaging 12 or 13 percent and with falling production almost everywhere, the president reversed course within a few months. In late 1974, now focusing on jobs and trying to cure recession, Ford projected a budget deficit of some $60 billion and asked Congress for a tax cut. This plan was designed to increase retail spending and to create a demand for manufactured goods. After several months of politicking, Congress finally passed a tax-cut package. Meanwhile, the Federal Reserve Board forced down interest rates to around 8 percent. Taken together, these measures prompted a modest economic revival during the summer of 1975. Inflation, however, also resumed, once again rising toward double-digit rates. The economy continued to oscillate between recession and inflation, both worsening with each swing and both undermining America's economic position internationally.

While economics bedeviled Americans, other issues widened the gap that had opened between the White House and Congress during the Nixon years. Afraid that dependence on Arab oil might weaken U.S. foreign policy,

Ford wanted to raise the price of domestic gasoline by boosting federal taxes and ending all price controls on oil. The marketplace would "ration" gasoline and, in effect, force down consumption. Democrats in Congress countered that Ford's approach would only accelerate inflation and unfairly hurt low-income people, while giving oil companies windfall profits.

Other factors complicated an easy resolution of the differences between the president and Congress. In the 1974 elections, held in the wake of Nixon's resignation, voters had sent many younger, more liberal Democratic representatives to Capitol Hill. These new legislators, together with some of their more experienced colleagues, recoiled at some of the business-as-usual politics of logrolling. By early 1975 they had ousted several powerful committee chairs who had long blocked liberal legislation. Moreover, many legislators saw an opportunity after the Watergate scandals to reassert their prerogatives. This feisty, heavily Democratic Congress outlined its own energy program. But Ford vetoed bills that would have maintained price controls and allocated funds for mass transit, while publicly denouncing government gasoline rationing as unworkable. Lacking unified leadership—more than ten Democratic senators, for example, were maneuvering for their party's 1976 presidential nomination—Congress enacted laws to improve gasoline mileage in American cars and increased taxes on gas guzzlers. The absence of any coherent response to the nation's economic and energy problems illustrated the drift that beset public policymaking since the early 1970s.

NIXON, KISSINGER, AND WORLD POLITICS

The Three-Dimensional Game

Henry Kissinger, Nixon's national security adviser until February 1973 and thereafter his secretary of state, viewed himself as a master of geopolitical strategy. He talked of detente with the Soviets, but his later memoirs make it clear that his detente was not a policy of passivity, acceptance, or compromise. Instead, it involved "a firm application of psychological and physical restraints and determined resistance to challenge." It was a beefed-up form of containment. Detente, according to Kissinger, was *realpolitik*—political realism exercised forcefully; unrelentingly; and with a great variety of political, economic, and psychological methods.

Arranging America's geopolitical cards to maximum advantage involved introducing a new player—China. Triangular diplomacy might put maximum pressure on the Soviets and gain substantial advantages for the United States as each of the bitter communist rivals courted America's support. Throughout the Nixon-Kissinger years, Americans negotiated with the Soviets and opened channels to China in what Kissinger called a "three-dimensional game" of diplomacy.

After 1969, the Soviet Union and the United States intermittently discussed nuclear arms control—proposals to regulate future growth, not to scrap existing military hardware. In 1969 both powers pledged not to build underwater installations and agreed to begin strategic arms limitation talks (SALT) in April 1970. Such negotiations required intense bargaining over intricate technical issues as well as over broad questions of strategic balance. Yet after mid-1971, when the United States formally accepted the principle of nuclear parity, diplomats made rapid progress.

Reassured by the progress of SALT, the Nixon administration took up a more visible but even less familiar task: normalizing relations with China. Small courtesies started a chain reaction. Nixon spoke of the People's Republic, not Red China, and told journalists of his desire to visit "that vast, unknown land." Nervous about their ancient enemy, Russia, and about Japan's surging economy, Chinese leaders reopened Sino-American talks through both countries' ambassadors in Warsaw. Nixon eased trade restrictions against China in early 1971, and the Chinese reciprocated with an invitation for a ping-pong tournament. Then in July Kissinger made a secret trip to Peking to arrange a presidential visit for 1972. The announcement of Nixon's trip startled both liberals and conservatives in the United States and refashioned world politics. The United Nations admitted the People's Republic three months later, rejecting the American two-China proposal, which was designed to preserve membership for Jiang Jie-Shi's regime on Taiwan.

On February 21, 1972, one of America's most celebrated anticommunists traveled to Peking to shake hands and bow gently with Mao Zedong, the world's archetypal anticapitalist. The president and his wife walked atop the Great Wall, mingled with communist dignitaries, and ate a twenty-two course state dinner. But public goodwill, carefully televised, could not dissolve longstanding animosities. Four days of negotiations with Premier Zhou Enlai produced primarily a list of postponements. The United States agreed that Taiwan's future was "an internal matter," but China pledged to deal with Taiwan "peacefully." Nixon reminded Chinese leaders of America's friendship with Japan, and Zhou broached the subject of "Tokyo's militarism." Mao voiced sympathy for "the people's struggle" in Indochina; Kissinger responded with references to "self-determination" and America's "eventual withdrawal." Though the new contacts went on—especially scientific exchanges, token shipments of grain from the United States, and relaxation of trade and travel restrictions—movement toward compromise on fundamental differences remained slow.

The prospect of Sino-American detente apparently pushed the Soviet Union into some technical concessions at SALT and toward an invitation, eagerly accepted, for Nixon to visit Moscow in the spring of 1972. There, Nixon and Soviet leader Leonid Brezhnev initialed arms-control treaties called SALT I, which terminated the development of antiballistic systems (ABMs), defensive shields that American scientists had deemed exorbitantly expensive and probably technologically impractical anyway. It also capped the number of nuclear missiles that each side could own, although the Americans and later the Soviets quickly expanded their stocks of MIRV missiles, containing multiple warheads on each missile. Thus, both sides could abide by the treaty yet still expand their numbers of deliverable weapons. The

United States had a two-to-one lead in total warheads. SALT I's actual results did little to cool the arms race, but the treaty did provide the experience of and precedent for arms-control negotiations. A year later Brezhnev visited the United States, and Nixon returned to Moscow in mid-1974. The momentum of detente continued and seemed to prove the advantages of triangular diplomacy.

As the Watergate scandals unfolded, Nixon increasingly sought redemption by stressing his international accomplishments. His personal diplomacy with China and the Soviet Union rated high in domestic opinion polls, and Kissinger was the only prominent member of Nixon's inner circle who emerged unscathed from the Watergate scandals.

The War in Southeast Asia

Despite the popularity of detente, the war in Vietnam still threatened the president's reputation and sapped America's strength. Nixon angrily told the nation that the United States would not "become a pitiful, helpless giant."

In 1971 Nixon continued negotiations in Paris while widening the war into Cambodia and Laos. Cambodia's neutral government of Prince Norodom Sihanouk fell to a U.S.-backed, right-wing general, Lon Nol, in 1970, and the Nixon administration, taking advantage of the coup, decided to invade to "clean out" communist supply camps. As American bombing and destruction in Cambodia proceeded, amid an outcry of antiwar protest at home, Nixon also ordered attacks in Laos. In both countries the North Vietnamese counterattacked, and the American invaders were routed. In Laos terrified South Vietnamese troops dangled from helicopter skids trying to escape; American advisers reported wholesale desertions.

In Paris, several months of secret diplomacy between Kissinger and North Vietnam's Le Duc Tho stalled. Leaders in Hanoi, encouraged by their adversary's misadventures in Laos and Cambodia and already planning their own military offensive, insisted that Nguyen Van Thieu and his followers must go. The Nixon administration, however, saw Thieu's presidency as the symbol of South Vietnam's self-determination. Slow bargaining against the luxurious setting of Parisian restaurants and elegant townhouses could not unravel the basic puzzle: If Thieu stayed on, the war would continue; without Thieu and his political organization the country would easily fall under communist control, for the NLF was its best-organized opposition force.

Both sides stepped up their search for a military solution. In late March 1972 North Vietnam attacked along a broad front, capturing An Loc, a gateway city only 30 miles from Saigon. Thieu's troops fell back on all fronts, and American air power failed to check the communist ground advance. With many in the Pentagon again predicting humiliating defeat, Nixon resumed bombing raids in North Vietnam and Cambodia and ordered the navy to mine North Vietnam's harbors, a risky move that Lyndon Johnson had carefully avoided because of the possibility of damaging Soviet or Chinese ships and triggering superpower conflict. With this new escalation, few military targets remained untouched, and civilian casualties and the number of refugees mounted.

The violent spring and the upcoming American elections at first spurred more diplomacy. Several weeks before the end of the 1972 presidential campaign, Kissinger announced another cease-fire. "Peace," he said, "is at hand." But as so often in the past, American leaders still believed that their sophisticated military technology could force a quick victory. In mid-December 1972, Nixon ordered an armada of B-52s to attack North Vietnam twenty-four hours a day "until they are ready to negotiate." Despite heavy losses, American bombers attacked North Vietnam's factories; ruined rice fields; and destroyed schools, hospitals, and other civilian facilities. This so-called Christmas attack was the heaviest aerial bombing in history. It caused an international uproar and a determination among antiwar members of Congress to end America's involvement in the Vietnam conflict.

The Christmas bombing marked the last desperate gasp of the American effort. In January 1973 the United States and North Vietnam signed the Paris Peace Accords, ending formal hostilities. Washington promised to withdraw its remaining 50,000 troops, dismantle its military installations, and deactivate mines in North Vietnam's harbors. No foreign troops were to remain in Laos or Cambodia, but Hanoi's forces could stay "in place" in South Vietnam. North Vietnam agreed to release American prisoners of war and to cooperate in national elections in the South. But the accords did not bring peace, only a withdrawal of U.S. troops. The war between the communist North and Thieu's dictatorship dragged on, 48,000 soldiers dying during the first eighteen months of the "cease-fire." By the summer of 1974 war had again returned to most of Indochina.

Meanwhile, Hanoi's almost legendary general, Nyguyen Giap, was organizing a coordinated assault by all his forces for the spring of 1975. Disintegration and demoralization in the South aided his plans. Thieu arrested opponents, banned opposition political parties, and closed down most newspapers. To consolidate his military position and possibly frighten the United States into sending more hardware, Thieu suddenly withdrew his armies from the three northernmost provinces of South Vietnam. But the planned retreat turned into a disorganized rout when Giap's troops took the opportunity to attack. Deprived of American air support, the dispirited South Vietnamese troops raced southward, pillaging their own villages as they went. The North Vietnamese followed, scarcely having to fight, while hundreds of thousands of civilian refugees crowded highways. Only at the gateway to Saigon itself, the provincial capital of Xuan Loc, did the South Vietnamese army make a stand. But Thieu's regime collapsed, and the communists overwhelmed the city in less than a week. On May 1 North Vietnamese and NLF forces entered Saigon, while the last American officials were frantically escaping from the U.S. embassy by helicopter.

Face-saving maneuvers followed. Military airlifts flew over 100,000 South Vietnamese, mostly those closely identified with the United States, to new homes in America. Meanwhile, Kissinger and the new President Gerald Ford tried to block the diplomatic and psychological consequences of the communist victory. Quietly reassuring allies in Western Europe, the secretary of state denied that his country would yield to "neoisolationists" at home. The administration also successfully countered congressional efforts to reduce the numbers of American soldiers stationed overseas and to pare military spending. To regain an image of diplomatic initiative, Kissinger gave a green light to a CIA project to supply and bankroll friendly forces in the Angolan civil war. (America's secret intervention in Angola prompted large-scale Soviet and Cuban aid to the other side; when Congress discovered and terminated this CIA adventure in Africa, the Soviet-backed faction came to power.)

In Cambodia, Lon Nol's U.S.-backed regime had succumbed to communist Khmer Rouge forces under Pol Pot. In late May 1975 the new Khmer Rouge regime seized an American merchant vessel, the *Mayaguez*, and imprisoned its crew for allegedly carrying contraband within Cambodia's territorial waters. President Ford, determined to flex American muscles and recoup his sagging popularity at home, dispatched a naval task force and some 2,000 marines to rescue the 39-man crew. Critics denounced the gunboat diplomacy that cost America 38 dead and 50 wounded, but most Americans supported their president. Clearly, although the communist victory in Vietnam may have marked the limits of American power, the Ford administration still wanted to demonstrate worldwide reach.

The long struggle in Vietnam proved more costly than anyone had imagined. It provoked bitter divisions at home and ended the cold war consensus of the post-World War II period. It also heightened the goverment's preoccupation with secrecy. The Watergate scandals and the revelations of CIA activities gave glimpses into the secret government that had grown during the war. At the international level, the war strained the American balance of payments and built up pressure on the dollar. Defeat hurt the credibility of American commitments abroad, chipping away still more at the dollar's strength. Through Vietnam, Americans discovered the consequences of power used unwisely.

For many years after the war, Americans seemed to want to forget their defeat. The idea that a small Asian nation could have, after a ten-year struggle, forced the retreat of the United States, a country at the pinnacle of its power, seemed almost beyond comprehension. Unlike the returning veterans of World War II, for example, Vietnam veterans were often shunned and their needs ignored. Even the government that had ordered them into combat tried to dodge its responsibility for the Agent Orange–related disorders that afflicted many veterans. Agent Orange was a deadly defoliant used to level the jungles in Vietnam. After a long court battle, during which it was revealed that the Dow Chemical Company and government officials had known in advance about the chemical's hazards, the government set aside a compensatory fund. But the amount was small in comparison to the number of veterans afflicted, and many chose not to join in the settlement at all because they perceived it as deficient.

If slightly submerged for a time, however, domestic division over the war and important nagging questions remained. Slowly, interest in the Vietnam War rekindled, and within a few years, a battle over how to interpret "the lessons" of the struggle emerged. Not surprisingly, these evaluations tended to reflect the positions held at the time of the war.

Hawks continued to present the case that the war could have been won. Some blamed the lack of a government-censored media and claimed that journalists had drained the American people of the will to persevere. Some complained that the war was lost in Washington by the politicians who would not commit themselves to the military measures necessary for victory. Some blamed the antiwar movement and argued that defeat took place in the streets of America. Most hawks argued that the military itself was not at fault but was the victim of a nonsupportive domestic milieu. But even within military ranks disagreements developed. One analyst propounded the thesis that the war was lost because the military emphasized counterinsurgency tactics rather than the kind of conventional warfare in which America excelled.

Wartime doubters and dissenters expanded their case that the war was in the wrong place, at the wrong time, for the wrong reason. Vietnam held little strategic importance for the United States, and U.S. leaders had mistakenly made the land into a symbol of American honor. The North, most argued, waged a "people's war," whereas Americans came to be seen as foreign invaders, the inheritors of a colonialist tradition. Some segments in the military bolstered these arguments, demonstrating that victory could have no operational meaning in a struggle that required the destruction of a land and its people in order to win.

Interestingly, amid the welter of arguments on all sides emerged a central point of agreement: In Vietnam, the ends had not matched the means. Military leaders warned that they would never again become the tools of a no-win policy, and most Americans wanted no more engagements that demanded an expenditure of lives and treasure for hazy goals and problematic national interest. In short, American governments ought more carefully to weigh gains against costs and not simply assume omnipotence; no one wanted another Vietnam.

The Middle East and Latin America

As Americans disentangled themselves from Southeast Asia, the Middle East exploded in war. In the fall of 1973, on the Jewish holy day of Yom Kippur, Egypt and Syria attacked Israel, determined to regain the territory lost in the 1967 war. With U.S. diplomatic support and large donations from American Jews, the Israelis first weathered the assault and then drove deeply into Arab territories. Anxious to defuse Arab-Israeli hostilities, Kissinger argued that the United States could best help Israel by negotiating with its enemies, not fighting them. He launched nearly two years of dramatic shuttle diplomacy, which eventually achieved a tentative settlement: Israel would pull back from part of the Sinai, and the United States would grant military aid to both Israel and Egypt. Best of all, according to Kissinger, his shuttle diplomacy eased the Soviets out of playing a role in Middle East settlements.

Kissinger's efforts to jockey for geopolitical advantage and reduce Soviet influence throughout the world translated into a simple formula: Support friends and punish enemies. In pursuing this policy, Kissinger did not worry much about the character of his friends' internal policies. His realpolitik held that as long as these countries provided a regional bulwark and were hospitable to American economic interests, issues of morality were beside the point. Kissinger's grand design for world stability through regional policemen aligned American's global interests with some of the most oppressive dictators in the world: Shah Reza Pahlevi in Iran, Park Chung-Hee in South Korea, Ferdinand Marcos in the Philippines, and the military leaders of Brazil. In Africa, Kissinger's so-called "tar-baby" report of 1969 concluded that black African insurgent movements were not "realistic or supportable" alternatives. The Nixon-Kissinger policy therefore continued to look primarily to South Africa (which received 40 percent of U.S. investments in Africa) and European colonialists to provide stability in the region and to form close ties with the military regime in oil-rich Nigeria.

America's military assistance and military training programs fed these dictatorships. Private foreign sales of American arms also skyrocketed, reaching $10 billion by the end of the Nixon presidency. Arms sales ameliorated America's serious balance-of-payments problems and contributed short-term stability, but they incubated more military dictatorships. In Latin America during the Nixon years, for example, countries in the southern cone—Uruguay, Chile, Argentina—experienced coups that interrupted traditions of stable, civilian democracy and brought brutal, U.S.-backed military dictatorships to power.

The case of Chile demonstrated the punitive measures the United States could employ against a regime that tried to pull out of its sphere of influence. In 1970 Salvador Allende, a Marxist, was elected president of Chile, a country with a strong tradition of civilian government and an apolitical military establishment. Greatly alarmed by Allende's campaign pledges to nationalize American-owned copper companies and move the country toward socialism, Nixon and Kissinger met with CIA chief Richard Helms, who emerged from the Oval Office with these notes:

One in 10 chance perhaps, but save Chile!
worth spending
not concerned risks involved
no involvement of Embassy
$10,000,000 available, more if necessary
full-time job—best men we have
game plan
make the economy scream
48 hours for plan of action

With an unlimited budget and full authority for any maneuver to "save Chile" from its elected ruler, the CIA first attempted to arrange a military coup to prevent Allende from taking office. This plan ran against the Chilean military's traditions and thus, at that point, failed. CIA encouragement did, however, lead to the assassination of one of Chile's most respected generals, a man who persistently opposed a military takeover. Next, Helms urged an economic offensive: The government ceased its aid to Chile; the World Bank cooperated by dropping Chile's credit rating; private banks suspended loans; and International Telephone and Telegraph (ITT) and American copper companies, which Allende had nationalized, worked tirelessly to promote his downfall. As chaos overtook the Chilean economy (Chile had huge foreign debts because of the large loans extended under JFK's Alliance for Progress), CIA dollars helped finance a trucker's strike that brought distribution to a halt. Shortages mounted, and the middle class increasingly blamed Allende. In 1973 the military finally decided to intervene. The leaders of the coup killed President Allende and thousands of his supporters and installed a regime so oppressive and barbaric in its use of torture that it quickly became an embarrassment to many in the U.S. government. Over Kissinger's protest, Congress subsequently suspended aid. And after the new Chilean government managed to assassinate Allende's former ambassador to the United States, right on the streets of Washington, D.C., relations between the two countries broke down almost completely—at least on an official level. On a private level, however, U.S. enterprise and investments again flooded Chile, attracted by the ironfisted stability.

THE CARTER PRESIDENCY

Jimmy Carter: Compassion and Competency?

James Earl Carter, soon to be known around the globe as Jimmy, capitalized on popular disenchantment with runaway intelligence agencies, political corruption, political insiders, and economic disarray. Emphasizing his rural roots, his born-again Christianity, and his lifelong distance from Washington, the naval commander turned peanut farmer promised voters that he would never sail a crooked ship of state. Beginning the 1976 race for the White House in 1973, the former governor of Georgia presented himself both as a plain person of the people—"a Southerner and an American . . . a farmer . . . a father and a husband, a Christian"—and as a skillful technocrat—"an engineer . . . a planner . . . a nuclear physicist." These diverse talents, he suggested, made him the ideal person to answer the "two basic and generic questions" facing the nation: "Can our government be honest, decent, open, fair, and compassionate? Can our government be competent?" Thus, Carter campaigned for the Democratic nomination and then against Gerald Ford for the presidency as an honest, neopopulist manager, someone who could balance both the nation's moral accounts and its national budget. He avoided strong stands on difficult issues—such as the government's role in defining social justice or in attacking inequality—and tried simply to project a straightforward, down-home image.

Criticized for drowning in day-to-day details while president, Jimmy Carter gradually won wide acclaim for his continued public service after leaving office. *Source:* Jimmy Carter Library.

Carter's meteoric rise was aided not only by his own personality but also by his staff's ability to operate in the new political climate of the 1970s. Popular disillusionment during the Vietnam and Watergate eras had contributed to a decline in party loyalty and in voter turnout, and the upheavels of the late 1960s and early 1970s had brought significant changes in the ways in which the two national parties, especially the Democrats, selected delegates to their national conventions. By 1976 local party machines and prominent party leaders had lost considerable clout. Carter's strategists realized that they could appeal directly to party activists, either in person or through the media, and make an end run around party stalwarts. Thus, Carter outmaneuvered more established Democrats, most of whom could not match his energy (holding no political office, Carter could devote full time to campaigning) or his shrewd, young campaign staff.

Another outsider with plenty of time to run for office, California's former Governor Ronald Reagan, almost snatched the GOP nod away from Gerald Ford, who was even less exciting as a candidate than as a president. Had Reagan only started a little sooner or had the GOP's primary process been as democratized as that of the Democrats, Reagan might have pushed aside Ford and captured the Republican nomination in 1976.

Taken together, the new political climate and the new political ground rules made Carter's ultimate victory over Ford seem the product of new democratic trends and the erosion of elitist patterns. Those party activists who did participate, especially in the Democratic primaries, saw their votes counting for more than they had in previous elections. In 1968, it should be remembered, Lyndon Johnson could virtually hand the nomination over to

Hubert Humphrey, and in 1972 George McGovern could gain the nomination by winning only eight presidential primaries. In contrast, Jimmy Carter had to survive nearly four years of caucus battles and primary fights—what one journalist aptly labeled a political marathon—before he could even claim the nomination. Thus, Carter's electoral triumph owed relatively little to the traditional power brokers and a good deal to the new politics of the late 1960s.

But once anointed by the voters, Jimmy Carter still needed to convince powerful interest groups of his capacity to lead. Events of the late 1960s and early 1970s had affected the rules by which candidate Carter captured the presidential sweepstakes, but they did not greatly change the larger political and constitutional structure, the one in which President Carter had to operate. As critical observers noted, the nation's postwar constitutional system was dominated by powerful vested interests. This system produced very valuable rewards for the organized—including tax deductions, government subsidies, and lucrative public contracts—but gave the unorganized largely the leftovers. Johnson's Great Society sought to extend the boundaries of the welfare state, but it made little effort to change the basic distribution of power. Well-organized elites tended to view the relatively unknown Carter, and his rhetoric about populist democracy, as another threat to a political-constitutional system that seemed already under siege. Many of Carter's difficulties as president, then, grew out of the unorthodox route by which he had come to the White House and his self-proclaimed status as an outsider.

From the very outset, Carter struggled to impress powerful elites. His much-publicized ties with the Trilateral Commission—a group of business leaders and academics who favored closer cooperation among the world's industrial democracies and more comprehensive economic planning by the national government—helped relatively little. Carter selected several of his new inner circle, including his first secretary of the treasury (Michael Blumenthal) and his national security adviser (Zbigniew Brzezinski), from the commission's membership. But Carter, even more than Nixon, underwent lengthy scrutiny by important corporation executives, prominent bankers, and other leaders of powerful institutions and interests. Carter's problems were complicated by the fact that he confronted a Congress filled with incumbents who had close working arrangements with the very interests that distrusted the new president. Carter owed his position to his direct appeal to a shrinking electorate, while traditional interest groups, based on geography and economic self-interest, retained much influence in Congress. Given this structural situation, it was not surprising that Carter soon found himself under sharp attack for his allegedly weak leadership, political naiveté, and inability to understand the complexities of power in Washington.

Carter's Foreign Policy

The Kissinger-Nixon-Ford years saw breakthroughs, such as the opening of a dialogue with China, but the government's willingness to shrug off glaring violations of human rights by many of its allies provoked growing outrage abroad as well as at home. Jimmy Carter's promise, as a presidential candidate, to encourage respect for human rights in international affairs won him popularity. Forming alliances with hated despots, Carter argued, was neither morally right nor strategically sensible: Opposition to terror and despotism in many countries had, under Kissinger's policy, become identified with opposition to U.S. influence. Once America abandoned its image as a benevolent power, Carter claimed, it lost its major strength in international affairs and its most powerful weapon in the cold war.

The human rights policy proved difficult to effect. President Carter appointed a full-time officer to oversee implementation of the policy, supported the weighing of human rights records in granting foreign aid, and stopped America's role as a supplier of instruments of torture. But rapid changes could not help but affect America's global position. In fact, Carter quickly assured many of America's dictator-allies that U.S. national security commitments would continue to take precedence over their internal conduct. Thus, governments such as those in Iran, South Korea, and the Philippines felt few punitive measures under the new human rights policy, but they did feel increasing pressure to ease up on the most flagrant violations. Other countries, such as Chile and Argentina, felt the new administration's disapproval much more dramatically.

As Carter's critics had predicted, the human rights policy gave heart to popular liberation movements in several countries and brought dilemmas to Carter's policymakers. The contradiction between the emphasis on human rights and the previous geopolitics of Henry Kissinger surfaced most notably in Nicaragua and Iran. In both countries popular uprisings swept the hated regimes of Anastasio Somoza and Shah Reza Pahlevi out of power in 1979. Despite severe pressure from domestic Republican allies of both regimes, the Carter administration, after a few attempts at compromise solutions, did not intervene to save the despots. After so many years of profiting from a close alliance with dictators in both countries, however, the United States should not have expected the new governments to be particularly friendly. In Nicaragua the new regime headed by the revolutionary Sandinista movement increasingly adopted a Marxist orientation antagonistic to the United States. In Iran, Carter faced an even more difficult situation that ultimately proved to be his administration's undoing.

After Shah Pahlevi's ouster in Iran, a long-exiled religious leader, the Ayatollah Khomeini, established an Islamic Republic dedicated to wiping out the influences of Americanization. In late 1979 a group of Islamic revolutionaries entered the compound of the U.S. embassy and seized about sixty Americans. The Iranian government demanded custody of the shah, who had been admitted into the United States to undergo medical treatment for cancer, in exchange for the release of the hostages. Khomeini also talked of gaining possession of the shah's personal fortune and of placing some of the American hostages on trial for spying, using evidence captured in the embassy takeover. Despite the shah's departure from the United States and various attempts at mediation, U.S.-Iranian relations worsened. Iran cut off oil shipments to the

United States; the American government froze Iranian assets, instituted full economic pressure against the ayatollah's regime, and attempted—against the advice of Secretary of State Cyrus Vance—an unsuccessful military mission to rescue the hostages. In this climate of extreme tension, even the shah's death in the summer of 1980 did not bring swift release of the hostages. Finally, in a frantic round of diplomacy in the closing days of the Carter administration, freedom for the hostages was exchanged for complex economic settlements, but relations between the two countries remained poor.

At home, Carter came under immense criticism. Many Americans across the country tied yellow ribbons to trees to symbolize the hostages' plight. One television network began a nightly news program called "America Held Hostage." In the wake of Vietnam, the Iranian crisis seemed one more example of American weakness, and Jimmy Carter got the blame.

Despite difficulties, President Carter's human rights emphasis redressed the previous drift of American policy toward alliances with repressive, unpopular regimes. It encouraged the forces of democratization that would sweep Latin America in the late 1970s and 1980s, especially the return to civilian rule in Ecuador, Peru, Brazil, Argentina, and Uruguay. And Carter also engineered rapprochement with black Africa. United Nations Ambassador Andrew Young, a black veteran of civil rights struggles in the South, gained Africans' trust as had few high-ranking Americans before him. Although Young was forced to resign in 1979 after he lied to the State Department about engaging in talks with representatives of the Palestine Liberation Organization (PLO), a group with which the State Department had forbade dealings, the new look in African policy continued anyway. For example, President Carter stood strongly behind British efforts to force the white minority government in Rhodesia (Zimbabwe) to effect a peaceful transition to black rule, a transition that signaled the end of an important bastion of white rule in Africa. If the Carter presidency seemed a particularly unsettled period in American foreign policy, the difficulties can be traced, in part, to earlier alliances with oppressive tyrants and unpopular regimes.

Unlike the human rights policy, many of Carter's major negotiating achievements—those in Panama, the Middle East, and China—built on the initiatives of his Republican predecessors.

In September 1977 the United States and Panama signed two treaties covering the ownership, operation, and defense of the Panama Canal. United States control over the Canal Zone, a strip of 550 square miles slicing through the middle of Panama, had caused bitter resentment for years and brought serious riots in 1964. Denounced in Latin America and throughout the Third World for still holding this land acquired in the days of territory-grabbing imperialism, the United States under President Johnson committed itself to the negotiation of a new treaty. Talks took place over the next thirteen years. After heated debate and a full application of presidential leverage, the Senate ratified the new treaties in 1978. Under their terms, the Canal Zone ceased to exist, and Panama assumed general jurisdiction; the United States retained primary responsibility for operating and defending the canal until the year

2000 but with ever-increasing Panamanian participation; and Panama agreed that the canal should be permanently neutral—open to all vessels with no discrimination on tolls. In addition, Panama would receive a share of canal revenues and a substantial commitment of American loans (not grants). Although critics charged that the treaties represented a rollback of America's strength, the Carter administration stressed that the increasingly obsolete canal was no longer the economic and strategic lifeline it had once been. Moreover, ratification would deflate anti-American sentiment in Latin America, a goal of growing importance to Carter's negotiators, as Mexico, Ecuador, and Peru were discovering new fields of petroleum.

Fresh from the battle over the Panama treaties, President Carter turned his full attention to the Middle East. Kissinger's efforts at shuttle diplomacy between Tel Aviv and Cairo had stalled after the breakthrough of partial Israeli withdrawal from the Sinai Peninsula in 1975. But Egypt's president, Anwar Sadat, surprised the world by traveling to Jerusalem. Sadat's visit to Israel indicated the economic exhaustion that ongoing confrontation had brought to both Egypt and Israel. The time again seemed right for progress. For thirteen days in 1978, Carter, Israeli Prime Minister Menachem Begin, and Anwar Sadat remained in near isolation at the presidential retreat at Camp David, Maryland. When they emerged, they issued for TV audiences an emotional three-way statement that outlined the beginnings of a negotiating process, subsequently ratified by treaty.

The Camp David agreements provided only a framework, not the substance, of a settlement. The most difficult issue—the future of the West Bank and Gaza—remained unresolved. Israel categorically forbade any official participation by the Palestine Liberation Organization in the negotiations, even though the PLO was the major representative of the Arab Palestinians in the West Bank and Gaza. The PLO and most Arab states charged that Sadat had negotiated matters that were not his to negotiate. The split within the Arab world widened as Israeli-Egyptian divisions narrowed. Some domestic critics, observing that the exclusion of the PLO and the antagonism of other Arabs made substantial solutions even more difficult than before, wondered whether Carter, Begin, and Sadat had created the illusion of settlement to raise their images at home. But optimists argued that the importance of the 1979 peace treaty lay in the momentum of negotiation. Clearly, the Egyptian-Israeli peace firmly established U.S. hegemony and eliminated Soviet influence in Egypt. Carter, like Nixon, dangled the large carrots of American aid and more arms sales to keep the appearance of negotiations alive.

Carter's diplomacy with China had less ambiguous results. On January 1, 1979, the United States and the People's Republic of China established formal relations, and over the next year they signed a number of cultural, scientific, and economic agreements. A joint economic committee cochaired by the secretary of the treasury, worked to enhance trade, and the United States zoomed up to fourth place among China's trading partners. In January 1980 Defense Secretary Harold Brown's trip to China (coinciding handily with the Soviet invasion of Afghanistan) signaled the opening of a military relationship as well. The new technocrats who succeeded to Chinese leadership after the death of Mao were bent on accelerating modernization by borrowing from the capitalist West, and the lure of the China market once again enthralled the American business community.

Renewing the Cold War

Toward the end of 1979 the counselor for the Department of State summarized the general view that had initially guided the Carter administration's foreign policy worldwide: "It is not a sign of weakness to recognize that we alone cannot dictate events elsewhere. It is rather a sign of American maturity in a complex world." More negotiation, more compromise, and greater attention to human rights marked Carter's early foreign policy.

External events and political pressures at home gradually led Carter to revise his foreign-policy emphasis. By 1978 policymakers talked more of larger military spending and cold war dangers. Then in December 1979 the Soviet Union invaded Afganistan. The Soviet action, the first armed Soviet invasion since the incursion into Czechoslovakia in 1968, probably reflected the Soviets' fear of a unified Islamic movement and their desire to solidify their shaky sphere of influence. Coming at a time when Americans were exceedingly nervous about the security of Middle Eastern oil supplies because of the Iranian revolution, the Soviet invasion touched off feverish cold war rhetoric reminiscent of the 1950s.

Critics of Carter's foreign policy leaped to their election-year podiums, denounced America's presumed weakness, and clamored for a response. The Carter administration warned Americans that overreaction was as dangerous as underreaction but announced reprisals against the Soviets. Carter ordered a halt to exports of grain and high technology to the Soviet Union, began to arm Pakistan, publicly highlighted the secretary of defense's trip to China, organized a boycott of the Olympic Games held in Moscow in the summer of 1980, withdrew the SALT treaty from the Senate, and reinstituted registration for a military draft. Despite such measures—the strongest response possible short of some type of military action—more and more Americans began to charge that Carter had presided over an erosion of American power that had opened the way for the Soviet invasion of Afghanistan. Neoconservative groups such as the Committee on the Present Danger constructed a litany of signs of America's weakness: the shah's ouster in Iran, the Soviet-Cuban presence in Africa, the growing power of Soviet-aligned Vietnam in Southeast Asia, and the revolutionary ferment in the Caribbean. The promise of rebuilding U.S. power became the theme of Ronald Reagan's presidential campaign of 1980, as public-opinion polls showed that 82 percent disapproved of Carter's handling of foreign policy.

Carter knew the political perils of soft-line diplomacy. Afghanistan, he said, shattered his previous illusions about Soviet behavior, and he promised to lead the nation in more forceful directions. A rift became increasingly apparent between Secretary of State Vance, who believed in detente and the negotiating process, and National Security Adviser Brzezinski, a hard-liner with a bipolar view of world politics and a deep distrust of the Soviets. When Carter ordered an ill-fated military mission to rescue the hostages in Iran (whose lengthening captivity had become a major political liability), the secretary of state resigned his post. Vance indicated that he was out of sympathy not only with what he considered a rash and risky military incursion into Iran but also with the new confrontational policy in general. With Republicans goading the administration about a weak defense, Carter complemented cold war rhetoric with promises to revitalize America's strategic posture. He began refurbishing military bases throughout the world and beefing up American military capabilities in critical areas, such as the Indian Ocean and the Caribbean; he increased defense spending and promised more emphasis on new high-technology weapon systems (satellites and lasers); and he strongly backed the controversial and costly MX missile system. His advisers even began to blur the traditional distinctions between nuclear and conventional military action, leaving the Russians to speculate publicly that Americans no longer considered limited nuclear strikes unthinkable.

Although the new cold warriors drew alarming pictures of an expansionist Soviet Union, the Soviets were themselves feeling embattled. Suffering major economic problems, threatened by growing dissent at home, and wary of a resurgent and hostile China, Soviet leaders also faced a decline in geopolitical power. Kissinger and Carter had both outmaneuvered the Soviets in the Middle East and effectively excluded them from influence in that area. Signs of discontent in Eastern Europe—especially the successful strike by Polish workers in August 1980—highlighted strains within the Warsaw Pact.

If both American and Soviet leaders felt increasingly insecure about their global roles in the early 1980s, it was because the rest of the world was struggling to avoid the tight grip of bipolar alliances and to build new power blocs. The movement of nonaligned nations; OPEC; the Committee of 77, which represented the Southern Hemisphere in the so-called North-South debate; the new power of Islam; the rising economic power of Japan; and a variety of regional pacts all illustrated the growing intricacy of world politics. Yet, as in the era of the first cold war, the leaders of the superpowers appeared to resort to a simplistic bipolar analysis to explain away the complexities of neutralist or nationalist aspirations.

THE NEW EGALITARIANISM

The Meaning of Equality

Perhaps the most perplexing social issue facing the nation in the 1970s was its commitment to equality. Nearly all of the Republic's founding documents—including the Declaration of Independence and the Constitution's

Fourteenth Amendment—affirmed the idea of equality. Yet one of the undeniable themes in the nation's history had been the persistence of inequality—political, legal, and economic.

The search for greater equality during the 1960s and 1970s revealed some fundamental differences over the meaning of equality and over the desirability of making it a key national goal. As the nation approached and then passed the bicentennial of its birth, debates about equality became more heated. In the late 1970s, polarization over this issue, though less visible than a decade before, was no less intense, especially in journalistic and academic circles.

Throughout most of the nation's history, *equality* seemed to mean "equality of opportunity," the chance for every citizen to join in the race for individual success. The sweetest victories and the largest rewards, it was assumed, should still go to those who ran the swiftest. But everyone should have a chance to get to the starting line, and no one should have to jump hurdles while their more fortunate competitors sailed along an obstacle-free track. Yet even equality of opportunity, though much celebrated, remained a dream for many people. The race-for-success ethos had worked as well as it had, it might be argued, because so many people never really got into the contest at all. Women, African-Americans, ethnic minorities, homosexuals—these and other groups carried handicaps that prevented them from even getting to the starting blocks. A traditional blues song summarized the way many black people saw the great American race:

> If you're White, you're all right,
> If you're Brown, stick around,
> But if you're black, O' brother,
> Get back! Get back! Get Back!*

Many of the political and legal battles of the 1960s and of the 1970s aimed at preventing people from being "moved back," at rehandicapping the race, and at removing old hurdles. Thus, the demands of the civil rights movement involved the elimination of various obstacles, such as segregation laws and discriminatory hiring practices, that prevented African-Americans from entering the gates of national institutions. Similarly, women's groups channeled their energies toward passage of the Equal Rights Amendment, an attempt to end discrimination through legal and constitutional change.

While the struggle to eliminate obstacles to equality of opportunity was still proceeding, the victories in this area began to change the perspective of many activists. As they looked at the race-for-success ideal, these "new egalitarians" began to argue that efforts to allow everyone to enter the race and to remove the old system of hurdles were not enough. Renewed commitment to the principle of equality of opportunity would probably not change the fact that only a few people were leading the race for economic success, that many people were bunched in the middle of the pack, and that a sizable portion

* Source: Carrousel France.

had fallen permanently behind. In the distribution of both income and wealth, the United States in 1980 remained a very unequal society: At the top of the scale, 5 percent of the population received 20 percent of the nation's income and owned more than 50 percent of its wealth; the lowest 20 percent, in stark contrast, gained 3 percent of the income and held less than 0.5 percent of the wealth. According to the new egalitarians, such inequality of condition and of results meant that there were all sorts of subtle and hidden handicaps in the system. If the United States were to be a truly egalitarian society, there must be vigorous and affirmative action to achieve greater "equality of condition" rather than simply a spurious equality of opportunity.

In the late 1960s and especially the early 1970s, the agenda of egalitarianism changed. Not only should students of color be protected from discriminatory procedures that barred them from educational institutions, the new egalitarians argued, but also there should be "affirmative action" programs to ensure their admittance and their graduation. In the area of employment, proponents of affirmative action urged programs to ensure that women and persons of color were not simply interviewed but were then hired and promoted on an equal basis. Proof of substantial progress was increasingly measured by comparing the percentage of women and minorities in educational or business institutions with their percentage in the total population, a process that opponents condemned as inevitably leading to the institution of quotas.

The quest for greater equality of condition involved more than pressure for affirmative action programs in educational and corporate institutions. Looking at the gross inequality of wealth and income, many egalitarians argued that the nation must confront the issue of income redistribution. After surveying the problem in *Inequality* (1971) and resurveying it in *Who Gets Ahead?* (1979), the sociologist Christopher Jencks claimed that social science data showed that attempts to equalize people's "personal characteristics," especially their educational backgrounds, was an "unpromising way of equalizing incomes." If people truly wanted a more equal economic order, Jencks concluded, efforts to "redistribute income itself" offered the "most effective strategy."

But as George McGovern discovered during the 1972 presidential campaign, redistributive proposals were difficult to sell to voters. Although many of Richard Nixon's "forgotten Americans" would have benefited from McGovern's proposed changes in inheritance laws, for example, most voters saw his ideas as too radical. "They must think they're all going to win a lottery," complained McGovern. In fact, many people viewed redistribution as hostile to their interests. It seemed to strike at the deeply rooted commitment to "propertarianism" and at the faith that no matter how unjust the general economic system might appear, something would turn up for them. (Public-opinion polls taken in the late 1970s revealed a similar phenomenon: People expressed considerable pessimism about the general economic situation but a striking optimism about their own prospects.)

Yet the movement for equality spread, and some of the new egalitarians went beyond purely economic issues to argue that everyone should have an equal opportunity to enjoy, without risking penalties, their chosen style of life. Some of the most bitter battles in the struggle for equality were fought over the issue of homosexuality. During the late 1960s and throughout the 1970s more and more homosexuals "came out of the closet" and joined a growing gay and lesbian rights movement. Gay and lesbian rights activists first wanted acknowledgment of their right to privacy, their right to satisfy their own sexual preferences with other consenting adults. Increasingly, they also demanded that gay and lesbian people be treated, in their public roles, no different than heterosexuals. The movement pushed for state and municipal laws ending traditional patterns of discrimination and sought greater police protection against physical abuse. Although the gay and lesbian rights movement won significant support, especially from civil liberties elites, it also produced a considerable backlash among those who feared the spread of what they considered an immoral way of life.

Efforts to create greater equality for women also raised controversy. Here, it was the American family, the bedrock of the social order, that became the issue. Proposals to expand government funding for day-care centers—necessities for most women who wanted both children and a job—angered those who claimed that the state should stay out of private matters and those who argued that more day-care facilities would only upset an already unstable family structure. In addition, most employers displayed little enthusiasm for such ideas as flexible work hours and job sharing, arrangements that could benefit both men and women who wanted families and careers.

The New Right

Fervent opposition to the new egalitarianism helped unify the new conservative coalition of the 1970s. Although some commentators had predicted that the "Goldwater caper" of 1964 signaled conservatism's imminent collapse, right-leaning leaders inside and outside the GOP quickly regrouped. As conservatives gained new visibility and greater self-confidence, a New Right emerged as an important political force.

Several things distinguished this New Right from the conservative movement of the 1940s and 1950s. First, conservatives now gained broad popular support, especially through their alliance with rapidly growing evangelical religious groups. Conservatives, who had once had to search for roots in the distant past, could now join the religious right in rallying around contemporary institutions such as the American family. (For the emergence of the religious right see Chapter 8.) In addition, conservatives mastered the latest media and organizational techniques. Conservative speakers, such as William F. Buckley and Milton Friedman, became skilled television performers, and conservative fund-raisers mounted highly sophisticated direct-mail appeals for donations. Following the lead of Goldwater's 1964 campaign, conservative political strategists were often more innovative than their opponents on the political left. Although many members of the GOP had opposed the changes in campaign-financed laws that grew out of Watergate, Republican-oriented pressure groups on the political right skillfully used loopholes in the new

measures, especially the provision allowing unlimited spending by indepen- *PAC'3*
dent political action committees—PACs.

The New Right also enjoyed a livelier and broader intellectual base than
the conservatism of the 1950s. During the 1970s, an informal conservative
coalition benefited from a steady flow of prominent refugees, particularly East
Coast intellectuals, from the cold war liberalism of the vital center. Some of
these neoconservatives settled into research positions at well-funded, right-
leaning think tanks (such as the American Enterprise Institution in Washington); others occupied newly funded chairs and programs at universities and
smaller colleges; and most wrote for a variety of lively scholarly and popular
journals.

Neoconservatives blended the old with the new. Espousing a more
cautious and extremely nervous version of the old anticommunist liberalism *NEo-*
that had been forged during the early postwar era, neoconservatives de- *CoNS*
nounced familiar enemies—international communism, Marxism, domestic
radicalism, and mass culture. Their favorite causes—political gradualism, enlightened capitalism, economic growth, and high culture—also had been the
bedrock of their ideology during the period of Truman's Fair Deal. But the
leftward drift of liberalism and the emergence of a new cultural and political
radicalism during the 1960s propelled many neoconservatives toward the
New Right during the 1970s. Norman Podhoretz, editor of *Commentary*
magazine, proudly pointed out that he had published Paul Goodman in the
early 1960s and had broken ranks only after realizing the "sinister" implications of that decade. The counterculture, Podhoretz claimed, was winning,
and sober intellectuals must take a firm stand against "irrational" ideas and
"dangerous" values.

Critical of what they considered a cowardly appeasement of communism
overseas and a soft-headed tolerance of cultural and political radicalism at
home, chastened liberals like Podhoretz, Irving Kristol, Daniel Bell, and
Nathan Glazer formed the intellectual core of neoconservatism. In addition
to their own numerous publications, they helped to popularize some of the
more conservative social science literature, especially the work of Edward
Banfield and James Q. Wilson. The resulting battles between the neoconservatives' set of academic experts and those of the left were fierce. Many of the
leading neoconservative theorists possessed backgrounds in both academia
and journalism, and they combined these talents to produce sprightly
polemics for *Commentary* and more scholarly pieces for *The Public Interest*, an
influential periodical edited by Kristol and Glazer.

Although neoconservatives found the United States—indeed, Western
civilization—entering a period of profound crisis, the specter of the new egalitarianism frightened them almost as much as did the Soviet Union. Some
neoconservatives were disturbed by the new efforts to achieve the traditional
goal of equality of opportunity, at least when such equality was sought by militant feminists, cultural radicals, and homosexuals. Kristol and the political scientist Walter Berns, for example, endorsed more vigorous censorship of cultural materials, and Ernest van den Haag warned that the new militancy of
gays and lesbians threatened traditional values based on heterosexuality.

The attack on the new egalitarianism, however, centered on what neoconservatives denounced as "equality of outcomes." Glazer condemned affirmative action as an insidious form of reverse discrimination, a doctrine that discriminated not simply against white males but also against all people of true merit. When applied to African-Americans, the political scientist Robert Sasseen argued, affirmative action really affirmed an "arrogant contempt" for blacks: It disguised a "paternalistic policy" that consigned its purported beneficiaries to "perpetual inferiority" and to a life as "special wards of the state." Midge Dector denounced militant feminism as a revolutionary attack on motherhood, as a sign of deep-seated self-hatred, and as the manifestation of the "desperately nihilistic idea" that there were no "necessary differences between the sexes." Kristol blamed most of the controversy over equality on "an intelligentsia" that despised liberal capitalism and "that is so guilt-ridden at being implicated in the life of the society that it is inclined to find even collective suicide preferable to the status quo."

The National Government and the Riddle of Equality

The struggle over the meaning of equality was not, of course, limited to rhetorical clashes. The egalitarian currents of the 1960s and 1970s, as wary neoconservatives recognized, touched most areas of public life, especially educational and corporate institutions. Did affirmative action programs that set aside a specified number of classroom seats or jobs for certain minorities constitute reverse discrimination against others who claimed they were more deserving of the places on the basis of their individual merit? Should, for instance, students of color be admitted to a law school, whereas whites with higher test scores were rejected? (Such questions became especially difficult and emotional when the persons rejected came from ethnic groups, such as Jewish- and Italian-Americans, who had once suffered from discrimination themselves.)

The controversy over affirmative action and reverse discrimination raged throughout the 1970s, and the U.S. Supreme Court finally entered the lists. In the much-discussed *Bakke* case of 1978, a deeply divided Court struck down a plan that set aside a certain quota of seats at a California medical school for "minority" applicants. But more significantly, a majority of justices also indicated that they were not willing to invalidate all affirmative action programs. The Court upheld a private plan devised by Kaiser Aluminum to upgrade the positions of minority workers and approved a congressional requirement that 10 percent of all contracts awarded under a public-works program would go to "minority business enterprises."

Affirmative action was just one of many issues related to the economic policies of the 1970s. Following the retirement of Lyndon Johnson, no president gave the issue of economic inequality much attention. Richard Nixon offered the poorest one-fourth of the population "benign neglect," while he courted the "forgotten American"—middle-class and lower-middle-class citizens who worked hard and paid more than their share of taxes. Although Nixon shut down Johnson's Office of Economic Opportunity, expenditures for social welfare, measured as a percentage of the GNP, actually continued to rise under Nixon and then under Gerald Ford. By this standard, the growth was faster under two Republican presidents than under Johnson, though these funds still failed to alleviate deeply rooted inequalities. Meanwhile, Nixon's promise to the forgotten American went largely unfulfilled as soaring inflation rates eroded most workers' real income.

President Jimmy Carter seemed more interested in procedures and planning than in broad policy arguments or political philosophy. Carter's first proposals for national action sounded no clarion calls for social justice but stressed managerial and technical issues—reorganization of the executive branch, streamlining of existing welfare programs, and new budget procedures. Carter did talk about energy conservation as "the moral equivalent of war," but his "wartime" strategy followed rather conventional paths. Most important, the Carter administration's plans assumed that the old liberal *deus ex machina*—economic growth—could be restored and could provide, as it had in the past, a means of avoiding a direct confrontation with the problem of inequality. If, through the magic of new energy-producing technologies, the economic pie could once again expand, even the smallest slices would be bigger.

The Carter administration, however, was no more successful than the Nixon or Ford administrations in promoting real economic growth. Throughout the 1970s, under Republicans and Democrats, the American economy failed to perform as well as it had done in the 1960s—or even in the 1940s and 1950s. Although the United States still produced more than any other country, the gap narrowed as America's economic productivity—its output per worker—grew more slowly than that of other industrial nations. Even Britain and Italy, countries with serious economic problems, could boast of higher productivity rates than the United States. At the same time that productivity languished, inflation flourished. The inflation rate for 1979 stood at nearly 14 percent, and the monthly rate for early 1980, when figured on a yearly basis, ran as high as 20 percent. According to one study, a family of four that had earned $13,200 in 1970 would have required an income of more than $25,000 to maintain the same standard of living in 1980. Although the salaries of most upper-income professionals kept pace with inflation, most American workers suffered a decline in their real income.

The nation's economic difficulties contributed to the unsettled political climate. In 1976 Carter exploited the popular distrust of political institutions; as president, he became the victim, rather than the beneficiary, of popular cynicism about government. And in charting his political course he had to deal with a party structure that was undergoing constant shifts and sags. Just as the Goldwater defeat had proved only a temporary setback for the Republicans in the 1960s, Watergate marked merely a momentary downturn for the GOP in the 1970s. While the Republican party regrouped behind Ronald Reagan and its refurbished right wing, the Democratic party splintered into even more factions than it had in the late 1960s. Carter and his strategists successfully built their own electoral machine, but many Democrats, especially social activists, expressed little enthusiasm for Carter's domestic policies.

Even if he had been blessed with only political assets and no liabilities, Carter would still have found it difficult to discover easy answers to the nation's economic woes. On economic questions there seemed no conventional wisdom to which Carter—or any president—could turn. The economist-social critic Herman Daly, for example, spoke for many advocates of the "small-is-beautiful" approach when he urged abandoning the old goal of economic growth in favor of a "steady-state economy," one that aimed at "sufficient wealth efficiently maintained and allocated, and equitably distributed—not maximum production." Other social critics also advocated major departures from the old liberal economic formulas. After surveying the growing pressures on the supplies of resources in the United States and in other nations, Richard J. Barnet predicted the onset of "the lean years." He urged greater government planning, reliance on "soft" rather than "hard" energy technologies (solar energy in preference to nuclear energy, for example), and greater democratization of the national and international marketplaces. The socialist writer Michael Harrington joined Barnet in condemning the misuse of power by the giant multinational corporations. In the age of monopoly capitalism, Harrington argued, unemployment, inflation, and a stagnant economy grew out of decisions first made in corporate board rooms and then accepted by political leaders. America's economic ills, Harrington contended, reflected underlying structural problems, conditions rooted in the very nature of an oversized capitalist economy.

Other observers offered a much different analysis. According to neo-conservative theoreticians such as Irving Kristol, traditional economists such as Milton Friedman, and representatives of large business corporations, economic problems could be traced back to the national government's interference in the marketplace and to "crushing" levels of taxation, especially on businesses. They blamed huge government deficits, unnecessary environmental restraints, ill-advised safety regulations, and the general burden of government-required paperwork for stifling economic growth. (As the economist Lester Thurow pointed out, though, those countries with higher productivity *all* had much *more* government regulation than the United States.)

These conservative writers promised no easy solutions. They urged massive government deregulation and substantial tax cuts, measures calculated to stimulate the "supply side," that is, the productive infrastructure of the economy. They also called for tighter control over the money supply and a sharp reduction of government borrowing to finance deficits, which, they claimed, deprived private business of necessary loans for research and expansion. They insisted that their proposals were good not only for business but also for all citizens. Conservatives did not ignore the issue of greater economic justice; but the problems of inequality could only be solved, they argued, by unleashing American capitalism.

Even the more conventional liberal economists, to whom Carter ultimately turned, offered him a variety of approaches to the key problems of productivity and inflation. Although the president endorsed the Humphrey-Hawkins bill, which pledged that the White House would reduce unemployment to 4 percent by 1982, his economic advisers focused on fighting infla-tion. First, they bowed toward the arguments of the deregulators and sought to lower prices by ending federal regulatory structures, such as those in the transportation industry, that supposedly raised prices. And though the Carter administration rejected a thoroughgoing system of wage and price controls, it announced voluntary wage and price guidelines. Finally, Carter and his eco-nomic aides pursued a policy of tightening credit (thus raising interest rates) and of cooling down the economy. Carter's monetary policies did drive down the inflation rate—though it still hovered near double-digit levels—but they also generated rising unemployment and increased social tension. By the summer of 1980 the nation had slid into a deep recession.

The Election of 1980

Lacking a broad base of political support and much experience in gov-ernment, Carter seemed confused in his approach to domestic affairs. As Nixon had done with his "Berlin Wall," Carter ducked behind a small group of fellow Georgians, skillful political tacticians who lacked a broad vision of na-tional priorities. Confidence in Carter's performance, as measured by various public-opinion surveys, steadily plummeted. By the time of the Democratic convention in August 1980, only 23 percent of the Gallup Poll's sample thought he was doing a good job. Carter's showing was even more dismal than that of Harry Truman during his final months in office or that of Richard Nixon during the dog days of Watergate.

Yet Carter amazed most political pundits and recaptured the Democratic nomination. As the nation's commander-in-chief, he ironically gained sup-port as a result of his own foreign-policy problems. With Iranians occupying the American embassy in Teheran and the Soviets invading Afghanistan, many Democrats rallied around their leader, even when his policies—such as admit-ting the shah of Iran into the United States—had contributed to some of the problems. Carter also benefited from the liabilities of his major Democratic rival, Senator Edward Kennedy of Massachusetts. Although Kennedy enjoyed generally favorable coverage before he declared for the presidency—and after his capitulation to Carter—his vulnerabilities, especially his own personal problems, dominated the media while he was an active candidate. Many Democrats, pollsters discovered, distrusted Kennedy more than they disliked Carter. Even many who saw the president as something of a bumbler still con-sidered him a decent and honest man. Finally, Carter effectively (ruthlessly, claimed the Kennedy camp) used federal patronage to build local ties. Al-though the White House lacked clear strategies for meeting domestic ills, it did dispense federal grants, both large and small, to Democratic mayors and governors. Thus, the Democratic National Convention of 1980 produced a cu-rious result: Delegates warmly applauded the person they had rejected for the presidency, Edward Kennedy (and incorporated many of his proposals into their party's platform), but unenthusiastically renominated a candidate, Jimmy Carter, who seemed a sure loser in November.

Election day proved a disaster for Carter and a serious setback for the Democratic party. The GOP's ticket of Ronald Reagan and George Bush carried 44 states, including most of those in Carter's native South, and captured 486 electoral votes. (Independent candidate John Anderson gained enough of the popular vote, 7 percent, to qualify for federal funds but failed to win any electoral votes.) Reagan and Bush cut into almost all of the traditionally Democratic voting blocs, especially union members, Jews, and white ethnic voters. According to one survey, 25 percent of Democratic voters supported Reagan. The oldest person ever elected to the presidency—Reagan was only a few months short of seventy on November 4, 1980—the former governor of California even outpolled Carter among voters under thirty years of age.

At the same time, Reagan's Republican party showed that it had recovered from Richard Nixon and Watergate. The GOP gained twelve Senate seats and took control of the upper house of Congress for the first time since 1954. A number of prominent Democratic liberals—including George McGovern—were turned out of the Senate. Although the Democrats managed to hold onto the House of Representatives, the GOP still picked up thirty-three seats in the lower house. In many other ways, however, the presidential result represented more of a repudiation of Jimmy Carter than an affirmation of Ronald Reagan. Nearly half of the eligible voters did not vote for any presidential candidate, so that Reagan's 51 percent of the popular vote gave him the support of little more than one-quarter of the potential electorate.

Reagan and his inner circle of wealthy advisers came to Washington to reverse the domestic political trends that had dominated the postwar political era. In contrast to Carter, for example, Reagan pledged not to reorganize government agencies but to dismantle at least some of them. His secretary of interior promised he would not even listen to environmental "extremists," and Budget Director David Stockman suggested that most government welfare programs should be eliminated. The new egalitarianism, Reagan's conservative supporters hoped, would be a thing of the past.

A master of political symbols, Ronald Reagan won rave reviews for presidential image making. The lavish inaugural proceedings—generously sprinkled with designer gowns, rented limousines, and Reagan's old Hollywood friends—recalled the early days of the Kennedy administration; Reagan's speeches, which called for rebuilding the American dream and for overcoming fears of new approaches, suggested the self-confident optimism of Franklin Roosevelt; and the president's narrow escape from an assassin's bullet, only a few months after taking office, placed him in the fearless western mold of John Wayne, a pop culture icon often invoked by Reagan himself.

ASSESSING THE 1970s

Despite numerous attempts to offer a comprehensive historical vision of the 1970s, scholars have come to emphasize very different facets of this complex decade. To some, it exuded a spirit of aimlessness in both public and private life. In a much-debated report prepared for the Trilateral Commission, the political scientist Samuel Huntington linked this spirit to a "failure of leadership" that ultimately stemmed from "an excess of democracy." The egalitarian demands of the late 1960s and the 1970s, in this neoconservative analysis, overburdened both the political and economic systems.

Other observers also detected a sense of aimlessness but drew different conclusions from those of Huntington. Finding a proliferation of "personal-growth" therapies, a spirit of self-absorption, and an apparent retreat from social concern among young people, Tom Wolfe (in a generally positive analysis) called the 1970s the "me decade." Pointing to similar trends, but interpreting the theme in a much less positive way, the historian Christopher Lasch saw the 1970s dominated by a "culture of narcissism."

Yet even Lasch, one of the decade's bitterest critics, could find other facets to the 1970s, including a remarkable growth of local, community-based self-help movements. Looking back on the "splendid decade," William Braden of the *Chicago Sun-Times* called the 1970s a time of "grass-roots revival." In small ways, often far from the glare of the national media, the "me decade" may have produced as much, if not more, ferment for social change as the 1960s. In one sense, the social initiatives of the 1970s avoided the tactics of the 1960s, especially the penchant for substituting mass-mediated political spectacles for grass-roots organizing. Yet in another way, social movements of the 1970s tried to build on impulses of the 1960s, such as the community-action programs of the Great Society.

Great Society programs had encouraged ordinary citizens to participate in community projects. Some of these efforts, such as attempts to gain community control of neighborhood schools, failed to topple oversized and centralized bureaucracies. But other local efforts met with limited, sometimes even striking, success. Local arts programs contributed to a grass-roots cultural revival reminiscent of the 1930s. Neighborhood clinics, legal-aid offices, and recreational and counseling services became regular features of everyday life during the 1970s. Meanwhile, community organizing, a strategy pioneered by Saul Alinsky's school for radicals in Chicago, developed broader goals and spread to other parts of the country and ideological spectrum.

The nature of the 1970s, as well as the legacy of the 1960s, also encouraged the emphasis on grass-roots self-help efforts. In a dialectical process, the growth of outsized institutions in an age of economic instability encouraged local counterresponses. In a trend thoroughly representative of the decade's complex reaction to oversized institutions, small group homes, in which people who were mentally or physically challenged could be helped in a community and family setting, came to offer alternatives to the large and costly mental-health facilities of the oversized medical establishment.

Many different groups participated in the decade's grass-roots approach to social change. Many African-Americans, for example, found it difficult to maintain, let alone expand on, the economic gains of the late 1960s and early 1970s. In 1978 there were twice as many blacks out of work as a decade earlier. The same year, the median income of African-Americans stood at only 55 percent of the median income of whites, the same percentage as in 1965, the year LBJ unveiled his Great Society. The concentration of African-Americans in decaying parts of central cities became even more intensive: By the late 1970s more than half of the nation's black population lived in the oldest, shabbiest portions of the inner cities. Meanwhile, the national black organizations and their white allies found it difficult to get significant new help from the federal government. Consequently, many concluded that the most effective strategy involved a return to their own communities and a renewed effort to develop new institutions and a spirit of self-help. Jesse Jackson, the controversial leader of Operation PUSH, headed one such movement in Chicago; Detroit became another city in which local organizations grew significantly; and a black-owned news service provided an alternative community network for small African-American newspapers across the country.

Members of other ethnic groups adopted similar strategies. During the late 1970s increased immigration (both legal and illegal) and high birthrates swelled the Hispanic population—largely Mexican-American and Puerto Rican—to about 6 percent of the nation's total. Without significant help from Washington or from local governments, many Hispanics turned to community-based institutions. César Chávez continued to be the most charismatic Mexican-American leader, especially in rural areas. But others, such as Ernie Cortes of Los Angeles' United Neighborhood Organizations, worked to organize urban communities, often relying on the resources and personnel of the Catholic church. Native-American leaders also eased away from dramatic clashes with white authorities, placing a new emphasis on self-sufficiency.

Efforts at local organizing were not limited to nonwhite minorities. Confronted with rampant inflation and with the continued surge of urban-development projects into their communities, the "unmeltable" white ethnics mobilized. In ethnic neighborhoods as well as in other parts of cities and suburbs there was a significant growth of local neighborhood associations. According to one estimate, there were literally millions of such groups. Many rural areas experienced similar examples of new grass-roots organizations. In Minnesota and Wisconsin, for example, farmers joined with city folk to protest the spread of nuclear power plants and the proliferation of high-voltage power lines.

Moreover, ferment went beyond ethnicity and geography. Older Americans, one of the country's fastest-growing interest groups, banded together to make "gray power" a reality. Feminist groups formed collectives that attempted to restructure everything from women's health care to literary forms to small-business organizations. Some blue-collar workers organized to demand more control over their job sites. Recognizing that new technologies might threaten not only their jobs but also their health, advocates of "workplace democracy" challenged claims about corporate responsibility and distrusted government inspectors who supposedly oversaw health and safety standards. In a few cases, groups of workers became owners, taking over plants that were being abandoned by large corporations and running them as worker-community ventures. Consumer cooperatives also flourished. In response to pressure from cooperative supporters, Congress created in 1978 the

National Consumer Cooperative Bank, a special institution that could provide loans to this new form of grass-roots enterprise.

What was the larger significance of all these grass-roots self-help movements? Given the political fragmentation of the 1970s, many answers were close at hand. Advocates of local activism saw such movements as tangible signs of a "new citizenship." At the backyard and neighborhood levels, people seemed ready and willing to reassert control over their lives and challenge big government, big business, and other established institutions of power. Such movements, their celebrants proclaimed, heralded the birth of new forms of community and a "new populist" spirit.

Other analysts and even participants in such movements were not so sanguine. They worried that individual organizations tended to focus on single issues and to ignore a larger vision of the entire nation's future. The successful effort by the gray-power lobby to extend the mandatory retirement age to seventy, for instance, only seemed to place another hurdle in the paths of women and minority workers. And pressures to raise Social Security benefits for the elderly resulted in Congress placing new tax burdens on younger wage-earners. Some political observers complained that single-issue pressure groups only further fragmented the political process and delayed formulation of general policies aimed at a broad socioeconomic reconstruction. And finally, even many people associated with these new efforts remained suspicious about linking up with other grass-roots organizations. In the western states, Native-American groups hesitated to cooperate with ranchers and farmers—longtime enemies—in a common stand on environmental and energy issues. Similarly, organizations of blacks and white ethnics traditionally drew a good deal of their individual energies from antagonistic rather than from cooperative relationships.

The highly publicized taxpayer revolts of the late 1970s highlighted the ambiguous nature of this new localism. On the one hand, the tax revolt seemed to confirm fears about the dangers of single-issue activism. Gaining momentum after Californians enacted Proposition 13 (a 1978 measure that cut state property taxes in half) and marching behind neopopulist attacks on big government, tax-cut leaders sold a seemingly simple proposal that had complex consequences, especially to low-income people who faced cutbacks in public services. On the other hand, studies of tax-revolt movements showed that rank-and-file rebels were not mean-spirited or selfish. Using the democratic process to fight what they considered inequitably apportioned taxes and unresponsive government bureaucracies, these taxpayers did not want low taxes as much as they wanted more equitable rates. They wanted better, not less, government. They still accepted the broad outlines of the postwar welfare state and endorsed government programs to meet "real" social needs.

Yet in the context of the fragmented politics of the 1970s, much of the neopopulist tax cutting failed to translate into any broader idea of community. Indeed, Ronald Reagan, with his individualistic vision of a new capitalism, seemed a major beneficiary of the impulse toward localism and self-help. Distrust of government institutions, especially at the national level, allowed the Reagan administration to argue against extending, and even for dismantling, social-welfare programs. Although many social activists continued to see community organizing and grass-roots action as the best path toward social change, the ascendancy of Reaganism at the national level would change the ways in which political and social issues would be defined in the 1980s.

SUGGESTIONS FOR FURTHER READING

Garry Wills, *Nixon Agonistes* (rev. ed., 1980), is a good single-volume introduction to Richard Nixon and his place in postwar political culture. More recent entries in the Nixon bookshelf include Bruce Odes, ed., *From the President: Richard Nixon's Secret Files* (1989); Stephen Ambrose, *Nixon: The Triumph of a Politician, 1962–1972* (1989); Roger Morris, *Richard Milhous Nixon: The Rise of an American Politician* (1990); Herbert Parmet, *Richard Nixon and His America* (1990); and Jonathan Aiken, *Richard Nixon: A Life* (1993).

On Watergate and the broader ethos of secret government, see Peter Schrag, *Test of Loyalty* (1974); Theodore White, *Breach of Faith* (1975); Athan Theoharis, *Spying on Americans* (1978); Frank J. Donner, *The Age of Surveillance* (1980); L. H. LaRue, *Political Discourse: A Case Study of the Watergate Affair* (1988); Stanley I. Kutler, *The Wars of Watergate* (1990); and Michael Schudson, *Watergate in American Memory* (1993).

On international issues during Nixon's presidency and the rest of the 1970s, see Paul Sigmund, *The Overthrow of Allende* (1977); John Stockwell, *In Search of Enemies* (1979); Walter LaFeber, *The Panama Canal* (1979); Barry Rubin, *Paved with Good Intentions: The American Experience with Iran* (1980); Franz Shurmann, *The Foreign Politics of Richard Nixon* (1987); Penny Lernoux, *Cry of the People* (1980); Gaddis Smith, *Morality, Reason, and Power: American Diplomacy in the Carter Years* (1986); Raymond Garthoff, *Detente and Confrontation: American Soviet Relations from Nixon to Reagan* (1985); and Garry Sick, *All Fall Down: America's Tragic Encounter with Iran* (1986).

On the political culture of the 1970s, see Peter Caroll, *It Seemed Like Nothing Happened* (1983), a general history of the entire decade; Harry C. Boyte, *The Backyard Revolution* (1980); Thomas Ferguson and Joel Rogers, *The Hidden Election* (1981); Walter Dean Burnham, *The Current Crisis in American Politics* (1982); Martin P. Wattenberg, *The Decline of American Political Parties* (1984); Gillian Peele, *Revival and Reaction: The Right in Contemporary America* (1984); Theodore Lowi, *The Personal President* (1985); Mark E. Kann, *Middle-class Radicalism in Santa Monica* (1986); and Thomas Ferguson and Joel Rogers, *Right Turn: The Decline of the Democrats and the Future of American Politics* (1987).

Betty Glad's *Jimmy Carter* (1980) is highly critical; Carter's own reminiscences are entitled *Keeping Faith* (1982). See also Charles O. Jones, *The Trusteeship Presidency: Jimmy Carter and the United States Congress* (1988); Erwin Hargrove, *Jimmy Carter as President* (1989); Burton J. Kaufman, *The Presidency of James Earl Carter, Jr.* (1993); Herbert D. Rosenbaum and Alexej Ugrinsky, eds., *The Presidency and Domestic Policies of Jimmy Carter* (1994) and *Jimmy Carter: Foreign Policy and Post-presidential Years* (1994).

On the complex issue of the new equality, see Christopher Jencks, *Who Gets Ahead* (1979); Paul Blumberg, *Inequality in an Age of Decline* (1980); Lars Osberg, *Economic Inequality in the United States* (1984); Philip Green, *Retrieving Democracy* (1985); Charles Harr, *Fairness and Justice: Law in the Service of Equality* (1987); Jay MacLeod, *Ain't No Makin' It: Leveled Aspirations in a Low-Income Neighborhood* (1987); Peter L. Berger, *Capitalism and Equality in America* (1987); Nathan Glazer, *Affirmative Discrimination: Ethnic Inequality and Public Policy* (rev. ed., 1987); Kenneth L. Karst, *Belonging to America: Equal Citizenship and the Constitution* (1989); Sara Evans and Barbara J. Nelson, *Wage Justice: Comparable Worth and the Paradox of Technocratic Reform* (1989); Irvin Solomon, *Feminism and Black Activism in Contemporary America* (1989); Karen Hansen and Ilene Philipson, eds., *Women, Class, and the Feminist Imagination* (1990); Iris Marion Young, *Justice and the Politics of Difference* (1990); Martha Minow, *Making All the Difference: Inclusion, Exclusion, and American Law* (1990); and Herbert Hill and James E. Jones, Jr., *Race in America: The Struggle for Equality* (1993).

10

Nostalgia and Nostrums: The United States in the 1980s

In his 1952 novel *Player Piano,* Kurt Vonnegut imagined a government system run by faceless technicians and presided over and made legitimate by a movie-actor president. Media politics, he seemed to predict, would merge with democratic forms until the mythmaking functions of electoral campaigns had wholly separated politics from governance. Less than thirty years later the United States did have a screen star as its chief of state, and Ronald Reagan promised that his presidency would inaugurate a new "conservative" era in American life, comparable to the "liberal" era ushered in by Franklin Roosevelt's New Deal.

Reagan became a skilled political performer; his old screen charm bloomed into a quality that had been lacking during the Nixon, Ford, and Carter years—presidential charisma. After Nixon's perpetual five o'clock shadow, Ford's stumbling, and Carter's furrowed brow, Reagan brought many Americans and the media a welcome change: an easy smile, rugged good looks, quick one-liners. Even frequent misstatements of fact in press conferences, incredible gaffes, and evidence of corruption by close associates failed to dent his image. Reagan, Representative Patricia Schroeder commented, was a "Teflon-coated president"—nothing stuck to him. Reagan instinctively knew how to tap into many popular dreams and national myths; this "great communicator" knew how to use the media. His was a presidency of symbolism, and—in that sense—perhaps did represent a period in American politics in which specific information and coherent ideas were less important than a general, cheerful, reassuring image.

One set of images on which Reagan skillfully drew stemmed from the early days of the cold war. The USSR, he warned, was an "evil empire." Reagan's world was populated by good guys ("freedom fighters") and bad guys (communists, except the Chinese, and "terrorists," a new category of villains that emerged in the 1980s). He depicted his foreign policies with all the subtlety of a child's Saturday morning cartoon show.

In domestic policy, Reagan's symbols, ironically, often contradicted the reality emerging from his policies. He often recalled a folksy, Norman Rockwell-style America of small towns, limited government, hardworking people, and old-fashioned morality. Yet his farm policies brought a rural crisis that threatened to shut down Main Street; he led an attack on labor unions, affirmative action, and assistance to the working poor; and he increased government spending to bring on soaring deficits. Reagan's politics and his appeal largely rested on nostalgia for a small-scale past, but his policies accelerated the giantism that had come to characterize American life in the 1960s and 1970s.

The Reagan years were ones of paradox: While the president's policies encouraged the concentration of power (and thus the feelings of powerlessness) in everyday life, he himself tapped the yearnings for simpler times in which "the people," not government bureaucrats, were in control. It was revealing that after eight years of living in the White House and presiding over rampaging budget deficits, Reagan could still rouse his supporters by denouncing "the big spenders in Washington."

SOCIOPOLITICAL CONFLICT IN THE 1980s

Presidential Politics, 1980–1988

Ronald Reagan promised to take the United States "back to the future." Certainly, he did help rekindle faith in national institutions and capabilities. But even though he dominated the political culture of the 1980s, controversy swirls around the precise nature and legacy of the "Reagan revolution."

Supporters depicted Reagan's successive electoral victories as seminal postwar events. In this view, his 1980 defeat of Jimmy Carter and 1984 drubbing of Walter Mondale, self-proclaimed heir of Hubert Humphrey, signaled the end of the welfare-state liberalism that had been associated with Humphrey, Harry Truman, Lyndon Johnson, and the dominant wing of the Democratic party.

Yet, on closer examination, the idea of any political revolution seems suspect. First, the appeal of welfare-state liberalism had been waning since the late 1960s; except for Social Security, primarily a program for the elderly, most welfare-state initiatives never enjoyed broad or deep support among the electorate. And after government regulations of the late 1960s and early 1970s, such as environmental and consumer protection laws, impinged on business decision making, a corporate-sponsored counterattack began to tap a deep antigovernment sentiment, especially among people who felt pressed by both taxes and inflation.

Though a Democrat, Jimmy Carter had also drawn strength from this backlash and anticipated some of Reagan's anti-Washington stance. When he began running for the White House in 1974, it should be recalled, Carter campaigned as an outsider who would bring small-town virtues and common sense to the wicked national capital. His bid, in fact, drew support from Pat Robertson and Jerry Falwell, prominent members of the Reagan coalition during the 1980s. In some ways, Reagan's domestic stance simply refined and extended Carter's antiestablishment populism.

Mondale's ill-advised attempt to revive the old Democratic vision contributed to Reagan's lopsided 1984 reelection victory. In this sense, the presidential contest of 1984 featured two candidates who looked backward, toward different perspectives of an older, pre-1970 America. Whereas Mondale recalled the welfare liberalism of Humphrey and Johnson, Reagan promised the kind of prosperity and international power associated with Harry Truman, Dwight Eisenhower, and John Kennedy. Against the backdrop of economic recovery, an unprecedented peacetime military buildup, and political apathy, more voters bought Reagan's nostalgic vision than Mondale's.

As both a challenger and an incumbent, Reagan primarily ran as Ronald Reagan and only secondarily as a Republican with a coherent philosophy and concrete program. In 1980, his victory depended on the strong no vote against Jimmy Carter, the highly unpopular incumbent; in 1984, Reagan gained both millions of yes votes for his personal performance and millions of no votes against Mondale, who seemed a decent-enough person but a dull, uninspiring personality. Going against political tradition, Reagan's landslide 1984 victory failed to carry his party; the GOP gained only fourteen seats in the House—remaining the minority party there—and actually lost two seats in the Senate. Finally, claims that the 1984 reelection validated any Reagan agenda must explain why exit polls suggest that 20 percent of those who voted for the president in 1984 had "serious" doubts about his domestic policies and that another 20 percent did not care much about any issues at all.

The peculiar nature of Reagan's support, especially among the New Right, further undercut his power. If the postwar Democratic party splintered over questions of race and culture, the post-1976 Republican party was divided by issues of religion and culture. Activists from the New Right, especially those from fundamentalist and evangelical religious groups with Democratic heritages, lacked deep loyalties to the GOP and, often, even to Reagan himself. With his ties to large corporate interests and his Hollywood background—which privately inclined him to more flexible attitudes on social, cultural, and religious issues such as AIDS and abortion than many of his supporters—Reagan was never the New Right's favorite; he simply seemed the most conservative political figure with the best chance to win the White House. Despite an alliance with the New Right, Reagan's ambiguity on a variety of issues again suggested that he led no mass social or political movement. Some of the most vocal leaders of the New Right, such as North Carolina's

Jesse Helms, continually criticized Reagan's policies as insufficiently conservative, especially on issues such as abortion and prayer in school. On a variety of other questions, Reagan also tested the faith of many of his supporters. What held his political coalition together, apart from his personal charm and tough rhetoric on foreign policy, were the familiar denunciations of welfare-state programs. Repeated calls for "getting government off our backs" and for lowering tax rates carried a broad, somewhat nostalgic, appeal. But when it came to pushing specific proposals through Congress or implementing policy via the federal bureaucracy, the Reagan administration achieved relatively little of the New Right's cultural agenda, and it trimmed, rather than completely dismantled, most domestic social programs. Moreover, from a cultural standpoint, the White House looked more often to the lavish life-styles of Hollywood and corporate board rooms than to the small-town culture of traditional conservatives and the New Right. To the extent that a loosely imagined set of preferences and prejudices amounted to a political and economic program, Reaganism envisioned a high-tech, fast-living, big-corporate style of neocapitalism that seemed fundamentally at odds with the Main Street values of old-style Republicans and the New Right.

Reaganomics: The Boom

Reagan's economic advisers promised to stimulate the most efficient and productive segments of the economy. According to the theory of supply-side economics, government policies should target economic producers, giving them incentives to save and invest, thereby increasing the supply of goods available for consumers and decreasing the inflationary pressures of the 1960s and 1970s. In addition, deregulation of the economy (which actually began in the airline industry during the Carter years) and revision of tax rates (an idea first embraced by the Kennedy administration) became centerpieces of Reaganomics.

Reaganomics initially seemed a disaster as the nation slid into its worst recession since the 1930s. The official unemployment rate soared to nearly 11 percent; industrial output plummeted; businesses, especially family-run farms in the Midwest, failed at alarming rates; the nation's GNP actually declined (or in the language of economics, "grew at a negative rate"); its balance of trade deficit reached record highs as did the federal government's budget shortfall. In the third year of Reagan's presidency, the budget deficit topped the $200 billion mark, and the accumulated national debt broke the trillion-dollar barrier. Although Reagan had promised balanced budgets, his economic advisers downplayed the deficit and other gloomy statistics; they confidently predicted that once inefficient producers had been wrung out of the economy and labor costs had been pushed down, supply-side economics would produce both a recovery and a more competitive economy.

Indeed, by late 1982, the promised "Reagan boom" seemed at hand. Budget deficits remained high, and Congress finally enacted the Gramm-Rudman-Hollings Act of 1985, which tried to legislate automatic budget cuts. But in light of the general economic growth, even many of Reagan's severest critics thought deficits were an issue that should be ignored; balancing budgets could mean a return to recession just when recovery was underway. Deficits, after all, provided economic stimulation and helped avert hard choices about spending priorities.

Most economic indicators improved dramatically during the mid-1980s. By 1987 the Dow Jones Industrial Average stood at more than 2,700, an all-time high. Even the "Black Monday" crash of October 19, 1987, which saw the Dow Jones set another record by plummeting 508 points in a single day, failed to dampen either general confidence in the Reagan boom or the stock market; economic expansion continued, and Wall Street fought back from Black Monday. By the end of Reagan's presidency the Dow Jones average again topped the 2,700 level.

Pundits created a new symbol for the success of Reaganomics: *Newsweek* dubbed 1984 the Year of the Yuppies—young, upwardly mobile, urban professionals who, supposedly, had been hippies during the 1960s. Allegedly marking the end of that decade's idealism, these aging baby boomers were represented, especially in films such as *The Big Chill* and *Wall Street*, as consumption-hungry profit maximizers, crass materialists with no time for moral and social issues. In addition to seeking a career in the fast lane, the stereotyped Yuppies focused on health spas, cholesterol levels, foreign-car dealerships, fern bars, trendy restaurants, and clothing boutiques. And as part of their general ethic of "wanting it all," according to one canard, calculating Yuppies even sweated themselves into shape for eating; in this way, they could enjoy the best in wine and food without having to suffer the usual drawbacks.

Advertisers certainly believed in the Yuppie. Racks of new "life-style" magazines featured vacation, decorating, fashion, and cooking tips for the upwardly mobile. Even Yuppie children became targets, as Saturday morning TV schedules aggressively pushed such products as Gobots and Transformers, disguised as cartoon shows. Just as suburbanites had once symbolized the affluent culture of the 1950s, the Yuppie became a central symbol of Reaganomics: At their 1988 National Convention, Democrats were encouraged to express contempt for eight years of Reagan by buying buttons that said, "Die Yuppie Scum."

The Reagan era also brought a new culture of extravagance (rather than one of mere Yuppie affluence). How could the very wealthy, who basked in the glow of Reaganism, hope to burn off their extra money? The media offered role models. "Lifestyles of the Rich and Famous" showed TV viewers how movie stars and corporate moguls lived in elegance. A young business tycoon from New York City became both an omnipresent media celebrity and a consumer product himself; an office tower, a gambling casino, an airline, an apartment palace, an autobiography, and even a board game all carried the name of Donald Trump. Malcom Forbes, publisher of the financial magazine bearing his name, rivaled Trump, especially when he motorcycled with Hollywood stars; threw a multimillion-dollar birthday bash for himself in Morocco; and published *Forbes'* annual tally of the nation's richest 400 individuals, a counterpart to *Fortune* magazine's more traditional list of the top 500 corporations. Supermarket tabloids splashed the comings and goings of Trump and Forbes across their front pages; being a tycoon again seemed to be in fashion. Many people—not simply Yuppies, the very wealthy, and large corporations—participated. Family-owned businesses thrived: At the end of the 1980s, one-third of the Fortune 500 companies were family-owned, and 60 percent of the nation's GNP was generated by family businesses. The percentage of women working outside their homes steadily increased, and members of ethnic minorities with marketable skills found improving job prospects. Some evidence even suggested that general economic prosperity, as Reagan's supporters had predicted, trickled down and benefited everyone. Celebrants of Reaganomics conceded that this expansion had not been perfect, but they deemed its problems easily manageable.

Reaganomics: The Bitter Legacy

Critics thought otherwise. Labor unions lost much of whatever countervailing clout they once possessed. Reagan's successful 1981 crushing of PATCO, the union representing air traffic controllers, set the tone. New conservative appointees to the National Labor Relations Board (NLRB) gave this national regulatory agency a decidedly antiunion tilt, and the federal courts, constantly restocked with Reagan-nominated judges, also showed little inclination to support organized labor. Meanwhile, the decline of the nation's old industrial infrastructure inevitably eroded the labor movement's traditional base, and organizers made slow progress in unionizing the growing service sector. By 1994, less than 15 percent of U.S. workers belonged to a union. The famed job expansion under Reagan had produced disproportionate numbers of nonunionized, low-paying service jobs.

Critics of Reaganism also worried about the nation's corporate structure. Much of the new wealth of the 1980s, for example, rested on a decade of corporate mergers, many of which were financed by "junk bonds," securities without the kind of backing required of more traditional commercial paper. The junk-bond craze of the 1980s, in fact, barely survived Reagan's presidency. Ivan Boesky, one of the decade's most celebrated merger moguls, plea-bargained a reduced jail term by agreeing to testify against other leading financial figures. Allegations of massive fraud, including insider stock market trading, rocked the entire merger-mania culture. And in 1990, the giant financial institution of Drexel Burnham Lambert—which had specialized in arranging corporate mergers by floating junk bonds—declared bankruptcy.

Meanwhile, the savings-and-loan industry, which had apparently prospered after relaxation of government regulation in the early 1980s, also barely staggered into the 1990s. Many S&Ls overindulged on junk bonds and high-risk real estate schemes; others squandered money in old-fashioned ways, such as fancy living by owners and top management. Whatever an institution's particular poison, the entire industry—and the taxpayers who had to rescue it—faced tough times. According to one estimate, the government bailout plan for S&Ls, hastily enacted in 1989, threatened to cost the average taxpayer $3,000 over the course of the 1990s.

The Politics of the 1980s in Everyday Life

Insolvency was not simply a problem for the savings-and-loan industry. During the 1980s, corporations, family businesses, and private citizens all came to depend more heavily than ever before on borrowed money; businesses relied on complex debt-restructuring deals, and ordinary consumers counted on their credit cards. The explosion of credit allowed Americans to run up record levels of personal indebtedness. In the 1970s, the average citizen spent 65 percent of his or her income, after purchasing necessities, on paying the interest charges on borrowed money; by the end of the 1980s, the comparable figure going to debt service reached 90 percent! Bankruptcy proceedings, not surprisingly, also soared; ordinary people and former wheeler-dealers, such as the flamboyant Texan John Connally, had to concede that their personal boom had ended.

Ronald Reagan's presidency built upon his image as a movie hero, particularly playing upon western themes.
Source: National Archives.

Moreover, even the everyday life of the fabled Yuppie was not all fern bars and BMWs. Free-spending Yuppies undoubtedly existed, but they hardly represented the way of life of most baby boomers or young professionals. Less than 5 percent of the baby-boom generation earned enough—or could borrow enough—to live affluently; more than half of the baby boomers actually made under $20,000 a year. Even for young professionals on the rise, everyday life meant long work schedules and complex juggling of family responsibilities. According to one analysis, many young professionals suffered from deep fears about whether or not they could continue to prosper and from nagging insecurities about whether or not their sacrifices were even justified. Such pressures and doubts bore down especially hard on women who worked in male-dominated professions. The use of the term *Yuppie* as an epithet, one suspects, was sometimes employed to disparage and discourage young women who were struggling to follow nontraditional career paths.

Considerable evidence suggests that many young professionals, especially women, never held the political conservative values widely attributed to Yuppies. Although immersed in private issues, such as raising families and finding meaningful work, young professionals also worried about social questions such as abortion, day-care services, foreign policy, and the environment. And on issues such as government support for day care, comparable pay for women, and aid to the contras, opinion studies suggested that so-called Yuppies seemed no more, and probably less, inclined toward conservative positions than other people.

While most young professionals found upward mobility difficult, many other people found their economic status stagnating or slipping during the 1980s. Although severe inflationary pressures subsided, the average worker's take-home pay, according to Labor Department statistics, actually declined slightly during the Reagan boom. Between 1978 and 1988 the average wage rose to over $9 per hour, but when adjusted for inflation it slipped against the real cost of living. Women's wages continued to lag behind those of men, wages of people of color behind those of whites. As a consequence of dominant wage structures, many young working-class people, even families with two incomes, could not enter the home-buying market; for the first time since World War II, the percentage of people owning their homes began to drop.

The 1980s also saw significant transfers of wealth toward the already wealthy. According to careful studies of pretax income shares, between 1980 and 1985 the annual income portion going to the richest 20 percent of the population increased by about $44 billion, whereas the remaining 80 percent saw their share decrease by about the same amount. At the end of the 1980s, even the staunchly conservative *Business Week* magazine marked the growing income gap and shrinking middle class as a potentially serious national problem.

Many forces contributed to the growing inequality in income distribution. The flood of the young, baby-boom generation into the work force, together with the rising percentage of working women, swelled demand for entry-level jobs, even at lower wages. But critics could also assign at least part of the blame to Reaganomics. Reductions in tax rates, for instance, primarily benefited the top-income levels; according to one study, the wealthiest 1 percent of the population watched their taxes decrease by 25 percent during the 1980s, whereas those in the bottom 40 percent saw virtually no tax relief.

Similarly, cutbacks and spending reductions for social programs, part of the effort to "get government off people's backs," took their toll. Programs for public employment and job training, which had never been extensive, were trimmed back in the 1980s. And the disappearance of jobs in the declining industrial-manufacturing sector meant that many people, newcomers as well as workers who had been laid off, lacked the special knowledge and credentials to compete for high-paying jobs in other areas. In the early 1970s, for example, young workers with a high-school diploma still earned 86 percent of what the college-educated received; by the late 1980s, the percentage had dropped to about 65 percent.

The ethnic dimensions of this disparity were heightened by the declining number of African-American and Latino children, raised in middle- and low-income families, who were enrolled in college. At a time when high school completion rates were increasing, the percentage of low-income African-Americans who went on to college dropped by nearly 10 percent during the early and mid-1980s; the comparable figure for Latinos fell by about 7 percent. After 1986, data showed an increase in the total number of African-Americans enrolled in colleges and universities, a figure that largely reflected increased enrollment by middle-class students at private institutions. Meanwhile, college-completion rates for other ethnic groups, especially Asian-Americans, rose during the entire decade.

Social Issues of the 1980s

Variously labeled as the "underclass," the "truly disadvantaged," and the "persistently poor," millions of people could only glimpse the Reagan boom from afar. Throughout the decade, city streets filled with the homeless. Some suffered either from drug dependency or mental disorders—deinstitutionalization of the mentally impaired, a "reform" of the 1970s, often substituted bus and subway stations for state hospitals. But many others, including entire families, had simply been pushed out of the job or housing markets into the streets and into temporary shelters. Of the more than 30 million people officially classified as poor, more than one-third, 13 million, were children; nearly a half million children were estimated to be among the homeless.

Although homeless people became a familiar part of urban streets, the 1980s also recalled earlier observations about the invisibility of poverty-related problems in an affluent society. Only some spectacular event, such as the March 1990 fire in which eighty-seven Caribbean and Latin American residents of New York City perished at an unlicensed social club, seemed to focus the mainstream media's attention on everyday social and economic issues. In contrast to media stereotypes, for example, many low-income people did not live in identifiable, poverty-dominated ghettoes but could be found scattered throughout different communities, the most segregated of which were defined by ethnicity or by age. Similarly, nostalgic stereotypes of rural life continued to conceal harsh realities. Although the worst of the rural problems— farm foreclosures, bank failures, and personal despair—were receding toward the end of the 1980s, the fact that many farm families relied on food stamps and surplus commodities remained one of the grim ironies of the decade.

Both scholarly studies and muckraking magazines told even bleaker stories. A general twenty-year follow-up to the Kerner Commission Report, entitled *Quiet Riots*, charged that "unemployment, poverty, social disorganization, segregation, family disintegration, housing and school deterioration, and crime" were greater problems in 1988 than they had been in 1968. Welfare benefits, which had risen during the 1960s and early 1970s, leveled off and then declined; when adjusted for inflation, the average welfare recipient suffered a cut of about 25 percent in the value of payments and food stamps during the 1980s.

The quality of social services aimed at low-income people also dropped. One specialized study, which tracked African-American men during the early 1980s (before AIDS and crack cocaine presumably made life much worse), found that "black men in Harlem were less likely to reach the age of 65 than men in Bangladesh," one of the poorest countries in the world. The nation's infant mortality rate remained higher than in any other industrial country, and New York City's rate (which had been declining in the 1960s and 1970s) actually rose during the 1980s, an increase that public-health experts attributed to inadequate health- and social-service facilities and to soaring crack use among women.

The feminization of poverty was another trend of the 1980s. According to some studies, one-half of people living in poverty also lived in families headed by women. Whereas studies by conservative social scientists, especially Charles Murray's *Losing Ground* (1984), blamed the welfare system, particularly AFDC (Aid to Families with Dependent Children) payments, for encouraging women to stay on welfare rather than to look for work, other analyses highlighted structural and psychological explanations. The absence of both well-paying entry-level jobs and positive role models made reliance on declining welfare payments seem to be many poor women's best alternative. As one mother who wanted employment explained, "I get so nervous and scared going out looking for a job . . . I never know how to talk." And welfare, unlike most low-wage jobs, provided coverage of basic health-care needs, an essential consideration especially for women with small children.

People across the political spectrum agreed that the welfare system needed reform so that it did not perpetuate women's poverty and dependency but could, instead, assist women in gaining employment skills. The Family Support Act, passed in 1988, required states to implement some form of "workfare," new employment requirements for women on welfare. At best, workfare reforms might assist women in attaining job skills and make provision for child-care and health-care needs. At worst, workfare might become another program that stigmatized its participants as lazy or "bad." Dominant

286   *Nostalgia and Nostrums: The United States in the 1980s*

cultural institutions sent women very mixed messages: The "good" mother, so many cultural images still implied, stayed home with her young children. Clearly a major challenge for those favoring welfare reform involved designing work requirements that were not punitive but constructively geared to promoting greater self-sufficiency. Questions about how social and employment policies should deal with gender issues received relatively little attention in either public-policy or mass-mediated discussions.

Controversies over Drugs, AIDS, and Abortion

Some social issues received extensive media attention. Both Ronald Reagan and his successor, George Bush, pledged all-out wars against drug dealers and drug use. Nancy Reagan headed a much-publicized but largely ineffectual campaign to get potential drug users to "Just Say No." Bush appointed tough-talking William Bennett, who had been Reagan's spokesperson on higher education, as a "drug czar" and charged him with stopping the flow of illegal drugs into the country and confronting the violent gangs that distributed them. Yet only a few blocks from the White House, drug dealers continued to peddle their wares, relatively free from official interdiction of any kind; no community, including small towns and wealthy suburbs, escaped drug dealers and problems of substance abuse.

Similarly, rich and poor alike faced a deadly new threat—AIDS. Acquired immune deficiency syndrome actually designated several types of invariably fatal viruses that were usually sexually transmitted. Throughout the decade, both the unknown and the celebrated died from AIDS; Hollywood's Rock Hudson, "Gunsmoke's" Amanda Blake (Miss Kitty), the old right's Roy Cohn, the New Right's Terry Dolan, and the fashion world's Ralph Halston were a few of the prominent people who succumbed.

Everything about AIDS seemed controversial. Initially, the disease primarily affected homosexual males, and this inclined socially conservative public officials to downplay efforts to fight, or even to publicize, its spread. Similarly, the association of AIDS with people from Africa and the Caribbean encouraged both misinformation and prejudice. Even scientists pursuing a cure became embroiled in nasty disputes over how AIDS was spread, which people were at greatest risk, and what team of scientists deserved the credit (and the money) for isolating its probable viral source. Meanwhile, activists complained that Washington was moving far too slowly to develop and license drugs that promised at least some relief from the ravages of AIDS.

Faced with intransigence and delay, gay and lesbian activists mounted self-help measures. Charging the Reagan administration with kowtowing to the New Right, by initially dismissing AIDS as a "special-interest" issue, gay leaders urged "safe sex" and monogamous relationships. Homosexuals continued, however, to oppose the kinds of sexual strictures favored by the New Right. Although right-wing libertarians opposed any government interference with gay and lesbian life-styles, most religious conservatives denounced homosexuality as sinful and urged criminal penalties, a stance that received the blessing of the U.S. Supreme Court in *Bowers* v. *Hardwick.* Reagan's own Surgeon General C. Everett Koop enraged the New Right by acknowledging the reality of sexual relationships outside the bounds of heterosexual marriages and promoting condoms as sensible precautions against the spread of sexually transmitted diseases.

The politics of AIDS was overshadowed by the furor over abortion. Here, New Right activists continued to preach a simple message: The government must say no to abortions, except in special cases such as rape, incest, or some life-threatening danger to a pregnant woman. Although opinion polls suggested that most people favored legal abortions in other circumstances, the antiabortion forces pressed their case through both direct action, including the kind of civil disobedience pioneered by the civil rights movement of the 1950s and 1960s, and more conventional political activities.

The antiabortion, or "prolife," coalition increasingly hoped that the Supreme Court would overturn the 1973 *Roe* v. *Wade* decision. In the fall of 1987, "prochoice" forces joined with civil liberties groups in successfully blocking Reagan's nomination to the Court of Robert H. Bork, an outspoken opponent of liberal activism by the Court. By a 58–42 margin, the Senate rejected the nomination of Bork, who many expected would provide the crucial vote needed to overturn *Roe* v. *Wade.* Anthony Kennedy, a quiet Californian who was probably more of a Reagan-style conservative than Bork, was finally confirmed.

Justice Kennedy did, in fact, provide a key antiabortion vote in the *Webster* case, a 1989 decision that further politicized the abortion issue. Here, by a 5–4 margin, the Supreme Court upheld a Missouri statute that severely limited women's access to legal abortions, thus opening the door for further state restrictions. But Justice Sandra Day O'Connor, another Reagan appointee, refused to join the four-justice bloc ready to overturn *Roe* v. *Wade.* As a result, both prochoice and prolife forces mobilized, all across the country and even in U.S. territories such as Guam, for state-by-state legislative and court battles over the abortion issue. Groups associated with the New Right, such as Operation Rescue, organized sit-ins outside of abortion clinics and picketed the offices and private homes of physicians who staffed them. Meanwhile, gaining access to safe and legal abortions became more difficult than it had been in several decades.

THE NEW COLD WAR

During the campaign of 1980, Ronald Reagan portrayed Jimmy Carter as a weak leader presiding over the erosion of American power abroad. Reagan promised to restore respect for the United States by aggressively confronting the Soviet's "evil empire" in every part of the world. Returning to the rhetoric and assumptions of the cold war and portraying the world as simply a bipolar battleground between the forces of good and evil, Reagan's early foreign policy stressed unilateralism, militarism, and crusading anticommunism. During his first term, the president launched a military buildup, abandoned detente with the Soviets, dragged his feet on arms-control negotiations, installed new missiles throughout Europe, pulled out of the UN Educational, Scientific, and Cultural Organization (UNESCO), beefed up the CIA, sent troops to Lebanon and Grenada, funded a mercenary army to fight the Marxist government of Nicaragra, and publicly provided covert funds for anti-Marxist troops in Angola and Afghanistan. Reagan seemed to tap a desire, after the nation's defeat in Vietnam, to assert American power aggressively and globally.

A massive military buildup, unprecedented in peacetime, became the dominant feature of the Reagan presidency. Huge new expenditures, accompanied as they were by tax cuts, tripled the national debt, increased the government's share of the GNP to over 25 percent, and transformed the United States from the world's principal creditor into its largest debtor. Critics charged that such large deficits undermined the nation's economic health, but Reagan requested deeper and deeper cuts in domestic social programs to alleviate the deficits. He refused to acknowledge what his first budget director, David Stockman, discovered: that reduction of social spending could never come close to bridging the tremendous gap between the military buildup and tax cuts.

In Reagan's vision, activism by the federal government was appropriate in the area of military protection, not in social welfare. The "Reagan revolution," which the president aspired to implant deeply in American life, required curtailing the government's domestic regulatory and welfare functions while expanding and managing its national security sector. The administration aimed at enlarging both nuclear and conventional capacity. It ordered more of the highly controversial MX missiles and B-1 bombers and enlarged its force of Trident submarines. Over grass-roots protests throughout Europe, America's NATO allies agreed to deploy American-made Pershing II and cruise missiles in Western Europe. Billions of dollars went into the military payroll and for modernization of equipment and bases. Congressional investigations also revealed gross abuses and mismanagement in the military-industrial sector: They found both massive (and sometimes deliberate) cost overruns by large contractors and small-time price gouging, including cases in which suppliers charged the Pentagon hundreds of dollars for common, inexpensive hardware-store items.

During his first term, Reagan used arms-control talks primarily to help fuel this defense buildup. As a candidate, Reagan condemned Carter's SALT II accords, which Congress never ratified but which both the United States and the USSR unofficially observed. As president, he opened new negotiations, which he relabeled START (Strategic Arms Reduction Talks), and then argued that only enlarged military budgets and an arms buildup could produce successful negotiations. But arms control proved politically popular at home, and a rapidly growing movement, which urged a freeze on nuclear weapons, blasted the administration for its apparent opposition to slowing the arms race.

Carrying military competition to outer space became the most important—and most controversial—part of Reagan's military agenda. In 1984, after several private meetings with Dr. Edward Teller, the "father of the H-bomb," Reagan surprised even close advisers by proposing a Strategic Defense Initiative (SDI), a space-based system that would supposedly shield the United States from incoming warheads. Widely called "Star Wars," SDI would theoretically provide more protection than the traditional policy of deterrence through "mutual assured destruction" (MAD).

Controversy over SDI mounted as scientists and politicians calculated its staggering costs (perhaps a trillion dollars!) and weighed its practicality. Many scientists warned that the computer software to operate a comprehensive space defense could never be made reliable. The dependability of advanced space technology became an even larger issue after the spring of 1986, when the space shuttle *Challenger*—whose mid-morning launch enjoyed well-publicized, live television coverage—exploded in midair, killing all seven of its crew. Moreover, some strategic analysts pointed out that a missile defense system would only prompt the other side to build more technologically elaborate missiles, thereby greatly escalating the arms race without improving national security. SDI divided the scientific community; some scientists pledged to accept no contracts for government work on SDI, whereas others welcomed the new pipeline of lucrative contracts. Though incredibly costly and probably impractical, the SDI proposal became a major obstacle to arms-reduction agreements with the Soviets and dominated foreign-policy and budget debates for several years. SDI was gradually scrapped after Reagan left office.

The militancy with which the Reagan administration pursued its new cold war policies intensified conflicts in the Middle East, Africa, and Latin America. In these areas, historic racial, ethnic, and religious divisions, as well as economic hardship associated with the foreign-debt crisis, underlay political turmoil. In many ways, though, the USSR was itself increasingly beleaguered: It was bogged down in a brutal, unpopular, and costly war in Afghanistan; it was challenged by the popularity of Poland's anti-Soviet Solidarity movement; it was saddled with the expensive aid still being supplied to Cuba; and it was straining to maintain its superpower status on the basis of a staggering, stagnant economy. Still, Reagan's hard-line advisers formulated policy through a prism in which every setback for U.S. influence meant an advance for the Soviets. Reagan's picture of the Soviet Union as a nation making aggressive gains worldwide provided the backdrop for assertive, militaristic policies by the United States.

In Lebanon the Reagan administration first showed its readiness to deploy military power. In 1982, Israeli forces invaded Lebanon to destroy and disperse the Palestine Liberation Organization (PLO). Lebanese Moslems, allied with Syria and backed by the Soviet Union, fought both the Lebanese Christians and the Israeli occupiers. After arranging Israeli withdrawal, the Reagan administration dispatched 1,600 American troops as part of a multinational force. But Moslem fighters renewed the struggle, now against troops from the United States. After 241 American troops were killed by a suicide commando mission in October 1983, domestic criticism of Reagan's Lebanese policy mounted. American military presence had aggravated, not lessened, violence and factionalism in Lebanon. Early in 1984, an election year, American troops withdrew, and Syria consolidated its influence over Lebanon. The Reagan administration's plan to limit Syrian gains and stabilize Lebanon through military power had failed.

Moreover, the perception among many Arabs that America's policy in the Middle East was almost identical to Israel's brought additional problems. Some Palestinian groups, fragmented and further radicalized after their expulsion from Lebanon, stepped up the use of terrorism and found support in Libyan leader Muammar Qaddafi. As Qaddafi railed against Zionism and the United States, Reagan denounced the Libyan leader as a terrorist and a "flake." In the spring of 1986 Reagan ordered the bombing of Libya, as part of a broader plan to eliminate Qaddafi from the scene. Bombs did considerable damage and killed Qaddafi's daughter, but his government survived. In the meantime, negotiations to end the spiraling bloodshed among Israel and its neighbors—by moving toward some resolution on the Palestinian problem—stalled.

Violence elsewhere in the Middle East mounted, as Iran and Iraq engaged in a prolonged and devastating war, and militant Islamic groups seized a number of hostages from Western countries they viewed as enemies. Publicly Reagan said he would not negotiate for the hostages' release for fear of encouraging more kidnappings. Secretly, however, the administration began to arrange a deal to sell arms to Iran in return for hostages.

Meanwhile, the president's advisers found easier, less risky places to assert military power. In counterpoint to the unsuccessful application of force in Lebanon, Reagan raised his ratings in opinion polls by invading the tiny Caribbean island of Grenada in October 1983. Justified as necessary to safeguard American medical students, who were allegedly endangered by a leftist, revolutionary regime, the invasion really aimed at overthrowing an unfriendly government that looked to Castro's Cuba for inspiration and material support. The task was quickly accomplished, though later assessments by military specialists uncovered major flaws in the Grenada invasion; only a Pentagon-imposed blackout on news coverage delayed reports of unnecessary casualties, bungled intelligence gathering, and uncoordinated battle strategies. But Reagan's popularity soared. Many people seemed eager to forgive the Lebanese fiasco and to bask in what the administration proclaimed as a clear-cut military success closer to home.

In Africa, Reagan's anticommunist crusade brought a stepped-up commitment to rebels seeking to overthrow the Marxist government in Angola and a more sympathetic policy toward white leaders in South Africa. The Reagan administration sided with the South African government in denouncing the African National Congress (ANC) as communists, even though it was the oldest black political organization in South Africa and enjoyed widespread support internationally and within the black community at home. Reagan's assistant secretary of state for African affairs labeled his South African policy "constructive engagement," arguing that American support for the white South African government would promote change in its racial policies faster than punitive measures.

Constructive engagement brought the administration into growing conflict with many black African leaders and sparked mounting dissatisfaction at home. South African Anglican Bishop Desmond Tutu, winner of the Nobel Peace Prize in 1984, charged that Reagan's sympathy toward white South Africans significantly worsened the situation for blacks and called for a change. Meanwhile, grass-roots street protests throughout the United States, smaller-scale versions of the civil rights and antiwar protests of the 1960s, pushed Congress and then the president into adopting some limited economic sanctions against South Africa. In 1985 an executive order curtailed loans to the South African government, prohibited importation of South African gold coins, banned most transfers of nuclear technology, and forbade export of some computers.

The Reagan administration centered its anticommunist crusade on Nicaragua. Determined to oust Nicaragua's Sandinista government—because of its Marxist leanings, its pro-Cuban stance, and its desire to shed historical dependence on the United States—Reagan's Latin American policy experts employed the by now classic techniques of covert action. An economic offensive induced shortages and discontent; a propaganda campaign portrayed the Nicaraguan government as nothing but a Soviet or Cuban client; and support and training for a counterrevolutionary army, called the contras, kept the Nicaraguan government under siege. Meanwhile, the United States expanded its military presence in neighboring Honduras and conducted ominous, massive "training exercises" throughout the Caribbean, clearly threatening invasion of Nicaragua.

Congressional opposition and adverse public opinion, however, restrained the president. Domestic opposition to the Reagan administration's campaign to overthrow the Nicaraguan government intensified after revelations that the United States had mined Nicaraguan harbors (technically an act of war) without congressional assent. And the United States suffered a blow to its international prestige when the World Court confirmed Nicaragua's charges that American aggression violated international codes of conduct. (The Reagan administration denied that the court had any jurisdiction in the matter.) In 1984 Congress cut off military (though not humanitarian) aid to the contras, after considering the mounting evidence of their terrorist tactics and corruption.

Undeterred, Reagan's policymakers redoubled their efforts. They stepped up economic destabilization measures against Nicaragua and secretly pressed foreign governments and ultraconservative millionaires to fund the contras' military efforts. In 1986 the fund-raising effort took a bizarre turn: Lieutenant Colonel Oliver North, an aide in the office of the national security adviser who was directing the secret fund-raising and arms-supplying effort to the contras, offered to sell weapons to Iran in exchange both for the release of

American hostages in the Middle East and to gain funds that could be then diverted to the contras. The head of the CIA, the national security adviser, and other top officials apparently knew of the scheme. Oddly, it was Reagan's close adviser and attorney general, Edwin Meese, who at a news conference inadvertently revealed the peculiar connection between North's Iran and contra projects.

When news of the Iran-contra scandal hit the front pages, Reagan's Watergate seemed at hand. (The media dubbed it "Irangate.") For a variety of reasons, the revelations of the affair, gradually emerging in televised congressional hearings during the summer of 1987, deeply discredited Reagan's foreign policy. First, North's plan violated the spirit of the congressional ban against military aid to the contras. Second, it contradicted Reagan's strong public stands both against negotiating with terrorists for hostages and against giving Iran military assistance in its ongoing war with Iraq. The Reagan administration was carrying out policies directly contrary to its public posture. Third, the whole approach to foreign policy raised serious questions about presidential leadership. As details of the scandal emerged, the president first seemed to deny knowledge of the deals but then accepted responsibility without seeming to comprehend the legal ramifications and policy contradictions.

The image of Reagan's presidency suffered from the Iran-contra scandal. Throughout lengthy investigations—by Congress, by a presidential panel, and by a special prosecutor—the public increasingly glimpsed an administration that was fragmented, excessively secretive, and even lawless. North and National Security Adviser John Poindexter, among a number of others, were convicted on criminal charges related to the affair. (They were later pardoned in the closing days of the Bush administration.) The former movie star turned Teflon president suddenly looked old, confused, and barely in charge. More and more people questioned the wisdom of his policies.

Sudden Thaw

During the last year and a half of the Reagan presidency, the new cold war, which the president had stoked with inflamed rhetoric and hard-line policies, suddenly thawed. In a dramatic irony, the Reagan presidency reversed course and took unprecedented steps toward detente.

In 1987, the administration that had launched the biggest military buildup in history signed a major arms-control treaty. A year earlier, at a summit conference in Reykjavik, Iceland, the first summit of the Reagan presidency, the Soviets had advanced the surprising proposal that both countries cut their nuclear weapons by half. Negotiations over such dramatic cuts, however, had stalled over the issue of SDI, Reagan's pet project that the Soviets wanted to end. Finally, in December 1987 a treaty reducing intermediate-range missile forces (IMF) was approved at a summit held in Washington, D.C. The IMF only slightly altered overall strategic balances, but the agreement was unprecedented in its political and symbolic significance. Both sides agreed to eliminate short- and medium-range missiles from Europe (including those that the early Reagan administration had pushed so hard to install) and approved on-site verification procedures, safeguards the Soviets had previously resisted. IMF signaled a major shift away from the arms race of the cold war. What triggered this sudden thaw? For both countries, the reasons were much the same: grass-roots pressure to redirect government priorities; top leaders who began to take a more pragmatic, less ideological, approach to policy; and urgent domestic economic problems.

In the United States during 1987, several trends jolted the Reagan administration into its foreign-policy reorientation. Grass-roots concern over nuclear weapons had grown rapidly, and politicians were becoming increasingly sensitive to popular fears about superpower conflict. As foreign-policy anxieties mounted, the Irangate scandal dramatized the excesses of secret government and the dangers of a heavily ideological, do-anything-necessary attitude.

Moreover, new advisers gained Reagan's ear. By the end of 1987, many of the officials who had shaped policy in the early Reagan years—among them William Casey in the CIA, Caspar Weinberger and Richard Perle at the Defense Department, John Poindexter and Oliver North in the office of the national security adviser—were no longer in the administration. New appointees, such as Howard Baker and Frank Carlucci, were less committed to anticommunist crusades and less beholden to the ultra-right wing of the Republican party, which had been so influential in the early Reagan years.

Perhaps most important, economic problems got the attention of business and policy elites and shook public confidence in Reagan's defense budget. Nearly everyone agreed that both the yawning budget deficit and the adverse balance of trade could portend a national security threat greater than communism: the threat of long-term economic decline. Academic publications and the public press trumpeted dire warnings about the end of the "American age." A scholarly history book, *Rise and Fall of the Great Powers* by Paul Kennedy, shot to the top of the best-seller list and helped popularize the theory of "imperial overreach." Historically, wrote Kennedy, heavy military spending had caused the decay of powerful nations, and this seemed to be the fate awaiting the United States in the late twentieth century. The *New York Times Magazine*, in an issue that featured Paul Kennedy and other prophets of America's decline, pictured the United States as an aged, balding eagle, supported by a cane. Such economic worries, combined with the Democratic victories in the 1986 elections, eroded congressional support for such weapons systems as SDI, allowing the Soviets to negotiate arms limitation without insisting on formal assurances of SDI's termination. As the public and policy elites became increasingly concerned over the deficit and trade balance, support for detente and arms control became more evident.

Changes in the Soviet Union also set the context for reduced tensions. Mikhail Gorbachev came to power in the USSR as part of a younger generation committed to major structural transformations in the communist system. Announcing policies of *glasnost* (a more open society) and *perestroika* (economic restructuring and liberalization) at home, Gorbachev also championed arms control and detente abroad. His initiatives brought him sympathetic coverage from the world press. As the image of "Gorby" as a forward-looking international leader blossomed, the Reagan administration seemed more and more a captive of the old and dangerous cold war thinking.

Gorbachev, of course, was as much the result of changes in the Soviet Union as their cause. By the late 1980s, the Soviet economy was in chaos, environmental damage was alarming, and the system simply could no longer afford the expense of maintaining the cold war and managing an increasingly restive empire. In Eastern Europe, deteriorating economic conditions and the advancing age of the Soviet-allied leadership portended a coming crisis for communist regimes. The Soviet's attempt to impose a client government on Afghanistan proved so costly and unpopular that Gorbachev finally withdrew Soviet troops, and the USSR's other international commitments also came under reconsideration. Moreover, Gorbachev and his reformist advisers realized that the economic integration of Western Europe, projected for 1992, would leave the Soviet Union and its communist allies falling further and further behind in economic development. Restructuring (glasnost and perestroika) needed to begin immediately, or the USSR's economic and imperial decline might be irreversible.

Leaders in both the United States and the Soviet Union finally acknowledged that the world was not bipolar. The robust economies in Japan and Germany, the projected integration of Western Europe, and rapid development in Pacific rim areas such as Korea and Southeast Asia began to reshape geopolitical and strategic thinking. The idea of a U.S.–Soviet cold war became an outmoded construct in a rapidly changing world order; and domestic and foreign policies had to be adjusted. Governments seemed to chase transformations as much as they led them.

THE CULTURE OF THE 1980s

The Culture of Nostalgia

Culture remained an arena for political and social battles during the 1980s. Nostalgia for products and images from the 1940s, 1950s, and early 1960s—a trend commonly associated with Reaganism—dominated mass culture. The popular board game Trivial Pursuit rewarded players for remembering the kind of shirts worn by the Beach Boys or the name of Ann Margret's first motion picture; a special set of questions for baby boomers focused entirely on cold war nostalgia. Meanwhile, two of the decade's most popular new TV programs, "Family Ties" and "The Cosby Show," offered updated versions of the family sitcom of the 1950s.

The major TV networks reprised the past. Programs with innovative story lines and production techniques, such as "The Lou Grant Show" and "Hill Street Blues," received cancellation notices or retreated to safer formats. The hottest "new" network products of the early and mid-1980s, prime-time soap operas such as "Dallas" and "Dynasty," merely adapted a familiar daytime format to nighttime viewing. By the 1990s, programmers for the three major networks seemed to be running out of both ideas and viewers, as surveys showed people turning to their own VCRs or cable television.

Cable television itself relied heavily on familiar formats. ESPN, for example, initially pioneered all-sports programming by introducing viewers to unfamiliar TV fare, such as Australian-rules football and table tennis; but by 1990, ESPN largely beamed a steady diet of boxing, football, baseball, and basketball. The premium cable channels, such as HBO and Showtime, did underwrite some original productions, and Nickelodeon developed new programs for children. But even these channels primarily reran older products, drawn from television and Hollywood, to fill their time slots. "Leave It to Beaver," "I Love Lucy," "Father Knows Best," and other black-and-white artifacts from the 1950s became cable-TV staples. Similarly, Ted Turner's new cable channel, TNT, drew on his company's vast holdings of Hollywood films.

Meanwhile, back in Hollywood, classical motion picture genres, which had begun their comeback in the late 1970s, continued to thrive. George Lucas and Steven Spielberg, blockbuster filmmakers who had been raised on television and the film fare of the 1950s, lovingly recalled their youth with expensive epics about monsters, rock-and-roll, alien empires, and powerful heroes. In two of the three *Indiana Jones* thrillers, the Lucas-Spielberg hero even fought those most familiar of cinema villains, Adolf Hitler's Nazis.

Nostalgia meant big business for male heroics. Sylvester Stallone's Rocky, a club-fighting journeyman in his film debut, went upscale in the 1980s, eventually winning the heavyweight championship; by *Rocky IV*, he even joined Ronald Reagan's fight against the "evil empire" and battled a communist superman—right on Soviet soil. Stallone's simplistic patriotism also garnered huge box-office revenues in his cycle of *Rambo* films, violence-filled epics featuring an embittered Vietnam vet. Though Stallone himself had missed the real Vietnam, his Nautilus-tuned character announced that defeat in Indochina—which *Rambo's* version of history attributed to journalists and cowardly politicians—could be avenged by a properly motivated, unencumbered superhero. Rambo joined an entire platoon of heavily muscled, tight-lipped vigilantes who created so much celluloid havoc that Hollywood devised a whole new rating category, NC-17, for films in which macho avengers violently blasted their villains.

With the increase in movie mayhem, women's roles generally fared badly. Although pictures aimed at specialized audiences (such as John Sayles's *Liana* and Yvonne Ranier's *The Man Who Envied Women*) might feature strong female characters and feminist themes, major distributors considered "women's films" risky ventures. Hollywood's moguls preferred women who stood by their men and stood up for traditional values, as they did in *Tender Mercies* and *Country*. Women who stepped out of narrowly drawn gender lines risked becoming the butt of cruel jokes—or worse. An antifeminist backlash was unmistakable in the new genre of "slasher" films: Women were not only sex objects but also potential victims for sadistic knife-and-chain-saw artists. Mainstream films were not exempt. Box-office successes such as *Jagged Edge* and *Fatal Attraction* carried strongly antifeminist undercurrents; similarly, the blockbuster *Batman* featured the casual brutalization of women by Jack Nicholson's antihero, the Joker.

Successful, mass-market films that touched on women's liberation generally soft-pedaled their messages. The highly publicized *Lives and Loves of a She-Devil*, though adopted from a celebrated feminist novel and featuring two strong women stars (Meryl Streep and Rosanne Arnold), attracted sparse audiences. In contrast, Jane Fonda's popular *9 to 5* leavened its feminist politics with fantastical and slapstick humor. *Tootsie*, in some ways the most successful "feminist" film hit of the 1980s, cast Dustin Hoffman in the picture's title "female" role.

Much, though certainly not all, popular music also revolved around nostalgia and male fantasies. All across the country, radio stations switched to "oldies" formulas; in larger markets, every decade from the 1940s to the 1970s could claim at least one spot on the radio dial. Risking once again the hazards of the road, aging rock superstars mounted new nationwide, and even international, tours. The Who and the Rolling Stones attracted the most attention and money, but many other middle-aged men, now sans drugs and young groupies, retraced paths of former glories. The top-selling African-American artist of the 1980s, Michael Jackson, bet much of his personal fortune on nostalgia when he purchased the rights to most of the Beatles' tunes. Many of his own songs expressed a kind of Peter Pan-ish retreat into childhood. And Jackson also joined millions of other people in making visits to Disneyland, the Magic Kingdom of the 1950s, a favorite pastime.

Reworking the Past

But looking backward could also take peculiar twists, not all of which meant nostalgia for the pre-Vietnam era. The music critic Nelson George, for example, coined the term *retronuevo* to characterize pop music that borrowed, often very consciously, from the past in order to create fresh new sounds; retronuevo, according to George, appreciated, rather than simply reprised, the postwar musical heritage. At their best, Prince and even Michael Jackson wove numerous musical traditions into exciting and novel productions.

Steven Spielberg's original *Back to the Future* (1985) captured some of the retronuevo spirit. Here, Marty McFly, a young man trapped in a dull and strife-torn family, is hurled, by errant technology, back to the pre–rock-and-roll 1950s. There, he finds his mother-to-be is attracted to him, rather than to his inept father-to-be. After "inventing" rock music, punching out the local hoods, and uniting his parents-to-be, Marty (played by Michael J. Fox of "Family Ties") scrambles back to "the future," the 1980s of Ronald Reagan. Having placed an imprint on the past, Marty finds the present remade: Because of *his* intervention, "history" will be transformed for the better.

Different people found very different messages in *Back to the Future*. Reagan quickly invoked its fascination with high-technology, borrowing a line from the movie for his 1986 State of the Union address: "Where we're going, we don't need roads." The president's critics found another Reagan-like message in the film—an ability to imagine that technology and simple optimism can solve complex, deeply rooted problems. Yet in other ways *Back to the Future* also expressed disquietude about both the present and the past that Reaganesque culture celebrated. Rather than simply offering an escapist trip to the 1950s, it also suggested a deeply felt desire for a significantly differ-ent present and implied that past mistakes, especially those made during the immediate postwar era, had helped to produce the dilemmas of the 1980s.

People found other, more complex examples of creatively reworking the past in cultural products identified as postmodern. An ill-defined but impor-tant cultural style that began to take shape in the 1970s, the postmodernism of the 1980s and early 1990s enthusiastically embraced forms from the past. Especially attracted by mass culture, postmodernists admittedly recalled the familiar, but in new and unusual ways. Postmodern architects, for example, re-jected the so-called international school, with its sleek, straight-lined, steel-and-glass skyscrapers. Ridiculing these "glass boxes" as soulless and preten-tious monuments to industrial and cultural elites, postmodernists celebrated the architecture of the ordinary, including highway billboards, Las Vegas casi-nos, and almost anything with elaborate ornamentation. In the AT&T build-ing in New York City, for instance, the architect Philip Johnson turned away from his internationalist past and designed a novel structure that resembled a nineteenth-century grandfather clock, topped by something that recalled Chippendale furniture of the eighteenth century.

Both approving and hostile critics agreed that postmodernists self-consciously blurred and often parodied traditional cultural forms. Postmod-ern culture delighted in transgressing old boundaries, such as those between mass and elite culture or between fiction and history. Woody Allen's *Zelig* (1983), for example, blended grainy film footage from the 1920s with new (though perfectly matched) scenes from the 1980s and created a pseudodoc-umentary about a fictional celebrity whom historians had supposedly forgot-ten. This approach encouraged viewers to imagine they were seeing Allen's character playing baseball with Babe Ruth and talking literature with F. Scott Fitzgerald. This postmodernist parody rejected both the conservative nostal-gia of Reaganism and the liberal commitment to the sanctity of accurate his-torical documentation.

Some critics even proclaimed the arrival of postmodern television, with shows that reworked, generally in clever parodies, earlier network texts. The first TV hit of the 1990s, "The Simpsons," offered a cartoon version of a strife-ridden, off-center family. Recalling "Father Knows Best" and classic cartoon families such as "The Flintstones," this show found a spot on a rival fourth net-work, Fox Broadcasting. Ridiculing, while it was recycling, traditional sitcom motifs, "The Simpsons"—and its even more controversial Fox network coun-terpart, "Married with Children"—offered an alternative to the carefully sani-tized and thoroughly predictable mainstream fare of the 1980s and early 1990s. In both "Married with Children" and "The Simpsons," conflict could not always be contained and order did not always prevail.

Other postmodernists went much farther in their search for new cultural forms. Some artists used the types of copying machines found in any college library or print shop to create new works of art. Others used computers and even fax machines, rather than the traditional brushes and easel, to "paint" their images. Simultaneously stretching traditional artistic boundaries and mocking the repetitive culture of advanced capitalism, such productions parodied the classic TV commercial that asked viewers to decide, "Is it live? Or is it Memorex?"

Cultural Conflict in the 1980s

During the 1980s, some products of mass culture challenged Ronald Reagan's claims of a steadily improving quality of life. In the era of TV satellites, for example, the alliance between music and social activism assumed new forms, as in the Live-Aid concert for African famine relief and recurring Farm-Aid productions on behalf of rural America.

Although these high-tech spectacles triggered relatively little controversy, other new cultural trends of the 1980s prompted considerable debate. Hip Hop, which had first emerged among African-American and Latino youth in New York City during the late 1970s, was one of the most complex, and controversial, cultural developments. Hip Hop expressed itself through flamboyant clothing, break dancing, and graffiti art on walls and subway trains, but rap music ultimately became its most powerful manifestation. Initially, popular disk jockeys became neighborhood celebrities by using powerful amplifiers to "sample" different musical backdrops, taken from a broad variety of popular styles, for break dancers and graffiti artists. Gradually, they took their amplifiers into local clubs and added new technical twists like "scratching," manipulating record turntables to produce unique sounds. More important, hip hop DJs added "rappers," young performance artists who recounted dramatic, often angry, stories about urban life over the sound of the music. Thus, rap music merged older traditions—including preaching, story-telling, and street corner boasting—with postmodern electronics to provide a means by which young people of color could express their rage against urban conditions and their hopes for social transformation.

Rap was immediately controversial. It graphically gave voice to the pent up emotions of young people, especially African-American men. Some raps rivaled heavy metal in their misogynistic lyrics; rappers sometimes angered Jewish-American groups; and some infuriated law enforcement officials by their "bad attitude"—a term denoting everything from fashion styles to "obscene" language to social outlook—and by the violence that became popularly associated with hip hop culture. Some law enforcement groups pressured record companies to censor rap lyrics.

At the same time, rap proved very popular. In 1980 The Sugar Hill Gang's "Rapper's Delight" (1979) became rap's first million seller, and rappers from outside New York City, such as 2 Live Crew from Miami and Los Angeles's "gangsta rappers," soon achieved prominence. MTV brought rap onto its playlist and eventually created "Yo! MTV Raps," a program devoted entirely to the new musical form. Meanwhile, a number of women rappers made their mark, reminding people that women had been part of hip hop culture from the outset and showing that artists like Queen Latifah could blend anti-misogynist and feminist themes into rap discourse. Indeed, by the end of the 1980s, some of rap's original admirers argued that it was becoming too commercial, a trend that resulted in outright fakes such as the white rapper Vanilla Ice and cross-over artists such as M.C. Hammer.

But rap's admirers continued to emphasize its energy and its connection to everyday experiences and generally neglected social problems; many rap artists, recalling the politics of Black Power, went beyond songs about sex, drugs, and violence to produce ethnically assertive lyrics such as "Proud to Be Black" and "Fight the Power." Rap music underscored the complex cultural conflicts of the 1980s.

Despite the dominant nostalgia, the nation's culture *was* changing, especially as the result of a new wave of immigration. After forty-five years of decline, immigration had been steadily rising in the post-World War II decades; but in the 1980s, the number of immigrants not only expanded dramatically but the countries of origin also changed. Immigrants from Asia, principally Vietnamese and Cambodians, made up nearly half of the total, and newcomers from Latin America and the Caribbean constituted the next largest groups. Settling in specific areas—such as southeast Florida, Los Angeles, Texas, New York City, and the San Francisco Bay area—the new immigrants quickly made their cultural imprints.

Newcomers from Latin America, for example, joined a Latino population that was already expanding much faster than the nation's non-Latino population. At that rate, before the second decade of the twenty-first century, Latinos would surpass African-Americans as the largest ethnic minority in the United States. Of course, the broad category of Latino actually included a number of different ethnic groups, each of which brought diverse cultural influences, ranging from salsa music to several new cable-TV networks, during the 1980s. Political attitudes also varied markedly, from arch-conservative, anticommunist refugees from Castro's Cuba to radical heirs of Chicano militancy in the 1970s. But while popular music, journalism, and television all felt the impact of Spanish-language products, the decade also witnessed signs of a cultural backlash. In the face of vibrant and growing Spanish-language cultures, a number of states proclaimed English as their official language and attempted to roll back movements for bilingual education.

Even when new cultural forms, such as salsa and rap, achieved commercial success, other controversies erupted. Spike Lee's movie *Do the Right Thing*, for example, sparked bitter debates, especially since its cinematic images of racially divided, violence-filled neighborhoods paralleled noncinematic conflicts in cities such as New York, Miami, and Boston. Although this young African-American writer-director was doing no more—though no less—than exploring the widely acknowledged problems of racism and poverty, conservative critics claimed that *Do the Right Thing* advocated violence as a solution for social and racial ills. Hollywood's Academy Awards completely bypassed this film and named *Driving Miss Daisy*—a picture featuring an elderly southern white woman and her African-American chauffeur—as the best motion picture of 1989. In a similar vein, the controversial, postmodern documentary *Roger and Me*, also ignored in the Academy Awards, angered powerful economic interests and cultural patrons with its anti–General Motors—as a symbol of uncaring big business—message.

The Mass Culture Debate Revisited

The question of how to respond to controversial cultural products cut across many different media and political alliances. Pornography, explicit works that represented the ambiguous legacy of the sexual revolution of the 1960s and 1970s, exemplified many of the dilemmas. What kinds of expression, for example, even qualified as pornographic? To some, the fact that works could be exhibited on some art gallery's walls, rather than on magazine racks, did not mean that they might not still be pornographic. The sexually explicit and homoerotic photographs of Robert Mapplethorpe, for instance, prompted widespread controversy in several major cities. A heated debate over public funding of the arts resulted from cancellation of a Mapplethorpe exhibition at the prestigious Cochrane Gallery in Washington, D.C. Although a few leaders of the artistic community sympathized with the Cochrane's fear of jeopardizing funding with such contested subject matter, most condemned the gallery for allegedly caving in to censorship and the political sensibilities of the New Right.

Other types of sexually explicit products, such as commercially distributed magazines, books, and videos, prompted different types of controversies and political alignments. Angered by a rising tide of violence against women, a powerful wing of the feminist coalition blamed pornographic materials for helping to incite the epidemic. Most pornography, they charged, had little to do with healthy eroticism and everything to do with exploiting, degrading, and endangering women. In spearheading legal campaigns against pornography, the antiporn feminists saw themselves acting on a long-standing conviction that the personal and the political could not be separated. Similarly, some veterans of the countercultural 1960s, who now were raising families in urban neighborhoods, also supported the padlocking of businesses that dealt in sexually explicit materials; cleaning out peep shows and magazine racks seemed part of a larger crusade to rekindle a spirit of neighborhood uplift and community building.

The antipornography movement confronted an equally diverse opposition. Making cultural judgments that accorded with those of the New Right instinctively unsettled many in the artistic community. Rallying around the banner of free expression, they joined civil libertarian groups (such as the American Civil Liberties Union, or ACLU) in condemning antipornography initiatives as violations of constitutional guarantees. Many of these people and groups had been struggling since the early cold war era to expand First

Amendment rights, and they feared that lowering any legal barrier against censorship would only embolden cultural and political know-nothings. The antipornography movement also troubled many feminists: Was not this new censorship, even though framed in terms of protecting women, part of a broader crusade to revive small-town, Main Street values, including older notions about the proper roles into which women should be contained?

Similarly complicated debates swirled around other cultural products, especially rock music. Even before the furor over rap, a campaign to censor rock lyrics gathered momentum; worried about government intervention, the major record labels rejected the pleas of free-speech advocates and adopted a system of warning labels for songs with images of violence or sex.

MTV, which debuted as a cable-TV network in 1981, also stirred debate. With its initial format, twenty-four hours of nothing but rock videos and commercials, MTV raised the stakes for people in the music business: A hit video joined a gold record, a platinum album, and a movie soundtrack as the markers of musical success. Market research suggested that MTV exerted significant influence over what albums and singles consumers decided to purchase. Here, MTV's role was controversial because it initially relied on slickly produced videos from Britain, featuring such all-white New Pop groups as Duran Duran, The Thompson Twins, and WHAM! As a consequence, critics charged MTV with favoring style over substance, established groups over newcomers, and white artists over musicians of color. Moreover, many women found MTV serving up anti-female images only slightly less objectionable than those in porno films.

At the same time, however, MTV proved a great success with its targeted youth audience and also gained admiration from a new generation of cultural critics. MTV's admirers credited it with a willingness to experiment with unusual media imagery and with an interest in postmodern cultural styles, both of which were evident in video's such as "You Might Think," by the Cars. Similarly, *Miami Vice*, an otherwise familiar police show, gained critical kudos, and high ratings, by transferring a good deal of the MTV look to network television.

Beginning in 1983, MTV began both to broaden its video playlist and to bring greater structure to its programming schedule. Although it still relied upon a single musical genre, with North American-based heavy metal replacing Britain's New Pop, MTV became increasingly committed to expanding the types of music and musicians that it programmed. In 1984, Tina Turner was without a record contract; the following year, after her new record company featured Turner in several videos that ran on MTV, she won a Grammy award and had a hit album, *Private Dancer*. The rise of Madonna and Michael Jackson, who used MTV to become international mega-stars, was much more spectacular. Their work, including videos such as "Like a Prayer" and "Thriller," became the subject of extensive journalistic and academic commentary. Critics claimed to find important religious themes in the work of both Madonna and Jackson. MTV, in short, helped music videos become an increasingly powerful, respectable form of musical production. By the mid-1980s, even country

music, the most traditional sector of the music industry, could claim two na-
tionally-available cable-TV channels.

At the same time that MTV was helping to change the production and
distribution of music, it was also changing its own format. In place of a con-
tinuous flow of visual imagery, which encouraged claims that MTV was *the*
postmodern medium, MTV steadily regularized its daily schedule until it resembled that of more traditional networks. Specific time slots became devoted
to the "Top 20" hits; to alternative musical forms, such as grunge; to postmodern videos, like those of Michael Penn; to rap, as hip hop entered the American mainstream; and to non-musical programming, such as the clever game-
show parody, *Remote Control.* A video-inspired documentary reprise of the
1980s even won MTV a prestigious award for journalistic excellence.

The Culture of Sleaze

Nostalgia for the culture of the late 1940s and early 1950s, ironically, paralleled revival of one of the least desirable aspects of that earlier era—widespread corruption or, at the very least, the perception that corruption flourished nearly everywhere. As the Reagan administration was preparing to leave
office, a widely respected Republican rhetorically asked, "For God's sake, are
we not entitled to hope that the next administration will be a little less sleazy?"
Indeed, the "sleaze factor" appeared oozing into many areas of American life
in the 1980s.

Political culture seemed to reek of it. More than a hundred members of
Ronald Reagan's administration were either convicted of crimes or cited for
ethical violations by various government watchdog bodies. Several top-ranking officeholders, including two cabinet officers, resigned while under fire.
The department of Housing and Urban Development (HUD), another scan-
dal-tainted cabinet office, paid outrageously large "consulting" fees to prominent Republicans and channeled scarce housing and redevelopment funds
into a series of questionable projects. Meanwhile, appointees in the Pentagon
pleaded guilty to accepting bribes, and investigative journalists claimed that
Reagan's $2.2 trillion worth of defense expenditures included huge cost over-
runs on faulty products and unnecessary expenditures for vastly overpriced
spare parts.

Reagan's Democratic adversaries also had their troubles. During the
1988 presidential primaries, candidate Gary Hart challenged journalists to
scrutinize his personal life: "If anybody wants to put a tail on me, go ahead.
They'd be very bored." Quite the contrary. Journalists quickly discovered
Hart, who campaigned as a family man, sailing off the Florida coast and sneak-
ing around Washington with another woman. Although some traditionalists
thought such scandal-hunting overstepped the longstanding maxim that the
private foibles of political figures were not news, journalists rushed to find
new sleaze. Several prominent Democrats, including House Speaker Jim
Wright, were forced to leave office in the wake of stories, pressed by both journalists and Republican activists, about questionable financial dealings.

Powerful religious figures also had their problems. Reverend Jimmy Swaggart, head of a vast TV and religious publishing empire, fell into disgrace and (even worse for an evangelical preacher) media oblivion when a rival minister revealed Swaggart's patronage of prostitutes. Oral Roberts, a long-time leader of the electronic church, confronted falling TV ratings and de-clining revenues after a media campaign in which he claimed that the Lord might strike him down if donors failed to fill his coffers. And perhaps in the biggest sleaze spectacle of the 1980s, Jim and Tammy Bakker lost their reli-gious theme park, TV network, personal fortune, and each other when a sex and money-skimming scandal enveloped their "ministry."

The culture of sleaze also became big business. CBS's "60 Minutes" used stories about scams and schemes to reach Neilsen's top ten, and ABC's "Night-line" received its highest ratings when it featured an interview of the Bakkers. By the mid-1980s, imitators of "60 Minutes," such as "Hard Copy" and "A Cur-rent Affair" flooded TV's syndicated market, peddling stories and formats considered too sleazy to meet network standards. One popular cultural form, professional wrestling, also thrived on sleaze: Treachery and double-dealing were required behavior, and one night's hero could become the following evening's villain. Meanwhile, supposedly legitimate sports wallowed in scandal as sports pages detailed allegations of players betting on games, accounts of heavy (often illegal and sometimes fatal) drug use, and even stories of fixed games and point shaving. By comparison, the earlier sports scandals of the late 1940s and early 1950s seemed minor-league affairs.

Two of the biggest nonsports heroes of the 1980s failed to escape taint during the 1990s. One of the former decade's central icons, Donald Trump became tabloid fodder when tales of his marital and financial troubles be-came public. Similarly, Ronald Reagan's Teflon coating began to be stained by sleaze. Reagan, most people continued to believe, was personally innocent of sleazy behavior; but political observers suspected that he had paid too little attention to the sleazy people and events connected with his presidency. Reportedly, for example, he once mistook Samuel Pierce, head of scandal-ridden HUD, for a big-city mayor. Reagan seemed similarly oblivious to mounting evidence of corruption in the savings-and-loan industry. After he had been out of office a year, opinion polls showed his approval rating below that of another former president, Jimmy Carter, the person whom Reagan had handily out-polled only a decade earlier.

SUGGESTIONS FOR FURTHER READING

A good place to begin looking at the 1980s is in the census data. See Andrew Hacker, ed., *US* (1983); and for a controversial, though provocative, interpretation of the nation's place in the world, see Paul Kennedy, *The Rise and Fall of the Great Powers* (1988).

Interpretations of Ronald Reagan himself include James E. Combs, *The Reagan Range: The Nostalgic Myth in American Politics* (1993); Stephen Vaughn, *Ronald Reagan in Hollywood* (1993); Lou Cannon, *Reagan* (1982); Robert

Dallek, *Ronald Reagan and the Politics of Symbolism* (1984); Michael Rogin, *Ronald Reagan the Movie* (1987); Garry Wills, *Reagan's America: Innocents at Home* (1987); Sidney Blumenthal, *Our Long National Daydream: A Political Pageant of the Reagan Era* (1988); Robert E. Denton, Jr., *The Primetime Presidency of Ronald Reagan: The Era of the Television Presidency* (1988); Jane Mayer and Doyle McManus, *Landslide: The Unmaking of a President, 1984–1988* (1988); and Kurt Ritter and David Henry, *Ronald Reagan: The Great Communicator* (1992). Bruce Franklin, *M.I.A. or Mythmaking in America* (1992), critically dissects one of the continuing issues of domestic and international politics—the claim that many U.S. prisoners of war were left behind in Southeast Asia.

Attempts to assess the broad impact of the Reagan years include Sidney Blumenthal and Thomas Byrne Edsall, eds., *The Reagan Legacy* (1988); Ryan J. Barilleaux, *The Post-modern Presidency: The Office After Ronald Reagan* (1988); Kathleen Hall Jamieson and David S. Birdsell, *Presidential Debates: The Challenge of Creating an Informed Electorate* (1988); William F. Grover, *The President as Prisoner: A Structural Critique of the Carter and Reagan Years* (1989); Richard O. Curry, *Freedom at Risk* (1989); John Kenneth White, *The New Politics of Old Values* (2nd ed., 1990); Harold H. Koh, *The National Security Constitution: Sharing Power After the Iran-Contra Affair* (1990); Michael Schaller, *Reckoning with Reagan* (1992); Kathleen Hall Jamieson, *Packaging the Presidency* (2nd ed., 1992); and Daniel Wirls, ed., *Buildup: The Politics of Defense in the Reagan Era* (1992). William C. Berman, *America's Right Turn: From Nixon to Bush* (1994), offers a broad overview.

Economic and social welfare policies are the subject of Michael Boskin, *Too Many Promises: The Uncertain Future of Social Security* (1986); William Greider, *Secrets of the Temple* (1987); James Tobin and Murray Weidenbaum, eds., *Two Revolutions in Economic Policy: The First Economic Reports of Presidents Kennedy and Reagan* (1988); Martin Anderson, *Revolution* (1988); Dennis Swann, *The Retreat of the State: Deregulation and Privatization in the UK and the US* (1988); Roger E. Meiners and Bruce Yandle, *Regulation and the Reagan Era* (1989); James K. Galbraith, *Balancing Acts: Technology, Finance, and the American Future* (1989); Kenneth R. Hoover, *Conservative Capitalism in Britain and the United States: A Critical Appraisal* (1989); Otis L. Graham, Jr., *Losing Time: The Industrial Policy Debate* (1992); Christopher Jencks, *Rethinking Social Policy* (1992); and Michael A. Bernstein and David Adler, eds., *Understanding American Economic Decline* (1993). See also the relevant chapters of Edward D. Berkowitz, *America's Welfare State* (1991).

Foreign policies are discussed in Walter LaFeber, *Inevitable Revolutions: The United States in Central America* (1983); Strobe Talbot, *Deadly Gambits: The Reagan Administration and the Stalemate in Nuclear Arms Control* (1984); Thomas Walker, ed., *Reagan versus the Sandinistas* (1987); Kenneth Oye et al., eds., *Eagle Resurgent? The Reagan Era in American Foreign Policy* (1987); James A. Bill, *The Eagle and the Lion: The Tragedy of American-Iranian Relations* (1988); Morris H. Morley, ed., *Crisis and Confrontation: Ronald Reagan's Foreign Policy* (1988); Roy Gutman, *Banana Diplomacy: The Making of American Policy in Nicaragua, 1981–1987* (1988); H. Bruce Franklin, *War Stars: The Superweapon and the Amer-

ican Imagination (1988); Coral Bell, *The Reagan Paradox: American Foreign Policy in the 1980s* (1989); William E. Brock and Robert D. Hormats, eds., *The Global Economy: America's Role in the Decade Ahead* (1990); Theodore Draper, *A Very Thin Line: The Iran-Contra Affairs* (1991); and Donald R. Baucom, *The Origins of SDI, 1944–1983* (1992).

Other issues of the Reagan presidency are covered in Elder Witt, *A Different Justice: Reagan and the Supreme Court* (1986), and C. Brant Short, *Ronald Reagan and the Public Lands: America's Conservation Debate, 1979–1984* (1989).

On social and cultural issues of the 1980s, many of the works cited at the end of the two previous chapters are relevant. In addition, see Robert Bellah et al., *Habits of the Heart: Individualism & Commitment in American Life* (1984); Michael Omi and Howard Winant, *Racial Formation in the United States: From the 1960s to the 1980s* (1986); Mark Friedberger, *Shake-out: Iowa Farm Families in the 1980s* (1989); Valerie O'Conner Sutter, *The Indochinese Refugee Dilemma* (1989); Randy Shilts, *And the Band Played on: Politics, People, and the AIDS Epidemic* (1988); Fred Harris and Roger W. Wilkins, eds., *Quiet Riots: Race and Poverty in the United States: The Kerner Report Twenty Years Later* (1989); James Coates, *Armed and Dangerous: The Rise of the Survivalist Right* (1989); Luciano Mangiafico, *Contemporary American Immigrants: Patterns of Filipino, Korean, and Chinese Settlement in the United States* (1988); William Julius Wilson, *The Ghetto Underclass* (1989); Barbara Ehrenreich, *Fear of Falling: The Inner Life of the Middle-Class* (1989); Carlos Munoz, Jr., *Youth, Identity, Power: The Chicano Movement* (1989); Neil Miller, *In Search of Gay America: Women and Men in a Time of Change* (1989); Russell Ferguson et al., eds., *Out There: Marginalization and Contemporary Cultures* (1990); Paul James Rutledge, *The Vietnamese Experience in America* (1992); Andrew Hacker, *Two Nations: Black and White, Separate, Hostile, Unequal* (1992); Toni Morrison, ed., *Race-ing Justice, En-Gendering Power: Essays on Anita Hill, Clarence Thomas, and the Construction of Social Reality* (1992); Dallas A. Blanchard, *The Anti-abortion Movement* (1994); Cornel West, *Race Matters* (1993); Manthia Diawara, ed., *Black American Cinema* (1993); and Robert Gooding-Williams, ed., *Reading Rodney King* (1993).

On the cultural battles of the 1980s, see Charles Jencks, *Post-modernism: The New Classicism in Art and Architecture* (1987); E. Ann Kaplan, *Rocking Around the Clock: Music Television, Postmodernism, and Consumer Culture* (1987); Linda Hutcheon, *A Poetics of Postmodernism* (1987); David Harvey, *The Condition of Postmodernity* (1989); Linda J. Nicholson, ed., *Feminism/Postmodernism* (1990); Mark Poster, *The Mode of Information* (1990); Douglas Kellner, *Television and the Crisis of Democracy* (1990); Nicolaus Mills, ed., *Culture in an Age of Money: The Legacy of the 1980s in America* (1990); James Davison Hunter, *Culture Wars* (1991); Timothy Corrigan, *A Cinema without Walls* (1991); Marsha Kinder, *Playing with Power in Movies, Television and Video Games* (1991); Susan Willis, *A Primer for Daily Life* (1991); Mimi White, *Teleadvising: Therapeutic Discourse in American Television* (1992); Celeste Olalquiaga, *Megalopolis: Contemporary Cultural Sensibilities* (1992); Lawrence Grossberg, *We Gotta Get Out of this Place: Popular Conservatism and Postmodern Culture* (1992); Henry Jenkins, *Textual Poachers: Television Fans and Participatory Culture* (1992); Andrew Goodwin,

Dancing in the Distraction Factory: Music Television and Popular Culture (1992); Carol J. Clover, *Men, Women, and Chain Saws: Gender in the Modern Horror Film* (1992); Elizabeth G. Traube, *Dreaming Identities: Class, Gender, and Generation in 1980s Hollywood Movies* (1992); Greg Tate, *Flyboy in the Buttermilk* (1992); Simon Frith, Andrew Goodwin, and Lawrence Grossberg, eds., *Sound & Vision: The Music Video Reader* (1993); Jim Collins, Hilary Radner, and Ava Preacher Collins, eds., *Film Theory Goes to the Movies* (1993); Wayne Munson, *All Talk: The Talkshow in Media Culture* (1993); and Susan Jeffords, *Hard Bodies: Hollywood Masculinity in the Reagan Era* (1994).

11

Toward the Twenty-first Century

THE PRESIDENCY OF GEORGE BUSH

The Election of 1988

The thaw in the cold war, occurring shortly before the presidential election of 1988, removed many issues from the center of political debate. The Reagan legacy seemed to fit on every side of foreign-policy issues, and the Democrats lacked firm ground. Most Democrats neither wanted nor were able to outflank Reagan in cold war crusading. Yet with the progress on arms control and the mellowing of the Soviet threat, the Reagan administration could also claim credit for detente and a safer world. Both George Bush and Democratic nominee Michael Dukakis, the governor of Massachusetts, tried simultaneously to project "toughness" in foreign policy and to endorse the easing of the cold war.

The presidential election of 1988 resembled other recent contests: It turned more on the personalities and the symbols identified with the individual candidates than on policy differences. Dukakis, an uninspiring campaigner in the Walter Mondale mold, cautiously talked about reversing the Reagan animus against social programs but offered no startling new proposals of his own; rather, he primarily presented himself as a competent economic manager who could bring the "Massachusetts miracle" to Washington. While stressing his years as Reagan's loyal vice-president, especially his emphasis on voluntarism (symbolized by the image of "a thousand points of light"), Bush also promised a "kinder, gentler America." The controversial selection of J. Danforth ("Dan") Quayle, an inexperienced and apparently uninformed senator from Indiana, as his running mate gave Bush only momentary problems. Advised by tough, young GOP strategists, such as Lee Atwater (the first head of any major party who could play the electric guitar), Bush's media managers portrayed Dukakis as big on taxes, soft on crime, and the captive of special interests (such as prochoice forces and Dukakis's former rival Jesse Jackson). Their candidate, in contrast, pledged no new taxes and stressed his reverence for national symbols, particularly the right to bear arms and the Pledge of Allegiance to the flag.

The Bush campaign of 1988 outshown even the earlier Reagan efforts in its use of the mass media, especially TV advertising. Bush's TV ads, for example, invariably bathed Dukakis in gloomy shadows, captured his face while contorted in a frown, and highlighted his heavy beard. In contrast, they filmed the vice-president with strong backlighting so that he was enveloped in a warm, Disney-like glow. The most infamous political commercial of 1988—which received more airtime when replayed on public-affairs talk shows than when originally broadcast as a paid advertisement for the Bush campaign—linked Dukakis to a sexual assault committed by a black man, Willie Horton, who had fled from a Massachusetts prison while on a furlough program. Slow to react, Dukakis defended the program by noting how many furloughed prisoners had returned without incident. Because Dukakis seemed unable to fathom the depth of popular feeling about crime or appreciate the racist appeal of the Willie Horton issue, the Bush campaign was able to attach Horton's image to Dukakis's bid for the presidency. Bush won the election comfortably—426 electoral votes to 112, 40 states to 10.

Bush's Domestic Policies

Conservatives had never considered George Bush one of their own, and their suspicions grew as they watched his domestic policies unfold. Why had John Tower, a staunch conservative and Bush's nominee for secretary of defense, failed to achieve confirmation? Had Bush done too little to support him? Conservatives also wondered about the speed with which the Bush administration swiftly replaced Reaganites with their own appointees. Bush pleased conservatives when he vetoed the Civil Rights Act of 1990, condemning it for allegedly setting up quotas for the hiring of women and people of color, but later mystified them by agreeing to a 1991 Civil Rights Act that seemed virtually indistinguishable from the earlier version. Ronald Reagan had appointed three staunch conservatives—Sandra Day O'Connor, Antonin Scalia, and Anthony Kennedy—to the Supreme Court, but Bush's first nominee, David Souter, was a scholarly moderate who quickly showed his reluctance to support the right-wing opinions of Scalia and Chief Justice William Rehnquist.

As a result of their suspicions, conservatives placed special importance on Bush's campaign pledge of "Read my lips. No new taxes." Economic problems, however, immediately conspired against Bush's antitax promise. As the unemployment statistics steadily rose and the rate of economic growth leveled off, the budget deficits piled up. Even Bush's own advisers recognized that the White House had to present an economic package that included new taxation. Finally in 1990, the president agreed to "tax revenue increases." Bush's media spin doctors claimed that there was an important difference between "tax revenue increases" and "new taxes," but everyone, especially betrayed conservatives, could read the president's lips.

Bush never recovered from his reversal on the taxation issue. Rather than develop a broad economic stimulus package, even when unemployment reached 7 percent, the Bush administration simply hoped that conditions would improve. Public-opinion polls showed Bush's approval rating, which had once stood at 70 percent, steadily plummeting. More broadly, people complained about the gridlock in Washington, the political stalemate in which neither a Republican White House nor a Democratic Congress seemed able to move ahead in dealing with important issues such as economic recovery, health-care reform, and urban problems.

Urban issues had been pushed to the background during Reagan's presidency, and Bush did no better. Initially, he raised hopes by appointing Jack Kemp as secretary of housing and urban development. A free-market conservative, Kemp urged job-creation efforts targeted at low-income urban neighborhoods and proposed several innovative programs, including one to allow tenants in public housing to purchase their apartments. Kemp, who formerly represented an urban district in Congress, was one of the few Republicans who urged a campaign to bring more people of color into the Republican party. Once Kemp was confirmed, however, Bush showed little interest in his secretary's ideas until violence convulsed South Central Los Angeles in April 1992 after the acquittal of four white police officers who had been charged with beating an African-American motorist, Rodney King. Several days of racial conflict devastated parts of the city; fifty-three people died, thousands were injured, and property damages totaled more than $1 billion. Bush responded by a flurry of visits to low-income areas, but no urban program ever emerged from the White House during his presidency.

George Bush, it seemed evident, had relatively little interest in domestic policy. A former ambassador to China and to the UN and a former head of the CIA, Bush was always more interested in foreign than domestic issues.

Foreign Policy under Bush

Bush hardly settled into the Oval Office before a chain of dramatic events reshaped international affairs. For at least two years it had been obvious that the cold war order was about to unravel, but no one anywhere predicted the rapidity of change that began in the summer of 1989.

In late 1988 Mikhail Gorbachev had, in effect, renounced Leonid Breshnev's doctrine forbidding any nation from renouncing communism. "Freedom of choice is a universal principle," Gorbachev declared. And Eastern Europeans quickly tested his words. Poland ousted its communist government in favor of a new one based on the popular, noncommunist labor movement,

Solidarity. East Germans dismantled the Berlin Wall, forced their communist government to resign, and moved quickly toward reunification with West Germany. Czechoslovakians, Hungarians, Romanians, and Bulgarians all mounted massive street demonstrations, tossed out their communist rulers, and then struggled to establish new systems with market economies and parliamentary governments. A few months before, winds of liberalization had swept China, but the Chinese government abruptly halted the movement, killing thousands of student protestors in Tianenmen Square in Beijing and tightening its grip over social and economic life. Such repression, though, did not come to Eastern Europe; there, most countries enjoyed a fairly peaceful transfer of power.

Americans seemed dazzled by the pace of events. "No one was expecting the Eastern bloc to go out of business in a month," one State Department official exclaimed. "It's as though there is a fire, and we are chasing the trucks to the scene." Some saw opportunities: McDonald's quickly opened restaurants in Budapest and then in Moscow; *Playboy* became the first American magazine sold in Hungary.

The abatement of the cold war reverberated in events throughout the world. In Africa, tensions in some trouble spots had already eased. Long-negotiated settlements finally brought independence to Namibia and the beginning of the withdrawal of Cuban troops from Angola, both areas in which cold war tensions had exacerbated and prolonged disputes. Early in 1990, the South African government recognized the African National Congress, the black nationalist group it had long labeled as communist, and freed its most prominent leader, Nelson Mandela. Another startling thaw came in Nicaragua, where the Sandinista government, which the United States had long tried to undermine, held a free election and was voted out of power. The new government and the Sandinistas both talked of trying to work toward national reconciliation. Clashing interests and ideologies remained in all of these places, but confrontation—at least in public rhetoric—went out of fashion.

Soviet leaders became increasingly preoccupied with internal matters. The Baltic states of Latvia and Lithuania, dominated by Soviet power since World War II, declared independence, and the major provinces that had made up the Soviet Union itself also seized the powers of self-government. The president of the new state of Russia, Boris Yeltsin, defiantly and successfully resisted a countercoup by hard-line communists in August 1991, and his popularity rapidly eclipsed that of Gorbachev. Yeltsin championed the establishment of a new Commonwealth of Independent States; on December 12, 1991, the Parliament of Russia ratified such a plan, and eleven ex-Soviet republics joined. The United States suddenly faced the task of opening new embassies and developing diplomatic relations with dozens of new states.

The Bush administration began to shape a new foreign policy for a post–cold war world. The secretary of defense projected a slowed pace of defense spending, and members of Congress began to talk hopefully about a "peace dividend." Still, if the Soviet threat seemed to be diminishing, Bush's policymakers pointed to new foreign dangers. Pentagon planners began to chart a new mission for the military. Future actions, they suggested, would probably involve rapid, targeted strikes, perhaps to solve new kinds of problems in the developing world. Bush turned to the military, for example, to fight the war against drugs that he had promised to wage during the election campaign. Panama became an example of the style of post–cold war military action.

The government of Panama, under dictator General Manuel Noriega, was deeply implicated in the drug trade. The Reagan administration had indicted Noriega for drug trafficking and tried to force him from power through economic pressure. Although Reagan's tactics severely damaged the Panamanian economy, Noriega only tightened his own political grip and denounced Yankee meddling. Despite fears that Noriega, who had once worked closely with the CIA, might embarrass the United States by exposing intelligence secrets, the Bush administration decided on military action against the general. The United States needed a friendly and responsible government in Panama to complete the successful transfer of the Panama Canal to Panamanian sovereignty. The U.S. marines landed in Panama on December 20, 1989, and during the first week of January 1990, Noriega surrendered for extradition to the United States, where he stood trial. Not only did American intervention in Panama gain Bush wide popularity at home and reestablish a friendly government with which to complete the gradual transference of the canal to Panama, but also it seemed a warning of strong action to other drug dealers in the hemisphere.

Other U.S. military actions against drugs, such as an attempt to blockade the coast of Colombia to interdict drug shipments and to support aerial destruction of coca fields in Peru, became increasingly controversial. Drug-exporting countries urged the United States to pay attention to the law of supply and demand: to reduce consumption at home and to become more attuned to incentives that might cause coca producers to shift to other cash crops. As tension rose, however, new domestically produced synthetic drugs grew in popularity. The futility of going after the producers of drugs and blaming foreign nations for an alarming domestic trend became manifest.

Besides drugs, another candidate for a successor to the cold war was the environment. No less a figure than George Kennan, the so-called father of the cold war containment doctrine, now ranked environmental degradation as the most pressing threat to national security during the 1990s.

Environmental dangers stemmed from many different causes. Scientists documented deterioration in the life-protecting ozone layer. Human practices that made desert out of productive land spread famine in Africa and elsewhere. Rain forests, which are needed to clean and produce oxygen for a healthy planet, suffered accelerating destruction. Water systems and animal habitats came under attack from acid rain and chemical poisons. Perhaps most ominously, experts debated whether or not the planet was beginning to experience the onset of the dreaded "greenhouse effect"—global warming caused by the heat from industrial processes—that could alter climate patterns and dramatically disrupt the daily lives of every person on earth.

It was in this context that Earth Day II, the twentieth anniversary of what had been a small consciousness-raising festival held in 1970, became an elaborate global event in April 1990. In one sense, Earth Day II offered the kind of star-studded spectacle that increasingly marked mass-mediated culture: Hollywood and rock music stars were the headliners. International drug cartels and environmental hazards, however, were quickly overshadowed as the most pressing post–cold war problems.

The Persian Gulf War

On August 2, 1990, President Saddam Hussein of Iraq ordered his troops to seize control of Kuwait and convert it into the nineteenth province of Iraq. Although Hussein had been massing troops on the Iraq-Kuwait border and denouncing Kuwaiti oil producers, his bold move surprised U.S. officials. Anxious not to underestimate Hussein's ambitions a second time, intelligence experts now warned that Saudi Arabia, the Middle East's largest oil exporter and a long-time ally of the United States, might be next on the list. George Bush even compared Hussein's territorial ambitions to those of Adolf Hitler.

Bush organized an international response and pressured the Saudi government, initially reluctant to allow Western troops to enter their devoutly Muslim society, to accept U.S. military installations. Only four days after the Iraqui invasion of Kuwait, Bush announced operation Desert Shield and dispatched 230,000 troops to the Middle East. After consulting with Western European leaders and with Gorbachev, Bush approached the UN, which denounced the invasion of Kuwait and imposed economic sanctions against Iraq. Later, the U.N. gave Iraq an ultimatum: If it did not withdraw from Kuwait by January 15, 1991, the United States would lead a UN military operation to liberate the country. Bush raised the stakes further by deploying 200,000 additional U.S troops in the Middle East.

Bush's domestic critics worried about a protracted war ("another Vietnam") against Iraq's supposedly battle-hardened army, and they warned that such a conflict might only produce greater instability in the Middle East. In addition, some charged Bush with blatant economic imperialism to preserve the West's access to cheap oil.

Hoping to counter this growing antiwar movement in the United States, the president asked Congress for a resolution supporting the use of force. Although debates in both Houses were heated and the prowar resolution passed the Senate by a mere five votes, Bush claimed a mandate for military action. By moving so quickly, he outflanked the antiwar forces at home. Bush claimed the nation had a moral obligation to "free" Kuwait (and thus restore one of the most reactionary political regimes in the world), and he also emphasized the economic peril that Iraq might pose to the West's supply of cheap oil. Secretary of State James Baker bluntly summarized what the ordinary U.S. citizen had at stake in Kuwait: "Jobs."

As the UN's January deadline approached, Iraq promised a long, bloody war. Hussein hinted about unleashing potent, new weapons if the United

States tried to move into Kuwait or Iraq itself, and his threats prompted some military analysts to speculate about his intentions. Would he retaliate by striking Israel with chemical, bacteriological, or rudimentary nuclear warheads? Would he risk an environmental nightmare by torching Kuwait's oil wells?

The United States prepared for a new kind of TV war. Dubbed Desert Storm by the Bush administration, the gulf war was designed to fit the routines of network television and the aesthetics of the small screen. The initial bombing assault on Iraq was timed so that it coincided with the evening news back in the United States, and journalists for CNN broadcast the opening salvos from their hotel rooms in Baghdad. Indeed, throughout the brief conflict, both Iraqi and U.S. officials turned to CNN for information about what the other side was doing. As in Panama, media pools of journalists, whose movements were carefully controlled by the U.S. government, worked symbiotically with the military and broadcasted only what the Pentagon wanted viewers to see—charismatic military leaders, such as General ("Stormin'") Norman Schwartzkopf, and the military's super-sophisticated, very expensive arsenal of post-Vietnam weaponry. In video game fashion, TV screens showed "smart bombs," explosive devices equipped with complex guidance systems, hitting their targets with supposedly surgical precision and, later, Patriot missiles intercepting Iraq's Scud attacks. Only after the war had ended did critical scrutiny drastically deflate the accuracy of the smart bombs and success rate of the Patriots.

On February 24, the United States began a ground offensive against Iraq. Five weeks of saturation bombing and economic embargo had taken their toll on Saddam's troops, and four days of heavy pounding ended the war. Controlling the skies with air power, the United States kept its casualties to fewer than 150 battlefield deaths, whereas Iraqi military casualties were estimated at 100,000 deaths, many of them caused by merciless bombing from above as troops staged a panicked retreat back toward Baghdad. Before retreating, Iraqi forces torched more than 500 of Kuwait's oil wells, producing a black inferno that required many months of firefighting to extinquish. Despite the brevity of the war, the economic, transportation, and communication infrastructures of both Iraq and Kuwait lay in ruins. Although some officials wanted to continue the assault on Iraq and topple Saddam Hussein himself, Bush feared the uncertain consequences of these moves and pulled back U.S. forces.

The gulf war represented a strong show of force by the United States and the United Nations. It undermined Hussein's prestige and his pretensions to leadership of an anti-Israeli, anti-Western bloc in the Middle East. As the old Soviet Union's support for radical Arab movements declined, the end of the gulf war also brought a slight easing of tensions throughout much of the Middle East. Growing moderation provided the backdrop for a historic agreement between Israel and the Palestine Liberation Organization on August 28, 1993. The PLO recognized Israel's right to exist in return for Israel's acceptance, in principle, of Palestinian authority over the Gaza Strip and Jericho on the West Bank as a first step toward self-rule in these Israeli-occupied areas.

Although the gulf war boosted George Bush's image as a world leader, the president proved unable to articulate the kind of long-term diplomatic initiatives needed in the chaotic, post–cold war world. The international economic picture did gradually improve. Huge debts, which Third World nations owed to U.S. banks, threatened in the mid-1980s to shake the entire American banking system, but most were renegotiated by the end of the decade. New free-market economies began to evolve in ex-communist states, and Western Europe planned major steps toward economic integration. Bush also made progress toward a North American Free Trade Agreement (NAFTA) that would join Canada, the United States, and Mexico into the largest free-market zone in the world. But these gains seemed overshadowed by new instabilities and problems. Civil turmoil convulsed several of the ex-Soviet provinces, and the transition to a private property, free-market economy proved difficult in all parts of the former USSR and in the socialist states of Eastern Europe. The former Yugoslavia disintegrated, and Serbia embarked on a brutal campaign of territorial aggrandizement and "ethnic cleansing" against Muslims in Bosnia. In the Far East, American officials complained that unfair business practices contributed to Japan's economic strength and to the adverse trade balance between Japan and the United States. In Africa, severe famine produced so much instability in Somalia that Bush ordered American troops to help establish humanitarian relief efforts.

The end of the cold war certainly eliminated some foreign-policy problems, but it simultaneously destroyed many of the traditional guideposts for what constituted national security. The policy of standing strong against communism, which Bush had followed throughout his long public career, had suddenly lost much meaning. He talked about shaping a "new world order," but neither he nor his advisers could explain how this broad concept translated into concrete goals or specific priorities.

CULTURAL POLITICS IN THE 1990s

Although no magic line separates political from cultural issues—a truism dramatically underscored during the 1960s—cultural politics gained new intensity during the early 1990s. The controversy often centered on debates over "political correctness" or simply "PC." The PC debates, which had begun during the late 1980s as educators pondered curricular changes that were designed to bring new multicultural perspectives to all levels of education, quickly spread to the mass media and, then, into national politics.

The Rise of the "PC" Controversy

A broad coalition of educators, building on the cultural politics of the 1960s, began pressing schools and colleges to represent more fairly both the nation's multicultural heritage and its current conditions. Historians who espoused multiculturalism paid greater attention to the roles that women and people of color had played, while literature professors supplemented the traditional "canon," works generally authored by European-American males, with texts that represented a greater variety of racial, ethnic, and gender perspectives. At the same time, as a way of creating a better environment for learning, many educators also considered multicultural teaching methods that might eliminate the kind of subtle sexism and racism that, in their view, prevented women and people of color from fully participating in educational life. Many institutions established guidelines for multicultural, gender-fair education, while some drafted speech codes with penalties for teachers or students who failed to respect differences, particularly those involving race and sexuality, both inside and outside the classroom. To their defenders, these new educational initiatives and speech codes merely acknowledged the reality of cultural diversity and the fact that words, when pointedly or even carelessly spoken, could produce harmful consequences.

Multiculturalism, however, quickly became controversial. During the 1980s prominent members of the Reagan administration, such as William Bennett (who headed the National Endowment for the Humanities [NEH] and then the Department of Education) and Lynne Cheney (who replaced Bennett at NEH), had denounced multiculturalism as a political ploy, by feminists and other cultural radicals, to subvert the cultural heritage of the West and politicize education. Similarly, Alan Bloom's surprise best-seller, *The Closing of the American Mind* (1987), had blamed multiculturalism on the cultural excesses of the 1960s, particularly when educators abandoned time-honored works by established authors in favor of the latest fashions in mass-produced culture. During the 1990s, these kinds of attacks escalated, especially as conservative philanthropic foundations funded authors and organizations who opposed multiculturalism.

The critiques of the 1990s quickly went beyond multiculturalism to broader condemnations of a cultural climate allegedly dominated by political correctness. (Ironically, multiculturalists, in a playful spirit of *self*-criticism, had initially coined the term political correctness, but their opponents soon made the phrase their own.) To its critics, PC signified an illiberal cultural impulse that required narrowly-conceived thought, behavior, and attitudes, particularly on issues related to race and sexuality. In this view, authoritarian educators were not only indoctrinating students with trendy works but insisting that they read classical texts, such as those of Shakespeare, in terms of contemporary political concerns such as gender relationships or imperialism. Professors who did not toe the line, according to the critics of PC, risked having their classes undermined by politically-correct colleagues or disrupted by student activists. What began as an attempt to open up the educational environment became caricatured in a wide variety of popular publications as an attempt to stifle freedom of expression and to impose rigid, almost puritanical standards.

PC's critics encompassed more than the political right. Many traditional liberals argued that multiculturalism comforted, rather than challenged, students and ignored common values in a misguided effort to highlight diversity.

Camille Paglia, a flamboyant media personality who styled herself a feminist, denounced the search for PC values—especially on issues involving sexual harassment and even date rape—as the kind of puritanicalism that the sexually "liberated" 1960s were supposed to have discredited. And Katie Roiphe, a young feminist whom the mass media immediately hailed as a spokesperson for Generation X, charged that concern for political correctness on gender relationships encouraged a conservative agenda, rather than the kind of progressive cultural politics that the "twentysomething" generation should embrace.

The PC debate became equally complex when the focus turned to race. While running for President in 1988 Reverend Jesse Jackson's call for multicultural politics won him a sympathetic hearing on many college campuses. At the same time, though, Jackson had refused to break with more race-conscious African-American leaders such as Minister Louis Farrakhan of the Nation of Islam. By the 1990s, Jackson's "Rainbow Coalition" was in tatters, while Farrakhan was a rising force in African-American youth culture, especially when the teachings of the Nation of Islam merged with calls for "Afrocentric" education.

Afrocentrism was an impulse that affected all levels of culture, from African-American studies programs at universities to the hip hop songs of rappers like Paris. Afrocentrism hailed the accomplishments of a black cultural tradition that was often traced back to ancient Egypt. Some of its proponents seemed to jettison multiculturalist premises when they argued for the superior values of an African-derived culture that, in the view of some, had been deliberately undermined by people of European descent, including Jewish traders who had, according to a controversial book published by the Nation of Islam, allegedly dominated the 17th and 18th century slave trade. Controversies over multiculturalism and campus restrictions on speech became more and more acrimonious and complex.

The Culture Wars

The PC controversy, especially when it involved issues of gender and race, extended beyond educational institutions. The Senate Judiciary Committee's 1991 hearings on the Supreme Court nomination of Clarence Thomas, an articulate African-American conservative, epitomized the new cultural politics. Just when it appeared that Thomas's opponents could not block his nomination, another conservative African-American, Anita Hill, charged Thomas with having harassed her with sexual innuendos while both had served in the Reagan administration. Although Hill had never brought a formal complaint under the federal laws against sexual harassment, Thomas's critics argued that Hill's testimony, which they judged credible, disqualified Thomas from the Supreme Court because of his insensitivity to both the law and social proprieties.

The confrontation between Hill and Thomas raised a variety of cultural issues. Thomas, who had steadfastly been portraying himself as a traditional conservative with a "color-blind" view of legal and political questions, suddenly confronted his critics with the cultural politics of race. While denying the veracity of Hill's charges, he also pictured himself as a victim of white racism and denounced the all-white Senate Judiciary Committee for conducting a "high tech lynching." Meanwhile, some people who opposed Thomas's conservative legal agenda felt that Hill's allegations, even if substantiated, had little to do with Thomas's qualifications for the Supreme Court. A number of African-American writers charged that no white nominee would have had his or her private life so ruthlessly scrutinized.

Hill's supporters saw the issues quite differently. Feminists accused Thomas's supporters on the Judiciary Committee with engaging in sexual harassment while they cross-examined Hill; moreover, they chastised anti-Thomas members of the all-male Judiciary Committee for failing to understand the serious nature of Hill's charges. As the African-American author Toni Morrison complained, Hill's interrogators "dressed [her] in the oppositional costume of madness, anarchic sexuality, and explosive verbal violence."

The Hill-Thomas confrontation, which resulted in Thomas being confirmed by a very close vote, reverberated throughout the political culture. Feminist organizations used Hill's treatment as a rallying point. Buttons proclaiming "I Believe Anita Hill" became part of a nation-wide organizing effort that resulted in the election of a number of women, including two new Democratic Senators from California and another from Illinois, to the United States Senate in the November 1992 elections. On the other hand, critics of this kind of cultural politics and anti-feminist writers continued to condemn the treatment of Thomas and, more broadly, the insertion of political correctness into national politics.

Meanwhile, talk radio and tabloid-TV shows continued to serve as important sites for the conduct of cultural politics during the 1990s. Supplanting the New Right religious preachers of the 1980s, a new group of moralizing, but entirely secular, commentators denounced feminism, political correctness, and multiculturalism. Rush Limbaugh, a former sports publicist and radio disk jockey, featured episodes such as the Thomas-Hill hearings in his growing multi-media empire: best-selling books, a radio show, a syndicated TV program, and a line of audio cassettes. A few radio and TV talk shows adopted a tone sympathetic to feminist and multicultural issues, but the vast majority tracked Limbaugh's conservative path. His soaring popularity even prompted a number of bars and restaurants to create "Rush Rooms" in which fellow conservatives could lunch to the sounds of Limbaugh's daytime radio program. After the 1992 elections, Limbaugh made Bill and Hillary Rodham Clinton his major targets.

Limbaugh's style of cultural politics took a new turn in the spring of 1994 when Paula Jones sued President Bill Clinton for sexual harassment. The incident had allegedly occurred in 1991, while Clinton was still governor of Arkansas and she was a state employee. The lawsuit was unprecedented, and legal experts differed on whether or not the courts should even hear this kind of case against the nation's chief executive. Meanwhile, in contrast to the Hill-

Thomas hearings, feminist groups invariably distanced themselves from Jones, while the conservative institutions that had denounced Anita Hill, particularly the *American Spectator* magazine, suddenly discovered that sexual harassment was an important national issue. As in the Hill-Thomas controversy, the narrow question of who was telling the truth became less important than broader cultural-political issues. Was sexual harassment serious enough to dominate a presidency that faced issues such as health-care reform and relations with the former Soviet Union? Or was something that would have been passed over only a generation earlier now a legitimate part of American politics?

Although the Hill-Thomas and Jones-Clinton cases suggested that cultural politics might simply enliven traditional partisan conflict, the controversies of the early 1990s carried the potential to create new political alignments, especially within the Republican party. As the 1992 national convention dramatized, militant cultural conservatives, such as Patrick Buchanan, stood ready to challenge those older "paleoconservatives," such as William F. Buckley, who had reshaped conservatism during the 1950s, and the "neoconservatives," such as Irving Kristol, who had joined the Republican ranks during the 1970s. Buchanan's calls for warfare against multiculturalism and political correctness, some political analysts claimed, had seriously undercut George Bush's re-election effort in 1992. Moreover, militantly conservative, grass-roots activists began mobilizing to take over local school boards, providing the potential for further dividing the GOP just as it sought to regroup after its disappointments of 1992.

BILL CLINTON: A NEW DEMOCRAT

Election of 1992

George Bush's inability to articulate a coherent vision of either foreign or domestic policy proved politically fatal. Within his own party, the most conservative Republicans during the presidential primaries rallied behind Patrick Buchanan, the outspoken TV commentator who had severely criticized the gulf war—because, he claimed, it did not advance any clear national interest—and who decried Bush's failure to pick up Reagan's right-wing standard at home. Bush easily defeated Buchanan in every primary race, but he allowed the militant far right to set the tone at the Republican National Convention, where Buchanan declared "a religious war" for "the soul of America." Other speakers decried homosexuality; attacked affirmative action; denounced the prochoice movement; and identified the Democratic nominee, Bill Clinton, and his wife, Hillary Rodham Clinton, as purveyors of un-American values.

Clinton effectively countered his Republican critics by identifying himself as a "new kind of Democrat." Born in 1946, Clinton emphasized his admiration for two very different baby-boom heroes, Elvis Presley and John F. Kennedy. A Rhodes Scholar at Oxford, a graduate of Yale Law School, and a governor of Arkansas at thirty-two, Clinton also conceded, albeit grudgingly, his political liabilities. He admitted to having had rough spots in his marriage, to having smoked (but not inhaled) marijuana, to having avoided the draft during the Vietnam War, and to having participated in antiwar demonstrations while at Oxford. Although Republicans tried to capitalize on these episodes in Clinton's past—Bush himself denounced Clinton for lacking patriotism—most voters recognized that none of these actions seemed unusual for a person who had come of age during the Vietnam era. Meanwhile, Clinton broke new ground in presidential politicking by donning dark glasses and playing the saxophone on "The Arsenio Hall Show" and by informally answering questions before youthful studio audiences on MTV. Despite the fact that Tipper Gore, the wife of Clinton's running mate, Senator Albert Gore of Tennessee, had once allied with members of the religious right in an antirock crusade, the Clinton-Gore ticket enjoyed the unofficial endorsement of MTV.

Clinton also proved to be a different kind of Democrat on social issues, at least compared to Mondale and even Dukakis. He spoke about overhauling the welfare system by requiring job-training programs, by aggressively pursuing men who avoided financial responsibility for their children, and by limiting the time that people could expect to draw welfare payments. He also talked about developing a strong anticrime package, a stance that was bolstered by his support as governor of Arkansas for the death penalty. And in contrast to both Mondale and Dukakis, who had been charged with pursuing special-interest politics by courting Reverend Jesse Jackson, Clinton deliberately accentuated his differences with Jackson. At the same time, he sought out other prominent people of color—such as Ronald Brown, the African-American attorney who headed the Democratic National Committee, and Henry Cisneros, the former mayor of San Antonio—who had close ties to the Democratic party. In November, more than 80 percent of black and 63 percent of Latino voters supported Clinton. Finally, Hillary Rodham Clinton's long involvement in feminist issues, including child care and abortion rights, helped Clinton to capitalize on the gender gap that had been evident in Bush's 1988 campaign. Clinton carried a majority of women's votes in November.

By emphasizing Bush's poor record as an economic manager and by refusing to allow the Bush campaign to label him a traditional liberal, Clinton positioned himself perfectly for November. The unorthodox, independent campaign of billionaire entrepreneur Ross Perot, who launched his quest for the White House by becoming a recurring guest on CNN's "Larry King Live" and other TV talk shows, spent nearly $40 million on a fall media blitz. Although Perot won no electoral votes, he did attract nearly 20 million popular votes, compared to nearly 45 million for Clinton and about 39 million for Bush. Most surveys suggested that Perot's campaign hurt Bush more than Clinton, who won 370 electoral votes by carrying 32 states and the District of Columbia. Bush carried a majority among only one of the major voting blocs, white Protestants in the South.

The 1992 election was a humiliating defeat for George Bush, who only eighteen months before had basked in the glory of the gulf war victory. Taken together, the anti-Bush vote, for both Perot and Clinton, totaled more than 62 percent of the popular ballots cast. Moreover, the electorate seemed eager to vote against Bush, as more than 55 percent of eligible voters cast ballots; this unexpectedly large turnout reversed thirty-two years of steady decline in voter participation.

The Clinton Presidency

Clinton set an ambitious domestic agenda. In addition to changes in anticrime and welfare policies, he called for new approaches to health care, education, environmental issues, and economic development. As a "new Democrat," he promised to shrink, not expand, both the deficit and the federal bureaucracy.

Clinton quickly scored some significant successes and displayed a capacity for backtracking when confronted by political battles that promised to be too divisive. He abandoned several prominent nominees for whom the confirmation process looked difficult, but finally he recruited an unprecedentedly diverse administration. His cabinet included Ron Brown and Mike Espy, the first African-American Secretaries of Commerce and of Agriculture; the former mayor of San Antonio Henry Cisneros as Secretary of Housing and Urban Development; and Hazel O'Leary and Janet Reno, the first women to head the Departments of Energy and Justice. He passed over several better-known but controversial nominees to select Ruth Bader Ginsburg to replace Thurgood Marshall on the Supreme Court. Justice Ginsburg, who had aggressively litigated antidiscrimination cases as a lawyer but compiled a very moderate record as a judge on the Court of Appeals, became the second woman to sit on the Supreme Court. With his second Supreme Court appointment, Stephen Breyer, Clinton also bypassed more controversial choices.

During his first few months in office, Clinton moved much more aggressively on economic than on social issues. He worked with Congress to formulate a budget bill that held the line on spending while raising taxes on higher incomes and making a start toward reducing the federal deficit, one of the primary crusades of Ross Perot. Fueled by exceedingly low interest rates during 1993 and by returning consumer confidence, the economy continued the recovery that had begun toward the end of Bush's presidency. The federal deficit narrowed impressively, reversing the recent trend of growing government borrowing.

Clinton also scored some significant changes in social policy. He ended the Reagan-era ban on abortion counseling in family-planning clinics and steered through Congress a family-leave program for working parents. The Brady Bill, which instituted a five-day waiting period for the purchase of handguns, became the first of a series of anticrime measures that promised more aggressive sentencing of offenders, placed more police on the streets, and banned most assault weapons. Small, pilot programs to provide college tuition assistance in return for national service and to expand youth-training programs, both of which had attracted strong popular support during Clinton's campaign, also received limited funding. Clinton temporized on his campaign pledge of ending the military's ban on homosexuals by trying to accommodate the Pentagon's conservatives. Under the compromise policy, called "don't ask, don't tell," recruiters would not ask prospective service personnel about their sexuality, so that gays and lesbians who kept quiet could have military careers. Neither the military establishment nor gay and lesbian activists were pleased, but this solution suggested Clinton's compromising approach to controversial social and cultural issues.

The central feature of Clinton's domestic program was health-care reform. Hillary Rodham Clinton took the lead, heading a task force charged with designing a new system that would provide health care for all Americans and, simultaneously, hold down rising health costs. The task force's proposal, unveiled in late 1993, had several controversial features. First, health-care would be delivered to all Americans through large private organizations competing with each other for subscribers in a system of "managed competition." Conservative critics charged that such large and highly regulated health organizations would give bureaucrats, rather than doctors and patients, control over crucial medical decisions. Liberal critics charged that managed competition would simply substitute one costly and confusing health care system for another, and they argued for a single-payer system that would, on the model of Medicare, be administered uniformly through direct government reimbursement. Second, health-care would be financed through employers, who would be mandated to pay the premiums to insure basic coverage for employees, and through additional revenue sources, such as higher taxes on cigarettes. These proposals also prompted a variety of critics. Many worried that small businesses would be unable to afford the requirement to pay for employee health coverage; that payment provisions for part-time employees could get exceedingly complex and burdensome; that costs to cover the currently unemployed and uninsured would be far higher than projected. Third, Clinton's proposal aimed to provide all Americans with basic health care, but disputes flared over what would be included within a standard package of benefits. Would, for example, mental health be covered? As Congress and the country debated all of these issues about the structure of health-care reform, Clinton insisted that almost every feature was subject to negotiation and compromise except one: He would make no concessions away from his promise of some kind of universal coverage for all Americans. Controversies, however, slowly deadlocked health care reform.

In foreign policy, Clinton faced the daunting task of inventing, articulating, and implementing new policies relevant to the post-cold war environment. Calling for greater openness in government, he began to ameliorate the cold war obsession with government secrecy and to revise standards for declassification of information. Secretary of Energy O'Leary declassified long-held secrets showing past government complicity in testing effects of radioactivity on humans. A massive project to declassify information relating to the assassination of President Kennedy went forward. The CIA promised to open files on eleven covert actions of the 1950s and 1960s, the existence of which it had previously denied. The CIA came under even greater pressure to reorganize itself when, in the spring of 1994, a highly placed official was revealed to have been a mole who had, for years, passed U.S. intelligence secrets to the Soviet Union and Russia, causing the death of a number of U.S. agents, and had also passed along KGB disinformation to CIA analysts. Clinton's greatest challenge, however, was how to redefine America's commitments in the world without being distracted from his domestic agenda, the fate of Lyndon Johnson and other reformist presidents.

During the first few months of Clinton's presidency, the future of the U.S. military intervention in Somalia became the thorniest question. President Bush had ordered American troops to help move food and relief supplies to alleviate a devastating, politically caused famine in Somalia. President Bush had placed the Americans under the umbrella of a UN mission, the goals of which gradually became more political: stabilizing factional rivalries and facilitating installation of a new government. When UN leaders clashed with one of Somalia's strongest factional leaders, General Mohammed Farah Aidid, the UN and the United States subsequently declared Aidid an outlaw and attempted to arrest him. Throughout the fall of 1993, Aidid's faction in Mogadishu was attacking U.S. troops daily, and U.S. newspapers carried dramatic pictures of casualties. Americans had trouble understanding why an ostensibly humanitarian effort had become a fighting war.

Clinton weighed the options. On one hand, he could enlarge military involvement to protect the U.S. presence and to try to build a functioning government for Somalia. But Americans had little cultural understanding or strategic interest in Somalia, and a protracted military involvement would be unpopular. On the other hand, a sudden U.S. withdrawal might disrupt food distribution networks, bring renewed famine, and threaten the humanitarian progress that the intervention had achieved. Some analysts also warned that a complete about-face in U.S. foreign policy would undermine the credibility of the new administration.

Other trouble spots simultaneously raised similarly complicated questions about when, why, and where post-cold war military interventions should be used. In the former Yugoslavia, Serbian troops continued to besiege Bosnian Muslims, and many Americans pushed the United States and its European allies to take a stronger stand, including military strikes, to halt the ongoing massacres in Sarajevo and other cities. After a particularly brutal shelling of a marketplace in Sarajevo in February 1994, Clinton supported a NATO ultimatum to Serbs, threatening air strikes unless the siege of Sarajevo stopped. Serbia halted its shelling of Sarajevo but troops remained in the surrounding hills and much of Serbia's firepower was simply repositioned for use against other Bosnian cities. Meanwhile, Clinton continued to advance diplomatic initiatives, hoping to avoid direct military involvement. During the campaign, Clinton had also vowed to help reestablish the elected government of Haiti, whose leader, Bertrand Aristide, was in exile in the United States. In October 1993, Clinton moved American troops to Haitian ports as part of a UN plan to reinstate Aristide, but he then pulled them back when angry throngs of Haitians gathered to denounce American intervention. Meanwhile, rumors that North Korea was close to having an operational atomic bomb brought strong denunciations from Clinton, but there was debate over what mix of diplomatic and military pressure would be most effective against the North Koreans.

Clinton's top policymakers weighed the pros and cons of military interventions as they charted America's new post-cold war foreign policy. Was refusal to take military action a sign of a new isolationism that turned a deaf ear to human rights claims and bolstered, through inaction, brutal dictators and aggressors? Or, by resisting interventionism, no matter how well intentioned, was Clinton avoiding open-ended and vague commitments that U.S. military power could not possibly fulfill?

With Somalia, Haiti, Bosnia, and Korea dominating international news during the fall of 1993, Clinton worried about the fate of his domestic agenda. In addition, he worried about allowing military controversies to dominate foreign policy issues. Gradually, he tried to shift away from the Reagan-Bush focus on military shows of strength. He announced that American troops would withdraw from Somalia in the spring of 1994 and engaged in negotiations with General Aidid. In Bosnia, he backed off from military confrontation, hoping that economic boycotts coupled with negotiations could achieve change. Regarding the nuclear impasse with North Korea a tentative agreement was reached. In September 1994, Clinton ordered American troops into Haiti to restore electoral processes. Critics charged Clinton with vacillation and weak leadership in foreign policy.

Clinton tried to move the principal focus of his foreign policy to international economic growth and recovery. Building on the Reagan-Bush legacy of trying to lower trade barriers and expand markets, Clinton consummated several historic trade agreements. He strongly backed NAFTA, despite opposition from labor unions and other groups in the Democratic coalition. After adding certain safeguards on labor and environmental issues, in December 1993 Clinton muscled the bill through Congress in a close vote that depended mostly on Republican support. He then traveled to the Far East to complete trade agreements with nations of the Pacific rim and, in February, 1994, normalized trade with Vietnam. After difficult negotiations in the final so-called Uruguay Round of GATT (General Agreement on Tariffs and Trade), agreements were also completed in late 1993. GATT established a World Trade Organization to mediate otherwise unresolvable trade disputes. Clinton hoped that these measures, in addition to the new popularity of free-market economies in Eastern Europe, Asia, and Latin America, would stimulate more rapid economic growth in both the U.S. and in the global economy. Post-cold war foreign policy under Clinton attempted to downplay military force and focus on economic growth.

Clinton's ability to concentrate on health-care and foreign policy faltered in the spring of 1994, however, as the press pursued investigations into his personal life. The Clintons had invested in an unsuccessful real estate development in Arkansas called Whitewater while Clinton was governor. Questions arose about whether their business partner, whom Hillary Clinton's law firm represented, had received favorable, insider treatment in connection with a bailout of his savings–and–loan company. The Clintons maintained that no corruption or illegal personal profit had been involved, but Republican charges forced the President to appoint a special prosecutor with full powers to investigate all circumstances surrounding Whitewater.

During the 1994 mid-term elections, Clinton's declining popularity hurt Democratic candidates. The electorate, which seemed angry at government and fearful about crime and other social issues, turned toward Republicans on election day. Republicans gained control of both houses of Congress for the first time in nearly fifty years, and also won a majority of governorships. The new Republican leadership, promising a "Contract with America," pledged to pursue the most conservative economic and social agenda of the postwar period.

RETROSPECTIVE

Any era is a culmination of previous trends, but the 1980s and 1990s, more than most, seemed a watershed. In the 1980s, most decision makers remembered, often nostalgically, the high degree of national consensus that had seemed to exist during World War II and the 1950s. In these Reagan-dominated years, Republican leaders seemed to want to move "back to the future." But with Clinton's election, the World War II generation passed from the scene, and a younger generation came into major positions of power. That generation had matured within the fierce social and political struggles of the 1960s and early 1970s, struggles that had elevated a multicultural vision of American life, worry about the overuse of military force and secretive government, and acceptance of more equal relationships between men and women. Within this generational shift, what new agendas would be set? What new visions would inspire the country? The future, as always, would be what people could make of it.

SUGGESTIONS FOR FURTHER READING

On politics from Bush to Clinton, see Charles Kenney, *Michael Dukakis: An American Odyssey* (1988); Sidney Blumenthal, *Pledging Allegiance: The Last Campaign of the Cold War* (1990); Stephen Gillon, *The Democrats' Dilemma: Walter F. Mondale and the Liberal Legacy* (1992); Thomas Byrne Edsall and Mary D. Edsall, *Chain Reaction: The Impact of Race, Rights, and Taxes on American Politics* (rev. ed., 1992); Jack W. Germond and Jules Witcover, *Mad as Hell: Revolt at the Ballot Box, 1992* (1993); John Podhoretz, *Hell of a Ride: Backstage at the White House Follies, 1989–1993* (1993); and Charles Kolb, *White House Daze: The Unmaking of Domestic Policy in the Bush Years* (1994).

On foreign affairs and the gulf war, see Michael J. Hogan, ed., *The End of the Cold War: Its Meanings and Implications* (1992); Roger Hilsman, *George Bush vs. Saddam Hussein* (1992); Douglas Kellner, *The Persian Gulf TV War* (1992); Hamid Mowlana, George Gerbner, and Herbert I. Schiller, eds., *Triumph of the Image: The Media's War in the Persian Gulf* (1992); T. M. Hawley, *Against the Fires of Hell: The Environmental Disaster of the Gulf War* (1992); Robert E. Denton, Jr., ed., *The Media and the Persian Gulf War* (1993); and Lawrence Freedman, *The Gulf Conflict, 1990–1991: Diplomacy and War in the New World Order* (1993).

On the culture wars of the early 1990s, see the works cited in Chapter Ten.

Index

Students for a Democratic Society (SDS), 169–70. *See also* Hayden, Tom; New Left; Weathermen
Suburbia, 71–73
Suez Crisis of 1956, 108–9
Sun Records, 87
Supreme Court, 38, 91–92, 146, 188, 287
abortion rulings, 287
and equality issues, 38, 91–92, 287
Nixon appointments, 135
Warren Court, 133–35
See also specific cases and justices
Sweatt v. *Painter*, 38
Symbionese Liberation Army, 186

Taft-Hartley Act, 31, 33
Taft, Sen. Robert, 30–31, 44, 47, 53
Taiwan, 14, 16, 104
Taxpayer Revolt, 273–74
Taylor, Sen. Glen, 33, 34
Taylor, Gen. Maxwell, 149, 154
Television, 83–85, 217–20, 294–95, 297, 301–2, 303, 308, 313, 317, 319
and Gulf War, 313
and politics, 85, 308, 317, 319
public television, 219–20
Thieu, Nguyen Van, 158, 249
Thomas, Clarence, 316–18
Three-Mile Island disaster, 208
Thurmond, Strom, 33, 145
Tijerina, Reies Lopez, 191
Tower, John, 308
Trade, 2–4, 242–43
Tri-Lateral Commission, 256, 271
Truman, Harry S, 1, 8, 18, 24, 26, 27–41, 58, 62, 122, 128, 129, 133, 269, 277
and anti-Communism, 39–43
and civil rights, 33, 35, 37–39
domestic social programs, 34–38
election of 1948, 31–34
foreign policies of, 1–20
internal security programs of, 40–41
and Korean War, 15–17
leadership of, 28–30, 37, 38, 58
and scandals, 43, 57–58
Truman Doctrine, 10–11, 16
Trump, Donald, 280–81, 303
Turkey, 10, 104, 116
Twenty-Second Amendment, 30

U-2 affair, 107
Underground press, 174

United Auto Workers (UAW), 28. *See also* Reuther, Walter
United Nations, 5–6, 33, 312–13
"Unmeltable Ethnics," 196–98
Urban issues, 97–98, 129–31, 141, 170, 211, 271–72, 284–85, 309. *See also* Great Society: Moses, Robert

Vance, Cyrus, 258, 261
Vandenberg, Arthur, 10, 32
Viet Minh, 110, 111
Vietnam War:
atrocities, 159, 160, 183
bombing, 157, 158, 161
Cambodian front, 181–83
economic impact of, 163, 251
and election of 1968, 160, 177–81
and election of 1972, 235, 236, 250
fall of South Vietnam, 249–50
Gulf of Tonkin, 154–56, 158
National Liberation Front (NLF), 112, 113, 152, 153, 156, 157, 159, 160, 161
origins of U.S. involvement, 110–13
Paris Peace Talks, 249, 250
Pentagon Papers, 238
and President Johnson, 153–61
and President Kennedy, 152–53
protests against, 158, 172–73, 183–84
search and destroy missions, 156–57
teach-ins about, 172
Tet offensive, 159–61
Vietnamization, 182
See also Cambodia
Vital Center, 35
Vonnegut, Kurt, 52, 276
Voting Rights Act (1965), 129, 131–32, 189

Wallace, George, 92, 134, 137, 177, 179–80, 181
Wallace, Henry, 9, 33–34, 48
War on Drugs, 311
Warren, Earl, 32, 125, 133–35. *See also* Supreme Court
Warren Commission Report, 125
Watergate, *See* Richard Nixon
Watts, violence in, 140–42
Weathermen, 183
Westmoreland, Gen. William, 159, 160
Whitewater, 324
Wilson, Charles, 63, 104